The First Industrial Woman

The First Industrial Woman

DEBORAH VALENZE

New York   Oxford
Oxford University Press
1995

Oxford University Press

Oxford   New York   Toronto
Delhi   Bombay   Calcutta   Madras   Karachi
Kuala Lumpur   Singapore   Hong Kong   Tokyo
Nairobi   Dar es Salaam   Cape Town
Melbourne   Aukland   Madrid

and associated companies in
Berlin   Ibadan

Chapter 3 originally appeared as an article in *Past and Present*, no. 130
(February 1991), pp. 142–69, and is reprinted with kind permission.
(World Copyright: The Past and Present Society,
175 Banbury Road, Oxford, England.)

The author has made every effort to obtain permissions from copyright holders
to reprint or reproduce material for this book. In some cases
the copyright holders and/or their whereabouts
were unknown.

Library of Congress Cataloging-in-Publication Data
Valenze, Deborah M., 1953–
The first industrial woman / Deborah Valenze.
p. cm.   Includes bibliographical references and index.
ISBN 0-19-508981-2.
ISBN 0-19-508982-0 (pbk.)
1. Women—Employment—Great Britain—
History—19th century.   I. Title.
HD6135.V35   1994
331.4′0941—dc20 93-50734

9 7 5 3   2 4 6 8

Printed in the United States of America
on acid-free paper

For
Timo, Emma, and Rosa

Acknowledgments

It has taken me years to realize that the subject of this book, women and industrialization, intimately connects my experiences of learning and teaching history. The topic of industrialization always preoccupied me as a student, and later, as a teacher, it became the medium through which I have tried to explain what I believe to be important lessons of history. The actual project began with my first book, a study of female preaching, which seemed, as one reader of that manuscript tactfully observed, overburdened with economic history. The problem of economic justice lurked in the margins of that study, and in this later work, by examining the production and distribution of wealth, I have tried to give it centerstage.

In developing my perspective on British and women's history, four teachers have played an especially important role. Eric Hobsbawm has been a mentor whose analysis of industrial capitalism and class is part of my daily life as an historian. I am grateful to him and Marlene Hobsbawm for years of conversation, advice, and hospitality. Joan Wallach Scott showed me how to think, research, and write about the history of women, and her generosity will always be an example to me. John Bohstedt taught me very early on that British history was what I wanted to study, and I am still trying to recapture the excitement I remember from his undergraduate seminar on class relations. And finally, the late Edward Thompson was a beacon and an anchor who helped me to understand the significance of the eighteenth century. His guidance was invaluable, and I am grateful to have been a part of a network of scholars deeply influenced by his work. I only wish he had been able to give the whole of this project the benefit of the intellectual rigor he applied to one chapter.

The creation of this project also depended on the experience of teaching history. As I passed through successive and sometimes difficult stages of my career while working on the manuscript, the support of friends and institutions made all the difference in the world. I wish to thank Chrissy Atkinson, Hal Benenson, Judith Bennett, Connie Buchanan, Jeff Cox, Jim Cronin, Leonore Davidoff, Laura Frader, Francis Gouda, Catherine Hall, Chris Holley, Maryanne Kowaleski, Beth Kowaleski-Wallace, Tom Laqueur, Ellen Ross, the late Ronald Sanders, Beverly Sanders, Dorothy Thompson, Judy Walkowitz, and John Walsh for their friendship, helpful comments, and counsel over the years. Temma Kaplan deserves special thanks for helping me realize how important my professional goals were at a critical time, and for her continuing friendship. Ruth Smith has always been there when I needed her; her intellectual kinship and common perspective are present throughout the entire book.

My students and colleagues at Barnard College have played a crucial role in the later evolution of this project. I owe thanks to the many Barnard and Columbia students who have listened to parts of the manuscript without knowing it and improved my work with their questions and animated discussions. The history department has provided a professional home with all the warmth and energy I could hope for. I am particularly indebted to Herb Sloan, whose intellectual companionship, helpful readings, and, yes, even footnote advice have been immensely important to me; to the late Bill McNeil, whose enthusiasm for this project and history in general sustained me more than I ever realized at the time; and to Nancy Woloch, whose humor, wisdom, and professional example will always be a great resource to me. I am also grateful to Dean Robert McCaughey and Barnard College for the leave time and travel funds that enabled me to complete this book.

Several friends and colleagues away from school gave a great deal to me as I wrestled with various stages of the project. Peter Weiler read and re-read the manuscript and gave me the suggestions and support of a true comrade. Nancy Carney reminded me of all the important things in life in addition to my work. Donna Andrew, Raymond Grew, Kim Hays, Jane Lewis, Michael McKeon, Peter Onuf, and Ruth Perry read chapters of the book and spent hours over coffee, at their word processors, or on the telephone in order to help me along. Nancy Lane of Oxford University Press applied the sunshine of her expertise to this project for several years; she has no idea how energizing she was at some critical moments. I am grateful to her for all her wisdom, insight, and foresight. I also wish to thank Catherine Clements for her many editorial skills marshaled so consistently.

The staff of several libraries assisted me in my research. I wish to thank the staff of the North Library of the British Library in London; the Kress Library and the Goldsmiths-Kress Collection in the Manuscripts Division at Baker Library, Harvard Business School; Langdell Library of Harvard Law School; the Houghton Library, Harvard University, and especially Susan Halpert; the Widener Library, Harvard University; the Schlesinger Library, Radcliffe College; the Boston Public Library; Butler Library of Columbia University; and Wollman Library of Barnard College. I would also like to thank the American Council of Learned Societies and the National Endowment for the Humanities for their fellowship support during the writing of this book.

Finally, I couldn't have created anything without the love and sustenance of my family. Emma and Rosa Gilmore have been a part of this project in every way, filling my days with their energy and affection, enduring my absences, providing countless works of art on the opposite sides of rough drafts, and reminding me of where my center is. They may understand more about the past ten years when they someday read these pages. We owe thanks to Tanya Braganti, Khy Buguey, Cindy Fallows, and Merav Gold for their spirited childcare while I raced off to libraries or sat upstairs at the computer. As for my husband, Michael Timo Gilmore, I doubt that I will ever express all the gratitude I feel for the ways he has nourished my professional and personal life. He has done more than simply sharpen my arguments, improve my prose, and rescue me from my worst moods. Through his love and support, he has made a multitude of goals a reality, including a strenuous commuting routine that has given all of us, but especially him, a deepened understanding of the problems related to gender and work. There isn't a page of this book that wasn't inflected by his presence.

Contents

Introduction: Finding the First Industrial Woman   3

1. Habits of Industry: Laboring Women and the Poor in Eighteenth-Century England   13

2. Economies of Survival: Laboring Women and Agricultural Change, 1750–1800   29

3. The Art of Women and the Business of Men: Women's Work and the Dairy Industry   48

4. The Quarrel with Women's Work: Spinning and the Displacement of Female Labor   68

5. A New World of Work: Female Labor and the Development of the Factory System   85

6. Invisible Breadwinners: Women Workers and the Declining Status of Cottage Industry   113

7. Women in the Age of Malthus: Political Economy and the Feminization of the Female Worker   128

8. Recasting Women in the Workshop of the World: Middle-Class Authority and the Female Poor   141

9. The Other Victorian Woman: The Domestic Servant in the Industrial Age   155

Conclusion   181

Notes   187
Bibliography   233
Index   245

The First Industrial Woman

Frontispiece from T. Firmin, *Some Proposals for the [I]mployment of the Poor* (1681). Reproduced from the Goldsmith-Kress Collection, Historical Collections, Graduate School of Business Administration, Harvard University.

Introduction:

Finding the First Industrial Woman

"The first industrial revolution" calls up a mixture of textbook images and ideas: dark satanic mills, the steam engine, the railway, new class relations, changing standards of living. Within these associations, women workers occupy an essential place. It is impossible to mention the advent of the factory without considering the factory girl, a virtual archetype of the era, who was condemned for her immoral behavior and pitied for her arduous workday. It is equally impossible to consider the accumulation of industrial wealth without considering the part that women played in supplying labor within the many enterprises that underlay England's takeoff as an international economic power.

A cursory look at the eighteenth and nineteenth centuries reveals startling contrasts: why were female workers praised for their industriousness in the eighteenth century, but a century later, damned or pitied? The earlier years represented a high-water mark of female industriousness: the female reaper with her shock of corn, the woman at her spinning wheel, the farmer's wife in her dairy—all acted as symbols of productivity and plenty. This is not to say that it was a "golden age" of women's work. A sexual division of labor characterized most forms of production, the male household head usually monopolized authority and status, and work was more often onerous and unpleasant than not. But quite apart from these constraints, the productive work of women was recognized and thereby acknowledged as a valuable contribution to the wealth of the nation.[1]

The nineteenth century, by comparison, lacked a vocabulary with which to praise its female workers. Victorians were ashamed of the factory girl and expended much energy cataloging her failings: she used coarse language, spent money on triflings, and was morally lax. She stood not as a bearer of the achievements of the industrial age, but as a casualty of the new system. Seldom a word was said about the actual work she successfully performed or the wealth she helped to create. Although many other women worked in less visible employments, they remained undiscussed, except in parliamentary inquiries seeking to limit their activity.

3

Theorists of economic development have long noted the negative impact that industrialization appears to have on the participation of women in the work force. Because the decline in the subsistence, or agricultural, sector of the economy usually occurs more rapidly than the growth of the industrial sector, women's participation often follows a U-shaped curve, recovering only when a later stage of development creates more jobs. Ester Boserup's classic work, *Women's Role in Economic Development* (1970), voiced concern that "in the course of this transition women will be deprived of their productive functions," which would in turn have negative consequences for their overall welfare.[2] Historians of the British economy have argued that women's employment in fact followed this pattern, regardless of the impression made by conspicuous factory workers. The many "invisible" trades pursued by women, often in domestic settings, seldom appear in surveys of economic development.[3] The argument that women retreat from economic activity thus highlights how they are squeezed out of mainstream industrial production and confined to low-paid, exploitative occupations that have earned them the designation as a vast "surplus army" of labor. Industrialization has not proven to be the progressive force for women workers that its celebrants have claimed.[4]

Opportunities for nineteenth-century women workers were narrowing not only because of structural economic developments. The exclusion of women from many industrial jobs resulted from the concerted effort to promote a domestic role that would curtail female activity outside the home. Victorian critics riveted their attention on the factory girl because she violated their sense of a woman's proper role as wife and mother. The negative attention directed to the plight of women workers was not only the product of a reforming conscience disturbed by inhumane working conditions, but also the result of a parliamentary campaign to press a domestic ideal upon the working classes. Working men interested in protecting their jobs from the incursion of cheap female labor united behind the effort. Though the Victorian age appears nearly unanimous in its support for cloistered femininity, the model engendered conflict within the working class. The economic contraints of working-class life would always pose a formidable barrier: an adequate male breadwinner's wage, necessary in order for the model to work, was more an ideal than a reality.[5]

Table I.1 Population of England and Wales (in thousands)

Year	Total	Female	Total Occupied	Male	Total Occupied
1801	8,893	4,638		4,255	
1851	17,928	9,146	2,819	8,781	6,554

Table I.2 Occupations of Female Labor Force, 1851

Occupation	Number (in thousands)	% of Females in Occupation
Public administration	3	4.5
Professional occupations and their subordinate services	103	38.9
Domestic offices and personal services	1,135	85.5
Transport and communications	13	2.9
Agriculture, horticulture, forestry	230	11.4
Fishing	1	2.7
Mining and quarrying, and workers in mines and quarries	11	2.8
Metal manufactures, machines, implements, etc.	36	6.3
Building and construction	1	0.2
Wood, furniture, etc.	8	5.0
Bricks, cement, pottery, and glass	15	16.7
Chemicals, oil, soap, resin, etc.	4	8.7
Skins, leather, hair, and feathers, etc.	5	8.3
Paper, printing, books, and stationery	16	20.5
Textiles	635	49.0
Clothing	491	54.0
Food, drink, and tobacco	53	13.2
All others occupied	75	14.6
Total occupied	2,832	30.2

Adapted with permission from Weidenfeld and Nicolson from "Table of Indoor Domestic Service in England and Wales," 1851–1881, p. 88, in Geoffrey Best, *Mid-Victorian Britain.* Copyright 1971.

Table I.3 Occupations of Female Labor Force, 1851

Occupation	Number (in thousands)	% of All Females Occupied
Domestic and personal services	1,135	40.1
Textiles	635	22.4
Clothing	491	17.3
Agriculture	229	8.1
Professional and their subordinate services	103	3.6
Food, drink, and tobacco	53	1.9
All others occupied	188	6.6
	2,834	100.0

Figures for Table I.3 were adapted from a larger table in Tranter, "The Labour Supply, 1780–1860," in *The Economic History of Britain since 1700,* 2 vols., ed. Roderick Floud and Donald McCloskey (Cambridge: Cambridge University Press, 1981), 1: p. 208.

The ideology of domesticity highlights how the problem of women's paid employment in the nineteenth century, as in every period, is imbedded within a specific historical context. Work, too, is a concept that changes over time. As anthropologists have shown, the tasks that constitute "work" in a preindustrial society differ from those in a modern wage-oriented society like our own. For our purposes, the late eighteenth century provides a critical point of transition in the history of work, when ideas about productivity and productive processes themselves underwent significant transformations. The outpouring of theoretical discussions of productive activity, Adam Smith's *Wealth of Nations* (1776) among them, marked a definitive acceleration in efforts to come to terms with Britain's economic power. At this juncture, an "idea of work in general" emerged, "that is, work considered separately from all of its particular forms in agriculture, manufacturing or commerce." The abstraction was implicated in important determinations taking place in the late eighteenth and early nineteenth century: the assignment of tasks to individuals according to age and sex, the correct level of wages, the notion of worker incentive, and the designation of wage earning according to gender.[6] The history of work thus informed the construction of gender and class during this critical period of industrial development.

Many standard treatments of industrialization, however, have taken these categories as given. Human agency has often taken the form of "great men in history," in this instance, entrepreneurs and inventors. Harold Perkin's influential study, *The Origins of Modern English Society* (reprint, 1991), characterizes the age as a "revolution in social organization," namely, an increase in "the size, complexity and degree of organization of the real unit of production, the working team under control and leadership of one man." Perkin's model, highlighting the heroic entrepreneur who overshadows lesser historical actors, obscures the real relations of labor and production:

> The entrepreneur, the active, working capitalist who both owned and managed his own enterprise, was the key figure in the revolution in organization. He it was who had to see and seize the market opportunity presented by the new technology within the context of existing or potential demand, who had to procure the capital or persuade partners to invest, find a site . . . superintend the building of the factory and the making and installation of the machinery, recruit, train, direct and discipline the workers, and purchase the raw materials and dispose of the finished article at remunerative prices. The trials and tribulations of Arkwright, Wedgwood, Boulton, Owen, Oldknow, Heathcote, and a great many other early entrepreneurs are well known.[7]

This interpretation not only relegates labor to the sidelines, where it is simply recruited and disciplined, but also depends upon a formulaic "role of the family" to accommodate all other aspects of social life. With the advent of the factory, work was taken out of the domestic setting.

"The migration of work outside the home . . . left the family free to concentrate on its more fundamental functions of home-making, child-bearing and rearing, and the emotional statisfaction of affection and companionship."[8] One would assume from this account that working-class women were satisfied imitators of a middle-class ideal—a distorted picture of the experience of working-class life during industrialization.

Another classic definition of the industrial revolution can be found in David Landes's *The Unbound Prometheus: Technological Change and Industrial Development in Western Europe from 1750 to the Present* (1972). Here the conceptual framework renders human activity, apart from invention, virtually invisible:

> [T]he substitution of machines—rapid, regular, precise, tireless—for human skill and effort; the substitution of inanimate for animate sources of power, in particular the introduction of engines for converting heat into work, thereby opening to man a new and almost unlimited supply of energy; the use of new and far more abundant raw materials, in particular, the substitution of mineral for vegetable or animal substances.[9]

In order to locate workers within the narrative, we must identify the way in which "production" is understood: in terms of rational versus tradition-bound ways of working. Gender is often embedded in this dualism, with male identity associated with the rational and female with tradition. Analyses of gender and science also point up the significance of the quest for technological mastery over nature, depicted as the advance of civilization against the forces of untamed nature. Landes's account fits into this framework. Compared to other places, he explains, Europe triumphed because of "the high value placed on the rational manipulation of the human and material environment." Technological progress sprang from an understanding peculiar to European and particularly British culture, that means must be harnessed to practical ends. Thus was born the determination to master nature, or what Landes calls "the Faustian ethic."[10]

The technological supremacy of Britain cannot be disputed. But this particular portrayal of the rise of industrialism is only part of a larger, less spectacular picture, one that successive generations of historians have revised many times.[11] Industrial capitalism had the power to disguise and obscure many of its less attractive features. Historians of class have pointed out that beneath the Faustian heroes of invention were many nameless handworkers who, in unseemly circumstances for low rates of pay, produced all kinds of commodities. "Mechanisation in one department of production was often complemented by an increase of sweating in others; the growth of large firms by a proliferation of small producing units; the concentration of production in factories by the spread of outwork in the home." Many of these domestic workers were women, who could be hired for rock-bottom wages to do work "between tasks" at home. As Chapter 6 argues, domestic outwork continued long after the introduction of laborsaving devices in the factory and contributed significantly to the accumulation of Britain's industrial capital, though not to the benefit of women workers.[12]

Studies of gender and technology have offered another way of looking at changes in the means of production. Privileging the rational often required suppressing other, perhaps equally sensible, ways of working in favor of methods that served to benefit particular interests. In many cases, "tradition" belonged to the practices of ordinary laborers. As competence and skill were redefined by new technology, both men and women struggled to defend their place in the work force, as new work in labor history has found. But among the many conflicts, certain assumptions have operated to affect women in especially detrimental ways. Skill itself is constructed, not objectively determined, and as such, it is often gendered as male. Conversely, the types of work women perform, such as sewing or "nimble-fingered" activities, are usually construed as unskilled and of little monetary value. The superseding of women's labor has consequently gone unnoticed. Recent historians of technology have emphasized that the introduction of machinery often brings about a division of labor that excludes women from a small coterie of elite workers and assigns them to the more numerous ranks of cheap labor. The differential in male and female access to training and capital also places women at a disadvantage within the work force.[13]

The distribution of rational or scientific knowledge also follows a selective pattern according to gender. An examination of the dairy industry in Chapter 3 shows how technical know-how came to be promoted by male agricultural writers and cheese factors in the later part of the eighteenth century. Dairywomen lost authority as the business of modernizing the industry challenged their methods and opinions. Seen as wedded to backward traditions, women lost status in relation to new male managers and commercial men who controlled later developments in the industry. A similar eclipse of women's authority took place in the unlikely area of infant care, as professional medical men asserted authority over the customary practices of mothers. William Cadogan's popular *Essay on Nursing* (1750) argued that "the business [of nursing] has been too long fatally left to the Management of Women," who presumed upon the "examples and transmitted customs of their great grandmothers, who were taught by the physicians of their unenlightened days." The "Knowledge of Nature," by which was meant a very specific form of empirical enquiry, was an eighteenth-century form of technology not available to women, even when it had to do with their own breast milk—or the milk of their own cows.[14]

Thus many critiques of old assumptions in industrial history have changed the way in which we must approach the history of women workers. It is not enough to simply recount what women did and how their employments changed. The most noted work in this vein, Ivy Pinchbeck's *Women Workers and the Industrial Revolution 1750–1850* (1930;

reprint, 1969), remains unsurpassed in its detailed evidence of women's paid employment, but as such, offers a rather limited, empirical interpretation. More recent studies have expanded the definition of women's work to include unpaid labor and have analyzed larger patterns of women's employment. Bridget Hill's *Women, Work, and Sexual Politics in Eighteenth-Century England* (1989) examines many unrecorded activities carried on within households and families, while Jane Rendall's *Women in an Industrializing Society: England 1750–1880* (1990) summarizes the gender divisions evolving within the work force. Yet it is still necessary to ask how the advent of "industrial progress" in textile production, to take just one example, not only impinged upon the history of women by altering what they did and where (Pinchbeck's approach), but how ideas about women impinged upon industrial progress. Understandings of women, affected by new forms of knowledge, constantly changed during this period of rapid economic development. The transformation of ways of working also reconstituted understandings of women. With considerable information available on women and work, we still need to consider how discourses about women workers became involved in a major reevaluation of their productive role in society.[15]

The intention of the following chapters is to examine a selective number of women's economic activities in the context of the classic era of industrialization. Turning back to the eighteenth century, we must isolate cultural definitions of economic activity and the valuation of women's work. We can uncover these through discussions about labor, looking for what was recognized as productive and valued. What social arrangements and hierarchies were part of laborers' lives? What definitions of the female laborer issued from government policy and social practices? Were laborers conceived as interdependent or as individuals? How did the onset of industrialization change these considerations?

Within this complex play of forces, contemporaneous debates about female labor played a crucial part in determining what paid employment would be assigned to women and men. The printed forum of the eighteenth and nineteenth centuries was highly influential: economic writers, journalists, magistrates, novelists, and publicists of all kinds entered the polemical fray. Nothing interested the eighteenth-century British public more than the topic of the wealth of the nation. The problems raised by the eighteenth-century poor insinuated themselves into discussions of creating new wealth. By examining these debates, we can see how constructs of the woman worker were constituted and mobilized on behalf of conflicting interests and goals.

Chapters 1 through 6 focus on problems facing the most typical women laborers over the course of the last half of the eighteenth century. The disappearance of "traditional" aspects of society, marked by small-scale, local economies and face-to-face relations, acts as a backdrop to these chapters. Chapter 1 explores the ideological reasons why, at the outset of our study, eighteenth-century women laborers could claim an

economic identity without question. The chapter lays out early eighteenth-century arguments for high employment and an "all-inclusive"
goal for utilizing labor, which favorably affected attitudes toward women.
In an age of agriculture, dispersed cottage industry, and small commercial
enterprises, women laborers were recognized as industrious and productive. Old attitudes associated with paternalism, founded on an understanding of society as hierarchical and bound by mutual obligations,
assisted these women and the laboring poor in general in their quest for
employment, bread, and a minimal subsistence.

Agriculture played a pivotal role in transforming Britain into the first
industrial nation. An efficient system of food production was necessary in
order to provide for a population that would gradually transfer into non-
agricultural pursuits. In Britain, the "agricultural revolution," which
extended over two centuries, reorganized landholding to promote the
production of wool and foodstuffs for trade centers. With very little new
technology, changes in agricultural techniques proved highly successful,
especially after 1750, when profits from agriculture were at a premium.
Along with increased output, the new system provided a laboratory for
scientific method. A profit-oriented agricultural base thus advertised the
benefits of private property and rational improvement for the wider society.

As Chapter 2 explains, these changes set the stage for a long-term
diminution in the status of laboring women. Declining overall employment in agriculture in the late eighteenth century led to high unemployment of women and their confinement to seasonal, underpaid jobs. While
women laborers had benefited from attitudes of benevolence and paternalism under the old system, they experienced attacks on their customary
prerogatives under the new. They perforce obtained earnings, food, and
other subsistence needs through work now designated "marginal" and
low-paid, or, in some instances, "illegal." The ideal of a male wage
earner, discussed in economic writings and tracts on the poor, was seldom realized. Yet at the same time, women's work went unacknowledged
and women became associated with a notion of the idle poor.

Transformation in fields of knowledge related to agriculture affected
the assessment of women's customary expertise in rural work. This
became clear in the development of dairying, as discussed in Chapter 3.
As greater wealth accrued from commercial expansion, women's authority came under scrutiny. The technological revolution in spinning,
roughly coinciding with the changes in agriculture mentioned above,
made its impact felt even more keenly. Chapter 4 discusses how laboring
women lost their connection to the notion of productivity attached to
domestic spinning and became stigmatized as intractable opponents of
improvement. An awareness of gender informed entrepreneurial decisions
to mechanize spinning, and criticisms of female spinners entered a more
general discussion of what to do with female labor. The eventual elimination of spinning as a universal domestic employment paved the way for

further erosion of both the economic security of laboring women and their image as productive members of society.

The textile factory represents the most typical example of industrial innovation and provides an opportunity to discuss mechanization and wage labor with regard to new forms of women's work. Yet the image of the mill girl, independent and intrepid, is deceiving. The factory had a much more complicated impact on the general condition of women laborers. Chapter 5 discusses how the new industrial factory system, from its beginnings in the late eighteenth century, sought and utilized the labor of women with the specific intention of exploiting their cheapness, and later, their availability. Over the long term, women were subordinated to male labor within the factory. These developments worked to solidify a definition of women workers as secondary wage earners and, as a later chapter shows, aberrant females existing outside their proper sphere.

The loss of spinning, compounded by declining work in agriculture, led women to search for other forms of paid employment. Chapter 6 examines the expansion of cottage industries, the most exploitative of industrial employments, in the last two decades of the eighteenth century. This coincided with laboring families' heightened need for earnings and the aggravation of problems associated with the poor in both rural and urban settings. Perhaps more than any other line of employment, cottage industry contributed to the degradation of women of the laboring classes, blurring the distinction between "poor" and "immoral" in the eyes of their contemporaries.

The rise of a new set of attitudes, promoted through political economy and associated with industrialism, marked a turning point in the general view of working-class women. From the mid eighteenth century, rising prices and a growing population had exacerbated the problem of the poor. Antipathy toward laboring women was apparent in changing social relations between landed classes and laborers, rich and poor. The era of the French Revolution challenged earlier assumptions of a charitable paternalistic society. By the early 1800s, the ideas of Malthus and Ricardo, disseminated in popularized form, helped to identify poor women as a problem in need of a solution. Chapter 7 shows how prescriptive roles for laboring women originated not in the writings of Victorian moralists, but in the ideas of economic and political theorists contemplating the needs of the emergent capitalist order. Female laborers emerged into the new industrial age as "women workers," part of an industrial working class with separate interests and identities.

As new models of behavior for women emerged, middle-class women took up the role of mentor by proselytizing among the lower classes. Chapter 8 focuses on relationships between laboring women and women of the middle class, which were conceived in religious writings and other didactic literature aimed at women and often authored by them. The model of the male breadwinner played an important role in the construction of new images of gender and social relations. A powerful middle-class culture was in the making, and constructions of womanhood, like notions of work, were often deployed through manuals on female philanthropic work and proper behavior. In a subordinate role to her upper-class female mentor, the nineteenth-century working-class woman emerged in contradistinction to the middle-class ideal.

As the largest female occupation of the mid-Victorian period, domestic service provides another view of typical work for young lower-class women. The category is important for what it reveals about middle-class thought and behavior as much as for its obvious impact on working-class girls. Chapter 9 analyzes the transformation of domestic service from the eighteenth to the nineteenth centuries, from a form of employment associated with aristocratic values of honor and duty, to a contractual job requiring menial domestic work and conferring status upon the employer. The experience of servants throws light on hidden dynamics of Victorianism, particularly the divisions between women of different social classes. This final chapter examines the exercise of female power within the middle-class home and the importance of women in transmitting nineteenth-century cultural norms. Through relations with their servants, wives and mothers of the middle class completed the social and discursive marginalization of working women begun a century earlier by political writers and entrepreneurs.

1

Habits of Industry:
Laboring Women and the Poor
in Eighteenth-Century England

*The landholder, merchant, manufacturer, mechanick, [and] labourer,
in every station are all linked together in one common interest; . . . so
the extending [of] our commerce on the one hand, and the number of
people to execute on the other, must be [in] the spirit of trade and the
interest of all.*

> [Anon.], *Populousness with Oeconomy,*
> *the Wealth and Strength of a Kingdom* (1759)

> *But chief by numbers of industrious hands*
> *A Nation's wealth is counted: numbers raise*
> *Warm emulation: where that virtue dwells,*
> *There will be traffick's seat; there will she build*
> *Her rich emporium. Hence, ye happy swains,*
> *With hospitality inflame your breast,*
> *And emulation: the whole world receive,*
> *And with their arts, their virtues, deck your isle.*

> John Dyer, *The Fleece*, (1757)

The work of women was everywhere in evidence in eighteenth-century
England. As rural laborers and servants, women helped to produce the
busy nation's food supply. Their skill in the dairy was undisputed and
universally acclaimed. Their spinning, knitting, weaving, stitching, and
lace making supported a network of trade, domestic and foreign. The
myriad trades of London depended on the large female population that

congregated there, including the many women who sought alternatives to domestic service. No commentary would have denied that women laborers were important producers of the nation's wealth.[1]

The fact of such widespread expectation of women's labor hardly seems remarkable from the vantage point of eighteenth-century society, but in retrospect, we know that it is worth noting. By the mid nineteenth century, women of the lower classes no longer laid claim to such universal labor, nor did public opinion praise their economic activity. Before exploring the relationship between their image and actual work, we must consider some of the prevailing assumptions governing economic activity in the early industrial age. The contexts of eighteenth-century life ultimately had as much to do with producing notions of women's work as the actual work process itself. A configuration of social settings, institutions, customs, and laws shaped the economic roles available to laboring women. These primary determinants of their working lives, specific to time and place, also produced understandings of what forms of labor women could and, perhaps more importantly, should perform. Transformations in perceptions of class, morality, and womanhood, as well as changes in the way people worked, initiated a very different depiction of the female laborer at the end of the eighteenth century.

I

Eighteenth-century England inherited many assumptions from the Tudor and Stuart state that affirmed economic identity for women. The prevalence of "one common interest" embodied in an enterprise that was both political and economic was a distinctly old notion. Its most current understanding was embedded in the ideology of mercantilism, which held that economic activity must be deliberately directed by the state for the material benefit of the nation. The fate of all laborers was thus tied to a corporate, or collective understanding of society, binding together all ranks and both genders in a common enterprise. No aspect of this pre-Malthusian age is more striking than its celebration of burgeoning numbers of laboring people. "There was virtual unanimity on one central point," a historian of economic thought has shown: "the great importance attached to a large, well-ordered, healthy and industrious population." In this indirect way, ideological assumptions sustained an inclusion of women laborers in the eighteenth century.[2]

More specifically, the ideology of patriarchalism governed attitudes toward the female sex.[3] As a formal theoretical construct of the seventeenth century, patriarchalism conceived of the social and political order in terms of a family, whose head was, obviously, the father. Though new liberal ideas regarding the individual soon displaced this theory at high levels of discussion, common discourse continued to invoke the notion of patriarchy as a social ideal. "The landholder, merchant, manufacturer, mechanick, [and] labourer, in every station are all linked together in one common interest," asserted an anonymous address to Parliament at mid-century:

> We shall find it binding for parents to preserve and cherish their children, from hence the analogy [of] fatherhood continued to all bodies of people, whether towns, cities, or kingdoms, the same law must be equally binding. We are one as to nation, one people, one great family, and every individual, unable to provide for himself, has a right derived from the first law to be taken care of.[4]

This model found reinforcement in the belief and practices of the Established Church, which actively promoted filial obedience for a century following the Restoration. Citizenship belonged exclusively to male familial heads (specifically, to those of the propertied classes), whose authority mirrored the greater power of the monarchy. Women, children, and servants, including apprentices and laborers living within a master's household, ranked as subordinates who received protection, care, and discipline from their masters. Throughout English society, patriarchal discourse enjoyed a common currency that liberal theories combated for at least a century more.[5]

Like their political and social identity, the economic activity of women was, in the words of one scholar of the period, "altogether vicarious." When laboring women worked, produced wealth, or experienced need, they did so under the aegis of their allotted households. Parish records rarely recorded women's occupations, identifying women through their fathers' or husbands' names and occupations. Yet this did not erase the importance of women's work in sustaining production. Women's labor was a crucial part of what historians have termed the "family economy" of the laboring classes. Households carried on several forms of economic activity that depended upon the work of all members, male and female, young and old. The historian must first wrest the work of women from this distinctive form of obscurity.[6]

We also need to identify women within the masses of eighteenth-century "laboring poor." This indefinite term sufficed to describe a spectrum of categories and walks of life, from street vendor to charwoman, that together comprised a significant proportion of the English population. In fact, little distinction existed between categories of "laboring" and "poor" since most eighteenth-century common people were both.[7] Statistics for the period are fugitive, but the best known, compiled by Gregory King at the end of the seventeenth century, publicized what contemporaries already knew: nearly half the English population consisted of laborers, cottagers, servants living out, and paupers who did not earn enough to get by.[8]

The number of women within the category of the poor was quite considerable. Recent estimates have shown that as much as 86 percent of the population classified as "poor" in 1755 were women; for 1801 to 1803 the percentage was roughly the same.[9] Their identity as women, however, was seldom discussed, even though much poor law administration, in its constant attention to bastardy and widowhood, appears to have had more to do with women than men. In their magisterial study of the poor laws, Sidney and Beatrice Webb argued that "the eighteenth century, even more than the seventeenth or sixteenth, thought of the poor in the lump, and scarcely ever discriminated in thought, or in the written records, between such categories as the able-bodied, the sick and infirm or the children."[10] One could certainly add gender to this list. Yet the impression given is that the eighteenth century, like our own age, saw a convergence of the categories of women and poverty.[11]

Widespread neediness was a daily reminder of the urgency of projects to employ the poor. Lawmakers, landowners, and writers alike engaged in an energetic debate over the most effective way of harnessing the nation's productive potential. What constituted the wealth of the nation? How could every man, woman, and child be enlisted in augmenting that wealth? And who was responsible for so many laborers?[12] The hope of turning the hands of every common person to remunerative industry was not misplaced, for local parishes were responsible for maintaining the poor and thus exercised some control over them.

Writers tacitly concurred that women, as part of the great mass of employable laborers, ought to work. "For having nothing but their Labour to bestow on the Society," argued Henry Fielding, "if [the poor] withhold this from it, they become useless Members; and having nothing but their Labour to procure a Support for themselves, they must of Necessity become burthensome."[13] Josiah Tucker assigned employments to "women and Children, as well as Men." "For no Person should be permitted to remain in a State of absolute Idleness," he argued, "if any Part could be found out, in which he might be usefully employed, without unreasonable Fatigue or immoderate Labour."[14]

But exactly how the vast reserve of labor should be put to work was another matter. The countryside afforded numerous opportunities for employment, not only in agriculture, but in domestic-based hand manufactures. Economic writers long understood that one of the best means of sustaining large numbers of laborers, both female and male, was through a combination of small-scale farming and cottage industry. In the words of Carew Reynel, writing in 1674, a "variety of husbandries" alongside a "variety of manufactures" promised to generate industry and wealth in a more evenly distributed fashion.[15] Such arguments survived well into the eighteenth century, particularly in the more market-oriented parts of the countryside, where mixed economies offered an alternative to the more recent trend of engrossing land for large-scale farming.

The jewel of England's commercial crown was the woolen industry, which employed men, women, and children in great numbers. Laborers in this area of economic activity "not only support themselves but enrich their country at the same time," argued a later writer, echoing the mercantilist arguments for advancing the national wealth before individual interests. As the crux of his argument, he presented a table (Table 1.1) that documented the number of days spent producing "*one* piece of superfine [Spanish] cloth."[16]

Women's work obviously offered a true boon to the economic well-being of the laboring family. "When our Woollen Manufactory flourishes, the wives and children of small Farmers, Cottagers, and Labouring Men, can earn nearly as much money by spinning at the wheel, as the man can get by his industry in the field," the author pointed out. He added, "[W]hen our woollen manufactory declines, the man alone must wield the labouring oar." The single male wage-earner, far from embodying a "breadwinner" ideal, represented a threat to the well-being of the laboring family. Eighteenth-century social theorists understood that the "melancholy frequency" of exactly this sequence of events accounted for the large number of applications for support from the parish.[17]

Tracts on the poor called attention to the productive capacities of laboring women. In a pamphlet best known for its proposals for the employment of children, Thomas Firmin implied that the bulk of his subjects were, in actuality, women. *Some Proposals For the imployment of the Poor, and For the prevention of Idleness and the Consequence thereof, Begging* (1681) exemplified how the identity of women and the needs of the poor were conflated. Its bold frontispiece, which depicted a spinster of pious simplicity sitting at the flax wheel, advertised the objective of

Table 1.1 Production of Superfine Cloth, 1773

	Men	*Women*	*Boys*	*Days*	*Number*
Dyeing	1	0	0	1	1
Beating and picking	0	2	0	4	8
Scribbling	2	0	0	5	10
Spinning the chain	0	8	0	7	56
Spinning the woof	0	8	0	7	56
Winding the chain	0	3	0	1	3
Warping, winding, quils, and weaving	2	0	1	24	72
Spinning the lift	0	2	0	2	4
Burling	0	2	0	4	8
Milling	1	0	0	1	1
Dressing	4	0	0	5	20
	80	135	24	Total	239

Firmin's plan; his repeated use of the female pronoun only underscored his intent. "Each Parish," he proposed, should provide work for women "as they might carry to their own Homes," namely, "Spinning of those vast Quantities of Yarn, which is every Year made use of, for the making of Bays, Sayes, Serges, and Stuffs of all sorts." Firmin's plan appeared unassailable in its logic. "I have taught several persons of about sixty years of age, to Spin," Firmin announced,

> who do constantly follow this Work, if they have no other; but if this answer will not do, the next should, which is this, if the Person cannot live of her Pension, and will not, being able, accept of such Employment as the Parish hath to give; let her get some other, by means of which she may help to maintain her self, so that she be not found begging in the Streets, upon pain of losing that Relief which she received from the Parish; to prevent which, 'tis like she would fall to work, from which, and her Pension, she might make a good Shift to live.[18]

Firmin's assumptions were those of his age: laboring women, like men, could support themselves; unlike men, they could always resort to the wheel for subsistence earnings.[19] His estimate of their earning power was not quite accurate—spinning and other preparatory tasks in textile production were notoriously ill paid—but his recognition of the simple fact that they produced wealth and earned a wage nevertheless represented an important difference between his age and a later one.

Women's work, according to timeless prescription, should adapt to the demands of the moment. Addressing the social effects of economic fluctuations, which often rendered whole localities inactive, Firmin recognized the capacity of women to alleviate the needs of their households through makeshift wealth-producing activities. Even the most essential branches of industry suffered periods of recession, he admitted, forcing many cottage workers into idleness. "If any of these should fail, as many times they do," Firmin noted, "had not then the poor People better spin than do nothing?"[20] Stopgap time at the wheel was only one of several means by which women could earn small sums. The enduring ideal of female virtue and industry informed contemporaries' view of the potential of women laborers to sustain their households in good times and bad.[21]

Women did, indeed, suffer periods of idleness and poverty. Circumstances specific to female lives accounted for much unemployment, and Firmin, for one, was sensitive to these conditions. In advocating domestic spinning over that performed in "Houses of Industry," Firmin argued that women's customary family responsibilites made going out to work difficult: "For suppose a Woman hath a sick Child, or Husband, or some Infirmity upon her self," he explained, "in all which Cases, she may do something at home, but cannot leave her own House." He was also well aware of the other primary characteristic of women's work, its seasonality and often its inconstancy:

As suppose a poor Woman that goeth three days in a week to wash or Scour abroad, or one that is imploy'd in Nurse-keeping three or four months in a year, or a poor Market-woman, that attends three or four Mornings in a Week, with her Basket, and all the rest of the time these folks have little or nothing else to do;

All of these assumed characteristics of women's lives—the responsibility of caring for others, confinement to menial and irregular jobs, as well as dependence on trades whose fortunes were subject to fluctuation—rendered women highly subject to the threat of poverty.[22]

It is not surprising, then, that women figured prominently as applicants for parish relief in the eighteenth century. This was particularly true when they lived outside the bounds of household and patriarchal structures, as in the case of single women, single mothers, and widows. English society prided itself in its longstanding attitude of responsibility for the poor. The famous Tudor legislation, familiarly referred to as "the 43rd of Elizabeth," established a wide-reaching legal foundation for provision of relief at the parish level. Poor law officers reviewed petitions for aid individually and doled out money, provisions, and sometimes even livestock or tools as they saw fit. One Elizabeth Atkin of Hawkshead received 3s. 6d."for her peats getting." In Warwickshire, officers paid for "2 loads of wood for Widd: Minas, she being a poore woman with several small children . . 12 [shillings]—."[23] As Roy Porter has pointed out, "In a multitude of small ways, the poor law served as a thorough-going system of support for and control over parishioners, complementing the family as the main regulator of life."[24] Most adult women depended on a combination of spinning and day labor in agriculture, work that proved to be highly insecure, particularly as the eighteenth century wore on. Because women generally received low wages for their work, they were more likely to need assistance in achieving a subsistence when they lived by themselves. Judging from the wide variety of allowances, poor law overseers saw the claims of a great many women as legitimate.

Offspring of the poor were entitled to parish-sponsored apprenticeship, and at the beginning of the eighteenth century, this could bring with it the opportunity to learn a relatively lucrative trade. As many as a third of all apprentices from the seventeenth to the nineteenth centuries were girls, who, like boys, completed entire terms in order to enter fully their chosen trades. The parish's frequent failure to discriminate according to sex when assigning poor girls to trades, compared to the nineteenth century, is inescapably striking: when dealing with the bottom of the social pyramid, authorities could choose expediency over categorizing by gender. Girls were apprenticed to a wide variety of occupations, from tailoring and blacksmithing to harnessmaking and shoemaking. A far greater number of female parish apprentices came within the all-embracing category of "housewifery," which encompassed skilled and unskilled work such as baking, brewing, and general servicing of the household.[25] The parish also placed many young women in the typically female-dominated textile and needlework trades, comprising a wide range of work, such as weaving and tailoring, in addition to knitting and spinning. Thus this sex-blindness should not be exaggerated: it pertained mainly to the very lowest strata of the laboring classes who relied on parish placements for their apprenticeships. Their employers probably took them on the cheapest possible terms. More discrimination was practiced among parents who could afford to pay the premium for a conventional apprenticeship. By the end of the eighteenth century, the parish appears to have favored only certain trades for girls.[26]

Eighteenth-century assistance had its limits: the poor laws were grounded in the geographical unit of the parish, and beyond this area, generosity did not extend. A special clause added to poor law legislation in 1662, amended but preserved in 1693, enabled overseers of the poor to remove any persons born outside the parish whom justices believed were "likely to be chargeable to the Parish."[27] A married woman derived her settlement from that of her husband, even when living apart, so the unattached woman was a particular target for the zealous overseer attempting to keep down the rates. These Settlement Laws produced an enormous mound of litigation in the eighteenth century. Cases frequently focused on removing single laboring women (sometimes pregnant, and, in some notorious instances, even in labor) or unattached women with children from parishes where they had no legitimate claim to residency. "1723 for removing of foure bige bellyd woemoen out of ye parish when like to bee chargeable . . 16 [shillings]—00" and "1722 To a big bellyd woman several days & nights at nursing at Robinsons, & conveying her to Chigivell after she had gathered strength to prevent her lying in here, she fell to pieces in 2 or 3 days there . . 17 [shillings]—7 [pence]" appear typical in parish records. As Dorothy Marshall observed from a general perusal of quarter sessions accounts, "When responsible parish officers adopted these tactics, it is no wonder that the roads were thick with wandering women in a pregnant condition."[28] While "the married labourer overburdened with children" was "the type of wage earner most likely to fall into distress," figures from eighteenth-century sessions books show independent women of all categories following as a close second (Table 1.2).[29]

The presence of laboring women was noticed and acted upon as a social problem. An act passed in 1744 extended the definition of idle and disorderly persons subject to arrest to include those who threatened or "actually do abandon wives and children, leaving them to the parish." Given the energy devoted to removals and the more general public outcry against rising poor rates, the "laboring woman question" emerges as a stark reality of eighteenth-century society.[30]

Settlement cases openly reveal how vulnerable to disaster such women were, regardless of whether they found places as servants. The mundane and often tragic circumstances of ordinary women are vividly inscribed in

Table 1.2 Status of Individuals Removed by Selected Parishes[29]

1699–1715

63 [married] couples
33 single women
14 widows   } 59 women of all categories
12 unencumbered widows
23 children, including bastards
17 single men

1716–32

81 [married] couples
42 women
12 widows   } 54 women of all categories
41 children
33 single men

1736–49

80 [married] couples
31 women
21 widows   } 52 women of all categories
13 children
16 single men

these legal records, which lavish generous attention upon the finest details of laborers' lives in order to determine their rightful place of origin. Lacking access to property or money and with limited opportunity to learn skills and trades, women became pathetically dependent upon their masters, their husbands, and their bodies for financial security. One Bridget Gibson, twice a widow, though probably not much older than thirty, was removed from Whitehaven, Cumberland, because she lacked a legitimate claim to residency there in 1782. The commanding influence of a colonial empire intruded into her otherwise restricted provincial life, in this case, through marriage: her first husband was a seaman "who belonged to the ship, *Violet,* in the *African* trade." Soon after he had departed on a voyage, Bridget gave birth to a daughter, and as a new mother, found employment as a wet nurse. She entered into a two-year "contract" with a Mrs. Anthony Benn, "to nurse her child for two shillings and six-pence *per* week wages, so long as the child should remain at the breast." During this time, Bridget's own child died. The records fall silent as to why, but the poignancy of Bridget's continuing service to the Benn baby is not lost. Perhaps in sympathy, Mrs. Benn offered Bridget further employment. "*Bridget,* I'll give you four guineas a-year, which is more wages than I ever before gave a nursery-maid," she was reported to have said. Bridget thus remained for two additional years, though no formal acknowledgment of the second term was made. This lapse would raise legal questions in years to come, but Bridget was in no position to quibble over details.[31]

During her second year of service, Bridget learned that her husband had died near Guinea, though the day or month of his death could not be ascertained. She eventually received at least part of her husband's unpaid wages owing to the intervention of Mr. Benn. Perhaps her acquiring so much money made her an attractive marriage partner, for in 1777, she married a William Gibson and commenced living with him in White-haven. When Gibson died (for reasons unstated) sometime around 1782, Bridget and another newborn child presented a potential financial burden to the parish. Because Gibson had told his new wife only that his settle-ment was "in *Yorkshire*," she had no exact notion of where her legal claim to relief was. The court finally ordered Bridget and her child back to the parish of the Benns at Hensingham, even though her life had changed considerably during the five years since her service to that fam-ily.[32]

Settlement records underscore how frequently women lacked knowl-edge of this crucial aspect of their own identity, either because they had been bereft of or abandoned by men who had never informed them of their rightful residence, or because their husbands simply had not known their own settlements. The conditions that sent women adrift are particu-larly revealing of the most salient economic and social forces of the age. Joseph Massie listed the "Wives or Widows and young Children of *Man-ufacturers, Labourers, Seamen,* or *Soldiers*" as typically experiencing this dilemma; yet it is difficult to imagine many eighteenth-century laboring men who did not fit into these categories. Many women were deserted by husbands who might have gone abroad to find a job, joined the army or navy, probably because they lacked employment, or simply ran away. Sarah Kidson, a former servant, and her six-month old daughter, Han-nah, were removed from Winlaton, Durham, in 1778, after the sessions verified that her husband, Benjamin Kidson, "a soldier in his Majesty's regiment of foot called the *Young Buffs*, now in *America*," was not legally settled where Sarah lived. "It is not known whether he is living or dead; that the place of his legal settlement is not known, and that there-fore the pauper [has] been removed to the place of settlement of the said *Sarah Kidson* before her marriage," read the record. Kidson and her daughter thus were forced to move to Ryton, Durham, where Sarah had worked as a servant for a year previous to her marriage. The legal records show the process by which many laboring women were rendered home-less and powerless; at the same time, perhaps ironically, they indicate how eager the late eighteenth-century courts were to reduce their financial responsibility for the poor. In the flurry of proceedings against poor women, resentment and hostility seem quite apparent.[33]

The poor laws were not expected to alleviate all the needs of the female poor; private charity and public philanthropy also came to the rescue. "Houses of industry," spinning schools, "houses of refuge," and charity schools offered a miscellany of solutions, many of them hopelessly amateurish. Public debate often cited the parochial custom of setting an entire family to labor as a tried and true method of addressing the problem of unemployment. At the same time, wealthy donors created new institutions in response to common forms of female distress. Among the major London charities established between 1740 and 1760, the Lying-in Hospital and the Magdalen Hospital dispensed care to pregnant women and prostitutes, decrying the most pronounced effects of poverty on laboring women.[34]

None of these schemes would be necessary, of course, if sufficient employment opportunities existed for laboring women. Long before the later part of the century, as agricultural and cottage employments noticeably declined, writers became aware of the lack of work for women. "I have often observed," remarked Sir John Fielding (half-brother of the more famous novelist) in his *Plan for a Preservatory and Reformatory, for the Benefit of Deserted Girls, and Penitent Prostitutes*, "that the Trades for employing Women are too few, that those which Women might execute are engrossed by Men, and that many Women have not the Opportunity of learning even those which Women do follow, on Account of the Premiums paid for learning the said Businesses[.]"[35] Many writers commonly held that idleness among the poor, female or male, led to crime and vice. Instead of reaping the returns from the productivity of laboring women and men, society was beleaguered by pickpockets and prostitutes.[36] At the end of the century, Priscilla Wakefield called attention to the same problem of narrowing opportunities in trade for women:

> The knowledge of a trade is a probable means, which ought not to be neglected, of enabling [women] to give their assistance towards the support of their family .... Men monopolize not only the most advantageous employments, and such as exclude women from the exercise of them, by the publicity of their nature, or the extensive knowledge they require, but even many of those, which are consistent with the female character. Another heavy discouragement to the industry of women, is the inequality of the reward of their labour, compared with that of men, an injustice which pervades every species of employment performed by both sexes.

But proponents for education for women in the trades were too few, and the disruption to the existing labor market too threatening to result in any large-scale plan.[37]

Philanthropic schemes offered certain advantages: such projects addressed immediate, local problems on an ad hoc basis and enabled reformers to highlight the dramatic healing effects of their efforts. More than the awkward operations of the poor laws, which seemed to reward those who did not work, these institutions encouraged industriousness among the poor.[38] Springing from the beneficence of interested individuals, charitable establishments appeared to knit together the social orders more effectively than legislative action.[39] Contemporaries never failed to applaud any material benefit flowing from such schemes, as proved by the enormous success of the Marine Society, which funneled boys into the Royal Navy. Admittedly, charities for girls promised less impressive returns. As Donna Andrew has explained, "women needed more sheltering and training, and earned less," and therefore "societies caring for women and girls appeared to be less profitable investments than other sorts of charities."[40] But the ubiquity of the female poor warranted some form of action. The unrealized productive potential of laboring women became one of the strongest arguments for directing attention to their needs.

While male laborers could always be enlisted to fill the ranks of the armed forces, expectations of poor women oscillated between the two stereotypic roles of servant and prostitute. Ideally, charitable institutions should reach young women before they slid from one line of work to the other. "What then must become of the daughters of [degraded] parents," one minister asked, "whose settlements are extremely difficult to be ascertained; especially the orphans of seamen and soldiers? [P]oor and ignorant as they are, they must be encompassed with every temptation; and necessity may make them prostitutes, before their passions can have any share in their guilt."[41] The Magdalen Hospital for penitent prostitutes argued that "such women will be found faithful and excellent servants . . . whose minds have been diligently cultivated with the best instructions; and whose industrious way of life in, and attendance upon, the business of the house, must necessarily qualify them for all menial offices." The governors shrewdly appealed to subscribers in two ways: as both donors and potential employers.[42] The guardians of the Lambeth Asylum, which schooled female orphans in "good housewifry, in order to qualify them for domestic servants," likewise believed that their goal would appear a worthy cause to potential donors. "Instead of being a nuisance and burden to the public," a minister told the guardians, the girls "become instrumental to its interest, and real blessings to their country."[43] Fielding's plan for a reformatory for deserted girls promised that "[t]he only Difficulty . . . is, the first Expence," since the charity would "prove a constant Nursery for a Body of useful Domestics, much wanted in this Town." The institution was actually planned to function as a "public Laundry."[44]

Joseph Massie's *A Plan for the Establishment of Charity-Houses for Exposed or Deserted women and girls, and for penitent prostitutes* (1758) revealed the extent to which contemporaries assumed that domestic service would act as an all-purpose source of employment for most women of the laboring classes. Under these circumstances, women could be expected to live and work under the authority of a male head of household who acted in loco parentis. According to Massie's observations, many "exposed" women and girls originally arrived in London in search of a "place" in service, either as a first position of employment, or as a replacement for some former one. Ill luck simply prevented them from finding safe harbor or a suitable alternative. "Some Accident, Disease (the foul one excepted), or a bad State of Health" rendered many others incapable of obtaining situations as servants. According to popular opinion, this pool of unskilled, often naive young females ultimately also supplied the city with its numerous prostitutes.[45]

Massie and many other philanthropists comprehended the remunerative potential—in many cases, already demonstrated—of so many females. "For there are great Numbers of Women," he declared, "who not only maintain themselves by honest Industry, but a Child or Children also, and, by such common sorts of Work as Women or Girls of ordinary Capacities may easily learn." "Manufactures" provided employment in the capital, and Massie strongly advocated putting former prostitutes and other unattached women to work in such industries. "If all the exposed or deserted Women or Girls in this Metropolis can be constantly Employed in some such Sorts of Work, without depriving any or many *British* or *Irish* Women or Girls of Employment, it would be happy indeed."[46]

Prostitutes were regarded as suitable candidates for productive work in spite of their fallen state. Some eighteenth-century philanthropists maintained that necessity rather than any predisposition to debauchery led these women down the wrong path, and that useful, remunerative employment would render them "pious, industrious, and frugal, [and] prepare them for a comfortable settlement in the world."[47] The typical background of a prostitute, according to Sir John Fielding, might even include a hard-working mother, whose only deficiency was that she had too few skills to provide for numerous children. The fathers of prostitutes appeared in a less favorable light:

> Infinite are the Number of Chairmen, Porters, Labourers, and drunken Mechanics in this Town, whose Families are generally too large to receive even Maintenance, much less Education, from the Labour of their Parents; and the Lives of their Fathers being often shortened by their Intemperance, a Mother is left with many helpless Children, to be supplied by her Industry; whose Resource for Maintenance is either the Wash-Tub, Green-Stall, or Barrow. What must then become of the Daughters of such Women, where Poverty and Illiterateness conspire to expose them to every Temptation? And they often become Prostitutes from Necessity, even before their Passions can have any Share in their Guilt.[48]

II

After midcentury, the positive image of the laboring woman characterized by her industriousness and economic potential was challenged by another, more critical view: she came to embody the undesirable impulses of human nature, including a general disregard for morality and the law, particularly that which related to property. The stereotype of the degraded female of the lower classes of course predates this period, but it is at this juncture that the negative image overshadows the more positive view of laboring women sustained by preindustrial settings. The fusing of women laborers and immorality occurred through a complex set of processes, several of which will be covered in the following chapters. Their denigration was linked to a general critique of the laboring classes emerging in the last decades of the eighteenth century alongside rising unemployment, urbanization, and sharpening class antagonism.

After 1750, the situation of the vast majority of the laboring classes worsened. Unemployment, poverty, declining nutrition and living conditions, and frequent periods of hunger marked the later years of the century. Historians have attributed many of these developments to the rapid growth of population evident from the 1750s. The rate of increase for England and Wales more than doubled in the second half of the century, pushing numbers from 6.20 million in 1751 to 9.16 million in 1801.[49] Food prices rose as a result, but new liberal market strategies contributed to distress by removing statutory controls on staple commodities. Thus the price of bread climbed and the availability of coveted commodities, such as meat, declined. Britain finally ceased exporting grain and, after 1765, became reliant upon imports to feed its own population. This, in itself, marked an important change in the economic life of the nation, one that called attention to vulnerability to economic fluctuations. Crowds protested against new policies and demanded that local authorities continue to regulate the sale of wheat and bread. A stable and cheap food supply was the backbone of a sound economy in the eighteenth century, and these later years would test the strength of Britain's social fabric.[50]

The age was also marked by periods of warfare: over half of the entire century was spent in conflict, and in the latter part, war with France between 1756 and 1763, the American Revolution from 1775 to 1783, and the French Revolution and Napoleonic wars from 1793 to 1815 produced fluctuations in trade and employment. Unemployment and poverty were perennial features of laboring life, but certain developments of the late eighteenth century rendered them particularly threatening to the laboring classes. Landlessness and dependence on wage earning (and hence, the purchase of food) left many laborers vulnerable to the inevitable vicissitudes of the economy. Rural laborers and cottagers, displaced by alterations in landholding, streamed into London and provincial towns. Joining their ranks were migrant laborers drawn from all parts of the globe, transported to England by colonial ventures and the British navy. London evolved into a metropolitan center crowded with warehouses, workshops, cheap entertainments, and gin shops. Critics of the poor laws strengthened the case for reform or abolition by pointing to the ever-rising level of taxation devoted to poor relief.[51]

These developments made their mark on current understandings of the laboring classes. Noteworthy after midcentury is the mobilization of an image of the poor as a social threat. In contrast with the sanctified notion of the poor as a blessing and sign from God, the belief in their nefarious-ness tapped the least inspired human impulses: resentment against those who accepted rather than gave aid; xenophobia against strangers, easily stoked in growing towns and especially in London; and paranoia among the increasingly wealthy, who felt that visible evidence of affluence ren-dered them vulnerable to attack. By the 1750s, the category of an under-class was coming into being, constructed as much from the fears of the rich as from the activities of the poor.[52]

In urban settings, laboring women were constantly thrust into an unflattering and often damaging limelight. The hard circumstances of their lives contributed to the deterioration of their public image. The growth of London called attention to the lack of employment for rural women, as migrants reportedly swelled the city's population of beggars, prostitutes, and thieves. During years of economic distress, crime rates for women appear to have soared. Single women were particularly numerous in cases of crime against property, which John Beattie has correlated with years of high prices and unemployment.[53] Rates of illegitimacy and infan-ticide were also sensitive to these factors. Hogarth's engraving of "A Woman Swearing a Child to a Rich Merchant" (that is, testifying to the paternity of her baby *in utero*, a notorious means of obtaining monetary damages for illegitimate children) wryly depicts a pregnant laboring woman, presumably a servant, utilizing a legal strategy that engendered great resentment and antagonism in the eighteenth century. The print exposed the frailty of the law, undone by the alleged immorality of women.[54]

A tarnished image emerges from many legal discussions of laboring women during the latter half of the eighteenth century. Contemporaries most likely expected the lower-class female to be bold and, for the most part, dishonest in her dealings with others. Handbooks on servants warned of her tendency to help herself to food, silver, jewelry, and money. Theft of a master's property became one of the first crimes to be made a capital offense when laws were reformed in 1706, and theft from a home with belongings valued over forty shillings was added in 1713. "If the true extent of petty theft by servants could be measured," John Beattie has pointed out, "the level of women's crime would be much higher than appears simply from the court records."[55] Theft of manufac-turing materials rivaled domestic theft as a source of suspicion and anxi-ety aimed at women. In the North, research shows, women pilfered raw materials, such as wool and cotton, in their dealings with middlemen. In London and port towns, their role as "chip-women" (gatherers of "chips" or wood scraps from shipbuilding) was as familiar as the gleaner of rural areas. Laws against such practices multiplied as well, demonstrat-ing how intractable this type of customary appropriation remained and how sentiment against it grew. It is no surprise that Samuel Richardson made his heroine Pamela win her fantastic reward not only by being chaste, but by her simple honesty as well.[56]

Low wages and powerlessness in determining the conditions of work probably justified these infractions in the minds of the women who committed them. As one looked further down the social hierarchy in urban areas, theft became ever more definitive in determining survival for poor women. "For . . . poor People *set their Wits to work that they may eat*," Massie pointed out in describing women in London; "and I am persuaded that if it was possible to know the Value of what they every Year *beg*, *pilfer*, or *steal*, in this Metropolis, it would amount to more than, with proper Management, would decently maintain them all."[57] A vague awareness of the extremes of urban poverty generated a chronic anxiety within the breasts of the propertied classes. Perhaps this was why charities in London experienced a crisis in support from the 1770s. Doubts about the beneficial effects of population growth very likely influenced the decline in support for the Lying-in Hospital.[58]

By the end of the eighteenth century, any sympathetic understanding of the exigencies of the female poor seemed anomalous among so many critiques of the behavior and habits of the laboring classes. It became clear that the "one common interest" of earlier times could no longer describe the spirit of the age. While the shadow of the urban population played a conspicuous role in this development, changes in rural society also helped to generate negative sentiments toward the poor. The place of women laborers within this declension can be understood by turning first to the transformation of English agriculture. New priorities became apparent as promoters of improved farming advanced the rights of private property against the claims of the poor. Customary images of female productivity, so important to the positive assessment of the female poor, had been embedded in traditional forms of agriculture. As alterations became prevalent in the latter half of the eighteenth century, the value of laboring women within rural society inevitably came into question.

2

Economies of Survival:
Laboring Women and
Agricultural Change, 1750–1800

When Harvest comes, into the Field we go,
And help to reap the Wheat as well as you,
Or else we go the ears of Corn to glean,
No Labour scorning, be it e'er so mean,
But in the Work we freely bear a part,
And what we can, perform with all our Heart.

Mary Collier, *The Woman's Labour* (1739)

According to most eighteenth-century authorities, rural England was the true source of people and produce; there also lay the foundation for a stable civic order. England was, after all, a predominantly rural society. An estimated 70 percent of the population of England and Wales lived in the country in 1780. While London and a few provincial towns were prominent in political and cultural affairs, the countryside figured as the repository of seemingly timeless ideals and values.[1] But signs of change, detectable in any age, were becoming increasingly evident by the 1750s. The conspicuousness of "deserted women and girls" congregating in the capital led the economic writer Joseph Massie to publish a proposal for charity houses for females. He added substantial commentary on rural problems, which he felt were growing more urgent each year. The well-being of the entire nation, he argued, was threatened by "removing multitudes of people, from our natural and fixed basis, land, to the artificial and fluctuating" economic activity of the city, trade. Massie added his voice to a growing chorus of opinion on the changes in the countryside that were disrupting the lives of the laboring classes.[2]

29

"Custom" and "tradition" are powerful and often deceptive concepts that can inhibit our understanding of historical change. Yet they do help us to describe aspects of rural laboring life in the eighteenth century. Massie's observations reveal a typical understanding of how customary arrangements were believed to accommodate the needs of laboring women. In families with access to land, women as well as men assumed economic responsibilities recognized as essential to the livelihoods of all. Rights to common land, referred to as "customary," would bring prosperity in years of plenty and provide sustenance in difficult times. Women's work in this realm was highly productive and time-honored. Furthermore, a solid foundation in land enabled common people to achieve a measure of self-sufficiency, apart from waged work for large farmers or in cottage industry. This fact appeared to engender an independent spirit that kept common people off the parish relief rolls. Political and social theorists expatiated on the value of such arrangements in fostering virtues like loyalty and bravery, and they argued that women and children greatly benefited from the resulting household stability.[3]

Rural women's lives were never as prosperous and secure as theorists would have hoped, but agricultural settings did offer the possibility of scratching at least part of a living from the soil. In the later part of the eighteenth century, though, this option disappeared, as customary rights were eliminated by agrarian capitalism. The restructuring of landholding according to restrictive definitions of property ownership curtailed informal work involving growing or gathering food and supplies from common land or wastes. Laboring women, by implication, stood to suffer by this turn of events. Their reliance upon work now prohibited by more efficient, "scientific" agriculture forced them to turn to forms of wage work, which, as we shall see, offered little recompense. Furthermore, in the course of these changes, laboring women came to be seen in a negative light. Their positive image depended not only on their association with productivity, but also on their regard for the law. As upholders of "custom" now seen as retrograde and even illegal, women laborers fared badly in the otherwise auspicious years of agricultural transformation.

I

Despite their numerical preponderance, the laboring classes were in possession of remarkably little land in the eighteenth century. Landlords held approximately 75 percent of the countryside, freeholders owned between 15 and 20 percent more, and the remainder, a mere 5 percent, was left to smallholders, mainly cottagers, who also labored for wages.[4] Unlike the typical European peasant, who farmed a family holding and was relatively self-sufficient, the English rural inhabitant depended on employment on the land of others in order to make a living. The consolidation and pri-

vatization of holdings in sheep-grazing areas in the Midlands created the
most pronounced example of this system of landholding in the seventeenth century. Many laborers there were forced to turn to cottage
industry as a partial or total means of support. Large landowners in parts
of the South and East, where land was most suitable to market agriculture, employed men and women laborers on a large scale. In other
regions, an array of small farming establishments bridged the gap
between the large landowner and the landless poor. But by far the
majority of common people at the bottom of the social pyramid owned
no property at all.[5]

Laboring families managed to get by simply by having access to land,
exercising what were known as "use rights." Exclusive or private rights to
property were as yet relatively insignificant in setting the terms of eighteenth-century rural life. The old open village system instead established
several different bases from which inhabitants could share or individually
use land. Varying according to locality, a typical arrangement frequently
comprised three types of land: arable fields sectioned into strips belonging to different families; common meadows devoted to hay and similarly
partitioned; and commons and waste (uncultivated land), open to all,
which functioned as pasture throughout the year, or, if part remained in
woodland, provided firewood and opportunities for game-hunting.
Laborers could raise their own crops on a patch of waste, graze livestock
on the common, gather firewood from the local lord's woods, and glean
from a landowner's field after harvest. Years of such practice established
these activities as law and justified their defense in manorial courts.
Dependent upon such arrangements were not just landless laborers but
also considerable numbers of smallholders and cottagers. Common rights
of all kinds thus coexisted alongside more individualized arrangements,
with contemporaries seeing little incompatability among them.[6]

Laboring women were direct beneficiaries of this loose system of property ownership since they cultivated family allotments and carried on
many of the activities governed by common rights. In fact, without the
considerable effort of the woman of the household, simple access to land
yielded few benefits. Male laborers joined in cultivating their small
acreage only after their waged work was done; large landowners were
sensitive to the competing demands of small holdings, and it was difficult
for laborers to spend much time on their allotments to the detriment of
their regular employments. In most cases, the woman of the household
undertook the responsibility for the work, growing potatoes, wheat, and
vegetables, with occasional assistance from her children and her husband.
Such responsibility required continuous labor, which enhanced the laboring woman's image of industriousness in the eyes of her contemporaries.[7]

The efforts of women cottagers could be prodigious and not without
up-to-date technical know-how. One woman, the wife of a collier at
Shrewsbury, lavished such care upon her minute holding (totaling a mere

one and one-sixteenth acre) that she was able, "chiefly by her own labour," to grow a sizable quantity of food, "good crops, and of late fully equal, or rather superior, to the produce of the neighbouring farms, and with little or no expence." She cleverly alternated plantings of potatoes and wheat, fertilizing the ground with manure from her pig. By using a three-pronged fork to dig up the potatoes, she was at once able to cultivate the ground and cover wheat seed for the following year. Nothing was wasted: the family pig consumed small potatoes, boiled turnips, and peas from her crops, producing in return more manure; at the end of eleven months, it weighed about three hundred pounds. Her wheat crop generally averaged a greater output per acre than that of her neighbors; most of it was turned into bread for her six children and husband. In addition, she grew vegetables for the table and for market, providing not only a varied diet for her family, but pin money for purchased items, most likely for shoes and clothing for the children.[8]

For those too poor to rent land, the waste provided a logical place to build cottages and cultivate small plots of ground. Even while enclosure proceeded in earlier centuries, enough land remained so that parish overseers relied upon the waste to grant small allotments (less than the four acres required by Elizabethan statute) to the poor. In one case, "forthwith upon notice hereof pvide some convenient place of habitation for Thomas Chernock, his wife and 3 poore children so that they be not starved by lyeing out of doors unless they show cause to the contrary at the next session here to be held or otherwise upon contempt." These assignments of waste show how a small parish, acutely aware of the needs of its inhabitants, responded to poverty with the best solution imaginable: land.[9]

Perhaps most in need of a piece of wasteland was the single woman, whether widowed, abandoned, or unwed, often with children. As mothers, many were hampered in finding work for wages; they could not live in as servants, nor travel long distances to labor in the fields. An allotment on the waste could enable them, quite literally, to earn their bread. Access to common fields or wastes made the difference between appeal to the parish poor rates and a minimal independence.[10]

In fact, the proportion of female-headed households among laborers dependent upon wastes and commons was strikingly large. Using land set aside by their landlord as commons, the ten cottagers in Table 2.1 displayed the diversity of living arrangements among the poor.[11] Here women accounted for about a third of cottagers with cows, and none received poor relief at the time. Such persons were able to sustain themselves quite adequately. A single cow, well tended, could supply a widow with a fair quantity of milk for butter and cheese; dairy by-products, in addition to a small crop of turnips, sufficed as feed for a pig. Depending on the region, such women could also spin or engage in domestic industries in order to supplement their living on the land. Recognizing their need, parish overseers sometimes allocated livestock and spinning wheels

Table 2.1   Cottagers in the Parish of Horbling, Rutland, in 1801

| Names | Rent | | | Stock | Family |
	£	s.	d.		
Eliza Delawaters				1 cow, 5 pigs, 3 sheep	4
John Howit	10	7	0	2 cows, 1 pig	4
Eliza Weathers	3	13	0	1 cow, 2 pigs, 3 heifers	5
William Sutton	7	5	0	2 cows	6
J. Taylor	6	6	0	2 cows	3
Samuel Witherington	3	18	0	1 cow, 2 pigs	3
John Field	3	13	0	1 cow	4
William Broad	8	8	0	1 cow, 1 pig	6
Eliza Bothroyde	17	0	0	2 cows, 1 pig, 2 heifers	4
John Sutton	4	0	0	1 cow, 1 pig, 6 sheep	4

as a form of relief. No single activity could provide a total subsistence, but without any one of them, such women would not have been able to survive independently.[12]

The expansion of capitalist agriculture was poised to alter such arrangements. The trend toward enlarging estates and working them for profit was already visible in the seventeenth century.[13] But probably the greater incentive to adopt "businesslike" attitudes toward property in the next century was rising food prices. After 1750, the price of wheat began an almost relentless upward spiral; levels never descended below 30 shillings per quarter after the 1740s, and between 1750 and 1774, averages rose by nearly 20 shillings.[14] Even the smallest landholder grew acutely conscious of the monetary benefits accruing to conscientious cultivation practices, as the cost of renting land rose with prices. "Formerly people were used to think[ing] nothing of dung," one Gloucestershire dairywoman observed, "but now every body is scraping all they can together; for since the rents have been raised, they could not live if they did not help their land."[15]

Thus the age of improvement and experimentation on the land was born. New scientific methods of agriculture captured the interest of estate holders across England. Publications on the subject proliferated; magazines, journals, and even travel books recounted crop rotations, methods of seed drilling, and schedules of hoeing and weeding that promised vast increases in output. Even George III was reputed to have subscribed to Arthur Young's *Annals of Agriculture* and followed that popular journal's latest recommendations.[16] Young (1741–1820), who has been called "the greatest of English writers on agriculture," enjoyed international acclaim and was influential in promoting policies favorable to improvement. The government created a Board of Agriculture in 1793, naming Young as its secretary. The fashion for modifying farming techniques seemed irresistible and, at the time, was much more widely followed by the public than any industrial development.[17]

Introducing new techniques such as drainage, manuring, and stock breeding required the outlay of considerable expense and time. To facilitate these improvements, as well as to assure sole benefit from such investments, farmers strove to consolidate many small holdings into fewer large ones. Thus a system of enclosure transformed the common fields and scattered holdings of early modern England into the consolidated, privately held farms of the nineteenth century. The process entailed "(1) the laying together of scattered properties and consequent abolition of intermixture of properties and holdings; (2) the abolition of common rights; (3) the hedging and ditching of the separate properties," or "the actual 'enclosing' which gives its name to a series of processes it completes."[18] Strategies differed greatly among regions, and changes occurred unevenly over the next eighty years. A standard procedure, entailing a private act of Parliament, was established, replacing agreements that had run their course by the eighteenth century. By 1760, 75 percent of England was enclosed, 28 percent having come under enclosure since 1600.[19] A General Enclosure Act was passed in 1801 in order to simplify further the process, for some areas, such as Cambridgeshire and Bedfordshire, still had far to go. The movement had run its course by the 1840s in most areas: the great majority of common fields, commons, and wastes were turned into private farms, with the bulk of land distributed among large landlords, and relatively little left in the hands of cottagers and laborers.[20]

Debate raged around the process of enclosure from its start. While agricultural improvers of the eighteenth century lauded its impact on capital investment and the implementation of new techniques, others condemned its effects on small farmers and the poorest villagers. Higher yields from the newly enclosed farms were, of course, very desirable. A growing population required more food, and the new agriculture responded to the need for greater productivity and the extension of arable land. But in most instances, larger farmers earned greater efficiency and higher profits at the expense of their laboring neighbors, who lost badly needed access to strips of land in the common fields as well as areas of commons and waste. Many small farmers and cottagers also surrendered, unable to maintain their holdings because of higher rents. In addition, the new arrangements introduced different patterns of employment, which accentuated the dislocation created by the loss of land.[21]

Women figured only indirectly within the contemporary debate, yet they were a distinct presence in discussions of the open field system. As early as the seventeenth century, advocates of improved farming techniques criticized the wastefulness of open pastures, and in so doing, denigrated the customary work of women. In dairy country, an early proponent of enclosure mocked the worth of the cottager's practice of keeping cows:

among them (cows) a great many small ones, which are hardly worth the keeping; but the encouragement is, and many pernicious commons we have, which, for the flush of milk in a few summer months, makes the poor buy cows, to starve them in the winter, and to spend so much time running after them, as would earn twice the worth of their milk by an ordinary manufacture; when as, if the commons were enclosed, some would feed them well all the summer, and others would yield hay for them in the winter, whereby there would be always a tolerable plenty of milk, from which would spring many more considerable dairies.[22]

The account failed to point out that cows under the new system of enclosure would not belong to the cottager. Though advocates of scientific farming omitted them from the picture, women were the noisome keepers of skinny stock and defenders of ill-kept commons.

II

As the new system of agriculture advanced, it carried with it an intensified notion of private property that promoted individual interests against those of the larger community. The spread of agricultural improvements only reinforced this development, as expertise and expense were invested in farms oriented toward profit making. In England, the process of transforming the legal system attached to customary agricultural production rendered many forms of common rights illegal. Hunting (or poaching), wood gathering, and gleaning were transformed into violations of trespass and theft. An ambiguous definition of land ownership and use thus receded before a more exclusive, modern one.[23]

Historians have examined this phenomenon, the transformation of "custom into crime," in relation to the activities of both men and women laborers.[24] Focusing on gender enables us to see how conventional critical attitudes toward women could be enlisted against customary work to legitimate the values of the new system of property ownership. While both men and women were forbidden to enjoy common rights, misogynist attitudes could be enlisted to further the ends of modernization. Women could be construed as typically stubborn, intractable, or simply ignorant. At the same time, the new system of agriculture did not endorse or even condone these customary activities of women. Their subsistence work was thus negated or at best ignored.[25]

One common right particularly affecting women was the license to glean after harvest. So longstanding was their practice of gathering the remains of the harvest after the sheaves were tied that the eighteenth-century legal historian Blackstone simply cited "Mosaical law" in defending the right: "And when ye reap the harvest of your land, thou shalt not wholly reap the corners of thy field; neither shalt thou gather gleanings of thy harvest; . . . thou shalt leave them for the poor and stranger" (Lev. 23:22).[26] Medieval manors had regulated the custom in earlier times, stipulating who might glean, certain times to gather, and entrances to the field; local regulations were also enacted in the seventeenth century.[27] In the eighteenth century, gleaning was "a general customary right" seldom closely monitored. Most women simply moved into the fields, supplied with large sacks and accompanied by their children, after the sheaves were bound and carried. In some regions, only women too old or disabled to work at harvest gleaned. In others, every woman, and occasionally men, worked at the job from the early hours until dusk.[28]

Gleaning could make a considerable addition to the annual family income. Eighteenth-century rural economists, as well as the laboring poor, regarded the proceeds from gleaning as an essential component of the laborer's household budget. One historian has calculated that gleaning provided 2.7 percent of the family's total annual earnings; contemporaries arrived at higher estimates (3.5 and 4.1 percent) when considered with other casual earnings.[29] Pinchbeck's research indicated that a woman could glean five to six bushels of corn each season. By the end of the eighteenth century, a bushel was worth two times the weekly wage of a laborer, thus making a woman's gleanings worth ten to twelve weeks of work—or about one fifth of a year's wages.[30] More significant than its strict monetary value, however, was the way in which gleaning supported the overall financial life of the laboring family. Earnings in kind, obtained and used according to need, made the difference between utter want and getting by; gleaning provided "in times of hardship, a safety net which could partially support the labouring poor."[31]

In 1788, a court case challenging the custom of gleaning captured the public eye. Arguing that the practice entailed trespassing on private property, the legal debate expressed in vivid terms two quintessentially different orientations toward the poor at a critical time.[32] A Suffolk landowner appealed to a relatively new notion of the inviolable rights of individual ownership. "The farmer is the sole cultivator of the land," argued the court, "and the gleaners gather each for himself, without any regard either to joint labour or public advantage." The argument went further to carefully dispute the custom as a right at all. The law in no way obliged the farmer "to leave *something* for the poor." "The soil is *his*, the culture is *his*, the seed *his*, and in natural justice *his* also are the profits." The practice therefore was a privilege and not a right.[33] In a bold replacement of religious principle by theories of classical economics, the case claimed:

> The law of *Moses* is not obligatory on us. It is indeed agreeable to Christian charity and common humanity, that the rich should provide for the impotent poor; but the mode of such provision must be of positive institution. We have established a nobler fund. We have pledged all the landed property of the kingdom for the maintenance of the poor, who have in some instances exhausted the source.[34]

In a straightforward way, the court affirmed the values of private property.

The subject ignited into a more public controversy in the pages of Arthur Young's *Annals of Agriculture*, which circulated among improving gentlemen and farmers across the nation. Thomas Ruggles, a Suffolk landowner and historian, attacked the custom of gleaning as "very near to theft and rapine;" his adversary, Capel Lofft, a famous radical and popular London orator, defended the practice on the basis of custom, charity, and humanity. The latter, described by the Hammonds as a "humane and chivalrous" magistrate, was reputed to be a champion of the poor. The series of articles was remarkable not only for its energy and eloquence, but also for its testimony to the dissemination and practical application of principles of classical economics in the eighteenth century.[35]

While Ruggles argued the need to adhere to the letter of the law, which described gleaning as a privilege and not a right, Lofft referred to its spirit—in this case, chapter and verse of Old Testament teachings embodied in "ancient" and established legal texts. Lofft invoked the principles of distributive justice, derived from "the spirit of our constitution" as well as "the spirit of Christianity." From religion, came a sense of "a community of interest"; from the law, a desire "to moderate the particular prerogatives of one class, by annexing other peculiar franchises to another." Within this framework, the needs of subsistence were recognized as universal. "Our necessary dependence as creatures," he noted, "our common wants and enjoyments are a proper basis for a custom." The claims of laboring women, as "the indigent, and those who are not of strength or habit to the more profitable labours of the field," warranted defense by the state.[36]

It was clear that purveyors of the new system had little truck with the customs of the laboring woman, whether or not such practices provided subsistence. "How many days, during the harvest, are lost by the mother of a family and all her children," inveighed Ruggles, "in wandering about from field to field, to glean what does not repay them the wear and tear of their cloaths in seeking." The custom only gave further proof of the irrationality of the common woman, a failing that now was seen to have moral consequences. Gleaning encouraged "idleness and loss of time" and served as a temptation to the laborer "to gather his employer's corn in a careless and slovenly manner." "It would open a door to fraud, because the labourers would be tempted to scatter the corn in order to make a better gleaning for their wives, children, and neighbours." It also acted as "an early and great inducement to children to pilfer from the swarth or shock." What had been an innocuous, albeit inefficient, means of securing subsistence now aroused annoyance and suspicion. Dismissing "Mosaic custom" as irrelevant, Ruggles marshaled soaring figures on the collection and payment of relief in England. "Can the principle which applied to the children of Israel," he asked, ". . . existing in a very early stage of society, apply to a country where such enormous sums are raised for the maintenance of the poor?" Property owners contributed to the poor rates, and hence, had no obligation to support the poor through such donations in kind.[37]

The attempt of some landowners to curtail the custom of gleaning did not go unchallenged. Women took collective action against farmers who closed fields to them, assaulting landowners and stoning them off their own property. Gleaners resolved to continue their practice, and the number of assaults perpetrated by landowners against persisting gleaners is eloquent testimony to the determination of these women. Moreover, gleaners in these circumstances were often able to obtain redress in court, proving that in these instances, local justices were unwilling to enforce a strict concept of private property. Gleaning proved to be a customary right difficult to extinguish.[38]

Unable to deny laboring women their customary rights, landowners could attempt to transform the context in which gleaning took place. Controlling the custom was one way: some landowners allowed gleaning to continue only under specific circumstances. In the 1788 judgment, the court cited the example of Basingstoke, where "a prudent regulation" stipulated the time and duration of gleaning (allowed only after the crops have been carried off) and the gate through which laborers might enter and leave the fields. Respect for property, as well as deference to an ethos of work, figured prominently in these provisions. A later case in Oxfordshire revealed a more subtle shift in emphasis. Here the gleaners were allowed to continue, but in granting them their wish, the law now designated the landowner's permission as an act of charity: ". . . no person has a legal right to lease without the consent of the occupier of the land; . . . the practice of leasing is an indulgence founded on benevolence, and ought, when permitted, to be exercised with gratitude and respect."[39]

New concern about the problem of poverty, often related to anxiety over rising poor rates, gave rise to such "benevolence." But rather than representing positive feelings about the poor, this shift heralded critical attitudes toward poor women that, as we shall see, cast them as dependent and idle.

The transformation of custom into crime obviously affected the ways in which laboring women were able to maintain their households. The responsibility of gathering wood for fuel, for example, often fell to the woman of the household, usually assisted by her children. In a seventeenth-century riot against enclosure of the Forest of Braydon, in Wiltshire, the leader appeared dressed in woman's clothes, enacting the typical ritual linking women and subsistence needs in popular disorder.[40] Women and children appear repeatedly in eighteenth-century evidence of fuel gathering, particularly in reference to the smaller types of wood. Custom regulated what kind of wood could be taken and methods of gathering considered acceptable. In Hampshire, laborers helped themselves freely to "what is called 'snapwood'; that is all the fallen branches, and such as they can snap off by hand, or break down with a hook fixed in the

end of a long pole."[41] Taking wood "by hook or by crook," applying to
the branch "only the effort of snapping it off," was permissible; sawing
low-growing wood was not. The rights to live wood were "clearly open
to much dispute," but the firewood that women were more likely to collect, best found on the ground, was considered yet another form of charity in kind.[42]

Intolerance of this activity grew, however, and by the late eighteenth
century, opposition to the right to gather fuel mounted into fierce
reprisals. Legislation was passed in 1766, strengthening a statute of 1663,
rendering wood gathering illegal. Laborers were not permitted to "wilfully
cut or break down, bark, burn, pluck up, lop, top, crop, or otherwise
deface, damage, despoil or destroy or carry away any Timber tree."[43] In
Wiltshire, justices of the peace frequently fined women for cutting wood
on the land of yeomen.[44] One incident during the 1780s involved a laboring woman taking wood from a hedge near Ogbourne St. George (Wiltshire); she was tried and convicted, and publicly whipped at the stocks for
the offense.[45] The law worked to erase the ambiguity around such loosely
defined forms of "charity"; wood gathering now became theft, and those
who committed the act were clearly criminal. Laborers may have continued to collect firewood without regard to property, but the language used
to refer to the practice had changed. In summarizing the expenses of cottagers and laborers, Arthur Young did not obfuscate their means of
obtaining fuel; the category read simply "Firing—steal it."[46]

Tracing public opinion on these issues reveals how the language of
morality was mustered to condemn customary activities. By the 1790s,
Sir Frederic Morton Eden's influential *The State of the Poor* (1797) set a
new style for surveys of the coming century. Arthur Young had been
unruffled by the custom of stealing firewood in the 1780s, but Eden
roundly condemned the practice. In taking account of a laborer's family
budget, he warned:

> Nothing is stated for fuel. If the labourer is employed in hedging he is
> allowed to take home a faggot every evening, while the work lasts: but this is
> by no means sufficient for his consumption: his children therefore, are sent
> into the fields, to collect wood where they can; and neither hedges nor trees
> are spared by the young marauders who are thus, in some degree, calculated
> in the art of thieving, till, from being accustomed to small thefts, they hesi-
> tate not to commit greater deprivations on the public. . . .[47]

Women were nowhere in evidence in Eden's account; the laborer's customary subsistence work was transformed into juvenile delinquence.
Eden recognized that the male laborer's payment for work was "by no
means sufficient for his consumption" needs, yet his recommendation
that farmers sell wood "somewhat below the market price" required the
laborer to purchase what he lacked. The market, not distributive justice,
henceforth would govern the way such needs would be met.

III

Little evidence reveals the actual voices of laborers, still less, the concerns of women. Yet the few surviving parliamentary counterpetitions and written protests to enclosures indicate that small owners and cottagers feared the loss of commons and wastes and tried to halt the process. Jeanette Neeson's study of Northamptonshire "shows that enclosure was more generally unpopular and more widely resisted" than previously recognized by historians.[48] While improvers delivered their documents to Parliament, cataloguing the steps toward reorganization of their localities, humble parishioners counterpetitioned against enclosure. Such action was most often a final—and often futile—step in local opposition, for when enclosure had advanced to the parliamentary stage, little else could be done. Compared to other circumstances generating riot, full-scale revolt against enclosure was relatively infrequent since most victims lacked the "independence, physical stamina, and networks of social communication" so vital to mounting protest by collective action. But in the few examples found by one historian, women and the poor figured prominently.[49] Local studies have uncovered covert and illegal forms of resistance ranging from fence breaking to riot and theft. Women and children sometimes participated, as, for example, when they joined men in cutting wood from the newly enclosed fields and common of Denton in 1775, or when they took down young trees in a recently enclosed plantation in Warmington. In one instance, after the failure of a parliamentary counterpetition, village women and several shoemakers led a riot at Raunds in which they "pulled down fences, dismantled gates, lit huge bonfires and celebrated long into the night." The disappearance of posts and rails was so common that, as Neeson has pointed out, "it is hard to define where enclosure protest ends and the need for fuel begins."[50]

The loss leveled on the diet of the laboring classes from enclosure is incalculable. Judging from the prevalence of laborers' complaints regarding the lack of access to grazing land for cows, historians have been forced to look more closely at the value placed upon livestock by the poor. A survey of enclosures in 1808 encountered the lament repeatedly: "The condition of the labouring poor much worse now than before the enclosure, owing to the impossibility of procuring any milk for their young families." "The poor have not the same means of keeping cows as before." "To my knowledge, before the enclosure, the poor inhabitants found no difficulty in procuring milk for their children; since, it is with the utmost difficulty they can procure any milk at all. Cows lessened from 110 to 40."[51] One historian has gone as far as to say that the loss of livestock definitively "forced husbandmen and peasant labourers into a category that some historians today would describe as a proletariat."[52] With the rising price of bread at the turn of the century, as well as a decline in the practice of providing room and board for farm servants, a marked deterioration in the standard of living occurred. Potato growing required less land and hence became a common way of supplying some, if any, food for domestic consumption. The potato replaced bread as the staple food of the laboring classes in some parts of the country, and those who continued to consume bread most often consumed wheaten, rather than white bread, an unpalatable substitute when eaten without any bacon or cheese.[53] In *The Case of the Labourers in Husbandry* (1795), the Rev. David Davies of Berkshire conveyed a more immediate sense of the change in the quality of the laborer's diet; he believed that while "wheaten bread may be eaten alone with pleasure," "potatoes require either meat or milk to make them go down." He added, "you cannot make many hearty meals of them with salt and water only."[54]

For the most part, laboring families were forced to purchase their food, a development that, given the instability of prices during the wars against France, proved disastrous. Whereas under earlier arrangements, laborers "might go for weeks without needing more than a few shillings to make up occasional deficiencies," they now required a steady income of money in order to live week to week.[55] Contemporaries like Davies recognized the change:

> Formerly many of the lower sort of people occupied tenements of their own, with parcels of land about them, or they rented such of others. On these they raised for themselves a considerable part of their subsistence, without being obliged, as now, to buy all they want at shops . . . . But since those small parcels of ground have been swallowed up in the contiguous farms and inclosures, and the cottages themselves have been pulled down; the families which used to occupy them are crowded together in decayed farm-houses, with hardly ground enough about them for a cabbage garden: and being thus reduced to be *mere* hirelings, they are of course very liable to come to want.

A reliance upon wage earning and money spelled vulnerability. Moreover, the preference that the new rural economy showed for male wage earners affected the extent to which women could redress the situation. The subsistence work of women had been swept away and little remained in its place. Female earning power was minimal under the new system of agriculture since women's jobs were confined to menial and part-time tasks. As Davies observed,

> And not only the *men* occupying those tenements, but *their wives and children* too, could formerly, when they wanted to work abroad, employ themselves profitably at home; whereas now, few of *these* are constantly employed, except in harvest; so that almost the whole burden of providing for their families rest upon the *men*.[56]

The new arrangements thrust poor laboring women and their children into a precarious state of dependence.

IV

Cast as economic burdens rather than assets, women could no longer be regarded as mutual supporters of the laboring household. As these developments suggest, the construct of a male breadwinner within the rural family was the product of a confusion of historical circumstance and economic theory. The notion would remain more ideal than real for the laboring classes in general.[57] The rural laboring family's reliance on wages continued to evolve in the late eighteenth and early nineteenth centuries as employment opportunities and actual tasks changed with the times. One trend seems clear: when women did turn to agricultural wage work, their options narrowed over time. When parliamentary commissioners inquired into the employment of women in agriculture in 1843, they unearthed information on conditions of a generation before. Women in their forties and fifties recounted to the examiners the details of their childhoods as "apprentices" in agriculture in the first decades of the nineteenth century. Their jobs changed by the day and season. "In the fields," one Devonshire woman remembered, "I used to drive the plough, pick stones, weed, pull turnips, when snow was lying about, sow corn, dig potatoes, hoe turnips, and reap. I did everything that boys did." She added, "I took a pride to it, when I used to reap, to keep up with the men." "Anything that came to hand, like a boy," another woman asserted when asked. In recalling how she led horses and bullocks to plough, she commented, "Maidens would not like that work now."[58] As they related their stories to their questioners, women laborers revealed their acceptance and enjoyment of hard physical labor. They also seemed aware of the fact that the present rural world operated according to very different standards.[59]

Before the massive curtailment of the practice of living-in in the nineteenth century, a girl of the laboring classes usually began her working life as part of the household of a local landowner. "Servants in husbandry," as they were designated, made up around 60 percent of the population between the ages of fifteen and twenty-four from the late sixteenth to the early nineteenth century, and of that total, women constituted about 40 percent in the late eighteenth century.[60] Contracts lasted for one year, though some servants chose to change masters before their terms expired. Their long-term future depended upon whether they married or not; usually they did, somewhere around the age of twenty-four or twenty-five. In almost all cases, service in husbandry functioned as a transitional period providing both employment and training for later years. Those who remained single joined an increasing number of poor women, including many widows, in search of work to support themselves, and possibly a number of dependents.[61]

While women and men shared some agricultural tasks (harvesting enlisted all available labor), a sexual division of labor did in fact obtain in many respects in the eighteenth century. Women were involved in dairy work, caring for poultry and other livestock, and tasks associated with maintaining the mistress's household, such as food preparation and cleaning. They also worked in the fields at tasks requiring dexterity, such as planting and weeding, though in many areas, they were also called upon for brute strength, without regard for their gender.[62]

Women's pay was customarily low and attitudes toward their behavior on the job could be condescending. Negative portrayals of women laborers certainly existed in the earlier period, even while the productive roles of women were taken for granted. Stephen Duck's account of women working in the fields, immortalized in *The Thresher's Labour* (1730), exhibits an ageless form of misogyny that played upon the low status of women in the hierarchy of farm laborers:

> Soon as the rising Sun hath drunk the dew
> Another scene is open'd to our view:
> Our Master comes, and at his Heels a Throng
> Of prattling Females, arm'd with Rake and Prong,
> Prepar'd, whil'st he is here, to make his Hay,
> Or, if he turns his back, prepar'd to play.
> But here, or gone, sure of this comfort still,
> Here's Company, so they may chat their fill:
> And were their Hands as active as their Tongues,
> How nimbly then would move their Rakes and Prongs?[63]

Duck suppressed any suggestion of the productive role women played in haymaking. Mary Collier, the famous "washerwoman poet" who published a response to Duck's poem, took offense at the omission: "And you of your annual Task have much to say,/ . . . But can't conclude your never-dying Theme,/ And let our hapless Sex in Silence lie/ Forgotten, and in dark Oblivion die[.]" *The Woman's Labour*, published in 1739, addressed the very question of Duck's representation of idle female laborers:

> For my own part, I many a Summer's day
> Have spent in throwing, turning, making Hay,
> But ne'er could see, what you have lately found,
> Our Wages paid for sitting on the Ground.
> 'Tis true, that when our Morning's Work is done,
> And all our Grass expos'd unto the Sun,
> While that his scorching Beams do on it shine,
> As well as you, we have a time to dine:
> I hope that since we freely toil and sweat
> To earn our Bread, you'll give us time to eat.[64]

The laboring woman's voice was neither believed (the third edition of the poem included a testimony signed by Collier's neighbors authenticating her work) nor particularly heeded. But it shed light on an image of women's work unmatched in any other source.

A condescending forbearance toward farm servants and a ridiculing tolerance of female behavior, commonplace in other forms of literature, turned hostile in eighteenth-century discussions about agriculture. Innovative techniques could spring from these very dissatisfactions among farmers. Jethro Tull complained of the lack of industry among his own farm servants and commended his course of horse-hoeing husbandry as a means of eliminating the need for at least some female labor. "But the Thing that is most detrimental to *perpetual* Crops of Wheat," he reported,

> is the Deceit and Idleness of the Weeders, that are necessary to cleanse the Partitions and Rows from Weeds, by *Hoes*, or Hands, or both, especially after they have been a Year or two neglected, their shattered Seed in that Case overstocking the Ground. These Weeders are the same Sort of People that *Mr. Duck* describes as *Haymakers*, their Tongues are much nimbler than their Hands; and unless the Owner, or some Person who faithfully represents him, (and is hard to be found) works constantly amongst them, they'll get their Heads together half a Dozen in a Cluster, regarding their *Prattle* more than the Weeds; great Part of their Time they spend in Play, except a few of them who bring their own Work with them, some their sewing, some their knitting, and these must be paid for doing their own Work upon my Land: This Wrong I have seen done both to myself and my Neighbours; and it has put me upon endeavouring to find a Way of disappointing the Weeders . . .[65]

Tull's solution, to plant a field in such a way as to enable a horse-drawn drill to perform the task of hoeing, considerably reduced the need for female labor. Such motivations should not go unacknowledged in assessing the factors generating improvement schemes.[66]

Criticism of farm servants was aimed at men as well as women; one often encounters attitudes of suspicion and exasperation in accounts of traditional laboring classes. This view was not universal; many contemporaries believed just the reverse in advising farmers' sons to mix as much as possible with the laborers in order to obtain a practical knowledge of farming. Advertisements for labor also reveal the surprising extent to which innovation was introduced *via* hired men who had already practiced new techniques.[67] More common, however, was the characterization of the laboring poor as "an alien and objectionable race," which, over the course of the nineteenth century, became frozen into the male stereotype of "Hodge," the remote, impassive creature much discussed in literature.[68] Discussion of laborers' skill, occurring infrequently, almost always applied to male labor, with dairying being the only exception with regard to women's work.[69]

The prevalence of a negative image of agricultural laborers reflected the growing distance between classes in rural society. Service in husbandry, the annual hiring of laborers or servants living in, was replaced by the practice of hiring laborers who lived out for shorter terms. This held true for women as well as men, though in large rural establishments, girls continued to live in as domestic servants with fewer if any responsibilities for farm labor. Declining gradually over the course of the late eighteenth and early nineteenth century, service in husbandry disappeared for reasons varying according to region and locality. The new system was, in part, an economy measure, as the rise in relief expenditure across the countryside contributed to a drain on the expenses of farmers. Many farmers were eager to avoid giving laborers settlement in their parish, which would ultimately render a landowner responsible for their support in the event of unemployment. Underscoring this reasoning was the tendency for well-to-do families to shun the society of their hired hands. The custom of sharing eating and living quarters with common laborers survived only in areas and establishments where prosperity had not inspired a growing distance between classes.[70]

Keith Snell has pointed out that while enclosure was not the sole cause of women's unemployment, it hastened a trend that was already in place by the mid eighteenth century. Enclosure enforced a pattern of seasonal employment that restricted women to "relatively poorly paid spring and early summer activities: weeding, stone-picking, the calving and dairying season, or haymaking." Women were more likely to be unemployed for the rest of the year. Because employment opportunities for both men and women were declining, competition in the "labor market" became more fierce, and what jobs remained were more likely to fall to male laborers. This was especially so "where male unemployment and rising real per capita poor relief in the south raised . . . persistent problems for the local social order." Thus, for women, the chances of finding work in agriculture, at least in the major corn-growing regions of the south and east, grew slimmer toward the end of the eighteenth century and worsened later on.[71]

The pattern of employment established by enclosure was key to the fate of women in nineteenth-century agriculture. Women were regarded as a cheap and elastic source of labor; large numbers of women, often with children in tow, were employed when needed and easily dispensed with when not. Their work enabled farmers to extract maximum yields from their lands; but as essential as the tasks of cultivation were, they nevertheless were regarded as marginal and unskilled. Women laborers thus earned wages that averaged from £3 10s to £5 a year, roughly half the male wage.[72] In his survey of poverty in the 1790s, Sir Frederic Eden regarded their low wages with some discomfort. "The women who here do a large portion of the work of the farm, with a difficulty get half as much . . . . It is not easy to account for so striking an inequality, and still less easy to justify it."[73] The seasonal, part-time employment of women, along with the considerable underemployment of men, remained typical in the English countryside for many years. The introduction of machinery was delayed well into the middle decades of the nineteenth century owing to the availability of cheap labor, as well as the widespread opinion that the laboring classes would not tolerate any further diminution of employment.[74]

The slow introduction of new harvest technology, extended over nearly eighty years, reinforced the relegation of women to secondary roles in agricultural production. For centuries, women usually took part in the reaping of grains with sickles during harvest; mowing with the heavier, more cumbersome scythe was restricted to male labor. But the trend to using the scythe, especially in an age of improvement, was inevitable: it reduced the number of men and women needed for harvest and it also cut the crop closer to the ground, leaving less wastage behind. From 1790, and especially after 1835, adoption of the heavier tool became widespread. Thus women were displaced from reaping and restricted to the job of raking behind mowers at comparatively lower pay. Some localities continued to employ women with sickles in spite of this general shift, preferring the neatness of the smaller tool.[75] But overall, the sickle remained in use only on small holdings or in very remote areas of Britain. This development contributed to the general failure of nineteenth-century agriculture to offer women remunerative employment.[76]

The laboring woman found herself unable to provide subsistence through gathering and use rights, while her wage-earning power, as well as that of male members of her family, was significantly diminished. Contemporaries were aware of the significance of these developments in generating widespread poverty. In 1802, the Society for Bettering the Condition and Increasing the Comforts of the Poor published an account "of the superior advantages of dibbling wheat, or setting it by hand." Rather than offering the typical plan for a benefit club or a school for industry, the article envisioned a more labor-intensive mode of agriculture, in this instance, employing women. The author recounted how he had prevailed upon a neighboring farmer to try his "experiment," with great success: it yielded a bountiful harvest and, even more importantly, restored women to remunerative agricultural employment. "If this mode of cultivation were adopted in every kind of land, to which it is suited," he pointed out, it would increase production and "give healthful and satisfactory occupation, and means of subsistence, to thousands of women and children, at the *dead season* of the year, when there is a general want of employment."[77]

The writer failed to comprehend the irreversible nature of recent agricultural changes, but he was cogniscent of a shift in the economic structure of the laboring household:

> It is at this period that most women and children consider themselves as laid up for the winter, and become a burthen upon the father of the family, and in many cases upon the parish. The wife is no longer able to contribute her share towards the weekly expenses, unless (which is seldom the case) she has any peculiar skill in knitting, spinning, or sewing, or other merely domestic work.—In a kind of despondency she sits down, unable to contribute any thing to the general fund of the family, and conscious of rendering no other service to her husband, except that of the mere care of his family.[78]

Advocates of the laboring poor saw that when women were reduced to the "mere care" of the household and family, their significant productive capacities were being wasted. As wages in agriculture fell in coming years, female unemployment would represent an even greater loss. Yet the new agriculture had laid the foundation for a modern sexual division of labor. From the point of view of new economic theory, the male breadwinner, as the sole source of income, was a harbinger of a new and better age.

The transformation of agriculture had diverse effects on the lives of laboring women: it eliminated their work in growing and gathering food, collecting fuel, and tending stock; it rendered their customary activities illegal; and it narrowed the availability of wage work in the fields. Through this complex process of marginalization, women laborers lost their claim to traditional rural images of female productivity. Folk customs continued to uphold the part of women in the harvest. According to one account of the eastern and midlands counties, "[a] woman must always bind at least one sheaf in the field at harvest, and she must come to do this if she is ever so busy. It is believed that the harvest will not be good unless a woman has had a hand in it."[79] But the new world of agriculture conveyed its own notions of value: resourcefulness and remunerativeness would now be attached to a more rational style of farming. This shift became most apparent in the dairy industry, where the longstanding authority of women confronted the forces of improvement in yet another form.

3

The Art of Women and the Business of Men: Women's Work and the Dairy Industry

An almost universal complaint of employers of girls . . . is that they are almost entirely unable and unwilling to give up methods of work inherited or once learned in favour of more efficient ones, to adapt themselves to new methods, to learn and to concentrate their intelligence, or even to use it at all. Explanations of the possibility of making work easier, above all more profitable to themselves, generally encounter a complete lack of understanding.

Max Weber, *The Protestant Ethic and the Spirit of Capitalism* (1958)

When Max Weber searched for the antithesis of the "spirit of capitalism," he found his model embodied in "women workers, especially unmarried ones." Here, he pointed out in 1905, one could see a living remnant of the obstacles that had confronted industrial capitalism in its earlier years. This disposition, so unlike the willingness of typical protestants to see remunerative labor as a worthwhile end, Weber labeled the "stone wall of habit." Weber voiced a widely held opinion that women stood in the way of progress by clinging to tradition and opposing rational alternatives.[1]

Anthropology has demonstrated the timelessness of this now familiar equation of female with nature and male with culture.[2] Yet at certain crucial historical junctures, this depiction of women workers as bearers of unreason has had a definitive impact on the structure of economic activity as well as on the status of women. Nowhere was this clash of images more grandly played out than during the formative period of industrial capitalism in the second half of the eighteenth century, when the imperatives of a new economic order came to dominate the spheres of both agricultural and industrial production. A complex dialectic developed between the mandates of a growing market economy and existing organizations of production that included women as key workers. Agriculturalists, political economists, and commercial men examined and evaluated the work of women, measuring their effectiveness in producing marketable goods. This ongoing assessment of female labor was of interest to a reading public associated with new scientifically oriented improvement societies. Within this forum, the role of women as producers came under attack, as commentaries on labor described their agency as incompatible with systematic and profit-oriented methods. While these writings did not dictate material reality, they nevertheless helped to shape attitudes and influence decision making in a way that was crucial to the creation of a public receptive to economic change. The transformation of the English economy could not have advanced without this intricate interplay between market pressure and popular opinion.

The debate over women's work in the dairy is particularly revealing for it depicts a conflict between customary ways of working associated with the agrarian world and a newer rational notion of production informed by commerce and capitalism. The growing business of selling butter and cheese directed attention to this seemingly mysterious bastion of womanly arts, where the new scientific agriculturalists, joined by men of commerce, made serious efforts to lay bare the dairy's store of secrets. Formerly the unchallenged preserve of female authority and labor, the dairy became contested territory. Female capacities were perceived as tradition bound and thus unacceptable to new standards of dairying, even while dairywomen adapted customary technique to the demands of the market. Profitable industry became joined to a model of organization and productivity associated specifically with men.

The following account of dairying will not provide quantitative data concerning women's contribution to production, nor will it chart the course of women in dairying history within specific regions of England. Instead, it will analyze key discussions of women and dairy work that reflect contemporary understandings of gender in order to place them in the larger context of a transformation of knowledge at the end of the eighteenth century. The declining power of women in dairying can be related to similar shifts taking place within the manufacturing sector, where female spinners were displaced and ultimately denigrated. These new notions of gender, which privileged male rationality and subordinated female labor, joined with the market in renovating conceptions of work and productivity in the early industrial period.[3]

I

As a ubiquitous domestic enterprise, dairying was women's work in the eighteenth-century rural world. Whether carried on for petty income by poor laboring women or as a useful pastime for gentlewomen, the production of butter and cheese was regarded as a female activity. In earlier centuries, it was hardly distinguished from other household duties. "Make butter and chese when thou may," instructed Fitzherbert's *Boke of Husbandrye* (1534), in between meeting the daily needs of the household and caring for the livestock. As an adjunct of food preparation, the dairy was both literally and figuratively attached to the kitchen in the farmhouses of gentry; cleanliness and convenience also dictated that the dairy be close by, so that constant supervision and attendance could be combined with other responsibilities within the house and yard.[4]

Dairying was associated with enterprises large and small in the eighteenth century. Possession of a cow and a few simple pieces of equipment entitled a cottager or a small farmer's wife to join in the relatively primitive production of butter and cheese, either for consumption or sale. On a modest scale, dairying could provide income for single women and widows lacking other means of support. The practice of marketing small quantities of milk, cheese, and butter was so well established in rural communities that overseers of the poor on occasion aided poor women through the purchase of a cow, so that, with rights of common, they might be self-sufficient. In grazing districts, these women could earn a living by selling their produce to the non-farming population.[5]

Dairying generated essential income for the small farm. Everyone recognized, like the homespun Poysers in *Adam Bede*, that "the woman who manages a dairy has a large share in making the rent."[6] Proceeds from the dairy in many cases exceeded the annual rent, and men often depended upon the successes of their wives in cheese and butter making for financial survival. Dairy cattle required "comparatively large amounts of labour in relation to capital" and so was ideally suited to the capabilities of smallholders and even cottagers. In areas like northwestern Wiltshire, where family establishments were the rule throughout the eighteenth century, the production of butter, cheese, beef, and bacon relied on family labor only. Wives and daughters provided the linchpin of such small-scale dairies throughout the northwest and southwest of England, as well as in parts of Suffolk and Yorkshire. Farmers often combined dairying with other agricultural pursuits, such as sheep grazing and the raising of stock, or with weaving or other domestic industries. While men tended livestock and fodder crops, women exercised a free hand in the dairy itself, organizing as well as carrying out the production of cheese, and possibly butter, for the market.[7]

Large-scale dairying, much the norm in parts of Gloucestershire, Cheshire, and Norfolk, depended on the same configuration of labor; women were indispensable, from the rank of farmer's wife down to the equally necessary dairymaid. Since the seventeenth century, serious commercial dairying flourished in these regions, promoted by the further concentration of land ownership and improved methods of agriculture.[8] In some instances, a "manager," either female or male, replaced the farmer's wife as overseer of the dairy, though the distinction between manager and farmer was sometimes blurred in dairying reports. A sexual division of labor similar to that of the small farm prevailed: men made decisions regarding stock purchasing and breeding, management of fodder crops and marketing transactions, while women supervised and participated in the actual production of cheese and butter. Women nevertheless understood the principles of stock management and contributed to the growing store of knowledge pertaining to breeding and feeding the animals they cared for.[9]

Contemporaries attached great importance to the personal attributes of the woman who exercised such noteworthy influence upon the traditional dairying establishment. Ordinarily, the role of manager devolved automatically on the wife and daughters of the farmer, and though not all of these women could be expected to rise to the distinction of "superior dairywomen," they nevertheless brought to the job the crucially important requisite, loyalty to the enterprise. Shirking the obligations of the family economy could mean considerable material loss, so the incentive to do the job well was built into the office of housewife. Tusser warned the woman who failed to participate in the activities of her own dairy:

> The housewife, to make her own cheese,
> Through trusting of others, hath this for her fees;
> Her milk pan and cream pot, so slabbered and sost,
> That butter is wanting, and cheese is half lost.[10]

So dependent was the small farmer on the free and careful labor of his daughters that the misfortune of having only sons could force him into livestock farming over dairying in the interests of economy.[11]

In the larger establishments, even greater responsibility automatically devolved upon the mistress of the dairy, and her qualities were mystified in proportion to her importance. "A superior dairywoman is so highly spoken of, and so highly valued, in this district," Marshall reported, "that one is led to imagine every thing depends upon MANAGEMENT. Instances are mentioned of the same farm, under different managers, having produced good and bad cheese: even changing a dairy *maid* has been observed to make a considerable difference in the quality of the produce." On smaller farms, where the superintendent took part in nearly every operation, the distinction between manager and assistant was not great in terms of hours of labor and actual tasks. Experience made the ultimate difference, endowing the mistress of the farm with arbitrary power and also making possible the appointment of a dairymaid as an "ostensible manager."[12]

Dairymaids, too, garnered praise for their expertise. In Gloucestershire, "the best of thin Cheese" owed more "to the Skill and good Management of the Dairymaid, than to the Grass or Herbage the Cows feed on." William Ellis underscored the value of these young women: "Farmers are so jealous of their Skill being made known in other Parts," he attested, "that they take care, in time, to hire and keep them to themselves." Thus the "Berkley Dairy maid" seldom worked far from her place of birth, "for if she quits one Place, she is almost sure to be hired in to another" close by, in order to maintain exclusive rights to her skills. Hertfordshire boasted the "strong hardy Girl" known best for her unflagging strength and energy, a "true Slave" for both household and dairy work. With "red plump Arms and Hands, and clumsy Fingers," this type of girl could milk the cows at great distances from the barn, in "all Weathers," including freezing temperatures, and carry the milk back to the barn without assistance. Differences of opinion existed as to how much autonomy the maid should enjoy, but a farmer might expect a dairymaid to come to the job with methods of her own and laud her knowledgeable independence.[13]

Dairying for profit, sometimes according to new scientific methods, became more urgent and widespread from the middle decades of the century. Higher rents forced even the most humble farmers to learn ways of extracting more produce from their holdings. The growing demand for food also affected dairying districts during these years, as a rising population created a large market for cheese and butter. William Ellis's serial publication, *Modern Husbandman* (1744), exemplified the market-oriented attitude that was current by midcentury. "Why Making Butter and Cheese is more profitable, than Suckling Calves," announced the subtitle of one installment. "This brings in Money without laying out any," Ellis pointed out simply, "whereas, in Suckling, there is a Charge, and Trouble of going to Market to buy Calves, and then no more Profit, than bare Suckling." John Lawrence echoed Ellis in a similar assessment of the profitability of dairying. "Were it demanded of me, generally, what is the most advantageous application of land, I should be inclined to answer, that of dairying, or feeding a large number of cows, for the produce of butter: but," he added, "with the reserve, that the business be conducted with great variation from the common modes." Lawrence went on to describe the need for assiduous supervision by a profit-conscious "dairyman." Treatises on marketing milk followed suit, indicating that the dairy was being subjected to a vigorous course of renovation.[14]

This expansion owed much to a growing market for cheese, generated by a burgeoning working-class population, particularly in London and large provincial towns. Because it was cheap, nutritious, and convenient, cheese enjoyed wide consumption by the laboring classes. Low-grade varieties (those types made with skimmed milk in particular) made up part of the staple diet of agricultural and town laborers. Particularly when times were hard, laborers ate little or no meat and relied on a diet of bread, cheese, and salt fish. Eighteenth-century workhouses fed cheese to inmates regularly, and the navy purchased enormous quantities. Institutional needs must have accounted for a considerable rise in consumption if the Greenwich Hospital, which served $2\frac{1}{4}$ pounds per week to each pensioner in 1802, can be seen as representative. Rising prices of other foodstuffs only amplified demand for the commodity throughout the early nineteenth century.[15]

Also in rising demand, butter enjoyed the status of a more universally coveted commodity and represented a barometer of household prosperity. It occupied an indispensable place on bread and even ale and was so essential to the consumption of peas and beans that its price was driven upward during the vegetable growing season. The laboring classes in the towns used butter far less widely than rural laborers and often purchased low-grade products (the lowest denoted as "grease") to wet their bread. Though much was probably rancid or thinned with water by the time it reached poorer purchasers, growing sales of butter (including quantities imported from Ireland) reflected both a rising population and higher standards of living among middle-class consumers.[16]

The intensification of dairying had a decided impact on the way in which labor was conceived and prescribed, for market pressures demanded more exacting standards of quality and uniformity from every supplier. The nature of the dairying industry, characterized by a multitude of small suppliers scattered about the countryside, lent itself well to the activities of a middleman, or factor, who played a prominent part in the business beginning in the seventeenth century. By purchasing products locally in order to sell in bulk to distant purchasers, he tied the remote dairy to cosmopolitan centers of consumption.[17] The markets of London generated sufficient demand to warrant a large combine (union) of cheesemongers, with their own network of factors scattered throughout Cheshire and the surrounding region, and a fleet of sixteen ships, who operated between London and Liverpool. As dairies acquired a reputation for money-making potential, some farmers leased their barns and cows to professional dairymen. Though this practice was probably limited, the very structure of the leased dairy, with a male manager at its head, calls attention to the most salient characteristic of the new business of dairying, a critical attitude toward the role of women and their ways of working.[18]

II

A proliferation of literature on agriculture in the eighteenth century inevitably affected dairying, as treatises, periodicals, and pamphlets strove to redirect methods of farming into more scientific channels. The drive to improve agricultural practices borrowed from the contemporary interest in natural science and empirical methods. The two impulses had much in common; relatively little distinction existed between "scientific" and "useful" knowledge in English enlightenment culture. Many advocates of the new scientific experimentation in physics and chemistry were gentlemen with interests in money-making endeavors, whose predilections for utility led them to foster an environment favorable to rationalized agriculture. From the highest echelons of the Royal Society of London to an array of unique provincial scientific associations, the promotion of agricultural improvements occupied an important place in publications and agendas. Alongside the familiar figures of William Marshall and Arthur

Young stood numerous lesser lights, such as Richard Bradley, F.R.S. (1688–1732), James Anderson, F.R.A.S. Scot. (1739–1808), and John Lawrence (1753–1839), who combined interests in botany, chemistry, philology, and philosophy in their promotion of agricultural subjects. Influential circles of men sponsored essay competitions, the publishing of correspondence, and the awarding of prizes. So prevalent was the fashion to publish information on agriculture that the derogatory terms "book husbandry" and "book farming" were coined to lay censure on those who were "scholars only" or "mere theorists." Yet this forward-looking attitude enabled British agriculture to produce an adequate food supply (at least in relative terms) throughout a period of enormous population growth.[19]

Rationalized methods of agriculture represented more than a material solution to the problem of food supplies; they signaled the appearance of larger systems of thought that would conflict with existing rural attitudes toward nature, production, and consumption. Emanating from new centers of activity, scientific discourses infiltrated the world of dairying. In some instances, these modes of reasoning converged with generally held knowledge about tending animals and producing cheese and butter; in others, they challenged the very values and practices upheld by generations of dairying families. The new discourses both boosted and absorbed the force of market demands for dairy products. A regular supply of acceptable cheeses and butter was needed but not always available, given the unpredictable outcome of many dairying procedures. In an attempt to assure such regular quality production, the new agriculture allied itself with empirical discourse aimed at attaining "true," repeatable results. The assumption that an absolute, scientific truth existed in dairying, which could be achieved through repeated experimentation and standardized measurements, introduced a new hierarchy of authority that would alter the social relations of the dairying farm and community.

A competition arose between new and old styles of dairying. Those in possession of new knowledge asserted superiority over the less enlightened, and armed with the incontestability of reason, they campaigned against customary ways of making cheese and butter. Inevitably, this debate developed into a struggle between the informed man of reason and the ignorant practitioner, most often depicted as the tradition-bound dairywoman, and was fought out in the pages of the agricultural treatise. Dairywomen were not considered open to new methods or new objectives; they were too closely associated with the realm of nature and superstition to promise success in scientific improvement. The "*fair* professors" of dairying, William Marshall pointed out,

> tho' they may claim a degree of NATURAL CLEVERNESS . . . having tried their skill, *alone*, without obtaining the requisite degree of excellency, can have no good objection, now, to let us try our *joint* endeavours. And I call upon every man of science, who has opportunity and leisure, to lend them his best assistance.[20]

What appeared to be the "natural" aversion of women to learning new techniques was only underscored by a prescribed female subservience to men. This undeclared war between new and old was in fact a struggle against women's ways of working. Recognizing and responding to the material advantages held out by the new agriculture, farmers acquired knowledge in order to adopt the role of instructor and reeducate women.

Against the erratic practices of traditional husbandry, the new agriculture posed technique that was observed, recorded, and repeated in the best empirical style. Dairying was particularly susceptible to the printed dimension of the agricultural revolution, for it represented customary, unrecorded methods of farming par excellence. Dairying was seen as an art rather than a science; owing to its reliance upon apparently incalculable procedures, as well as its irregular results, dairying belonged to an occult branch of husbandry. Very little on dairying methods had been recorded before the eighteenth century, a fact that amazed contemporaries, as well as later historians. The move from oral to written knowledge constituted an advance over previous practices, as the act of printing and publishing would subject methods to the scrutiny of a wide audience and the test of further experience. "The art of agriculture must ever remain imperfect while it is suffered to languish in the memory, and die with the practitioner," wrote William Marshall in his treatise on Norfolk. Although he referred to farming as an "art," Marshall revealed his reverence for art's opponent, science: "RECORD, only, can perpetuate the art; and SYSTEM, alone, render the science comprehensible." It was no coincidence that Marshall's plea for making agriculture a recorded science appeared in the preface to a work on one of the major dairying counties in the nation. "What Dr. Johnson says of Language is applicable to Agriculture," Marshall added in a telling footnote. "'Diction merely vocal is always in its childhood. As no man leaves his eloquence behind him, the new generations have all to learn'."[21] Marshall's words ominously predicted the dawn of a new age of dairying, in which raising the art would also entail reconstituting its techniques. Through the writing and dissemination of these texts, male practitioners redefined the art of women and appropriated it as their own.

Much of the actual work of dairying appeared to defy rational explanation and systematic analysis. Cheese making demanded attention to minute details in a seemingly endless process. Many operations required determining proper temperature and time, measurements literally incalculable without modern instruments. The correct temperature for milk at the time of adding the rennet was, appropriately enough, "milk warm," and only the experienced hand of the mistress showed sufficient sensitivity. The rennet itself constituted a uniquely mysterious substance whose properties were not fully understood even in the late nineteenth century. Produced from an extract of the stomach of a calf according to as many methods as there were cheeses, rennet made possible the chemical reaction enabling curd to form from the milk and cream. Agronomists and dairywomen debated various ways of pickling, drying, and cleaning the "calf's bag" for nearly a century and a half.[22]

Other steps in cheese making varied according to countless regional factors and climatic conditions. Under such constraints, a seemingly mysterious matriarchal authority prevailed, and techniques often derived from several generations of women. "How unthankful an office it is," complained one treatise on dairying, "to attempt to instruct or inform Dairywomen, how to improve their method, or point out rules, which are different from their own, or what hath always been practised by their Mothers, to whom they are often very partial." To the outsider, such women appeared stubbornly set in their ways, and almost superstitious in their adherence to imponderable procedures. "There may be many variations as to the minutiae . . . as no two dairy women exactly follow the same method," a Cheshire farmer reported, "some pretending to have a secret, or nostrum, unknown to their neighbours." Arthur Young simply surrendered in the face of such obscurity. "The minutiae of dairy concerns would fill a book," he complained, "and after all would not be useful to any extent."[23]

Yet dairywomen were not oblivious to external pressures; long accustomed to selling their products, if only on a local basis, they showed considerable sensitivity to the ever-elusive predilections of the market. Yellow butter attained its golden cast not from nature, but from marigold blossoms, which the dairywoman carefully preserved for yearlong use in order to cater to the universal preference for a colored product.[24] Gloucestershire cheeses acquired a reputation for a variegated appearance through a "trick" of dairywomen adopted long before the inquiries of the eighteenth century. The oldest dairywoman with whom William Marshall conversed was unable to remember when cheeses were not artificially colored; by the 1790s, the practice was so standard that factors claimed that they could not sell the cheeses without their characteristic tint and therefore undertook the job of supplying their dairywomen with dyes.[25] Early in the eighteenth century, coloring cheeses had been seen as a form of adulteration and thus as a crime, particularly as the substances used were sometimes toxic. But by the end of the century, the coloring of cheese was seen as part of the dairywoman's skill in satisfying the purchaser, the cheese factor, and ultimately, the consumer:

> They colour it, now, through a kind of necessity, and with intentions as innocent as those of other manufacturers who change the colour of their raw materials. If the eaters of cheese were to take it into their heads, to prefer black, blue, or red cheese, to that of a golden hue, . . . they would do their best endeavour to gratify them.[26]

Marshall criticized some coloring techniques as "filthy practices," but less judgmental agronomists recounted methods with respectful exactitude. William Ellis offered several explanations for making figured cheeses, obtained from "*one of the best Dairywomen in the Vale of Alesbury*," including "a pretty way of making chequer'd Sage-cheese." Formerly construed as unlawful deception, these techniques now constituted art. Dairywomen also painstakingly produced cheeses in the shapes of pineapples, flowers, fish, and trees, and then colored them accordingly. The pressures of the marketplace thus influenced the alacrity with which women engaged in customary practices.[27]

Whatever managerial role that dairywomen played in the new world of commercial dairying was gradually erased in agricultural treatises. Writers effectively displaced women from positions of authority by appropriating the role of instructor and obliterating the agency of women in dairy production. The liminal status of the agricultural writer, straddling two worlds, contributed to this process: as a practical farmer, he was thoroughly acquainted with women's work in the dairy, but as authoritative writer, he communicated to a world of men. John Lawrence (1753–1839), a successful popularizer of improved farming techniques, demonstrated a noticeably ambivalent attitude toward these problems in his *New Farmer's Calendar* (4th ed., 1802). He inscribed his monthly offering "to the farmers of Great Britain" with the title page exhortation "Britons! Honour the plough." Judging from correspondence in Young's *Annals of Agriculture*, the readership of serial publications was almost exclusively male, with only one or two female exceptions. Lawrence could hardly have expected the dairymaid herself to read his advice to "beat the butter down with a hard wooden rammer, not *hot fists*." But in one instance, he explicitly addressed his comments to both sexes, and this was in his command to give milch cows "the most *patient*, gentle, and humane treatment." "*I say this to masters and mistresses, who, however regularly they may go to church, are guilty of a high breach of their moral duty, when they do not enforce, both by example and precept, the humane treatment of all animals.*"[28] While such moral advice constituted fit information for women, his remaining instructions were addressed to no one in particular. Presumably Lawrence aimed his *Calendar* at farmers like himself, who would then take on the office of instructing others.

Though the female dairy manager was absent as an essential character in the pages of Lawrence's work, she was nevertheless the source of his expertise: he admitted that he obtained his knowledge of the dairy from his wife. "The few loose hints I have to offer on DAIRY-MANAGEMENT," he explained in passing, "are from my wife, who has been accustomed, from her youth, to the superintendance [*sic*] of the dairy, as well as the business of farming and gardening in general."[29] Lawrence was not alone in relying on his wife for information; his more sophisticated contemporary, James Anderson, F.R.S., LL.D., F.S.A.E. (1739–1808), also credited his wife, then deceased, in a postscript to his installment on dairying in *Recreations in Agriculture*. "To her gentle influence the public are indebted, if they be indeed indebted at all, for whatever useful hints may at any time have dropt from my pen," he humbly acknowledged. Anderson further obliterated signs of her independent contribution to the science of dairying by adding a bit of moral philosophy to his postscript. "A being, she thought, who must depend so much as man [*sic*] does on the assistance of others, owes as a debt to his fellow-creatures the communication of the little useful knowledge that chance may have thrown in his way." Concurring with his wife's apparent selflessness, he added, "Such has been my constant aim." Yet Anderson grasped the implications of transferring knowledge to a readership that was hungry for technical advice. Emblazoned on the title page was a quotation from Bacon: "Knowledge is power." His publications, like those of Lawrence, would undermine the authority of the dairywoman.[30]

Other writers displayed a more marked consciousness of the gendered nature of dairying skills. William Marshall's famous works on the rural economy of England, published from 1787 to 1798, provided perhaps the fullest account of dairying methods and explicitly acknowledged the prominent role of women in production. Obtaining information about this womanly art, however, was no simple task. "The dairyroom is consecrated to the sex," Marshall averred, "and it is generally understood to require some interest, and more address, to gain full admission to its rites." Like the altar of a primitive religion, the dairy occupied some nether region of female space. In publishing information on dairying, Marshall presented his findings as private information now rendered public. He contrasted the manufacture of cheese with the cultivation of land; while farming was a "*public employment*," cheesemaking was "a *private manufactury*—a craft—a mystery—secluded from the public eye." The "minutiae" of the industry are so obscured from view that "even . . . the master of the dairy" may not know them. He pointed out that his compilation of methods used in Gloucestershire and northern Wiltshire amounted to more information "than any individual of the two counties knew" at the time. "The knowledge, even of practitioners, is in a manner wholly confined to their own individual practice," he explained; "or perhaps to that of some few confidential neighbours." The published agricultural treatise now existed as a countervailing force against the tendency of dairywomen to maintain their privacy, and Marshall and others insured that science would replace secrecy.[31]

The flurry of information on dairying, like that on agriculture in general, had as its ultimate object the advancement of the individual dairy farmer over others. But the representation of the dairy as a private enterprise wanting exposure and publicity conflicted with the prevailing spirit of some dairying communities, where knowledge was both private and shared. The best and costliest cheddar came from regions of England where farmers and dairywomen depended to a great degree on cooperation for the production of cheese. In the Brue Marshes in eighteenth-century Somerset, for example, the residents of each township combined their milk daily to produce a cooperative cheese, known throughout England for its high quality. Celia Fiennes witnessed the same practice in Cheshire, where "the custome of the country to joyn their milking together of a whole village and to make their great cheeses" compensated for the fact that the herds of individual farms tended to be small in number during the first half of the eighteenth century. One need not idealize the eighteenth-century farming community to find practices that, according to rational considerations, benefited the entire community rather than the individual dairy farmer. Here quality and commercial success were compatible with customary methods.[32]

At times, the social practices of dairywomen positively enhanced the cooperative spirit that existed within rural communities. Cheese itself could be shared; as food, it satisfied a natural need linked to women in their customary role as producers of life and providers of sustenance. In his travels, William Ellis took note of a widely acclaimed custom of making "dolphin cheese," in decline by the middle years of the eighteenth century, which celebrated the event of childbirth. Produced from a specially carved wooden mould, the cheese "was much esteemed as an Ornament, as well as Service to a lying-in Woman's Chamber." The significance of this figure, symbolizing rescue from peril and resurrection from death, made it a popular item in country households; the moulds being scarce, they were "lent from one Neighbour to another, throughout a Town." The dolphin cheese thus served the multiple purpose of communicating neighborly good will, female art, and material sustenance at times of need.[33]

The typical eighteenth-century dairy presented a world of labor unto itself, topsy-turvy in its assignment of gender roles. The workforce, headed by a woman, was primarily female: the mistress of the farm commanded anywhere from two to twenty maids (each maid tending ten cows), driving the girls hard from four in the morning till well into the evening. This phalanx of female industry might be assisted by one or two men or boys, but male labor was generally unskilled and irregularly provided. Milking was a long and laborious process, often taking place in the pastures, so that some help from men was needed in getting the milk back to the barn. But the designation of "Odd Man" ("one that is to set his Hand to any common Business") indicated the anomalous nature of this category of employment.[34]

Turning the heaviest rounds of cheese, sometimes weighing over a hundred pounds each, presented the greatest problem for agriculturalists as they attempted to prescribe gender-specific roles to dairywork. Clearly women were capable of the task. In Cheshire, where cheese making was usually a large-scale undertaking, women simply did the work that was required. "The labour of turning and cleaning cheese is performed almost universally by women," Holland reported in his work for the Board of Agriculture; "and that in large dairies, where the cheeses are upwards of 140 lb. each, upon an average: this they do without much appearance of exertion, and with a degree of ease, which is [a] matter of surprise even in this county." A man might join in this later stage of production, but such assistance was by no means the rule. Men like Marshall blenched at the reality.

> It is customary, even in the largest dairies, for the ostensible manager, whether mistress or maid, to perform the *whole* operation of making cheese; except the last breaking &c. and the vatting; in which she has an assistant. But this, in a dairy of eighty or a hundred cows, is too great labour for any woman: it is painful to see it.

A Midlands cheese factor witnessed the same, and protested against it: "The weight of a large *Cheshire* Cheese," he stated, being too great to be wrought by a Woman, and turning, rubbing, washing, and cleaning, is more than one Man can easily perform." Though both writers observed women successfully performing such tasks, their revulsion caused them to obscure that fact beneath a general condemnation of traditional practice.[35]

The attributes of labor found in the eighteenth-century dairy contrasted strikingly with later models held out by industrial capitalism, where mental work was separated from manual. Marshall recognized that dairying required both "much thought, and much labour," a combination of talents rarely attributed to laboring women, much less to women anywhere in the public world of production. The qualities assigned to women and men virtually inverted the roles of the sexes: women combined decision making with industry and showed ceaseless commitment to a never-ending workday, while men appeared on the scene only sporadically in order to contribute unskilled labor. According to at least one observer, male laborers also displayed a recalcitrance and diffidence that nineteenth-century writers later associated only with women. Before the introduction of mechanization into larger establishments in the 1790s, butter making sometimes required male assistants to help in the long process of churning. But "men servants make many objections to this employment (which is certainly very laborious) and generally set about it with an ill will, often quit it before it is finished, and as often contrive to get out of the way, when likely to be wanted for this operation." In the area of milking alone, women were praised for a specifically feminine touch: "gentleness" was universally regarded as the best approach to extracting milk from a cow. Otherwise, dairying demanded endurance and strength totally absent in grace.[36]

Though associated with the female sex, the dairy did not display characteristics in keeping with prosaic images of femininity. Cleanliness was always of foremost importance; but that required of the dairywoman and her dairy was not "studied *outward neatness*" for show, but rather, cleanliness soberly manifested "*in reality.*" "A cheese dairy is a manufactory— a workshop—and is, in truth, a place of hard work," explained Marshall. Attention to "arrangement" and appearance there "would be superfluous."[37] What was pleasing to the eye was not necessarily desirable; and what seemed unattractive was not always regarded as such by the expert. Caring for cows required constant contact with their bodily parts and functions, including regular tending to their diet and excretions in order to monitor factors contributing to the flavors of milk, butter, and cheese. Cheese making similarly entailed dealing with strong odors and slimy substances that were often unpleasant, and sometimes fetid and repugnant. Yet skillful dairying demanded that the manager not only confront such elements of the job, but also inspect and analyze them. Too much heat surrounding a cheese as it aged created "heaved Cheese," detected by sticking the round with a taster to allow the air to "rusheth forth with a strong Wind, of a rank disagreeable smell, caused by the Air being discharged from putrid or undigested Curd." Through experience, a dairywoman might also determine what plants to sow to rid her cows of flatulence. Inevitably, women might also speculate upon the parallels between the production of cow's milk and their own; by no coincidence, a woman farmer discovered that frequent milking increased the production of her cows by a considerable amount. Nature cohabited with women in the dairy; in the eighteenth century, it was not a carefully contrived presence, but rather, a shameless and often slightly soiled one.[38]

Though Marshall was able to observe the "old established practice" in his tour of Gloucestershire in the 1780s, new attitudes had begun to whittle away tolerance of tradition in dairywork. Dairying as a science slowly overtook dairying as nature and art. The positive attributes of female labor in the family farm did not promise advancement in the new world of agriculture for they were circumscribed within a role of housewifery that was gradually separated from the realm of business and subjected to new standards. Business considerations acquired more force within the most successful establishments, and these farms led the way in fixing powerful norms for others. At the forefront of this transformation stood the cheese factor; as an agent involved in the procuring and marketing of cheese, his experience in securing sales and good prices led him, through success and failure, to skillful dairywomen, from whom he systematically obtained information in techniques and procedures. The factor was often a farmer himself, usually of a large holding and many cows. His labor force was largely hired, their schedules routinized, and his credits and debits carefully accounted for. When eighteenth-century "men of science" inquired into the dairy industry, they turned to factors (and, in some instances, cheesemongers) for the information they required.[39]

Marshall encountered such a man, suitably named Mr. Bigland, who was "purchaser of, perhaps, half the cheese which is made in the vale of Berkeley," "proprietor of a dairy of more than fifty cows," and most importantly, "a man of science." Contrasted with Marshall's other favorite, Mrs. Wade, who boasted "*education*," "natural abilities," "experience," and only forty or fifty cows cared for over twenty or thirty years, Marshall was led to overcome a distrust of "modern deviations" in order to investigate further the man of progress. Bigland was the person "most capable of giving me information," Marshall admitted, "in every department of the subject I was investigating." Moreover, "his ability of information . . . was exceeded by his liberality in communicating it." Hence followed several hundred pages of description of Bigland's dairy, so that the reader of Marshall's Gloucestershire tour was left to wonder at the disappearance of the venerable Mrs. Wade, who had ranked "among the first dairywomen of the district."[40]

Marshall's treatise was not alone in displacing the authority of the dairywoman with that of the male manager. In Josiah Twamley's *Dairying Exemplified, or the Business of Cheese-making* (1784), "the said art" of women became the "business" of men. The book claimed to be the first of its kind; "no Treatise or Book of rules, or method of making Cheese" had ever been set to paper. As a cheese factor plainly representing the best interests of the trade (his job was to contract good cheeses for later sale in a distant market), Twamley aimed to root out the exasperating irregularities that arose from the nature of dairying. "'Tis evident to a nice observer," he complained,

> of the different, yea, very different qualities of Cheese produc'd in different Dairys, or even in the same Dairys, when either the Dairy-maid is changed, or the usual method of Cheese making, by the Mistress or manager of each Dairy, is not strictly adhered to. A Remedy for this great deficiency is looked upon as an affair of great moment, especially by those, whose lot it is to be fixed in the Cheese Trade in a considerable Dairying Country . . . .

Twamley's observation echoed that of Marshall; but what Marshall simply marveled at, Twamley condemned. Labor—particularly of such an elusive variety—must not ultimately determine the quality of the final product. Twamley offered a blueprint for successful dairying that explicitly blamed the capacities of women for the inadequacies of the trade.[41]

The factor criticized the stubbornness, inability, and in one case, the "stupidity" of the dairywomen he encountered, railing against the "great number of inferior Dairys." In place of customary attitudes and methods, he offered uniform standards and techniques. "Good Cheese may be made by a good Dairy-woman in any place, or on any land," he claimed and boasted that his advice could transform poor produce into highly marketable commodities. He expected resistance: "What does he know of Dairying," the women would ask, "or how should a Man know any thing of Cheese making?" Superior knowledge stood as his defense; he could present, in a soundly reasonable way, solutions to problems that "the Dairywoman would fairly acknowledge she could not account for." The mystery of the dairywoman's art gave way to the reality of rational science.[42]

Twamley's treatise included many personal accounts of his adventures as a cheese factor, each revealing the clash between his scientific spirit and the traditional temperaments of the women he encountered. His project was greatly aided by the nature of his trade in a tightly knit dairy farming community; on the road, at fairs, in kitchens, and in barns, the factor availed himself of hospitality, information, and local gossip. A neighborliness not lacking in ordinary animosities, as well as dependent relations, prevailed among the dairywomen he interviewed. As a potential purchaser of cheese, he was greeted with eagerness, openness, as well as a fair amount of suspicion. His favorite strategy, to venture guesses at how cheeses were made, or what the taste of a cheese was before testing it, elicited amazement and disbelief from local women. Not having the benefit of Twamley's far-flung exposure to various cheeses, they were unable to fathom the source of his knowledge. One woman thought instead that he knew where she hailed from (constituting, in her mind, an explanation for his familiarity with her cheese), and she never totally relinquished the view that the factor practiced a form of prognostication. Tales like this, juxtaposed with methodical and precise explanations of dairying processes, assured the reader that Twamley had indeed stumbled upon a benighted art, one waiting to be liberated from a crippling irrationality.[43]

Twamley also used stories to recommend advice to the dairywomen he met, and in his treatise, he related what was clearly a favorite anecdote concluding with an instructive revelation. His observations had convinced him that "Cheese in general was made too much in a hurry." Happening to pass by a house "notorious for as bad a Dairy as I ever met with," Twamley reluctantly paid a visit. "Won[']t you call and look at my Cheese," the mistress of the establishment supposedly requested, "I am sure tis as good as my neighbour T—s, which you have been buying." "I fear not," replied the knowledgeable factor and, upon inspecting the dairy chamber, "told her it would not suit" him. But in casting a glance about the room, Twamley spotted one cheese that was "very blooming in appearance." "I should be glad to know the History of it," he inquired. Her response, in Twamley's eyes, only underscored her ignorance. "Why truly said she tis a strange one":

> One night when I had rendled my Milk, a person came running to me, and said, neighbour T— is groaning & you must come immediately; I said to a raw wench I had to help me, now be sure you don[']t touch this Cheese till I come back, I will be sure to come to you when I see how neighbour T— is; but it happened she was worse than I expected, and I could not leave her till after midnight. I said, my Cheese will be spoiled, but the poor Woman shall not be lost for a Cheese; when I came home I found it not so bad as I expected, put it into the Vat in a hurry, saying, it may possibly make a Cheese that will do for ourselves, but I little thought it would ever be a saleable Cheese.

The account revealed as much about the dairying community as the science of cheese making. Helping a neighbor had taken precedence over the fate of her cheese; ironically, this was the very woman with whom she competed. Neither did the dairywoman approach the accidental results with the same attitude as Twamley. "Well now—said I," Twamley recorded, "and is not this Cheese a proper lesson to you? don[']t you thereby plainly see that you have made the rest too quick[?]" The woman replied, "It might, if I had thought at all—but I declare, I never once thought about it." "Profound stupidity! thought I to myself," wrote the cheese factor, "and left her."[44]

Twamley was a prophet among an unenlightened people, spreading news of a brave new market in which his listeners had too little interest. Bound together by rigid custom and shared opinion, the dairying community needed to be divided and conquered by the new mentality. Twamley decried the "dangerous consequence, for a Factor to complain of any fault in the Cheese to the maker, or not give it sufficient praise." So tight was the fellowship of dairywomen that he could not afford to talk of the relative faults and merits of neighbors' cheeses for fear of alienating them all. His suppliers complained that all were given "nearly the same Price" for their cheeses, and thus were discouraged from improvement; yet no one appeared willing to abandon her loyalty to the group in order to overcome "mediocrity." The commercial world of dairying, Twamley tirelessly argued in response, ultimately must extend beyond narrow local opinion.[45]

Twamley's most revolutionary argument, that "dairy folks" must learn to compete in the marketplace, came disguised in the form of a homely proverb: "There is one best way of doing every thing, and 'tis what in every way of life is a cause of strife, a maxim I was taught in my youth was, never strive to be second-best, someone must prevail, and they that do must strive for it, the best way of doing a thing is as easy, when known, as the second-best." Production for the market meant making new alliances; rather than clinging to their neighbors' society, dairywomen must cleave to the cheese factor. Twamley pointed out that their interests were the same as his: improved goods that brought the best customers to the cheese factor "would of course give the command in price to those who supplied him." His very language attempted to demonstrate the joining of factor to producer, market to household, male to female. Dairywomen would discover, he argued, that "Ambition & Interest, their bosom friends, will point out a new road to them, in which they will travel, not only as swift & prosperous, as their rival neighbours, but will not leave them in an easy & composed state, till they have out gone them." Dairywomen were to adopt the values and traits of the cheese factor and the market; a love of competition and mastery over others marked the talents of the dairywoman in the modern age of cheese-making.[46]

III

The new standards set by agriculturalists and cheese factors by themselves could not displace women from primary positions in dairying. A number of smaller farms persisted in utilizing chiefly wives and daughters, who made important decisions and performed heavy work. Mid-nineteenth-century inhabitants of Wiltshire reported that dairy farmers' wives took "the hardest part of the work upon themselves"; this fact, they claimed, allowed agricultural laborers to enjoy a life that was not "so hard as it used to be." The controlling mistress was still in evidence in the 1840s:

"I know many dairy-farms where the mistress never allows a servant to manage or clean a cheese, nor to touch it after it comes out of the vat," claimed one land agent, "thus performing the severest part of the labour herself." A strong market for dairy products supported large and small farmers alike through the first half of the nineteenth century, enabling those who wished to remain loyal to customary work roles to adopt selectively the dictates of learned authorities.[47]

But large-scale dairy farmers interested in the latest improvements had enough capital to invest in laborsaving machinery, which warranted the employment of several dairymaids while obviating the need for the farmer's wife's traditional role. On such establishments, authority came from above, and the autonomy of women was clearly circumscribed. Machinery gradually performed much of the maids' actual work, while leaving a less skilled person in charge of supervising each task. At the bottom of the hierarchy, the ordinary dairymaid became part of the proletariat of the agricultural work force. Though considered more respectable than the average laborer owing to the fact that she did not mix with men on the farm, her hours were notoriously long and her position increasingly difficult to fill.[48] Her symbolic significance seems to have waxed as her status as laborer waned. As Charles Phythian-Adams has shown in a study of May Day rituals, the country milkmaid came to represent pure female sexuality, "chastity, modesty and clean, but hard, *country*-living," in contrast with the less acceptable attributes of male labor. The nineteenth-century milkmaid competed with other wage earners as a subordinate requesting the aid of wealthy elites, though this did not diminish the durability of her symbolic image, as the character of Thomas Hardy's Tess seems to demonstrate.[49]

The growing sophistication of the market played a strong part in determining the nature of social relations in dairying during this time; commercial considerations and transactions became paramount in establishing the chain of command in some dairying districts. An account of cheese marketing in Derbyshire in 1829 makes no mention of women in its explanation of the highly articulated "staple commodity" business. Factors or dealers made contracts with "small dairy-men," which included collecting the cheeses at the centrally located warehouses where the rounds were inspected and reinspected and readied for the huge market of London, for fulfilling government contracts or for shipping all over the kingdom. The extension of canal systems through the Midlands greatly facilitated business from the late eighteenth century, and by this time, it is clear that quantities of sale had multiplied by hundreds of pounds in weight. Only the small dairymen entered in a "ready-money trade" for smaller quantities; the rest of the farmers relied on credit and waited until higher prices were fixed by the factors at large fairs.[50] It is difficult to say, without more detailed research, just how women participated in this kind of dairy industry. Scattered references in agricultural journals to male managers suggest that some commercial dairies hired men to intercede

between the market and the milk bucket. It seems clear that the direction
of control, more than ever before, was from factor to farm.

By the 1860s, foreign competition and falling prices of foodstuffs promoted a new wave of attitudes toward labor in the dairy: the reduction of
labor and the standardization of dairy products became primary goals as
farmers sought to cut costs and maximize profits in a stiffer market. Leading authorities, all of them men, published essays and books giving precise instructions for techniques that were assumed to be incontrovertible.
"For many years past it has been our object to produce the *best cheese*
with the *least possible labour*," one dairyman indicated. His instructions,
like those of other authors, stipulated precise times, temperatures, and
measurements and boasted equally precise results. Such "principal
improvements in dairy practice . . . have enabled us to send into the market a superior article, increased in quantity 25 per cent., at a reduction of
the original labour of more than half," he pointed out.[51] Dairymaids were
usually the losers in these calculations; the object was to reduce the need
for labor so that the farmer's wife and perhaps his daughters might be the
only required hands. Yet the tension between articulated standards that
minimized or erased the authority of women and the resistance of the
ever-present farmer's wife continued. Harding himself must have relied
on his wife for some managerial assistance, for when he fell ill in later life,
she appears to have replaced him on the lecture circuit. But this sort of
power was conferred by familial connections more than from formal
channels of authority. It is difficult to find any mention of women in late
nineteenth-century accounts of the trade.[52]

The movement away from employing farmers' wives and daughters
seemed to be afoot under a different guise. With the entry of American
factory-made cheese around 1870, the Midland Agricultural Society
organized a project to build factories at home. One of the purported aims
of this movement, along with the obvious goal of obtaining greater uniformity and higher quality of cheese, was to put "a stop to the undue
labour . . . of the mistress of an ordinary home cheese-dairy."[53] Dairywomen themselves had little to do with this initiative. Only one woman
went on record as being behind the cause. "Soon after a speech by Lord
Vernon" that "insisted on" the need for factories in order to relieve farmers' wives of their responsibilities, one dairywoman submitted (significantly,
in a letter sent to J. Chalmers Morton after the public lecture) that "there
is really too much devolving on a farmer's wife who looks well to her
dairy, and wishes to do her duty in a domestic way." Higher standards of
domesticity must have exerted pressure upon prosperous dairywomen
after midcentury, but not all subscribed to the new ideology. When Morton attempted to press this issue with other dairywomen he met in
Cheshire, he found that "this [reasoning] would not . . . be allowed by
any of those to whom I spoke upon the subject." Dairywomen, as well as
their husbands, maintained that the work was not the "drudgery" that
advocates of the cheese factory claimed it to be, and that the quality of

their produce warranted the continuance of "home dairy management."[54]

In her comprehensive treatment of women and work in the industrial
revolution, Ivy Pinchbeck described a reorganization of dairy farming
that entailed the replacement of women by male managers in the first
decades of the nineteenth century. She attributed this shift to the "disin-
clination for the heavy work of the dairy" among wives of the more prosperous and respectable rural farming class.[55] Yet this later *embourgoise-
ment* of dairywomen, evident as increasing affluence during the French
wars afforded new styles of consumption among more substantial farmers, was different from the process described above. The expansion of
commercial dairying in the eighteenth century introduced new criteria for
production and instigated conflict over the value of female labor before
habits of gentility interfered with the dairywoman's work. And while
observers may have been quick to note the rural woman's retreat to the
parlor, it is not at all clear that the dairywoman herself initiated the
change.

Changes in commercial dairying can be related to a general transformation in the nature of work at the end of the eighteenth century. In a
provocative research proposal, Maurice Godelier sketched out the importance of historical and cultural factors in shaping the meanings of work in
any society. He pointed out that eighteenth-century European political
economy developed a concept of work that associated it with the creation
of wealth; by the nineteenth century, Marx identified the release of the
concept from its particular forms, a point at which "'work in general'
becomes conceivable as a practical reality, as the point of departure for
modern economics." This shift away from embeddedness in social relations (in this case, small-scale and household forms of production) paved
the way for a denigration of women's work. "Work in general" under
industrial capitalism was actually rationalized work tailored specifically to
men. Traditional women's work was seen as irrational, and thus, by
definition, less valuable. As Godelier pointed out from an anthropological
perspective, "In societies where men dominate, women's tasks are often
considered inferior and unworthy of men. The dominant social representations frequently are intended to 'prove' the inferiority of women's
tasks, when in fact they are inferior simply because they have been consigned to women."[56] Without articulating an explicit sexual division of
labor, the new industrial era displaced women from valued positions and
relegated them to a more vulnerable place in a system that purported to
be value free.

4

The Quarrel with Women's Work: Spinning and the Displacement of Female Labor

Come, village nymphs, ye matrons, and ye maids!
Receive the soft material; with light step
Whether ye turn around the spacious wheel,
Or, patient sitting, that revolve, which forms
A narrower circle. On the brittle work
Point your quick eye, and let the hand assist
To guide and stretch the gently-lessening thread;
Even, unknotted, twine will praise your skill.

John Dyer, *The Fleece* (1757)

Spinning constituted a ubiquitous employment in the eighteenth century, and everywhere it rested in the hands of women. It very often figured as an archetype of female industry in depictions of labor. Women of all classes were expected to be familiar with the art, whether for practical purposes or simply in the cultivation of virtue. Discourses on the ideal of womanhood praised the "good Mistress" who in accordance with biblical injunctions "seeks Wool or Flax, and worketh willingly with her own Hands." While the origins of "spinster" remain obscure, one of the earliest usages noted that the "Industry of female Manufacturers would be most laudably employ'd this way." "This Word intimates that a Woman's chief Praise consists in Domestic Industry, and in Simplicity," the tract read. So intertwined were the cultural definitions of the good housewife and the work of spinning that the very word "distaff" came to represent the female side of a family.[1]

In addition to its relationship to gender, spinning was an instrinsic part of the economic life of the poor. Because of the low cost of a wheel and the ready availability of raw wool, spinning constituted a viable, relatively profitable way of working for women in every part of England. Particularly in agricultural districts, where work was seasonal, carding and spinning kept most women busy throughout the year, filling the weeks unoccupied by other remunerative activity. Here, indeed, lay the quintessential "stopgap" measure of labor; or, in the words of Fitzherbert in his famous *Boke of Husbandrye* (1555), "A woman cannot get her livinge honestly with spinning on the dystaffe, but it stoppeth a gap and must nedes be had."[2] Fitzherbert implied the obvious fact that contemporaries never questioned: that spinning was underpaid, probably owing to its association with female domestic work. Nevertheless, estimates indicated that spinners "outnumbered all other workers" in the textile trade of the eighteenth century, and women and children may have predominated by a ratio of eight to one.[3] Even outside the weaving districts, spinning was a foremost by-employment, conveniently helping to support the large proportion of the population intermittently subsidized by poor law relief. For these same reasons, proposals for employing the poor never failed to recommend spinning as a suitable solution.[4]

This common household activity became the basis of a new world of industry. To Daniel Defoe, the remarkable industriousness of spinners virtually enacted the drama of English commerce. "There was not in all the Eastern and middle part of Norfolk, any Hand, unemploy'd, if they could Work," he expounded in characteristic fashion in 1723. Women everywhere appeared to be engaged in gainful employment, boosting the nation's prosperity as it became known worldwide. Though he was not directly aware of it, this flurry of domestic industry represented the first gust of a growing storm. The expanding business of textiles soon brought the issue of female labor before the public eye, where it exploded into a problem of serious proportions and really never went away.[5]

By the end of the eighteenth century, Defoe's simple picture of female activity had changed entirely. Though women had been central to the textile industries at the beginning of the century, new technology and capitalistic organization removed them from their primary role in production and deprived them of an accessible source of income. Displaced by innovations that necessitated large-scale investment and new management, relatively few women found jobs in factories as low-paid assistants under male supervision by the early nineteenth century. What had once been a ubiquitous domestic industry became isolated within certain regions, specialized according to new categories of skill, and firmly structured according to gender. The new system subordinated ordinary women in every instance.

I

Each traditional method of spinning—by distaff, small wheel, or large wheel—displayed a marked relation to the world of women. The distaff, the oldest and most primitive instrument, consisted of a cleft stick about a yard long, operated in conjunction with a spindle on which the spun thread was wound. The work proceeded slowly as the spinster pulled the yarn from the distaff, twisted it, and wound it, repeating the process again and again until the fleece had been transformed into thread. Of all the methods of spinning, the distaff produced the finest thread. Its main advantage, however, was its convenience, as it could be carried anywhere and even put to use while doing other things. As John Dyer's famous epic revealed,

> and many, yet adhere
> To th' ancient distaff, at the bosom fix'd,
> Casting the whirling spindle as they walk,
> At home, or in the sheepfold, or the mart
> Alike the work proceeds.[6]

Though hardly profitable when calculated by the hour, work with the distaff ultimately proved more productive over the course of a woman's day. Given the intermittent nature of women's work, with its repeated interruptions and its many simultaneous responsibilities, the distaff was supremely adaptable. This must account for its persistence through the eighteenth and even into the nineteenth century. "One rarely met with an old woman in the north of Scotland, that is not otherwise employed," an observer remarked in 1795, "but who has got a distaff stuck in her girdle and a spindle at her hand."[7]

More common throughout eighteenth-century England was the large, simple spinning wheel. Used primarily for wool, the wheel was visible in nearly every eighteenth-century house or cottage. Here, too, the work was time-consuming and tedious, demanding much perseverance and patience. The spinner drew out the wool with one hand while turning the wheel with the other, stepping backward and forward to accommodate the growing thread. Thus a woman might walk as much as thirty-three miles in a week by spinning. Sporadically, the spinner stopped to wind the thread on a separate bobbin. (The smaller Saxony wheel, developed by the middle of the eighteenth century, added a bobbin and flyer to the design of the larger wheel, but it was used mainly in spinning flax for linen.) Work at the wheel required more practice than skill, and mothers were quick to train children to take their place when they were occupied in other tasks. By the age of six or seven, a child could produce an acceptable thread. Like most domestic industries, spinning was not an exclusive activity; depending upon any available labor, it ultimately fell upon all the women and children of the household.[8]

Neither was the profession of spinning exclusive of other jobs. Women spun in addition to accomplishing other tasks, some of them outside the home. Spinning both complemented and was complemented by agricultural labor, gathering provisions, tending livestock, household work, and the care of family members. The sporadic nature of spinning enhanced its association with virtuousness, for in this way, women fulfilled the expectation of always being at work. Injecting a prescriptive note into an otherwise empirical discussion of technology, a Scottish writer quoted Benjamin Franklin when he pointed out the beneficial effects of spinning by hand: "Lost time is subsistence; it is therefore lost treasure." Thus spinning was recommended as a highly desirable way of utilizing the odd moments in a woman's daily routine; it reinforced the gender-determined shape of female productivity. "Spinning by the hand, in a country like Ireland," the writer reasoned, "where the sedentary occupations of the female must be so often interrupted, not only by domestic, but agricultural labours, is attended with one very striking advantage, namely, that it can be suspended and resumed without any inconvenience, and thus small intervals of time are filled up that would otherwise be lost." Considerations of gender had a great deal to do with the way in which spinning was allocated to women and, at the same time, undervalued.[9]

Spinning nevertheless offered an adaptability from which laboring women could derive enjoyment and material benefit. It afforded ample opportunity for sociability and communality among village women. They could gather together with their wheels without much trouble, and talk and mind children while they worked. A local historian of Yorkshire recalled such a scene of female industriousness, which vividly illustrated the freedom from constraint enjoyed by prefactory labor:

> . . . the women of Allerton, Thornton, Wilsden, and the other villages in the valley, flocked, on sunny days, with their spinning wheels to some favourite pleasant spot to pursue the labours of the day. In Back Lane, to the north of Westgate, rows of wheels might also be seen on summer afternoons.[10]

Women might also live and spin together in order to support themselves more successfully than if they lived alone. Overseers were known to organize spinsteries for several women in need of support in eighteenth-century Colyton. Spinsters also voluntarily banded together when their situations required it, living and working under the same roof, thus averting the need to rely on the parish for support.[11]

While conviviality was not always the rule, the common activity of spinning gave women similar concerns and points of view. In some localities, spinners themselves participated in the marketing as well as the production of their thread, enabling them to gain an acute sense of their work's worth. Day laborers fetched the wool for their wives and daughters, and the women sold it themselves at the best price. A scenario of woolen spinners in 1741 vividly depicted the "free" market and *ad hoc* arrangements typical of this intermediate form of organization:

> [T]he common way the poor Women in Hampshire, Wiltshire and Dorsetshire, and I believe in other Counties, have of getting to Market (especially

in the Winter-time) is, by the Help of some Farmers' Waggons, which carry them and their Yarn. . . . During the Time the Waggons stop, the poor Women carry their Yarn to the Clothiers for whom they work; then get the few things they want, and return to the Inn to be carried home again. . . . As to those who may live in or near the Market Town, there will be in Market time 3 or 400 poor People (chiefly Women) who will sell their Goods in about an Hour.[12]

The ritual of market day could engender a collective spirit and an interdependence among villagers that, at least momentarily, mitigated tedium or hardship. And while the need for woolen yarn remained acute, independent producers enjoyed an advantageous position: by seeking the best market, they could secure higher prices for their yarn while avoiding the cost of middlemen.[13]

More commonly, however, most spinners worked for a merchant or putter-out, who had regular access to large quantities of raw wool or cotton. The precise organization of the spinning industry has been a matter of historical debate. "[F]rom the beginning," one account has argued, "the employing capitalist was responsible for the organisation of the industry."[14] In southwestern woolen districts, for example, a large clothier might employ as many as 2,000 spinners dispersed over a wide area. Nearly all the women of laboring families there spun full-time for wages. Spinners relied upon the putter-out to deliver wool to their homes, or they congregated at pack houses in order to collect raw material and drop off finished yarn. Such businesses sometimes grew to gigantic proportions. In 1740, a Manchester merchant employing 5,000 spinners engaged the inventor Lewis Paul to develop a machine that would ease the inconvenience and expense of employing so many women. In the second half of the eighteenth century, when the shortage of prepared warp and weft grew even greater, more weavers may have taken over the supervisory capacity of middlemen, organizing their own spinning before producing and selling their cloth to merchants. Yet even in the hands of weavers, the system aimed at extracting a profit from the labor of spinners, exploiting their dual position as workers and as women.[15]

Stigmatized by its association with women's work, spinning never earned wages commensurate with the demand for thread. Though its history and rationale are nearly impossible to account for, the existing hierarchy of wages for work placed women's domestic labor very low.[16] Purchasers of spun thread, whether middleman or manufacturer, assumed that spinners came from households where male wages provided the primary means of support; thus they deliberately set wages for spinning low, often in complete disregard of other factors involved in the trade. Women were repeatedly trapped in contradictory circumstances. In agricultural districts, where work in the fields might supplement spinning, wages for spinning were abysmally low, while laboring men received low wages on account of the steady income provided by wives and children. The poverty of the full-time independent spinster was sometimes so conspicuous that parishes often supplemented their earnings with small allowances. Yet merchants, in turn, sometimes set wages lower in these places, relying on the parish to make up the difference.

Manufacturing regions varied more in their wage rates, yet even in the best of times, payment levels were rather arbitrarily determined. As one defense of spinners complained, the putter-out operated free from any sort of regulation and often took advantage of spinners by reducing payments owing to the catchall excuse, "dullness of trade." "Himself the judge and jury of his conduct," the unregulated employer aimed to turn the highest possible profit and did so at the expense of the spinster.[17] Despite her essential role in England's economic fate, the spinster received penurious wages for her work. "England's greatest industry," one historian boldly observed, "rested on the basis of sweated labour."[18]

The organization of the putting-out system enabled women to undercut the hierarchical structure of the industry that placed merchants and weavers on top and spinners at the bottom. Free from supervision, spinners struck back at arbitrarily low wages through illegal practices of false reeling and embezzlement of raw material. By "reeling short," a woman could retain part of the yarn distributed to her to be spun, spinning and selling it later to another buyer. Laws against fraudulent practices were passed repeatedly during the eighteenth century, attesting to the impotence of the courts in regulating the work of the laboring classes. Some contemporaries recognized that such dishonesty arose as a result of the poor pay earned by spinsters. "There is great reason to believe," argued one writer, "that were the poor to receive the full wages for their work, most of these complaints [against embezzlement and false reeling] would be effectually done away."[19] In the West Riding, Herbert Heaton pointed out in a history of the woolen industry, "there was a stronger capitalistic organization on the one hand, and a keen sense of solidarity of labour on the other. If the master dared to punish an offending workman, either for fraud or neglect, he generally called upon his head the wrath of the labouring classes in his locality, and might suffer severely for his temerity." In an unorganized but forceful way, preindustrial textile workers exercised some control over their relations with employers.[20]

Women spinners joined the battle even as masters resorted to the law to enforce their claims. Public punishment dramatized for all the cost of criminal action. In August 1764, "Lydia Longbottom, of Bingley, was publickly whipt thro' the market at Wakefield, for reeling false and short yarn . . . the town bailiff carrying a reel before her."[21] Such chastisement in Manchester resulted in reprisals from the crowd, particularly from women:

—This Day at Noon . . . Elizabeth Howarth was brought to the Stage a fourth Time, and had a few Lashes; but the Mob, especially some Women, beginning to be very insolent the whipping of three others was defer'd till about Four o'Clock, when the Military Force in Town was drawn out and the three Convicts were brought from the House of Correction by a Party with their Bayonets fixed and were whipp'd at the Cross, the Soldiers being drawn up round the Place.[22]

Though lacking in formal organization, women presented a formidable opposition to capitalists bent on carrying on their business. Despite such demonstrations of the supremacy of the law, spinners persisted in defying the rules of commerce.

During the 1770s, masters throughout Yorkshire, Lancashire, and Cheshire turned to Parliament for further help in restraining the impudence of spinsters and other perpetrators of embezzlement. Organizing committees for the purpose of petitioning Parliament, they ultimately obtained statutory provisions against fraud in the Worsted Act of 1777. Thus capital and the state joined hands, in this instance, mostly against disorderly women. Claiming that the intimidating power of "spinners and workpeople" had made further legal assistance necessary, the act set up a system whereby manufacturers chose inspectors who would be licensed by quarter sessions to carefully supervise distributors and spinners of raw material, checking for embezzlement and undue delay in returning finished material. The penalty for offenses was one month in the House of Correction.[23]

The "preponderance of female culprits" punished for "neglect of work," which entailed keeping material for more than eight days, suggested that "the law was invoked against women and very seldom against men." Even Heaton, not particularly sympathetic to the position of women, wondered if men were "especially law-abiding," or if "the 'solidarity of labour' which had frightened the masters at an earlier date . . . [was] also instrumental in causing the inspectors to wink at male offenders, whilst taking advantage of the disorganization of the women to pounce upon female transgressors." Evidence against numerous women nevertheless came forth and prosecutions against fraud abounded, conspicuous, Heaton pointed out, "if one turns to almost any copy of the Leeds newspapers from 1777 to the end of the century."[24] Certainly the constraints of women's labor, which often entailed many other responsibilities in addition to spinning for wages, could have hindered the completion of tasks in a set period of time as well as participation in any form of labor organization. Inspectors might have found this occasion a welcomed opportunity to punish women for their general part in slowing down the manufacturing process with their seemingly inefficient ways of working. By this time, as the early history of trade unionism shows, male textile workers had organized strikes and protests against numerous grievances, but women did not benefit from these activities. Heaton was probably correct in suggesting that the industry and the law took advantage of the organizational weakness of female labor.[25]

The attractiveness of the putting-out system, despite its vulnerability to fraud and its obvious inconveniences, owed largely to the hierarchy of gender imbedded in the organization of labor. Inexorably capitalist in design and promise, the textile industry offered the risk-taking merchant the chance of considerable profits and even social advancement. The business of putting out "provided a ladder up which the energetic man could climb,"[26] and given the relative permeability of class barriers in Britain, entrepreneurs could at least fasten their hopes on achieving a local reputation of some worth. The rise of the merchant capitalist was inevitably gained at the expense of the woman at the bottom. While merchants and middlemen had a strike at making a fortune, the most that spinsters could hope for was a regular wage. After the invention of spinning machinery, the scope of fortunes awaiting the ambitious man grew even greater, while the position of spinsters became wholly vulnerable to redundancy. Entrepreneurial success depended upon the ability to organize the labor force (in this case, women) and materials in such a way as to extract profit from the necessary costs. The ordinary spinster found little reward in a system that applauded "the short step from weaver to putter-out, and from putting-out agent to manufacturer." She was not destined to be the hero of the classic story of the industrial revolution, but she clearly made it possible.[27]

II

The technological transformation of spinning, beginning with the introduction of the spinning jenny, ultimately displaced customary ways of producing thread by the beginning of the nineteenth century. The eighteenth century's demand for spun thread remains legendary. The woolen trade, England's most longstanding textile industry, flourished in the 1720s and gave copious work to spinners everywhere. Experimentation with mechanized spinning equipment began early, not because a shortage of spinners existed, but rather as a way of solving the inherent difficulty of supervision and transport involved in the putting out of materials. Harvest time could create a shortage of labor in agricultural districts, and this problem might account for the interest of the French government in seeking improved methods of spinning early in the eighteenth century. But real interest in improvement appeared to follow upon a wish to control, as well as speed up, the already extensive production of thread. Lewis Paul, the inventor of the device generally recognized as the first in the cotton industry, complained of the irregular size and quality of much hand spinning, which clearly aggravated the periodic bottleneck in supply. Tales abound, apocryphal and otherwise, recounting the frustrated miseries of entrepreneurs who tinkered with apparatus until they landed upon some form of improved spinning machinery. Paul's machine with rollers, functioning in 1738, was intended for use in spinning wool as well as cotton, but apparently because of commercial reasons, it was applied only to the latter industry. The production of large quantities of cotton thread with extraordinary speed was growing into a major business activity.[28]

Discussions regarding the resulting displacement of labor ensued, carried forth at every level of society, from pamphlet literature to papers of the Attorney General's patent office. Contemporaries seemed acutely aware of a discussion of spinning as a form of employment, as it was universally perceived as a means of harnessing the labor of the poor. Carefully calculating the impact of spinning with rollers, John Wyatt concluded that against considerable gains to the parish and nation as well as the employer, only thirty out of a hundred spinners would be dismissed as a result of introducing the machine. The fact that these displaced "able people" were women played an important part in John Wyatt's defense of Paul's invention:

> It now remains to find employment for these thirty . . . and the chief of those which would feel the effect of [these machines] would be the young women, who at present for the sake of their liberty etc. (which by the way they seldom make the best use of) choose that way of living rather than in service[.]

Wyatt disapprovingly pointed to the preference young women gave to independent employment in domestic industry over its obvious—and often single—alternative, domestic service. Thrown out of work, such women would have to accept what was, in the opinion of Wyatt, for their own good:

> and whoever is acquainted with the just complaints of the farmers on that head, especially in the summer, will be convinced that if these two bodies of people [i.e., farmers and spinsters] are considered together they will not be hurt; and we do further presume that such services are the best protection for such young women, both with respect to their livelihood and moral[s].

According to Wyatt's paternalistic reasoning, these women would fall naturally into the hands of similar-minded rural employers; unlike the rest of his commentary, this plan showed remarkably little foresight and shrewdness. He nevertheless called attention to a social problem that, in later years, inventors felt no need to address at all.[29]

A more serious shortage of thread mounted in the 1760s, as the call for cotton fabric rose and the East India Company experienced difficulty in importing sufficient quantities from the East; home as well as continental markets grew and placed increasing demands on the production of British weavers. The delicacy of Paul's machine limited its application, and the search for further improvements continued. When the flying shuttle made its appearance in the same decade, entrepreneurs rushed forward to alleviate the resulting bottleneck need for thread. Sometime between 1764 and 1767, the weaver Richard Hargreaves developed his spinning jenny, which ultimately entered textbooks as the definitive invention. The original jenny replaced the single spindle of the spinning wheel with eight, and later versions increased the number to sixteen, then eighty. Its application spread slowly, but improvements continued. By 1800, large jennies carried 100 to 120 spindles. The machine could not produce strong enough yarn to be used in making woolens, but within two decades, it changed the map of Lancashire and environs by catapulting the cotton industry into a leading place in the British economy.[30]

Though historians assume that machine spinning made good business sense to just about everybody, reorganizing the industry was hardly a natural development, given the decentralized character of all economic activity. How did such rational attitudes, which privileged expeditious production and risk taking, triumph over the most customary of all industries? Certainly the lure of making money helped along the case for invention; the inconveniences of putting out also added impetus. Yet as one reads accounts of the attenuated struggles over control of the spinning process, an extensive and markedly female industry, another dimension of the transformation becomes evident. Introducing new technology would require a shift in attitudes toward female domestic industry, from one of general acceptance and praise to a more critical stance. The dimension of gender provides access to conflicting attitudes toward spinners as industrial laborers, for arguments in favor of mechanized spinning necessarily challenged their ways of working.

From its inception, spinning technology represented a very different world of work. The potential for a fantastic multiplication of productivity brought eighteenth-century scientific advancement down to earth. Baconian optimism, national pride, and economic success melded into one.[31] This powerful combination inspired John Dyer's *The Fleece* (1757), a didactic poem extolling the mundane details of English textile production and trade. Dyer's description of Paul's roller spinning device easily demotes hand spinning, as the workings of the machine take on the qualities of the Newtonian solar system:

> A circular machine, of new design,
> In conic shape; it draws and spins a thread
> Without the tedious toil of needless hands.
> A wheel, invisible, beneath the floor,
> To every member of the' harmonious frame
> Gives necessary motion.

In the pleasant form of poetry, Dyer presented a seemingly natural dichotomy between customary female labor and the machine: the "tedious toil of needless hands" was no match for a "harmonious frame" impelled by "necessary motion."

> One, intent,
> O'erlooks the work: the carded wool, he says,
> Is smoothly lapp'd around those cylinders,
> Which, gently turning, yield it to yon cirque
> Of upright spindles, which with rapid whirl
> Spin out, in long extent, an even twine.

The contrast between female spinners (the "nymphs," "matrons," and "maids" of an earlier stanza) and a solitary male machine minder becomes readily apparent: while the former contributed tedious manual labor, the latter performed by concentrating his mental capacities. Unlike the village spinsters, this producer spoke and even explained his craft. In every aspect, the machine asserted its superiority, in spite of the poetic flourishes liberally applied to feminine graces.[32]

Celebrants of the machine multiplied as the century progressed. Writers on the new science of political economy worried little about the resulting displacement of female labor and instead dwelled on the competitive superiority that the machine brought to English trade. An allegiance to practical science marked the mentality of these advocates: Quoting Bacon's *Atlantis*, Thomas Bentley inscribed a telling message upon the title page of his *Letters on the Utility and Policy of Employing Machines to Shorten Labour* (1780): "Upon every *Invention of Value*, we erect a *Statue to the Inventor*, and give him a liberal and honourable Reward." Defending spinning machinery in the wake of riots against the jenny in Lancashire, Bentley heaped scorn on the detractors of progress. "New truths, new machines, new medicines, and new improvements of all kinds, by which the condition of human life has been made more comfortable and happy, have always been persecuted by ignorant people and bigots," he commented. Mechanical innovations in spinning were to take their place alongside medical and scientific discoveries. These objective and rational endeavors inhabited a universe that was decidedly masculine and middle class. "A *tool-making animal*, or *engineer*, has by some been adopted as the best and most characteristic definition of man," he explained; these traits provided a critical distance from animals. Bentley and writers like him were loathe to surrender that margin of difference.[33]

The effort to obtain thread was, according to some accounts, a struggle between the sexes, as merchants and weavers pressured all the women within reach to satisfy their industrial requirements. The cotton industry, boosted by colonial trade of the eighteenth century, produced a seemingly limitless demand for spinners. One weaver could require the work of three women spinning full-time for an adequate supply of thread; counting the additional assistance necessary for preparation of the raw material, a weaver might rely on as many as six to eight people. The steady labor of a wife and several children often failed to meet a weaver's needs, and many weavers perforce turned to women outside the family for additional supplies. Scouring the neighborhood could be costly for the weaver, for spinners were well aware of their advantageous position in supplying a scarce commodity. "It was no uncommon thing for a weaver to walk three or four miles in a morning, and call on five or six spinners, before he could collect a weft to serve him for the remainder of the day," a contemporary historian explained; "and when he wished to weave a piece in a shorter time than usual, a new ribbon, or gown, was necessary to quicken the exertions of the spinner." The use of Kay's flying shuttle, widely adopted in the 1760s, only enhanced the demand for thread, as it enabled the weaver to work nearly twice as fast.[34]

Nineteenth-century discussions of the cotton trade reveal an awareness of the dimension of gender in the scramble for thread. They depict the weaver as a harried, hard-working man, harrassed by uncooperative females. "He had with much pains to collect [weft] from neighbouring spinsters," Baines's *History* lamented. "Thus his time was wasted, and he was often subjected to high demands for an article, on which, as the demand exceeded the supply, the seller could put her own price."[35] Little doubt existed as to who wielded power in this predicament. In his history of Manchester, Aikin conceded, "The weavers, in a scarcity of spinning, have sometimes been paid less for the weft than they paid the spinner, but durst not complain, much less abate the spinner, lest their looms should be unemployed."[36] Accounts spoke unflatteringly of spinsters, complaining of their "insolence" and "knavery," adjectives usually reserved for women or servants. Decrying the fact that at times these women obtained more for their work than weavers, contemporaries called attention to the seeming injustice of it all.[37]

In their adherence to a rather whiggish view of the history of technology, most accounts of industrialization have adopted a similar view of customary spinners, while celebrating the appearance of the spinning jenny. David Landes, establishing the generally accepted view in his *Prometheus Unbound*, throws a mocking aside to traditional production methods. "The spinning wheel, which had taken some centuries to displace the rock, became an antique in the space of a decade."[38] Phyllis Deane's account depicts an eager readiness on the part of laborers: "The family spinning-wheels were hastily consigned to the lumber room and their place taken by the new jennies."[39]

But the transition to new ways of spinning was not so sudden, and many historians have exaggerated the immediate impact of Hargreaves's jenny. As Maxine Berg recently pointed out, "There was no striking and revolutionary break between mechanized factory technology and cotton manufacture."[40] A large room or an upper floor of a cottage could accommodate smaller versions of the machine, so much of the industry remained at first in domestic and workshop settings. Women were able to operate the smaller jennies, and thus some were able to continue to produce large quantities of thread at home. In such cases, for a brief period at the end of the eighteenth century, a woman working at the jenny might earn more than her husband at the loom. As one apologist for the use of machines stated, "If it were true that a weaver gets less, yet, as his wife gets more, his family does not suffer." Depending on the availability and cost of the jenny, control of the machine was at first relatively dispersed.[41]

But laboring women and men responded to the appearance of the contrivance with great apprehension and often hostility. According to Baines, writing in 1835, Hargreaves "kept it as secret as possible for a time, and used it merely in his own business . . . but when it became the subject of rumour, instead of gaining for its author admiration and gratitude, the spinners raised an outcry that it would throw multitudes out of employment, and a mob broke into Hargreaves's house, and destroyed his jenny." Soonafter, Hargreaves moved from Standhill, near Blackburn, Lancashire, to Nottingham, reportedly in order to escape "persecution." Rioting against the jenny continued to ravage the area, touching Turton, Bolton, and Bury in 1769. Ten years later, further rioting around Blackburn reached new heights, as crowds singled out larger machines, including some that had been introduced into the preparatory processes, for attack:

> A mob rose, and scoured the country for several miles around Blackburn, demolishing the jennies, and with them all the carding engines, water-frames, and every machine turned by water or horses. It is said that the rioters spared the jennies which had only twenty spindles, as these were by this time admitted to be useful; but those with a greater number, being considered mischievous, were destroyed, or cut down to the prescribed dimensions.[42]

Authorities put down the rebellion, and "upwards of fifty men and women [were] sent to Lancaster Gaol, several taken up, their houses broken open at midnight, and hurried away on board . . . leaving their destitute and exasperated wives and offspring exposed to poverty and misery."[43]

Rioters were able to discriminate between one machine and the next; their opposition was not based on a simple antagonism to machinery, but to the organization of labor and system of ownership that was part of technological advance. As Pinchbeck has pointed out, "the grievance of the cotton workers was obviously not against the smaller machines, but against those they could not afford to buy and with which they could not compete." Petitioning Parliament, protesters aimed their attack not at the jennies, but the larger machines, as "the Jenneys are in the Hands of the Poor and the Patent Machines are generally in the Hands of the Rich."[44]

Weavers, too, feared the use of jennies and their mechanical successors, and they sometimes joined in registering grievances against their introduction. Machines produced finer thread than spinning by the wheel and thus affected the quality of the woven fabric. Some weavers were "afraid lest the manufacturers should demand finer weft woven at the former prices," which would take longer to produce.[45] Gentry as well as laborers showed little enthusiasm for the new machines. "Decreasing earnings from spinning affected the poor rates in every rural parish; and even if the use of machinery ultimately increased employment in the towns, it was bound to remove a source of income from the agricultural laborers' families at a time when, with rising prices, they needed it most."[46] Alarmed "lest the poor-rates should be burdened with workmen thrown idle," "middle and upper class" persons sometimes "connived at, and even actually joined in, the opposition to machinery, and did all in their power to screen rioters from punishment."[47]

Some sympathetic contemporaries were quick to identify the displacement of spinsters as part of a larger transformation of social values. Coming forward as advocates of the poor, critics of the new manufacturing interest saw spinsters as voiceless victims of an economic system that privileged the few at the expense of the many. Richard Sadler, a noted philanthropist, set his discontents to meter: "Who sings the SPINSTER shall not want a muse," he declared, in obvious allusion to Dyer's famous verses:

> Thus kindly labour, once, could yield relief
> To age, to childhood, poverty and grief:
> But now what *Turn* shall stead them—Hapless term!
> That none now steads them, lo! their woes confirm:
>
> Maternal Nature's all inclusive plan
> Design'd a competence to ev'ry man;
> But step-dame Art, with curst contracted view,
> *Wrongs* a whole region to enrich a *Few*.
>
> If manufacturers aught a State bestead,
> 'Tis to employ the POOR, and yield them BREAD.
> On *this* foundation, past dispute they stand
> The first of blessings in a thrifty land;
> Where still to industry their gain inspires,
> And yields to labour all that life requires[.][48]

What had been a general occupation of women had now devolved upon children and teenage girls. Defenders of the poor linked the appearance of the machine with supplanting "the general distribution of labour, and therefore of subsistence, to the industrious, but now starving poor."[49]

Opposition to mechanization in the textile industry was both a family and community affair; dissatisfaction spread beyond the displaced spinners to their kinfolk and neighbors, and local gentry and magistrates indicated their own doubts about the innovations through their hesitation in prosecuting rioters. Little direct evidence of women participants in the riots has survived; some historians have argued that when activity was planned and nocturnal, women often did not take part.[50] But this does not mean that women's interests, as part of the laboring family economy, were not represented. In fact, several Lancashire localities viewed the advent of machinery as a worthy concern of the government and thus got up a petition, which they sent to Parliament in 1780. Calling the introduction of machines "a Domestic Evil of very great Magnitude," the petitioners argued that the distress caused to the community by such innovations ought to be weighed against "the immense Profits and Advantages" brought to "the Patentees and Proprietors." Their calculations included careful comparisons between the earnings of women with single spindles pitted against machines with twenty-four. Local authorities stopped to listen. In the case of Wigan, "magistrates, principal inhabitants, and manufacturers met and agreed to suspend the use of all machines and engines worked by water or horses for carding, roving, or spinning, till the determination of Parliament on the subject was known." A parliamentary committee finally resolved that the industry should continue to operate its machinery, and the resistors at Wigan were effectively defeated.[51]

Resistance to mechanization varied from region to region, depending also on the type of machinery involved; while some areas in the North quietly adapted to the new inventions, the Southwest encountered much more difficulty in the introduction of jennies and other improvements in preparing yarn and finishing cloth to the woolen industry. Wiltshire and Somerset workers rebelled against jennies in the 1790s, in some instances driving manufacturers to other areas.[52] Most historians have argued that rioting against spinning machinery ceased, at least in the North, because the expansion of trade was able to absorb displaced labor. In the remoter areas of the Southwest, however, this was not always true. Activity shifted from market towns, which had distributed work to surrounding areas, to village locales, where available water power enabled manufacturers to set up mills.

III

The overall effect of the transition to machine spinning was to concentrate the production of textiles within specific regions, and for an industry formerly characterized by its universality, this clearly spelled distress for a great number of women and their families. Employment was highly localized: while a Gloucestershire clothier boasted, probably with a certain amount of exaggeration, "since the Introduction of Machinery there is much more work for the Women and Children in the Villages than formerly," the laboring poor in nearby Seend, Wiltshire, were now in dire straits.[53] Competition forced the woolen industry to the North and finally rendered the southern regions marginal by the second decade of the nineteenth century. Particularly in the Southeast, where almost no other opportunities for employment existed, poverty and distress now became a noted feature of laboring life.

Pinchbeck's assessment that a general increase in production created jobs for displaced spinners seems slightly too sanguine for what was, at first, a major displacement of labor. "[Fifty] persons . . . with the help of machines, will do as much work as 500 without them," commented Frederic Eden in one instance, and critics of the mechanization of the cotton industry in Lancashire systematically reported the reduction of hands in carding, doubling, twisting, and winding mills. "One or two persons, will perform as much work as would have employed and provided bread for eight or twelve," lamented one pamphlet. By the 1840s, manufacturers calculated that what had formerly taken six hundred and twelve hours of a woman's time, with the help of one or two children, now took thirty-eight hours for one woman spinning warp on a jenny and thirty-four hours for one man with two children making weft in a factory.[54]

Coupled with changes taking place in agrarian society, the loss of spinning meant that many families fell short of earning enough to get by and, hence, applied for poor relief to make up the difference.[55] Before the technological transformation was complete, an acute observer attributed the financial well-being of some agricultural laborers in the South to the industriousness of the women of the household; if spinning were eliminated, the family would inevitably suffer:

> Suppose the wife and girls *not* to have learnt to spin; then, instead of earning 2s. 4d. a-week, which comes to 5 l. 17s. a-year, they would only earn, like the common run of women, about 1 l. 10s.; and therefore, instead of a surplus at the year's end, there would be a deficiency of 4 l. 4s. unless by living harder they curtailed their expenses so much. It is owing to the money gained by spinning, that this family is enabled to keep out of debt, and to live so decently.[56]

Public opinion was quick to change, however: most commentaries on the subject regarded women's domestic spinning as a remnant of an obsolete age and decried the lack of foresightfulness in plans designed to teach "habits of industry" through the wheel. Pointing to the high poor rates in woolen districts, Arthur Young argued that fluctuations in the industry led laborers to turn to relief rather than working for small wages during hard times. Retreating from the paternalistic attitudes that favored regulating the course of industry, Young advocated a policy of laissez faire. As long as different branches of the textile industry lurched forward unevenly, no one step in the production process ought to be favored over another.[57]

The disappearance of this particular image of female industry struck a disturbing chord for some commentators. "Thus from time immemorial the Hand or Jazey Wheel, has been the pride of the English Housewife. In bad and good weather it equally was a resource," lamented one author. "But now the Wheel must be laid aside as a useless thing!"[58] Sadler's *Discarded Spinster* (1791) also invoked the notion of good housewifery, which was quickly becoming obsolete with a new mode of production. Underscoring the importance of women's work to the larger community, Sadler alluded to another bygone image, that of laborers constituting the strength of the nation:

> Whilst Arts existing in the fost'ring hand
> Of *living* Labour, *natural* to a land,
> Not all the Spies France ever kept in pay,
> Nor Spain's Armadas e'er can bear away.
> As well may they deprive the vernal air
> Of *sweets*, which only BEES can *gather there*,
> Such like a *Wife*, whom nothing can decoy,
> Remain a country's treasure, strength, and joy.[59]

The passing of hand spinning stood as a trope for the end of a certain form of national well-being, akin to a household with its loyal and dutiful housewife. While the role of woman was idealized, the model alluded to a more general significance attached to the change in technology, one that went beyond the immediate interests of textile production.

Since the triumph of technology over the spinning wheel, much has been done to discredit women's ways of working. With few exceptions, historians have preferred to depict spinning before the advent of machinery as a leisurely, sometimes pleasurable pursuit that, by definition, earned little. "It is true that [spinning] was only a supplement to the ordinary income of a farmer's family," Paul Mantoux pointed out unquestioningly in his influential study of the industrial revolution, "and the conditions of work were not arduous." He cited a nineteenth-century account of Yorkshire women spinning together outdoors as a way of illustrating the absence of "serious" labor.[60] Not only have industrial historians concluded that the ordinary work of poor women, attended to in "the common round of a day's toil,"[61] was not essential to a marginally sufficient household budget; they have tacitly agreed that female labor demonstrated a less systematic devotion to productivity and hence, under the pressures of industrial expansion, brought down obsolescence upon their own heads.[62]

In theory, the process of mechanization is distinct from changes in the organization of production. In the case of eighteenth-century spinning, new technology did not lead immediately to the reallocation of work in the factory. Signs of a wholly different organization of labor gradually became visible, however, when manufacturers realized that even greater gains could be had from more centralized production. Strategy and decision making were key factors in transforming what had been simply expanded domestic production into the formal setting of the factory. Following the pattern set by alterations in technology, the final move toward large-scale factory settings solidified the definition of labor as male for reasons that further discredited the work of women. The following chapter will examine the first half-century of the factory system.

5

A New World of Work: Female Labor and the Development of the Factory System

Touch'd with no interest, and without a fee,
For the poor SPINSTER pours a plaintive plea.
Poor worm! who now, discarded from employ,
Lies stript of all her hope, and all her joy;
Not jockied she (new arts new idioms give)
But jennied out of every means to live.

If manufacturers aught a State bestead,
'Tis to employ the POOR, and yield them BREAD.
On this foundation, past dispute they stand
The first of blessings in a thrifty land;
Where still to industry their gain inspires,
And yields to labour all that life requires[.]

Robert Sadler, *The Discarded Spinster; or, a Plea for
the Poor, on the Impolicy of Spinning Jennies* (1791)

No aspect of industrialization provokes more discussion than the advent of the factory. Raised to the level of an abstraction in most histories of western Europe, the factory has been made to represent the irrepressible force of progress. Herein lay the advance of technology, the modernization of production, and the salvation of backward local economies in need of rationalization. Against this view, critics have argued that the factory introduced tyrannical control of work, systematic exploitation of labor, and destruction of the environment. The working-class female is a principal character in this historical tableau. Standard accounts of industrialization virtually equate her with the definition of mill worker, depicting her emergence from the household to the factory as a chief innovation of the system. Historians of women thus have entered the debate in an attempt to gauge the effects of industrialization and capitalism. Did the factory represent an opportunity that ultimately benefited the laboring woman and her dependents, offering work free from the patriarchal confines of household production? Did independent wages give her spending power that improved the quality of her life? Or was factory work an unfortunate necessity that led to other forms of oppression, such as exclusion from skilled jobs and labor organizations, and wages that compared poorly with male co-workers?[1]

In order to address these questions, we must examine how the physical organization of production affected the employment of female labor. Quite apart from the list of familiar inventions associated with industrialization, we must consider the many managerial determinations that shaped the development of the institution of the textile factory. The choice of buildings that housed machinery for production, hiring practices, the assignment of jobs, supervision and discipline, and wage rates, to name only a few factors, influenced the work of women and men. At the same time, the activities of organized labor entered into a fitful dialogue with factory owners and government officials. The emergence of the factory, far from following a "natural" evolution, rested upon a complex series of experiments, conflicts, and negotiations.

In light of the diverse responses to this new organization of work, of what significance was the factory in constructing an image of the working-class woman? The second half of this chapter will explore various representations of the female factory worker and their implication in debates about women in general. By the 1830s, the notion of a woman's proper place being in the home was gaining currency, rendering factory work for women morally degrading and destructive of the fundamental relationships of the family. Government investigations, economic and social commentaries, and novels repeatedly focused on the female factory worker in order to define, describe, and evaluate her. "To the Victorians belongs the discovery of the woman worker as an object of pity," Wanda Neff wrote in her study of the subject, "and in the literature of the early nineteenth century one first finds her portrayed as a victim of long hours, unfavourable conditions, and general injustice, for whom something ought to be done."[2] Less sympathetic were the assessments of the independent factory girl, notorious for her promiscuity, coarse language, drinking, smoking, and sexual misbehavior.[3] The Victorian working-class woman became, in short, a problem, linked in a multitude of ways to the history of the factory.

I

The eighteenth-century industrial revolution did not bring a sudden, uniform change in the manufacture of cloth. Traditional histories have focused misleadingly on the major innovations of the age, fostering a "big bang" theory of industrial development.[4] In fact, many small efforts at improvement first occurred in insignificant places, and at least some of the inventors aiming to quicken or ease the labors of cloth production did not have their sights set on much money or fame. A tombstone in a Lancashire churchyard displayed one modest claim to posterity: there lay John and Ellen Hacking, "who invented the first carding engine that carded cotton for their neighbours and turned it by hand in Huncoat in 1772."[5] The obscurity of the Hackings' achievement, particularly when set beside the monumental triumphs of Richard Arkwright or James Watt, suggests a humble version of industrial history. Their carding engine was one of many neighborhood ventures growing out of manufacturing processes set in kitchens or workrooms. Unlike the progress outlined in history textbooks, this case of technological advance took place within the home. Here, the fact that carding was women's work meant that manufacturing incorporated female ingenuity; devising a better method depended on the expertise of Ellen Hacking. The participation of women, in this case, led to an acknowledgment of their labor.[6]

Many small factories still resembled their domestic ancestors, showing that, at least for a time, the organization of industry could take any number of courses. A list of equipment housed in 1780 in an establishment operating at Heaton Norris, Lancashire, made explicit its recent evolution from household industry. Organized on a small scale and unspecialized in its forms of production, this factory simply gathered under one roof several processes that had previously taken place in homes. Its premises contained the following:

an iron pot (probably used for washing cotton)
a stove
48 "flakes to dry cotton on"
"a large willey for cleaning and opening"
3 carding machines, and another "unfinished"
3 slubbing jennies of 46, 36, and 26 spindles
20 slubbers' wheels
13 spinning jennies: 3 of 120 spindles each, 3 of 100 spindles, 1 of 84 spindles, 1 of 80 spindles, 2 of 60 spindles, 1 of 59 spindles, 2 of 50 spindles
1 fine jack and feeders (probably for twisting)
3 Dutch wheels
1 warping mill and bobbins
7 looms
additional miscellaneous equipment, including raw material[7]

This form of machine manufacture harmonized with hand industry; many of the smaller makeshift factories of rural Derbyshire, for example, employed domestic spinners or weavers while mechanizing other processes. As long as the settings of manufacturing remained diverse, women of all sorts—young and old, single and married—stood a chance of employment. Though the manufacture of cotton warps was "almost from the beginning" a factory industry, weft spinning "remained . . . a domestic operation performed on the single spindle or the smaller jennies."[8] No dominant institution set an explicit standard for production or a hierarchy of labor. And as long as the break with household production was incomplete, women exercised some form of control, however limited.

The conversion of barns and outbuildings proceeded apace from the late 1780s to the turn of the century, creating what the early nineteenth-century historian William Radcliffe called "the golden age" of the small rural manufacturer. Even after Lancashire had superseded other regions in finer, more sophisticated methods of production, jenny spinning continued in the marginal areas of the Derbyshire Peak district, and even in Stockport and Wigan as late as 1811. A close look at enterprises often blandly categorized as "mills" or "factories" reveals relatively unambitious arrangements, for not all can be traced to true commercial firms or discrete buildings. Board of Agriculture surveyor John Farey counted as many as 107 "mills" in northern Derbyshire in the period 1807 to 1811. As it was applied in the textile industry, "the word 'mill' sometimes meant no more than 'a machine which performs its work by rotary motion.'" Many "jenny shops" were simply domestic buildings or outhouses containing a handful of spinning frames. One "Cotton Works" offered for sale in the *Derby Mercury* in 1787 contained only four frames.[9] As late as the turn of the century, the "coexistence of . . . many different manufacturing structures" lent diversity to a rapidly growing industry, in spite of a later growth in the scale of production.[10]

But the configuration of power was soon to change. Pitted against such homespun tinkers, shrewd entrepreneurs, often men of means, were able to organize and adapt the new inventions to more promising circumstances. "Economy" became the watchword; saving time, avoiding waste and fraud, eliminating inconvenience—these were the urgent imperatives of a new age. Though the two major innovations in textile production, the spinning jenny and the carding engine, had been used first in a domestic context, they sparked revolutionary changes when introduced to a factory setting. Offering profits that would multiply at a new rate, the early inventions induced men to seek their fortunes by rearranging machinery and workers. The carding engine, turned by hand in domestic settings, soon appeared in early factories in Derbyshire, Lancashire, Yorkshire, Nottinghamshire, Denbighshire, and Cheshire. Similarly, the spinning jenny, ranging from a domestic size of twenty-four spindles to an optimum capacity of several hundred, moved into workshops and factories. The burgeoning advertisement columns of Lancashire newspapers, offering machinery and mills, gave proof of the irrepressible force of capitalist enterprise in the 1770s and 1780s.[11]

The career of factory baron Richard Arkwright makes vividly clear the kind of drive that not only transformed the textile industry, but also endowed the role of factory owner with power and authority. Arkwright's determination to create a money-making business appeared obvious from the enormous outlay of capital used to establish his empire. Arkwright claimed that before any profit was made, he and his partners spent £12,000 between 1769 and 1774; by 1782, expenditures rose to as much as £30,000. Over the protests of manufacturers across the North, Arkwright pressed to retain a monopoly on his carding machine, even though similar contrivances were already in wide use.[12] Recognizing that others might want to copy his water frame, Arkwright and his associates confined it to the secrecy of a factory. They also restricted licences to units of a thousand so that the machine would never be reproduced on a domestic scale.[13]

Given the expense of this kind of venture, the factory owner absolutely depended on cheap labor. Any enterprising factory master saw that high wages drained returns from his investment, and reductions in the expense of labor also protected him against inevitable slumps in trade. It was no coincidence that women and children made up much of the work force of the early factory. The two groups were locked together in a category of worker that was "naturally" subordinate. The low level of women's earnings, long antedating the factory in domestic stages of production, characterized their factory wages from the start. Employers did not offer a "living wage" to the female or child since they assumed that she was dependent upon a household headed by a male and therefore did not depend only on her wages for subsistence.[14]

Many accounts have exaggerated the attractiveness of factory wages for women. Recruitment was not always easy, for wages were not high enough to draw workers already engaged in other employments in the towns. The Midlands hosiery districts, for example, posed a problem in the 1790s, as many young women were already gainfully employed in the stocking industry. Advertisements reveal the kinds of enticement required to people the early mills. One from 1787 illustrates the need to draw all members of the laboring family, even though women and children were most desired:

> Darley Cotton Mill. Wanted, Families, particularly women and children to work at the said mill. They may be provided with comfortable houses and every necessary convenience either at Darley or Allestry; particularly a milking-cow to each family. It is a very good neighbourhood for the men getting work who are not employed in the manufactory.[15]

Later factories would not offer such generous rewards in exchange for the labor of unskilled men, women, and children. Nor would the occasional incentive solve the problem of a general shortage of hands throughout the period. Early factory masters in Derbyshire were forced to import juvenile and female labor from Manchester and Nottingham. In Essex, Samuel Courtauld "deliberately sought to recruit hands from among the poorest sections of the female population, initially by employing young women and girls from the remaining workhouses."[16] By advertising for indentured juvenile and skilled labor in Nottingham and Derby newspapers, Arkwright was able to obtain enough hands at low rates of pay; at Bakewell, he employed "good-natured girls" from Manchester. Often the factory relied upon the unemployed as a reserve of labor. In the nineteenth century, factory owners turned to parish overseers for help in finding "needy and suitable families," culled from relief rolls, willing to work in the mills.[17]

Despite the fact that mill wages were low, historians have reached different conclusions regarding their acceptability. In a well-known early study, Frances Collier argued that because other occupations paid even less, the cotton factories around Manchester had a favorable impact on laborers' lives in the 1790s. Wage books "substantiate the view that the families of mill operatives at this time were in a better economic position than that of the average working-class family," Collier argued.[18] Her assumptions about the low position of women's work determined how she made her assessment. She showed that women's earnings varied from small sums—from 4s. to 8s. per week—paid for picking, to larger amounts paid by the piece for stretching—as much as 37s. 6d. Because women were paid by piece rates, however, their wages could amount to as little as 3s. 3d. a week. At another establishment, women and girls (it is impossible to differentiate them in some records) earned between 4s. and 10s. a week, with the majority earning 6 or 7s. Even at the lower end of the spectrum, wrote Collier, these figures appeared relatively attractive in comparison to estimated earnings of laborers' wives. The typical woman, she pointed out, was partially employed at casual labor, for which she might earn 6d. a week. The problem with part-time labor, Collier admitted, was that only by depending on a combination of earnings that included a male wage earner, his wife and several children could working-class families hope to meet their expenses. Even then, a total income of 23s. 6d. a week did not represent "enough to keep a family of six in comfort with prices as high as they were in 1795."[19]

More recent studies have taken a position more critical of the early factories. Even for men, who were privileged as spinners and overlookers in these establishments, wages "were paltry indeed." At Arkwright's Bakewell mill from 1786 to 1811, male "mechanics at the top of the wage-scale earned only 10s to 15s weekly," and overseers in cotton works at Wirksworth earned only 12s. a week. Compared to the earnings of a male laborer engaged as a carter in the 1790s at roughly 12s. a week, these wages were hardly attractive. Women's wages were not set according to more generous standards. Female and juvenile rates of pay in the Derbyshire area "were generally higher in the [domestic] hosiery industry than in the mills."[20]

In fact, the differences between male and female rates of pay in the factory were strikingly apparent. After the extensive inquiries into factory labor in 1833, a report issued by the government showed women earning an average of 9s. 8¼ d. per week, compared with 22s. 8½ d. for men.[21]

Such disparities reflected the fact that women were often segregated in lower-level jobs, rarely securing better-paid positions as supervisors. Women were usually paid piece rates, making their earnings more irregular and vulnerable than the flat rates of men. Moreover, women seldom experienced the same vertical mobility within the factory that men enjoyed. Thus their gender determined not only the jobs they were able to find and the pay that they received, but also their prospects for advancement within the system.[22]

Factory owners' preference for female labor was based not only on its cheapness: many women assumed the yoke of hard labor in the factories without complaint, and this fostered the widespread opinion that female workers were more docile, and therefore less likely to cause trouble than men. Jobs in the new mills demanded a submission to an arduous factory discipline that required long hours of work and regular attendance six days a week. Women were noted for their willingness to work, even into the evening hours, when male workers expected a regularly scheduled break. "They are more easily induced to undergo severe bodily fatigue than men," the factory commissioners believed, "either from the praiseworthy motive of gaining additional support for their families, or from the folly of satisfying a love of dress."[23] Unlike their male counterparts, they seldom questioned the orders of factory managers and overlookers, and they were much less likely to be involved in unions. Moving in and out of the work force in response to the ever-changing demands of others, as well as their own needs, many women clearly felt they had no choice but to comply.

Some women did choose to leave factory jobs, and judging from records of the Strutts' factory between 1805 and 1812, the reasons they gave suggest that employment there was not the elysium that optimists might have expected (see Table 5.1)[24] Among the women leaving for "other occupations," about half planned to go into service while another 38 percent planned "to stay at home," which probably meant temporary unemployment or some reliance upon a form of cottage industry. By comparison, only one of the seventy-eight men leaving for other occupations planned to take up service and the overwhelming majority planned to take up a trade. Factory work was one of many options for men, while for women, it functioned within a lesser class of occupations; for some women, it may have been the only alternative to the last resort of service. In their history of the early factory system, Fitton and Wadsworth point out that "the number who left because of positive objections to mill-work was small," owing, they speculate, to the Strutts' reputation "as good paternal employers." Yet in their tabulations, they choose to exclude the numbers of workers who left without notice, ran away, or were dismissed; these men and women might well have had "positive objections" to work in the factory. A more critical reading might find that the significant numbers listed under "insufficient earnings" and "dissatisfied with mill work" suggest that their paternalism was not wholly successful.[25]

Table 5.1 Reasons for Workers Leaving Strutts' Factories, December 1805 to July 1812

		Males	Females
Summary of Notices	Other occupations	78	82
	Leaving Belper of Milford	2	14
	Insufficient earnings	2	12
	Dissatisfied with mill work	3	9
	Pregnancy and health	1	147
	Miscellaneous	3	14
		89	278
To Take Up Other Occupations	To learn a trade	28	
	Nailer	17	
	Apprentice	15	
	Shoemaker	6	
	Framework knitter	2	4
	To work at his own trade (weaver)	2	
	Weaver	1	
	Filecutter	1	
	To learn the art of weaving calico	1	
	Wheelwright	1	
	Mason	1	
	Collier	1	
	To work at his trade	1	
	Service	1	40
	Milliner		2
	To go home		6
	To stay at home		30
		78	82
Insufficient Earnings	Cannot get sufficient wage		6
	Cannot (or will not) get enough wage		1
	Cannot earn her maintenance by picking cotton		1
	Too little wage		2
	Dissatisfied with wages	2	1
	Has a large family that wastes more in her absence than she gets		1
		2	12
Dissatisfied with Mill Work	Dissatisfied with place	2	6
	Says she's shifted about too much		1
	Says Wm. Winson uses her ill		1
	Cannot give satisfaction with her work		1
	Cannot give satisfaction in his place	1	
		3	9

		Males	Females
Miscellaneous Reasons	To attend school	2	4
	To live with relatives		5
	To be married		2
	To go to her husband		1
	Lives too far off		1
	To be at home with mother who is ill		1
	Dissatisfied about his wife not having her own place in mill again after having been ill	1	
		3	14

Adapted with permission from Manchester University Press from tables in R.S. Fitton and A.P. Wadsworth, *The Strutts and the Arkwrights, 1758–1830: A Study of the Early Factory System* (Manchester: Manchester University Press, 1958): pp. 231, 232.

Cheap female and child labor at first substituted for technological improvements in the factories. This was particularly true for the silk industry, for as long as protective tariffs kept up British prices, industrialists could rely on hand manufacture that was slower, but still inexpensive. But after the passage of the Free Trade Act in 1824, increased competition in silk manufacture encouraged the introduction of machinery that would cheapen production costs. At that point, factory owners could adopt machinery designed to be operated by women, which would keep labor costs down.[26] As the factory system became established, particularly in the cotton towns of Lancashire, industrialists were able to call the tune. The more general application of steam power after the end of the Napoleonic Wars in 1815 led to the dominance of a new, large-scale type of establishment set in more populated areas. Faced with an abundance of available labor, manufacturers were more likely to lay off or dismiss workers than to search for hands to fill positions. These powerful institutions eclipsed the smaller paternalistic factories of the rural villages, capturing the attention of the public and the state.[27]

Given current beliefs regarding mechanization, factory workers of both sexes were justified in their fear of redundancy. Apologists for machines hailed mechanical inventions as a laudable solution to "slackness of trade" and foreign competition. Taking the form of a paean to the human mind, one defense elevated the manufacturing process by associating inventions with high-minded scientific pursuits and the national interest:

[N]ecessity sharpens the human intellect; men's geniuses awake, and are animated; and discoveries are made that astonish the world. The Manufactures are greatly improved in quality, or cheapness, or both; and thus a whole country is frequently preserved from want and beggary, by the seasonable invention of a new *machine*.[28]

These arguments worked as powerful legitimation for what amounted to considerable human cost. Andrew Ure summed up the prevailing view: "it is the constant aim and tendency of every improvement in machinery to supersede human labour altogether, or to diminish its cost."[29] The widespread employment of children gave visible testimony to the drive to employ labor at its cheapest level, though by the 1830s, this practice was under attack and was subject to limited government regulation. One owner openly admitted that he "hoped to get rid of 'all the spinners who are making exorbitant wages'" and simply employ low-paid piecers.[30]

Many men believed that the employment of women was but the first step in a gradual elimination of better-paid workers, and women, too, would lose their jobs, ultimately to children. A male spinner in 1833 compared the use of the new self-acting mule with the older common mule as an illustration of such a trend. In this instance, the new mule employed three men where eleven once worked; the same number of children would be employed as piecers. "As the machine comes gradually into use throughout the spinning business," the spinner pointed out,

> it will throw out of employ an equal proportion of adult hands, and it will take into employ a greater number of juvenile hands . . . Now, I only mean . . . to show the effects of general improvements in machinery to be, to dispense with adult labour, and either to call for a greater proportion of juvenile labour, or to leave its amount pretty much where it is.[31]

Trade unions attempted to combat this trend, and male workers, far better organized than women, maintained a position of strength at the expense of women. By the 1820s, "even the women were combining and giving trouble," and workers' fears of being superseded by machinery were confirmed by experience.[32]

The celebrated story of the factory's beginnings, highlighted by the subsequent meteoric rise of industry in England, has obscured the disadvantageous position of women in these early years. Given the presuppositions of factory owners, as well as women workers' lack of bargaining power, female labor was not rewarded with high rates of pay or favorable working conditions. In its first decades, the factory was forced to compete with other forms of employment for women. But as work in agriculture, spinning, and domestic industries declined, the factory presented a precious opportunity to young working-class women entering a world of ever-increasing economic uncertainty. As factories grew in size and influence, male workers established means of conflict and negotiation with employers. Women workers meanwhile achieved little recognition or power and, instead, were defined as others saw them. These developments were part of a wholesale revision of attitudes toward the working-class woman and her place in society. Philanthropists, trade unions, and parliamentary commissioners would share in reconstructing expectations, as they brought pressure to bear upon factory owners to restrict the work of women and alter the conditions under which it would take place.

II

Organization and protest by women workers appears only sporadically in the historical record, but this does not mean that women were indifferent to their situation. New studies in women's labor history have analyzed the bias built into much labor history. As Ava Baron has pointed out, a new gendered labor history poses questions differently: "Rather than ask: Why have women been difficult to organize? it asks: What assumptions about gender have been structured into unions? How does union organization serve to recreate or challenge gender hierarchies? How has gender operated to define union issues in ways that make them irrelevant to women's concerns?"[33]

The policy of exclusion by male unions may have been the most important factor in the apparent dirth of women activists through much of the early nineteenth century. The Combination Acts of 1799 and 1800 restricted all formal union activity until repeal in 1824, and those trades that evaded the law often explicitly excluded women on the grounds of skill. Customs that were male-defined rendered women weak in the work place and made their vulnerability to low wages a serious obstacle to their gaining recognition and respect within the workforce. Hampered by their absolute need for employment, their limited options, and their frequent inability to work without interruption, women workers had little room to maneuver in the world of work. In most employments, women workers had difficulty organizing owing to their prevalence in work that was dispersed in homes, seasonal, or simply low-paid, unskilled, and isolated from organizational apparatus. The sociability of the pubs was closed to them, and their responsibilities as wives and mothers often prohibited them from participating actively in organizations. As male workers developed organizations and strategies, the disadvantages working against women became rationalized as the very reasons for their exclusion.[34]

The factory offered the noteworthy advantage of a centralized work place that facilitated an identification of common interests among all workers. But divisions between the sexes undercut the development of a mass movement among factory workers. Men organized to create craft status in many branches of industry and commonly excluded women according to practices protected by tradition. Male spinners were among the most successful in bargaining with employers through unions in the early decades of the nineteenth century. Their power was based on their ability to ban women from their ranks by preventing them from operating the spinning mules, even though women were capable of handling the machines. The "skill" required to operate spinning machinery became defined as work performed only by men. Thus the Grand General Union of the United Kingdom, organized at a conference of Lancashire cotton spinners in 1824, excluded women and girls.[35] The sexual segregation of the factory work force reinforced the subordinate position of women and inhibited their involvement in trade unions, particularly in spinning, for a large part of the nineteenth century.[36]

Nevertheless, women emerged as energetic participants in strikes carried out by power-loom weavers at midcentury.[37] Power-loom weaving differed dramatically from spinning in its employment of women and men on the same machinery at equal rates of pay. Crucial differences exist in the histories of labor organization in the two industries. Weavers' unions were open to women since male workers needed to keep women from breaking ranks and accepting lower rates of pay, and action against employers was a joint affair. One of the earliest recorded incidents of collective action occurred when weavers, male and female, struck at Stockport in 1818. When employers imported women and girls from Burton-on-Trent as blacklegs, the strikers forced them under a local water pump in demonstration of their contempt.[38] But such unity existed more in appearance than reality. Men predominated as supervisors in weaving sheds and retained the sole rights to tuning the looms; like mule spinners, their apparent skill in tending to machinery enabled them to protect their advantage over women workers. In fact, male weavers managed to design multiple ways in which they could earn more money and assert more power than their female co-workers, so that an actual hierarchy evolved among workers at the same level.[39]

The inspiration of Owenism in the 1830s boosted the cause of women factory workers within the trade union movement. An earlier effort in 1819 at organizing men and women across trades had failed, but the Grand National Consolidated Trades Union of Great Britain and Ireland, formed in 1833 to 1834, enabled women to distinguish themselves as equal members of the work force. Clearly the ideology of Owenism, stressing mutuality and fellowship, helped to bridge divisions between male and female labor. Conflicts nevertheless emerged, as Barbara Taylor has illustrated for the tailoring trade. Organizations by sex within separate trades avoided some of these difficulties, and the names of various groups remain inscribed in local records as evidence of their success. The Grand Lodge of Women of Great Britain and Ireland and the Grand Lodge of Operative Bonnet Makers numbered among Owenite demonstrators, and an obscure group known as the "Ancient Virgins" on one occasion joined forces with men at Oldham to agitate for a ten-hour day.[40]

The tension between labor organizations over sexual divisions may have diminished during periods of radical activity. Radical associations that sprang up during the Chartist activities of the 1830s and 1840s reveal men and women organizing together, drawing upon traditions established within the anti–Poor Law campaign of the early 1830s. Formally established in 1839, the Bradford Female Radical Association drew its membership from weavers and woolcombers, as well as from the factory operatives. Together, these groups formulated a plan to pressure local shopkeepers through "exclusive dealing," employing the power of the purse available to all women, regardless of occupation.[41] Details of individual lives are scarce, but the occasional record of some lively discussion gives the impression of energy and commitment among northern operatives. Dorothy Thompson uncovered a rare instance of a Bradford

woman who, before a mixed audience "composed of hundreds of thinking men," testified to the oppression of her class and the difficulties of
organizing against employers:

> Had Mr Trimble not discharged her brother, sister and herself for the high
> crime of attending a meeting on Good Friday "to take into consideration
> the means of bettering the condition of the Power-Loom Weavers", she
> would still have been the unreflecting slave of the power-loom without the
> cause being ascertained why she was a slave. Her father was discharged
> because her brother was chairman of the meeting alluded to, and her sister
> was discharged because she had accepted the office of treasurer; but she was
> thankful to Mr Trimble for that circumstance. . . . ere long they would find
> that the female workers in Bradford would be a powerful auxiliary in the
> onward march to 'a fair day's wage for a fair day's work.'[42]

The consciousness of the fundamental need for a fair wage was based on
the common interest of men and women in providing for their families.
Perhaps in times of radical activity this concern overrode conflicts over
sexual divisions. Evident, too, is the way in which the experience of work
itself contributed to the sense of solidarity and dignity shared by women
workers in the mills.[43]

When female militants combined within their respective occupations,
their efforts had a palpable effect on their situation. These women squarely
addressed the issue of their exploitation as women within their specific
trades. Manufacturers were not ignorant of their activities. "We had an
intimation that they had meetings," one manufacturer reported to a parliamentary committee in 1833, "and I saw a letter signed by a woman,
calling upon one house to raise wages to the same rates as paid to men."[44]
In another instance near Leeds that same year, women objected to the
insufficiency of their piece rates. "The card-setters in the neighbourhood
of Scholes and Hightown, chiefly women, held a meeting to the number
of 1500, at Peep Green, at which it was determined not to set any more
cards at less than a halfpenny a thousand," reported the *Leeds Mercury*.
The implications of these demonstrations were not lost upon the manufacturing interests. As the newspaper admitted, "Alarmists may view these
indications of feminine independence as more menacing to established
institutions than the 'education of the lower orders.'"[45] Determined and
angry women posed a real threat to the prevailing image of pliant female
labor, doubly subdued by gender as well as class.

III

Given the sheer volume of literature on women factory workers, then and
now, we must remind ourselves that factory work was not the most common form of female labor in the nineteenth century. As Louise Tilly and
Joan Scott have pointed out, "the impact of industrialization on women's
employment was more varied and far less dramatic than the standard
image of the mill girl implies."[46] Women working in textile factories in

1833 represented but a "tiny fraction of the national workforce,"[47] and by 1850, "less than half the total of persons of all ages and sexes occupied in textiles" alone "was working within factories."[48] Yet even though factory employment involved a small percentage of the working population, the debates surrounding it created important normative forces. Within these discussions, the public forged definitions of masculine and feminine, skilled and unskilled work, and even moral notions of right and wrong. Though not all working women were factory workers, factory workers influenced all working women. The importance of public opinion during the age of the factory in shaping the future for women workers should not be underestimated.[49]

Inevitably, the factory entered the maelstrom of debate related to women and the laboring poor at the end of the eighteenth century. One might guess, given the dearth of gainful employment for women by that time, that the new textile mills would be applauded as a sorely needed solution for the problem of the female poor. Some early industrialists and poor law officers must have ascribed to this view, judging from the arrangements they made to transfer workhouse inmates to the new factories. Advocates of industrial expansion also saw factory employment as a panacea for the apparent Malthusian crisis in the countryside. "What a contrast is there at this day, between the torpor and brutality which pervade very many of the farming parishes, as delineated in the official reports, and the beneficent activity which animates all the cotton factory towns, villages, and hamlets!" exclaimed Andrew Ure, one of the most famous champions of the new industry. His position harmonized perfectly with the theories of political economists, who welcomed machinery as part of a more productive economy.[50]

Women workers were not exempt from the factory's propitious influence. The regularity of factory employment kept them productively occupied and prevented them from marrying early and giving birth to "equally degraded progeny." A parliamentary commissioner investigating the deplorable condition of handloom weavers extolled the "progress of manufacturing industry" and its "tendency to raise the condition of women" through profitable employment. "Education only is wanting," he claimed, "to place the women of Lancashire higher in the social scale than in any other part of the world."[51]

But general public opinion was anything but unanimous in its response, and the woman worker soon became entangled in contentious debate over the impact of the factory on labor. Tory opponents excoriated the manufacturing establishment for its self-interested abuse of the working population. An illusory lure of riches, one critic inveighed, induced laborers to abandon "an occupation healthy, moral, orderly, simple, frugal, and temperate; for one diseased, dissolute, insubordinate, factitious, expensive, and drunken."[52] In their scramble to catalogue the detrimental effects of industrialism, critics of the factory articulated a wholesale critique of the female factory worker. They unfurled a long list of indelicacies to which she was prone: unseemly behavior created by the amassing of coarse workers, immodesty brought about by wearing scanty clothing because of the heat, precocious sexual development, fondness of drink and stimulants required by fatigue, solitary night travel necessitated by hours of work that lasted into the night, and cravings for excitement created by long hours of monotonous work. The factory female acquired a reputation as a fallen creature disposed to indecency. Even Frederick Engels, a champion of the interests of the working classes, invoked Victorian values in order to criticize factory girls when he marshaled statistics that illustrated the fact that three-fourths of all girls between fourteen and twenty were unchaste. Ironically, advocates of the factory used the same criticisms of working-class women as an argument *for* factory employment, citing the inadequacies and immorality of female handloom weavers and spinners as evidence.[53]

Within discussions of the 1830s and 1840s, one sees every aspect of the classic Victorian woman summoned up to point out the failings of the working-class female factory worker. Comparisons abounded as writers pointed out the working-class woman's failure to meet the standard of the middle-class "angel of the house." "Here," intoned Peter Gaskell, "will be found an utter absence of grace and feminine manners . . . . no delicacy of figure, no 'grace in all her steps,' no 'heaven within her eye,' no elegance of tournure, no retiring bashfulness . . . . " Gaskell's list went on, punctuated by pseudoscientific theories that confused cause with effect. The unwomanly voice of the factory girl, he explained, was owing to "too early sexual excitement," which produced "vocal organs closely resembling that of the male." And the disfigured condition of the working class mother's breasts, he pointed out with evident satisfaction in his relentless logic, was just as indicative of "perversion in the usual functional adaptation of parts." The "soft, flaccid, pendulous" breasts, offering little nourishment to the dependent infant, proved the destructive effects of her "occupation and habits."[54]

Victorians' fascination with factory girls led to lengthy speculations connecting their moral condition with their physical state; discussions of one were virtually indistinct from the other, as contemporaries hypothesized about the causality of their degeneracy. Medical doctors reported on the development of girls' breasts and their pelvic structures, noting the absence of color in their cheeks and their slightness of stature. A fine line of distinction separated these "professional" assessments from those of the ordinary man making observations about the female body. "They are such poor decrepit creatures," commented one machine maker, "that though I am now fifty-one, I would not marry them if I could." Adding that his own wife was "a stout woman" when she was young, he added, "Now . . . you may look in vain for any such at present, either for size or for bloom." His testimony nevertheless confirmed parliamentary commissioners' opinion that "the race of women" found in industrial areas was on the decline.[55]

Investigators viewed the discrepancies in pay for men and women in the factory as a blessing in disguise. By offering less incentive to join the factory work force, employers made the prospect of homemaking more attractive to working-class women, particularly mothers. "Factory females have also in general much lower wages than males," Ure pointed out in his *Philosophy of Manufactures*,

> and they have been pitied on this account, with perhaps an injudicious sympathy, since the low price of their labour here tends to make household duties their most profitable as well as agreeable occupation, and prevents them from being tempted by the mill to abandon the care of their offspring at home.[56]

While championing the factory, Ure remained loyal to the ultimate goal of assigning women to the home. His distance from eighteenth-century arguments valuing women's productivity is noticeable. In the industrial world, the low price of women's labor was an accepted fact and dealt with as such.

The critique of the factory girl would not have been possible were it not for the existence of an ideal of womanhood already grounded in middle-class prosperity and values. The notion of female virtue allied with domesticity evolved in the late eighteenth century, and Malthus demonstrated how the model could be applied to the problems of the laboring poor.[57] The early Victorian period witnessed a reconfiguration of these ideas within the working classes. Agitating for a limited workday, working people joined reformers in pressing for a Factory Act, which limited the labor of children and introduced the need for the provision of schooling in 1833.[58] This movement brought many different interests, including working men, into dialogue over the proper extent of the factory's power over working-class life. Through public discussions about female and child labor in the factories, philanthropists, parliamentary commissioners, and factory operatives thus applied a standard of domesticity to working-class women. In effect, working-class women were harried home by a multitude of voices.

When agitation for a ten-hours bill resumed, it took a slightly different direction: the discussion of restricting the work of children became inextricably bound up with the "problem" of the woman worker. The Short-Time Movement mobilized sentiment against working women "withdrawn from their domestic duties" and capitalized on the precedent of earlier protective legislation to remove women as well as children from the pool of free labor. Historians have differed over their interpretations of working-class involvement in this struggle. The demand for a restriction of women's hours, some have argued, was an alternative strategy based on a genuine desire for the restriction of *all* workers' hours. Yet the goal of working men appears to have been a desire for a "family wage" paid to a male breadwinner, making the employment (and thus the competition) of working-class women unnecessary.[59]

Working-class men agreed with middle-class observers in believing that factory women belonged in the home, though for a panoply of different reasons. With women eliminated from the pool of surplus labor, which pulled down wages, everyone, it could be argued, might enter on an upward spiral of improvement. The prospect of impoverishment and the workhouse must have contributed to working-class support for a "family wage" for the male worker. In a letter to a cotton spinner in 1835, Francis Place advocated pressuring employers to restrict the use of female labor by a form of work stoppage:

> If, then, the men refused to work in mills and factories with girls, as they ought to do, as other trades have done, in workshops, and for those masters who employ women and girls, the young women who will otherwise be degraded by factory labour will become all that can be desired as companionable wives, and the whole condition of factory workers would soon be improved, the men will obtain competent wages for their maintenance.[60]

Place hoped that removing women from their competitive position in the labor market would perform a dual function: male wages would rise, and the quality of working-class home life would improve. Place's argument failed to address the fact that most female factory workers were single, and those who were married worked because their families needed their wages to get by.[61]

Concern for their own job security obviously influenced male workers in their opposition to the employment of women; rather than arguing for the improvement of everyone's wages and work conditions, male workers chose a more divisive strategy. The influential mule spinners in cotton mills were among the working-class leaders of a movement to exclude women from privileged positions of employment and unions. As a self-constructed aristocracy of labor, these men assimilated the discourses of male breadwinner and female domesticity as part of their masculine identity. Historians of labor often quote the worker who, when pressed to explain how and why women should be removed from the factories, answered,

> [Factory women] grow up in total ignorance of all the true duties of woman. Home, its cares, and its employments, is woman's true sphere; but these poor things are totally unfitted for [this] . . . . It is an inversion of the order of nature and of providence—a return to the state of barbarism, in which the woman does the work, while the man looks idly on.[62]

These men were instrumental in promoting a concept of the male breadwinner within the working class.[63]

The antipathy that working-class men felt toward wage-earning women had its roots, at least in part, in changes in the status of male workers during this period. Women became necessary and important wage-earners within the working-class family at precisely the point at which displaced skilled workingmen "found themselves pushed into an unfamiliar dependence on wife (and child) earnings" because of the decline of their trades. By the 1830s and 1840s, "the wage-earning wife, once seen as the norm in every working-class household, had become a symptom and symbol of masculine degradation." Though male workers' exclusion of women from unions suggests a general attitude of "sex privilege and prejudice," Jane Humphries has argued, their opposition must be seen in economic terms. The debate was fueled, in part, by the decline of tailoring, stocking making, and other skilled trades. The introduction of low-paid female labor into such work had resulted in the deterioration of male wages and employment prospects and, to make matters worse for men, a reversal of the conventional household hierarchy. Much negative commentary on women's work thus emanated from artisan circles, which included Chartists and other radicals, in response to these developments.[64]

Studies of women and factory legislation have placed a great deal of responsibility upon the doorstep of one commissioner, Leonard Horner, whose plea for protection summed up the legal distinction between male and female workers under laissez-faire capitalism:

> Twelve hours' daily work is more than enough for anyone; but however desirable it might be that excessive working should be prevented, there are great difficulties in the way of legislative interference with the labour of adult men. The case, however, is very different as respects women; for not only are they much less free agents, but they are physically incapable of bearing a continuance of work for the same length of time as men, and a deterioration of their health is attended with far more injurious consequences to society.[65]

How Horner arrived at a determination of "much less free" has been a matter of speculation.[66] Like most advocates of protection, Horner played up the rapaciousness of industry and its tendency to take advantage of defenseless children and women. His report stressed the "illegal over-working" of young people, which he believed arose from an abundant supply of workers. Horner thus applied the Malthusian arguments of an earlier generation to the new context of factory industry. "A theorist may say that these people (women just over eighteen) are old enough to take care of themselves," he stated, "but practically there can be no such thing as freedom of labour, when from the redundancy of population is such competition for employment." This was no socialist critique of the slavery of capitalism, but rather, a gloomy judgment of the consequences of overpopulation.[67]

The opposition to women's factory work, furthered by a broad coalition of beliefs, breathed new life into negative assessments of the working-class female. By the Victorian period, women workers were circumscribed by definitions of domesticity and female virtue that rendered their work in the factory reprehensible. Legislation, however salutary, enforced these views: an act of 1844 limited the daily hours of work for women, along with those of children, to twelve. Another bill, passed in 1847, limited the hours of labor to sixty-three per week for women and young persons over thirteen.[68] The same concerns would ignite debate in the different milieu of the 1870s, resulting in protective legislation that was definitive in limiting the productive role of women workers while holding them responsible, without acknowledgment of their economic disadvantage, for maintaining a family.[69]

IV

Despite its obvious drawbacks, factory work nevertheless held out many enticements to female labor. By the early decades of the nineteenth century, factory employment was one of a declining number of options, and compared to its foremost rival, domestic service, it offered considerable advantages. With a bit of luck and a great deal of hard work, young women could make a living in the new factories. Most were young and single; as many as 53 percent of all single women in Stockport were factory operatives in 1851.[70] Some came to the factory town from nearby rural areas, while others were the daughters of local handloom weavers or factory workers. Compared to extremely low wages, or no wages at all, factory pay appeared quite attractive. The work was usually free from the unpleasantness of personal supervision and humiliation that domestic service entailed. And regular money wages could admit young women into a world of getting and spending that had particular allure in the new age of consumption.

Money earned meant different things to different women. For many, factory wages purchased the ordinary staples of life and then a little bit besides: contemporaries often noted ham, butter, eggs, and cream, as well as clothing as the commodities that factory women were fortunate enough to afford.[71] Some may have enjoyed the advantage of having actual spending money; girls were sometimes allowed to dispose of a fraction of their wages after the greater part had been contributed to their parents' households, and even small change promised incalculable freedom. Young women purchased rather than made clothing, and they often bought ribbons and other decorative items that observers never failed to comment upon. The ability to spend was a pleasurable and sometimes intoxicating power. In their correspondence with friends and family, American girls in early New England factories indicated their pleasure in receiving their own wages, earned outside the confines of their homes, and their enjoyment of purchasing clothing and gifts for themselves and their families.[72] It is easy to imagine that their English counterparts found equal satisfaction in having a single shilling to spend as they pleased each week, whether it was prudently saved or quickly squandered.

Factory employment might also mean a more independent way of life, free from the constraints of family supervision and protection. Elizabeth Gaskell summed it up in the words of a character in *Mary Barton* (1848): "That's the worst of factory work, for girls. They can earn so much when work is plenty, that they can maintain themselves any how."[73] The ability to obtain the necessities of life—a place to live, clothing, and food—without the assistance of others represented a considerable achievement for working-class girls. At sixteen or eighteen years of age, their wages reached a maximum, and thus young people came into early possession of their greatest earning power. "This premature independence," observers noted, "too often induces them to quit their parents' houses, that they may be more at liberty to follow their own inclinations."[74] Thus factory work could break the customary bounds of age and authority as well as gender.

Evidence of young people living in lodgings apart from their families of origin shows that some did escape parental authority. In Preston, Lancashire, for example, "somewhere over 10 per cent" of the age group ranging from fifteen to nineteen lived in lodgings during the first half of the nineteenth century.[75] The percentage grew considerably by midcentury, reaching 37 percent of migrant females.[76] But as Judy Lown points out in her study of Halstead, Essex, rather than escaping parental rule, female lodgers usually deferred to patriarchal authority in multiple contexts. They often sent the bulk of their wages back to their parents, while bowing to the authority of household heads in their new lodgings. In actuality, the households they entered were very much like the ones they left, with the important exception that they were located near places of employment.[77]

Whatever the reality of these situations, middle-class observers were acutely aware of the novel aspect of "female independence" made possible by factory employment. While some philanthropically minded critics waxed "indignant at the knowledge that women had to support themselves,"[78] "others were indignant that they *could* support themselves."[79] Factory girls' flagrant displays of finery, far more extravagant than middle-class observers believed befitting a laborer's station, provoked disapproving comments. As he inquired into conditions of work in a Manchester factory, a commissioner scrupulously noted the dress of an eighteen-year-old power-loom weaver. "[She] could not cut out and make up such a gown as she wears now. (It was of beautiful silk, and well made.) The gown she has on cost her 1l. 16s. 6d., her bonnet cost 1l. 9s. She wears silk gloves; they cost her about 1s. 6d. per pair; shoes cost her about 15s. a year."[80] The commissioner must have been awed by the young woman's resourcefulness, for upon inquiring, he discovered that in addition to her 13-hour day at the mill, she made and sold fancy caps for as much as 8s. a piece. The simple fact that some women had the freedom to earn and spend their wages however they pleased suggested a female independence that clashed with conventional standards of propriety.[81]

This much vaunted independence may have been more widely discussed than experienced. "As parents sent daughters off with traditional expectations," Joan Scott and Louise Tilly have pointed out, intending to carry on a family economy that included factory wages, "so the daughters attempted to fulfill them. Evidence for the persistence of familial values is found in the continuing contributions made by working daughters to their families."[82] Factory commissioners found in examining over sixty factory girls in Manchester that "all their wages went to their parents; as likewise all those of their brothers and sisters." Even when the young women were migrants from the countryside, they often sent wages home and brought other members of their families to the city to live and work with them.[83]

Many women and girls worked alongside husbands and fathers as assistants, or elsewhere within the same factory. Some mills hired families *in toto*. "Masters allowed the operative spinners to hire their own assistants (piecers, scavengers, etc.) and . . . the spinners chose their wives, children, near relatives or relatives of the proprietors." Thus the family economy of preindustrial production moved, intact, into the factory.[84] Michael Anderson's study of Lancashire revealed that 54 percent of Preston factory employees under the age of eighteen were hired by adult male spinners; 59 percent of all employees under eighteen were working under spinners throughout the county. According to Anderson, most spinners did not employ their own children at the mills, but many did engage the children of relatives.[85] And as many as one-half the women employed in a sampling of Yorkshire and Lancashire factories in the 1840s had husbands in the same factory.[86]

A Manchester woman, the wife and mother of factory workers and a former tenter and stretcher herself, gave evidence to parliamentary commissioners on the nature of this sort of family employment:

> Her husband is a fine spinner, at Mr. ——, where he has been from 1816, has five children. Her eldest daughter, now going on fourteen, has been her father's piecer for three years. At her present age, her labour is worth 4s. 6d. a week, and has been worth as much for these last four months; before, it was worth less. At present her husband's earnings and her daughter's together amount to about 25s. a week—at least she sees no more than 25s. a week; and before his daughter could piece for him, and when he had to pay for a piecer in her stead, he only brought home 19s. or 20s. a week.[87]

Financial necessity made it imperative that as soon as she reached a suitable age—around ten or eleven years—a daughter would become her father's assistant. In this case, the savings achieved through a young woman's work amounted to slightly more than the weekly rent of the family dwelling.

Far from destroying the working-class family, industrialization often strengthened kinship ties. Working-class families recognized the desirability of staying close to their relatives, as this was usually the only way to solve the ineluctable need for shelter, food, help with children, and companionship. And given the low rates of pay for all jobs, families heavily depended on the contributions of all members in order to get by.[88] Testimonies revealed again and again the intricate web of interdependence connecting factory girls to their families. Jane (b. 1815), an eighteen-year-old power-loom weaver, lived at home with her mother and brother.

Her weekly wage was 13s. a week; her brother, a warper, earned as much as a pound or a guinea (21s.) a week. By "looking after" several hand-looms, perhaps by renting out one or two and tending another herself, her mother was able to add to the household earnings; but of the three forms of income, handloom weaving was the least reliable. Jane reported that she gave her mother 7s. a week, "and keeps the rest herself; if mother wants more, gives her more." Financial independence was not an option, nor did she expect it to be.[89]

Another girl, Mary, seventeen, worked as a piecer for 5s. a week. She, too, was the daughter of a handloom weaver (in this case, her father) and understood her responsibility was to her parents' household. Three sisters earned 5s. a week as piecers, and her brother earned 8s. at the same job. While these five children attended work at the factory each day, another sister earned 8s. a week by handloom weaving alongside her father at home. They rented a third loom to a stranger, which brought in an additional few shillings a week. But as income from such work, particularly in silk, fluctuated greatly, their earnings could not be counted on. Situations like these convinced contemporaries that in one way or another, the factory supported most working-class households through its dispersal of many, albeit small, wages of women and children.[90]

Factory employment brings to light, perhaps paradoxically, the poverty of the working classes, for those women who seized such opportunity were usually desperate for work. Only roughly 15 percent of all working-class families could have escaped a period of poverty over the life cycle, Michael Anderson has shown, and in Preston, 20 percent of all families were below the poverty line even when the wife was working.[91] John Foster's figures for Oldham indicate a much higher percentage of families living in poverty within certain occupations. Among skilled factory workers' families during the distress of 1847, 52 percent were on or below the subsistence line.[92] None of these figures reflects the abject poverty experienced by women outside the conventional boundaries of the family, such as single women and single mothers, who sought employment in the factory. Joining them were the many women who sought temporary jobs as pickers, for example, when their fathers or husbands were out of work. They appeared for a time in factory wage books, and then vanished, working "at intervals, probably when they could spare the time or were in urgent need of the money that could be earned."[93]

The working married woman demonstrated the failure, as well as the inappropriateness, of the ideal of the male breadwinner within the working-class family. Seasonal male workers, such as masons, navvies, bricklayers, and jobbing laborers, suffered from extended periods of unemployment; many other men held jobs that were poorly paid and uncertain. In an effort to denigrate the practice of employing wives and mothers in industry, contemporaries often exaggerated the numbers of married women within the factory; about only one in six women, or approximately 10,000 of 61,000 women employed in 412 textile factories in

Lancashire in 1844 were married.[94] Yet the publicity called attention to circumstances that were obscured in many other ways during the Victorian period. The prevalence of lodging houses was only one instance of the more "covert" attempts of women to bring in an income in an increasingly cash-dominated society. Few if any working-class families could afford to support a wife who earned no money.[95]

More pronounced was the contemporary antipathy toward the "female breadwinner," the woman whose wages formed the basis of household income in the working-class family. Engels vigorously voiced these feelings in his investigations into living conditions in Manchester in the 1840s. General unemployment crippled urban areas across Europe during that decade as the industrial economy suffered one of its most dramatic slumps. Engels assessed the impact on the quintessential factory town. "The wife is the breadwinner while her husband stays at home to look after the children and to do the cleaning and cooking," he pointed out with disapproval. "In Manchester alone there are many hundreds of men who are condemned to perform household duties. One may well imagine the righteous indignation of the workers at being virtually turned into eunuchs." Engels took careful note of the statistical evidence of unemployed men married to factory workers; of 10,721 married women employed in 412 factories in Lancashire in 1844, at least 821 had unemployed husbands. (No information was available for 659 others.) Such a reversal of "natural" circumstances led, in Engels's view, to the "shameful and degrading" erosion of normal sexual attributes. As another writer on industry put it, women had more important work to do at home: "By feeding us—I don't mean earning our bread, but cooking it."[96]

Contemporaries also feared that the factory system was transforming the natural bond between parents and offspring into a monetary contractual one. Parents and children negotiated exchanges of wages, along with certain responsibilities. "I give my parents 7s. out of the 9s. every week," a young woman of twenty-six explained. "Till lately I gave them 8s. a week; but then my wages of an average were 10s. I live with them; they feed and lodge me; I clothe myself." The commissioner then added, "But does not pay for her washing."[97] Earning wages gave young people a basis on which to "bargain" with their parents; thus the factory could lead to different authority relations within the working-class household. "The children that frequent the factories," one critic noted, "make almost the purse of the family, and by making the purse of the family, they share in the ruling of it."[98] The wage-earning power of the woman within the family led to a similar challenge to patriarchal status. This example of the domestic world turned upside down led even Engels to recognize the social construction of the family. "If the reign of the wife over the husband, as inevitably brought about by the factory system, is inhuman, the pristine rule of the husband over the wife must have been inhuman too," he theorized. Engels's speculations prove how profoundly destabilizing the new world of the factory was for many contemporaries. Perhaps it is not surprising that Victorian philanthropists and reformers hastened to reassert patriarchal authority through institutions, publications, and legislation.[99]

The factory system signaled the emergence of women workers as wage earners, a status that brought both advantages and drawbacks in its wake. Barbara Hutchins, a Fabian and feminist activist of the early twentieth century, saw the wage contract as "an advance from [woman's] servile state" under other conditions. The concept of the female wage earner, though not entirely new, became more explicit with the introduction of the factory. The regular wage, attached to the institution of the factory, demanded that women be dealt with as autonomous individuals. Under this system, a woman's employment was "no longer bound up with personal dependence on her own family, or personal servitude in her employer's."[100] But the passage of protective legislation associated with mining in the 1840s had proven the vulnerability of this line of reasoning: the law decided that women were not "free agents" at all, but in need of restrictive protection.[101] Middle-class feminists of the 1870s persisted in upholding the freedom of the wage-earning woman, and though they found themselves among unlikely allies, they nevertheless strove to link the notion of a wage to other freedoms, including the vote.[102]

In spite of its contractual nature, wage earning was obviously vulnerable to gender bias: positing the autonomy of the female wage immediately exposed the fact that the level of a woman's earnings was determined by an assumption that her wage was a supplement to some other (most likely a male breadwinner's) wage. The idea of a woman's wage never really existed outside older patriarchal attitudes, but instead, defined itself in a dialectic relationship to them.[103] A woman's "worth" could be succinctly measured by considering her wage-earning power in the context of her household, whether she contributed wages to a family coffer or cared for her children and her home. This attitude informed government inquiries into the condition of female factory operatives; the commissioners' strategy showed that they were interested not only in whether women handed over wages to a male household head, but also in how the two forms of women's work compared in value. In squaring the idea of women as wage earners with their more conventional role as wives and mothers, the commissioners, perhaps ironically, confronted the value of women's work in the household.

As one commissioner queried of a tailor who had formerly worked in a factory, "Do those women who have been brought up at mills make useful wives?" "Not many of them," replied the man; "not useful wives with regard to household work." The exchange between the artisan and commissioner was redolent with an odd blend of old-fashioned patriarchy and attitudes born of the much-criticized factory age:

> Fortunately for myself, my first wife was a pretty good one, considering I had her out of the mill, with regard to her abilities in household work; but,

unfortunately for me, she was often sick, and lame in one ankle from over-strain during her factory work; so that, with her lameness and sickness together, we had very little pleasure the five years we were tied together. But with regard to my second wife, I have advantages which I had not with the first, her enjoying and her child much better health, and being more handy in household work, having been a servant in gentlemen's families.

Is she worth as much to you in a money point of view?—Yes, I consider she has the advantage by being able to get me what she does get at home, and at the same time being able to make me comfortable. By being not in such an emaciated and sickly state she retains her temper better, which enables us to live a more peaceable life.[104]

The values of the middle-class factory commissioner harmonized with those of the tailor in most respects, although it is doubtful that the inspector understood the financial circumstances that made women's wage labor a necessity in a working-class family. Besides the obvious prejudice against the female factory worker, the passage reveals how deeply the taproot of the cash-based economy had penetrated. Pleasure, comfort, sickness, and even children were assessed within a quantifiable budget of household activities. The question of women's wages inspired measurement without once challenging the meagre sums that were considered reasonable for women's work.

V

The factory acted as a powerful dispenser of societal norms, quite apart from its allegedly revolutionary impact on the economy. Legislative interference brought Victorian values of male economic dominance and female dependence to bear upon the working classes. In some cases, the factory itself imposed a carefully defined order upon many aspects of workers' lives. Close studies have shown individual owners adopting an explicit paternalistic role in relations with their employees and their local community. The Courtaulds of Halstead provide an early nineteenth-century example of this; factory discipline, housing, educational institutions, and local pageantry reflect the shaping hand of the master in producing a population that was dependent, loyal, and obedient. The Strutts and Arkwrights, and in a very different way, Robert Owen, offer other examples.[105] In the 1840s, according to one historian, these tendencies formed a distinct style of economic and political domination, identifiable as a "new paternalism." For the second half of the nineteenth century, "it was the social effect of the capitalist workplace that mattered most" in the North of England. The factory drew into its powerful vortex all aspects of life: education, religion, leisure, and the family "were not discrete areas of experience," but rather, components of a large culture created by the new mode of industry. "The degree to which the late nineteenth-century factory dominated the world of the operative," Patrick Joyce makes clear, "can hardly be exaggerated."[106]

For working women, this meant an increasing stress on "proper" feminine behavior, as well as expectations that replicated middle-class family structure and morality. Factory schools taught girls principles of hygiene and homemaking skills, boarding houses enforced strict rules of conduct, and punishments were meted out to those who bore illegitimate children or cohabited with men. Though female operatives showed little enthusiasm for these schemes (in one instance, the rules that were posted in a "Factory Home" for women were burned by the inhabitants), middle-class philanthropists maintained that such strategies were "useful" and necessary labors. "The female factory population of our large towns," the noted feminist and reformer Bessie Rayner Parkes pointed out, were worthy objects "to whom England owes much of her wealth, and whom she is bound to educate and protect."[107]

In some instances, middle-class women participated in the inculcation of proper values in the female factory worker. "The grand desideratum in politics," wrote Elizabeth Strutt Evans in 1793, "is the diffusion of knowledge and morals among the poor. This the manufacturer has it in his power considerably to promote and is culpable in the neglect of it."[108] In the early years of the nineteenth century, the effort could take the form of direct involvement. George Courtauld's four daughters helped to supervise his female work force, prescribing "perfect silence except [for] the singing of hymns which we find a useful relaxation and a help to industry, attention and orderly conduct."[109] In families originating in trade, the genteel status of the factory owner's daughter needed definition, and the role of disciplinarian and female mentor sometimes aided the process. In the Courtaulds' case, not until the next generation grew to majority in the 1840s did the feminine ideal realize itself in a life of total leisure.[110] Then the role of educator was passed on to an appointed instructor, in this instance, a Quaker philanthropist and nurse, Mary Merryweather.[111] Merryweather cited in particular "the wife of the senior partner" who "had been wishing to do more in the way of education and kindly oversight for the working-people of their largest factory." It was Mrs. Courtauld who finally engaged Merryweather as a free-lance assistant (her job was to "try to be useful amongst these factory women") at Halstead in 1847.[112]

Merryweather's account stands as a useful measure of middle-class female opinion of working-class women. Merryweather was trained as a nurse by Florence Nightingale and maintained an active interest in feminist philanthropic causes. One finds a curious mix of Malthusian condemnation and genteel disapproval in her discussion of factory workers. Her "first day's visiting" revealed "evidence of at least three of our social sores, all more or less connected with ignorance:—careless and too early marriages; unsteady, idle conduct in the young women; and total disregard to all sanitary laws." Despite her reforming spirit and her dedication to uplifting lower-class women, Merryweather's view of her "charges" was negative and censorious. Her sense of social distance from the "coarse, noisy girls, with no womanly reserve or modesty" indicated how hierarchical a notion of true womanhood could be. Indeed, Merryweather soon enlisted "about eight monitors" for her evening school, working-class deputies who would serve as intermediaries between her and the "disorderly" factory girls. She included in her *Experience* several letters from these monitors, exercises in composition and penmanship required of all students. Not withstanding the nature of the assignment, the monitors' letters demonstrate slavish deference, addressing Merryweather as "Lady," thanking God for her efforts, and expressing apologies for the girls' behavior. The self-deprecating references to speech and other aspects of working-class culture are almost painful to read.[113]

By the time the more influential Bessie Rayner Parkes wrote her introduction to Merryweather's *Experience* in 1862, the domestic ideals of Victorian womanhood had reached an unassailable height. As a founder of the *English Woman's Journal*, which aimed to explore the various aspects of women's work in order to improve training and expand opportunities, Parkes was greatly interested in women factory workers. Yet her stance as a feminist was based upon an explicit understanding of a separation of spheres. The socially volatile aspect of Victorian culture, the promise of self-improvement and advancement, was thus held out in different ways to men and women factory workers. The institution of factory schools lay bare the distinct expectations directed toward male and female students. "To give a [male] youth the means of obtaining a superior education," wrote Parkes in her preface, "is to afford him a chance of rising in the world, of changing his place, or obtaining a superior post. None can say, who look upon a hundred boys gathered together in the Factory Night School, what will be their individual path in after life, nor how far the superior instruction they there receive may not prove the stimulus fitted to lift this or that one of the number into another sphere."[114] She saw an entirely different set of possibilities for the women there:

> But among girls a different general principle prevails. As a rule, they are, and they must be, attached to the domestic life of the neighbouring district; to unfit them for that life would, as a general rule, be a misfortune and not an advantage to them. The great problem, for all who truly wish them well, must be how to repair the disadvantages of their industrial position; how to fit them for living well and wisely in an inevitable lot—that of the rulers of small households, the dispensers of small incomes, the mothers of a generation which, to all appearance, will be swept even more completely into the system of Factory Life.[115]

Parkes believed that working-class women, like women of other classes, must make the most of their important position as wives and mothers.[116]

The working-class woman bore an additional burden that extended beyond the simple maintenance of "domestic life." A crucial connection existed between her domestic and moral responsibilities and her husband's social mobility. "The only thing that enables a working man to rise," a Victorian economist argued, "and the foundation therefore of all his other virtues, is providence, and it is in a home that this must have its source . . . ."[117] A woman wielded considerable influence over the fate of her household; upon her behavior depended a wealth of economic and political rewards. A working-class woman's good nature, Peter Gaskell pointed out, can "do more towards making [a man] a good husband, a good father, and an useful citizen, than all the dogmas of political economy."[118]

The gendered education and protection of working-class women suppressed the recognition of their productive worth. This was not just the consequence of the ideology of domesticity, but the cumulative effect of decades of disparagement of the working-class woman's character and behavior. Though Victorian reformers might have wished to distance themselves from the less enlightened eighteenth-century critics of the poor, they adopted similar ideas and language with regard to the working-class female. Notions of hierarchy and subordination played a major part in carving out a place for the working-class female.

6

Invisible Breadwinners: Women
Workers and the Declining Status
of Cottage Industry

Mamma, it may be so, But then you lived full fifty years ago.
Then you might safely turn the spinning wheel
And not be counted very ungenteel.
But now the world much more polite appears
For fashions alter in a round of years.
Thus trade increases, the poor are daily fed
And thousands get their living by the head.[1]

Nicholas Rowe (1674–1718), *A Poetical Address to the Ladies of Bedfordshire*

Long before the coming of the factory, eighteenth-century England was
attuned to the call of rationality and profits, commerce and manufacturing. These developments, as we have seen, were narrowing opportunities
for work available to laboring women. By the 1780s, the transformation
of agriculture and the mechanization of spinning were forcing thousands
of women to seek alternative means of earning wages. In cottage industry, many women found readily available, if poorly paid, employment.
The compatibility between their needs and those of merchant manufacturers led to an auspicious marriage of convenience: the abundant, unemployed female work force in the countryside became a cheap, exploitable
pool of labor. Though this form of production had been present in England since the sixteenth century,[2] the configuration of the domestic system and merchant capitalists became a dominant feature of the economic
landscape between 1780 and 1815.[3] Minor industries such as lace making, gloving, leather, and straw plait, though difficult to measure,

113

expanded significantly during those years. The growing perception of laboring women as idle and ill-suited to better types of employment served to reinforce their predicament. Cottage industries became associated with impoverished circumstances, and women earned criticism, not praise, for engaging in such work.

From the start, relations between putters-out and women workers were unequal. Unlike urban handicraft industry, this form of production took its cues from merchants rather than from workers themselves; cottagers had no say over the terms of their work or the payment they received. Manufacturers strove to maximize profits through practices unknown to urban manufacture: arbitrary wage cutting, seasonal and partial employment, and the withholding of commodities in order to release them at advantageous times characterized the conditions of cottage industry. Adam Smith was highly critical of the system, which he believed was "carried on for the benefit of the rich and the powerful." Town merchants expected to pay as little as possible for the labor of country workers, and in the case of Smith's native linen industry, most were "poor people, women commonly, scattered about in all different parts of the country, without support or protection." He argued that the arrangement inevitably led to political and moral degeneration.[4]

According to feminist historians, the role of women within the family was at the heart of this configuration. In the case of the female worker, employers assumed that her earnings were subsidiary to others in the same household. Wages were never set at subsistence level (as they were presumed to be in the case of most male employments), but rather, as low as the pool of labor would bear. Women workers showed a remarkable capacity for self-exploitation, adapting to any condition or level of payment. The terms of cottage industry melded with the duties of wives, mothers, and daughters: women performed work at their own pace in their own homes, working as circumstances dictated. Mothers could enlist the help of children, the "capital of the poor man," who furnished a handy reservoir of labor, especially when time was short.[5] Cottage industry provided a way for women to support families when male wage earners experienced periods of unemployment. Economic writers were debating a theory of the male breadwinner at this time, but the prevalence of multiple wage earners in every family revealed how far from reality that notion lay.[6]

Yet this extended phase of development, however inequitable, "preceded and paved the way for industrialization proper." Identified as "proto-industrialization" (or "industrialization before industrialization"), the system enabled manufacturers to accumulate the capital, entrepreneurial skills, and technical expertise necessary for a general transition to factory industry.[7] In their attempt to rescue cottage industries from oblivion, historians of proto-industrialization have highlighted the crucial place of women within the laboring family, calling them "the vanguard of the peasant household industries."[8] Yet even in attempting to valorize the contribution of women, their discussions have subordinated women's work within the very hierarchy of employments they criticize. Their accounts refer to women's work as "marginal" and as part of "petty agrarian production," categories they have adopted as natural rather than created by developments in agriculture and mechanized industry. Thus they have reinscribed a historically constructed notion of "supplementary" upon the work of women.[9] The language habitually used to describe cottage industry actually impedes our understanding its meaning. As Robert Malcolmson has pointed out, "it may be misleading to speak of 'by-employments' at all, for it is often the case that one means of livelihood cannot be clearly identified as predominant and the other as subsidiary."[10] It is only with some difficulty that historians have set out various theories of the impact of cottage industries.

Historians of proto-industrialization have argued that the struggle for subsistence at times "necessitated a 'maximum . . . of familial cooperation'" and "could go so far as to erase the traditional division of labour between the sexes and the age groups." "Women as cutlers, nailmakers, and as organizers of the marketing of industrial products were as common as men in the roles of spinners and lacemakers."[11]

> Occasionally, this adaptation of the organization of familial work to the conditions of survival went even further. It could lead to the reversal of traditional roles: where the necessities of production compelled women to neglect household "duties," this "loss of function" could be compensated by the men's assuming traditional women's roles. . . . It was here that "men . . . cook, sweep, and milk the cows, in order never to disturb the good diligent wife in her work."[12]

Male agricultural laborers with sufficient employment experienced little change in their familial relations. But within the textile trades, men assumed an adaptive, cooperative position in maintaining the household or helping to produce for the market. In some cottage industries, such as glove making or lace making, men joined in the work itself. Thus

> the division of labour within the household showed no uniformity; it varied according to the branch of production, its developmental stage and its market conditions; it frequently deviated from the 'classical pattern' . . . in which the man was weaving, the wife was spinning, and the children were occupied with subsidiary activities such as the preparation of materials for the production process.

These variations in the sexual division of labor carried the potential for significant change, at least in terms of gender relations within the working-class community.[13]

It is possible that popular politics and plebeian culture *did* acknowledge the productive role of women more explicitly within this transitional period than in the mid nineteenth century, when working women "disappeared" from the public sphere.[14] The laboring classes readily incorporated both sexes in demonstrating their collective opinion in matters pertaining to subsistence. Women were prominent protesters against enclosures, the high prices of provisions, the imposition of machinery in the textile industry, and the introduction of the New Poor Law.[15] They also came forth as leaders in sectarian Methodism, organizing and preaching to cottage societies scattered throughout the countryside.[16] This chapter will examine their work in cottage industries as part of a larger picture of laboring life, a panorama that included many aspects of the laboring family's social identity.

The following discussion does not pretend to be a comprehensive history of women's work in cottage industries. It focuses on several minor industries as they developed alongside more "modernized" forms of production, such as spinning. For lack of space, several outstanding branches, such as framework knitting and the metal trades, have been omitted.[17] Ranging from relatively skilled work in lace making to the less demanding straw-plait industry, domestic industries present a complicated problem of interpretation. As recurrent as such industries were, those of the late eighteenth and early nineteenth centuries had an especially profound impact on understandings of work and productivity. Women's work in these areas contributed to a revision of their image within the new industrial regime, one that did not work in their favor. Work in cottage industries contributed to a long-term erosion of the status of laboring women: the degradation that came to characterize domestic outwork ultimately associated the nineteenth-century working-class woman with undervalued, low-paid labor.

I

Though cottage industries were not, by definition, crafts, they nevertheless commanded a certain degree of respect prior to the nineteenth century. Lace making, for example, required considerable training and skill; always facing stiff competition from Flanders, the finest English lace makers achieved a high degree of accomplishment in the eighteenth century. That women and children of the poor were its main producers did not affect the remunerativeness of the trade. "The wives of agricultural labourers frequently earned more than their husbands" by working at the pillow in some areas.[18] And while Defoe charged that lace makers came "from the most idle, useless and burthensome part of our people, viz. the younger women and female children," he admitted that they "were now made able to provide for themselves"—a laudable achievement in the eyes of contemporaries.[19] The plaiting of straw similarly earned relatively high wages in the early eighteenth century, even though the trade was not the sole pursuit of rural women and children. A petition to Parliament in 1719 defended the interests of "farmers' wives, children and servants," who "do at their spare hours earn some 10, some 20 and some £30 per annum by manufacturing their own straw which is a good article towards paying their rent."[20]

Yet we must combat the temptation to use categories such as "spare hours" to evaluate these activities: cottage industries were seldom simply a leisure pastime for women and children. Most if not all industries appeared in places where seasonal and part-time employment led to a serious need for remunerative work. Historians have analyzed the appearance of such industries according to regional variations in the economy; many, for example, flourished in dairying districts in the Midlands and North. The distinction between the "cheese" and the "chalk" areas of England, one devoted to mixed employments within a pastoral economy, the other to full-scale capitalist agriculture, may have provided a geographical and political basis of industrial growth extending back to the Middle Ages.[21] Parliamentary reports described the Yorkshire Dales as "one large grazing and breeding farm," where cattle and sheep replaced tillage almost everywhere. There cottagers earned their livings by knitting stockings, caps and jackets, or by making gloves.[22] Partible inheritance often encouraged an abundant population in these districts, and available commons attracted migrant poor in need of land for a cottage. Framework knitting spread through eighteenth-century Nottinghamshire, Leicestershire, and Derbyshire, where scarcity of land led to dense populations in unrestricted areas of settlement.[23]

We can explain the regional variation in the growth of cottage industry more simply: necessity, not geography, was probably most crucial in establishing industries in the countryside. "The common feature among all rural industrial workers, no matter what the period of time or region in which they were employed," a historian of lace making has argued, "was poverty."[24] The link between declining employment in agriculture and cottage industry was clear to contemporaries. Women took up straw plaiting and lace making in the eastern counties, where cereal specialization had reduced the overall demand for labor and confined them to low-paying, irregular jobs weeding or hoeing. In the Midlands, where the conversion to pasture also reduced the need for labor, rural industries absorbed women in search of employment.[25] Gloving supplemented agricultural regions where few women had work and men were paid very little. In the southwestern counties, around Worcester, Yeovil, Woodstock, Hereford, Ludlow, and Leominster, a parliamentary commissioner reported in the 1840s, "Gloving is a resource to the mass of people, and 'keeps many above want who could not work in the fields,' and on this account it is an advantage."[26]

Local authorities in some agricultural areas devised plans for the poor that trained women in various domestic-based trades. Associated with needlework, gloving appeared to offer an ideal alternative for poor women in Worcestershire and Oxfordshire. In 1818, when pressures on unemployment were exacerbated by the postwar slump, Burford (Oxfordshire) burgesses agreed "that a person shall be engaged to learn one person in every poor family to make gloves." Women comprised the bulk of the work force by performing the laborious task of stitching together the pieces provided by the master glover, while men worked in tanning, dyeing, and cutting the leather. Growing numbers employed in the trade in agricultural areas continued to indicate the need for such supplementary forms of employment alongside agriculture.[27]

Appealing to the same sector of the population, plaiting eventually replaced wool spinning as a means of support for single and poor women in the South Midlands. Parish overseers purchased straw for workhouse inmates and also doled out the raw material to poor women who applied for relief. The Society for Bettering the Condition of the Poor encouraged plaiting as a solution to the prevailing problem of unoccupied female laborers. Mistresses came from distant places in order to instruct local women and girls in the art, and gradually, the industry spread across the Midlands countryside. As a rival domestic industry, straw plaiting expanded in many areas just as the woolen industry declined in the late eighteenth century. Plaiting became the only means of earning wages for thousands of laboring women.[28]

The number of poor people earning some form of income from cottage industries grew to an unprecedented height in the eighteenth century.[29] Scattered across the countryside and carried on in private homes, the true extent of such industriousness among the poor became generally known only in times of crisis. A notable instance occurred in Worcester, when in the 1780s, a failure in the glove trade threw "upwards of 10,000 poor People in the said City, and its Environs, chiefly Women and Children . . . out of Employment, through a general and distressing Stagnation of their Trade."[30]

Contemporaries came to associate cottage industries with the very margins of survival. As poor women from all walks of life moved into domestic industries, public opinion maligned the work itself, categorizing it as marginal employment demanding no skill. Button making attracted the very poorest of the parish, including widows and orphans, who faced the necessity of supporting themselves with few skills and resources. Many were said to be "Weakly, Aged, and Decrepid," and the sedentary nature of the craft, like most domestic industries, enabled even the feeble to earn small sums. The overstocked condition of some trades led some observers to condemn women for diluting work formerly carried on by men. In London, according to one authority, female button makers had "reduced the Trade to small Profits, and a small Share of Reputation;"

> The Women are generally Gin-Drinkers, and, consequently, bad Wives; this makes them poor, and, to get something to keep Soul and Body together, work for a mere Trifle, and hawk their Work about to the Trade at an Under-price, after they have cheated the Lace-man of his stuffs.[31]

By forging a specious link between need and immorality, such accounts legitimated the degradation that the system of outwork imposed on its workers.

The periodic booms and slumps of the new industrial economy repeatedly confirmed the low status of cottage workers. Though workers in all trades faced periods of unemployment and considerable economic insecurity, cottage workers were particularly vulnerable to an employer's precipitous decisions. Little overhead restrained merchant manufacturers from completely shutting down operations at a moment's notice; and often needing to produce goods quickly and in great quantities in order to compete in a wider market, workers might experience abrupt changes in orders. The pin trade, which employed many women and children as headers and stickers, provides a vivid example. Trade with America influenced production between 1814 and 1821; sales were deadly slow in early 1814, but as war in America wound down in December, brisk trade followed and a Warrington manufacturer communicated to his partners, "You may extend the pin trade as far as our capital will hold out. I could sell £10,000 worth tomorrow." By the following November, however, American markets were saturated, and pins were sold off at auctions at a loss, sometimes by as much as 30 percent. "By 1818, an estimated "three-fourths of the pinmakers in Great Britain had either failed or retired from the industry."[32]

Underscoring this pattern of instability was the fact that many cottage industries relied upon the precarious market associated with the clothing trades, where changes in fashion, as well as import duties and methods of marketing, could wreak havoc in the demand for goods. When French gloves flooded the English market with the liberal trade policies of 1826, unemployment rose astronomically. "The poor rates were trebled . . . and at Woodstock and Yeovil they were almost doubled"; in Yeovil, "distress was so serious that dragoons had to be quartered in the town and immediate neighbourhood."[33] Critics of the new policy pointed to its disastrous impact on women workers. "The greater part of the imports from France consist of goods, which our *artizans, particularly females,* are deprived the benefit of making," complained one involved in the trade in 1834.[34] The decline in gloving continued through the first half of the century, until improvement in the quality of English goods enhanced their appeal and employment began to rise again.

Like glove making, the trade of straw plaiting fluctuated dramatically over short periods of time, rendering unstable the livelihoods of laboring women and their families. Straw plaiting enjoyed prosperity during the Revolutionary War years and suffered serious decline whenever foreign imports found entry into Britain. When fine plait imports from Italy ceased after 1793, the industry experienced its greatest boom. Improvements in the technique of splitting straw around 1800 enabled English trade to emulate the finer types of plait, and sales of home products soared. High duties following the war period also promoted the trade, and plaiters and hatters, as well as farmers involved in producing straw, prospered and multiplied accordingly. But prices for plait fell when better hats from Italy returned to the English market. By 1834, "the price of plait had fallen . . . to 20 per cent. of the price at the beginning of the century."[35]

Compounding the hardship stemming from the irregularity of trade was the insidious influence of seasonal demand. The bonnet industry inevitably slowed during winter months, though some plait could then be sold to basket makers and producers of other straw products. The winds of fashion were more difficult to predict. "The size of the bonnet was important," a historian of the craft pointed out, "for an increase of only two inches in the size of the ridiculously small bonnets worn in the middle of the [eighteenth] century would have required twice as much plait." Straw plaiters simply fell victim to all of these variables, and available work and wage rates fluctuated mercilessly, ranging anywhere from 6s. or 10s. to only 2s. 6d. a week.[36]

Subject to the same drawbacks associated with the clothing trades, button making also suffered dramatic fluctuations according to changes in style. With the growth of horn and pearl button manufacturing, covering buttons with cloth grew less and less remunerative after the first quarter of the nineteenth century. "Probably no article in extensive demand is more subject to the caprices of fashion than buttons," wrote one trade journal. "They not only undergo frequent changes in size and form, but also in material." Buttonmakers in the south of England surrendered their place to manufacturers elsewhere. Whereas a woman might have earned between 6s. and 7s. a week in the 1790s, by the 1830s, her earnings were as low as 2s. 6d. in some places, with only the highest levels reaching 6s. In 1843, average wages were no better: "a young woman, with her hands clean, and constantly employed" made 3s. a week, and "a girl of nine or ten, on an average not more than 1s. a week."[37]

The dual impact of the public perception of degradation and economic fluctuations trapped women in cottage industries in a circular bind. Exploiting these factors were middlemen, who made considerable profits at the expense of women workers through wage cutting and payment in kind. By transforming part of the payments into materials, middlemen were able to devalue the worker's labor by inflating the value of the materials beyond their actual worth. Payment in kind, often in the form of bread and candles, almost always worked to the disadvantage of the worker, for the goods she received in exchange for her work were valued at far more than their market price; in some cases, the goods were of poor quality or short of weight. Such payment also gave women less flexibility in obtaining the food, clothing, and other necessities that they required.[38]

Until middlemen began to enter the trade in the 1780s, straw plaiters enjoyed relatively more independence than button makers. Women obtained straw directly from farmers and carried the finished plait to local markets to obtain the best price. The expansion of plaiting far into the countryside, however, meant that some women had to sacrifice a day of work in order to attend market; in addition, many were reluctant to ply their trade by themselves. With the emergence of a flourishing hat trade in the late eighteenth century, mediated arrangements displaced these older methods of dealing in plait. Enticed by the promising London market, suppliers bought plait from country women and transported the material to urban hatters. Factors also joined in, buying raw straw from farmers and selling it to plaiters in sorted bundles, or buying and distributing bleached and dyed straw. The activity of so many middlemen marked the proletarianization of straw plaiters. To the poor local women involved in the industry, the plait dealer often appeared as the "sophisticated traveller from another world." They were in no position to challenge his terms or circumvent his system. At the behest of dealers or factors, they now worked for wages that seemed beyond their control.[39]

A new form of lace making began with the advent of Thomas Taylor's point-net machine in the 1770s. Far from diminishing the availability of outwork, Taylor's machine gave employment to an army of "finishers" who hemmed and stitched pieces of the lace at home. Following the invention of the "bobbin-net" machine in 1808 and the expansion of the trade by the 1820s, female employment in mending, "running," "scalloping," and embroidering spread throughout the East Midlands. Machine-made lace outstripped the bone and pillow lace industries of the South; their decline was nearly complete by the 1830s, though they enjoyed a brief second life as a luxury industry of the mid-Victorian period.[40] The system that evolved from the introduction of technology multiplied the number of middlemen (which included some women) involved in putting out work. Usually a mistress employed several young women, sometimes in her own house, but often in villages scattered about the area. These women, in turn, might hand out work to their children and neighboring "young persons."[41] By the mid nineteenth century, lace often passed through the hands of as many as three different mistresses, thus reducing the payment of the actual workers to greatly diminished sums.[42]

Few lace runners could find redress for low wages or seek work elsewhere. Many were poor women with several young children—and sometimes an unemployed husband—at home; others were young and relatively defenseless. "Those from the age of 12 to 18 or 20 suffer most by the system," reported one girl, "because they are most dependent on their work to obtain their living, and also because they frequently are paid by bread and candles, instead of money."[43] Mistresses were usually local women little better off than their underlings, and they countered any dissatisfaction among the lace workers with intimidation by threats or simple dismissal.[44]

The historical record nevertheless yields the occasional incident of organization and protest, and in one outstanding case in 1842, it was the mistresses who came under attack by women workers. Lace runners in Nottingham organized a turnout in protest against the unfair practices in distribution and payment. In a parliamentary inquiry into abuses in the trade, a leaflet distributed by the organizers came to light:

Sisters,

On Monday last, a meeting was held, in the Democratic Chapel, Rice's-place, Nottingham, to consider the best means of putting an end to the present injustice practised towards you, by those who call themselves mistresses;

you are well aware, that they are in the constant habit of going round to the warehouses taking out nearly all the work, and dealing it out to you, at what price they think proper to give; that you are not only obliged to take work from what are called "second-handed mistresses," but also from "third-handed ones;" that in consequence of this method of giving out work, the lace-runners in many cases receive for their work not more than one-half the original price, the mistresses reserving to themselves the remainder for that most useful of all purposes, walking with your work to the warehouse! . . . . no wonder that misery enters our dwellings—that we are in the depth of poverty, that our children are crying for bread, while there is a swarm of locusts hovering between us and the manufacturers, ready to devour one-half of our hire, it is not enough, that we have to compete with machines which, in many cases, supersedes needle-work; but are also robbed in the manner described above: is this state of things to exist? . . . . The Committee whom you appointed to manage your affairs, have agreed that there shall be a turn-out on Monday next, against this most unjust of practices, and we trust that the lace-runners will be at their post and show their oppressors, "that their occupation is gone."[45]

The lace runners attempted to engage the support of the manufacturers, as well as "the male portion of society," but their efforts came to nothing in a context in which most industry was unregulated, and most regulations were unenforced.[46]

III

Cottage industries frequently grew up in localities free from the rigid control of large landowners, and thus they gave rise to unconstrained economic and political behavior. A staunch sense of independence, often remarked upon by contemporaries, remained central to the social world of laborers in cottage industries. Lace makers in Devon acknowledged the distinctiveness of their circumstances:

> The people of Beer are a good deal cut off from all other neighbourhoods, and have "no gentry among them," one woman explained. "The men are fishermen, and, if they are not misrepresented, are all smugglers . . . . all the married women, as well as the girls, work [at lace making] at home, when not taken up with "tending the house."[47]

Cottagers' work arrangements left them free to determine their own pace of work and encouraged attitudes that seemed insubordinate to contemporaries. "Working often in their own cottages, owning or hiring their own tools, usually working for small employers, frequently working irregular hours and at more than one job, they . . . escaped from the social controls of the manorial village and were not yet subject to the discipline of factory labor." Acutely aware of local animosities and class tensions, independent cottagers were free to express dissatisfaction with economic and legal injustices. Ultimately, E. P. Thompson has argued, these people populated the crowds of protesters and rioters in the eighteenth century.[48]

Workers in cottage industry also enjoyed more freedom in their social and sexual behavior. In "open parishes," populations of poor people could grow unchecked, as the number of cottages and the immigration of laborers were not restricted by landlords. "Insofar as earnings, not property, became the pre-requisite for family formation and marriage," cottagers wed more freely and at younger ages. The industrialization of the cottage economy may in fact have been responsible for the declining age of marriage for women, from twenty-six to about twenty-three, during the eighteenth century.[49] And with this trend came a higher rate of fertility, as women spent more of their childbearing years within marriage and consequently had more children. Research on proto-industrialization has linked a growing population to the presence of cottage industry.[50]

Cottagers followed their own customs and culture, jettisoning institutional strictures and elite practices. The wages of cottage industry freed young people from parental authority, particularly with regard to courtship and marriage. Straw plaiters sometimes planned and carried out marriages without parental consent or formal betrothal. If they were able to save, young women enjoyed considerable independence. As one woman recalled from her own youth in a plaiting district, a girl could simply declare her intentions and draw her money from the bank. "We're both a goin' to draw out," asserted one beau, "and we're goin' to be married on the plait money. Ain't we, Mary."[51]

For cottagers outside elite culture, weddings were public occasions that recognized the couple's place in and need for the laboring community. Cottagers developed the custom of a "bidding wedding," which "revived and extended the old traditions of giving" while discarding all traces of paternalistic ritual. The marrying couple would hire a local bard (a "bidder") who would travel about the countryside announcing their wedding and requesting gifts, which would endow the newlyweds with the essentials they lacked. In a locality of Yorkshire, the custom acknowledged the contribution of the industrious female to the prosperity of the marriage: bidding took the form of carrying the bride or bride-to-be, posed as a spinner, on a wagon through the village. Friends responded by placing gifts of furniture and other necessities upon the wagon. At a time when elites were reducing the size of their weddings, making them more private affairs, "plebeians expanded theirs, simultaneously constructing a system of mutual giving that enabled many to marry who would otherwise not be able to do so."[52] The fragile economic base of cottage industry sustained popular practices that promoted an awareness of community and solidarity.

For women, cottage industry offered a relatively independent means of earning a living. Where domestic service and agricultural labor constituted the most common forms of female employment, women found greater freedom in cottage industry. They could migrate to nearby villages in order to live and work together, combining earnings in order to avoid dependency upon others, including the parish. This sense of independence may be the reason for lace makers' practice of celebrating St.

Katherine's Day, which commemorated their own wage-earning power, symbolized by Katherine of Alexandria, the patron saint of spinsters.[53] Complaints of their disrespectful behavior were commonplace. Encountering straw plaiting in Hertfordshire in 1804, Arthur Young railed, "It makes the poor saucy, and no servants can be procured, or any field work done where this manufacture establishes itself."[54]

That laboring women should escape the salutary influence of deferential relations particularly irked contemporaries, so much so that the industriousness of these women completely eluded middle-class observers. Well into the nineteenth century, many critics commented only on their apparent ignorance of housekeeping and child minding and their lack of manners. "They prefer plaiting, even . . . when the trade is so low, to the restraints of service," a parliamentary inquiry reported; "and having an extreme fondness for dress, they no doubt often resort to prostitution as a means of adding to their scanty earnings; and this they could not readily pursue in service."[55] Not even the more genteel trade of lace making was spared these same aspersions. "Many persons have informed me," one account went, "that the girls brought up to this business [of lace making] are helpless, and good for nothing else; that they earn so much, if good hands, that they will attempt nothing else, not even to wash their own linen."[56]

Nevertheless, their significance as wage earners seems to have endowed women cottagers with a wider range of roles and possibly a greater importance within their communities. The fact that women in cottage industry played a vital part in providing for their families impinged upon the particular form their consciousness took. Visible evidence of this mentality surfaced at times in the form of political action. In 1811, the female lace makers of Loughborough joined in the general unrest of Luddite activity by agitating for higher payments for their work. "A Spirit of Combination to dictate to their Employers, and to raise the price of their Wages, has within these few days shown itself among the *Women* who are employed in what we call *running Lace*," wrote a local magistrate in a handbill. "Meetings have been called and emissaries sent into all the neighbouring Towns and Villages to unite, and to collect Money for their Purpose."[57] The historical record falls silent following the magistrate's handbill; perhaps the women, who with girls and children numbered some twenty thousand throughout the entire Midlands area, were unable to muster forces among such a dispersed body of workers. Much Luddite activity was not only carefully (and secretly) arranged, but noctural as well, conditions that easily might have excluded women. The handbill nevertheless suggests that some effort at collective action did take place among domestic outworkers. It is possible that more careful research might reveal just how extensive such attempts were.

This form of protest often sprang from women's experience as material providers and care givers within laboring families. Conceived more generally, such action displayed what Temma Kaplan has called "female consciousness." Emerging "from the division of labor by sex, which assigns women the responsibility of preserving life," such consciousness results in a "collective drive" to secure rights associated with these obligations. While enhancing the power of women within the laboring community, women's work in cottage industry also may have propelled women into situations where political and social struggles were taking place.[58]

In 1835, for example, the introduction of the controversial New Poor Law at Ampthill, a plaiting district in Bedfordshire, provoked demonstrations and resistance to new methods of poor relief. The notable presence of poor women, many undoubtedly plaiters, testified to their determined commitment to the financial well-being of their households. An imposing crowd of women mobbed the new relieving officer as he arrived at the village of Lidlington, forcing him into a corner of the parish overseer's house and vowing "they would not have bread instead of money." The women freed the officer only after he turned over £3 16s, which he had desperately borrowed from the parish overseer. Protests against the new regulations continued the next day; five men and four women were taken into custody immediately, and eventually nineteen in all were arrested. The threat to the plaiters' fragile strategy for survival had warranted full-scale resistance to the interference of local poor law officers.[59]

A more sustained assertion of laboring women's interests occurred within the Methodist sects in the early nineteenth century. Though in no way an organization of labor, Methodist sectarianism offered cottagers the opportunity to form domestic-based religious societies that, drawing on plebeian customs and values, defended people against economic insecurity and hardship. Their lives disrupted by industrialization and the commercialization of agriculture, the laboring poor found in this form of "cottage religion" a means of preserving elements of popular culture while contradicting established religion. Women assumed a natural place as leaders within these groups. In 1812, Primitive Methodism grounded its separation from the parent body of Wesleyan Methodism on the right to certain practices, including female preaching, considered inappropriate by Wesleyans concerned with respectability. Following the Primitives were Bible Christians and others; all told, hundreds of laboring women rose to the fore during the first half of the nineteenth century to organize and lead societies. Here women could express a form of "female consciousness" directly related to their working lives and familial roles.

Available in towns as well as the countryside, outwork also enabled unmarried preachers to support themselves. Elizabeth Tomlinson, the aunt of George Eliot and the fictionalized subject of *Adam Bede*, took in lacework in Nottingham as a young woman.

> I used to work at my mending of lace until two or three o'clock in the morning, generally that I might be furnished with money and clothes, that I might not be a burden to any one; and this I did with great pleasure. I believe I had one of the best places in the town, I had very good wages and could earn fourteen or fifteen shillings a week, and did not as some may

have supposed, go out for loaves and fishes, nor for a husband, as I then believed I never should be married to any one. No, "Christ was all the world to me, and all my heart was love."[60]

Domestic industry at night freed Tomlinson to devote the remainder of her waking hours to religious activity: leading prayer groups, visiting the sick and infirm, and traveling to outlying villages to organize societies. Thus the female preacher figured as a helpmeet and inspiration to those who struggled in impoverished circumstances, whether single or married, young or old. For female followers plying the needle or laboring in some other industry, the tenets of Methodist sectarianism reaffirmed essential familial and neighborly cooperation. Cottage religion flourished where the theology of domestic security and plebeian independence coalesced with the consciousness of women at the fulcrum of their household economies.[61]

Often flourishing in areas where the poor enjoyed some political and social freedom, cottage industry fostered a vital plebeian culture. Within this milieu, laboring women were active, vocal participants who provided for their families and communities and defended their rights as workers and as citizens. Demonstrations of plebeian culture would remain the clearest evidence of the importance of women within this outcast world.

IV

As each year brought at least one round of unemployment for many male wage earners, women working in cottage industries at times supported their households. In the fishing village of Beer in Devon, women were, in effect, seasonal breadwinners. As a lace mistress pointed out, "the men are . . . out of employment in the winter, when the women and children 'support the town.'"[62] As the building trades, shipping, and other occupations experienced distress in the 1840s, many women supported their families by lace making or straw plaiting. One lace drawer reported that her husband, a joiner, had "not had more than half work for two months"; another was the wife of a "jobbing labourer . . . now out of work."[63]

Paradoxically, these circumstances led contemporaries to pass moral judgement upon the condition of laboring families, including the women who worked in domestic industries. As work in agriculture declined at midcentury, many women and children plaited to support male laborers. Even men with steady jobs earned little enough to make strawplaiting attractive to their wives and daughters. "A well-ordered family [could] obtain as much or more than the husband who [was] at work on [a] neighbouring farm," an observer commented in 1860.[64] Not surprisingly, some men abandoned agricultural work altogether, while their wives and children continued to work. This reversal of the norm drew criticism, since it appeared to indicate a declining state of morals. "[T]he men, a good many of them, make the women keep them when plait is good. Scores of men sell bonnets, plaits, and block hats, and won't go out to farm work," complained one poor law officer at Luton. "They have no shame about applying for relief, and a great many get relief who don't deserve it."[65] A gentleman made the typical association between working wives and profligate husbands:

> The women and children in past years could earn sufficient money to keep the household, while the men spent their own earnings too frequently in drink. For generations they have borne a bad character; most of them agricultural labourers, and always being in greater number than the surrounding farmers required, they have kept down the price of labour, . . . and have often to walk a distance of four or five miles to and from their work to a cottage presenting none of the features of what a home should be[.][66]

Criticism was not confined to men: as a result of their working, women were censured for their failure as homemakers: "The plaiters are untidy women, though such fine girls in dress, and often neglect their domestic duties, such as washing, mending, &c. I see on going into their cottages that they are not the tidiest people."[67] To this, a clergyman added, "A large number of the women have illegitimate children, and some at such an early age as quite to startle even those who are at home in criminal statistics."[68] It was no coincidence that in enumerating the causes of the "low state of morals" in a Midlands parish, a parliamentary commissioner listed "the straw plait," along with "want of education" and "the great number of public houses."[69]

While at times enhancing their power within families and communities, women's work in cottage industry ultimately damaged their social status and position within the work force. Their experiences in the late eighteenth and early nineteenth century solidified their association with the lowest forms of work and the lowest pay in the industrial economy. The inescapable identity of "secondary wage-earners within their families" forced women to adopt the same role in the modern industrial work force outside the home. In the Leicester hosiery industry, as Nancy Grey Osterud has demonstrated, when women's work moved from the cottage to the factory in the 1870s, their wages remained at the same low levels, "even though mechanization had multiplied their productivity."

> Both the nature of their labour and the timing of their employment were determined by their families' needs; paid labour was subsumed by their domestic role, rather than being independent of it. . . . Their employment in gender-segregated industries and gender-typed jobs divided them from working men. It allowed the development of wage differentials, and guaranteed that those would be maintained even when the nature and location of women's work was changing.

Women never gained entrance to high-paying jobs occupied by men, but instead, moved into wholly new positions, at low wages, created by changes in technology.[70]

7

Women in the Age of Malthus:
Political Economy
and the Feminization
of the Female Worker

. . . [L]et your beneficence be like the sun at noon day, that warms every heart; . . . let the fatherless and widow be amply provided for, and deemed, as they really are, a part of our wealth; and let every poor man that has a numerous family be looked upon as a great benefactor to his country; and all that have more children than they can comfortably maintain, be allowed sufficient to assist them.

[Anon.], *Populousness with Oeconomy* (1759)

To remove the wants of the lower classes of society is indeed an arduous task. The truth is that the pressure of distress on this part of a community is an evil so deeply seated that no human ingenuity can reach it.

T. R. Malthus, *Essay on the Principle of Population* (1798)

We have seen how a history of women workers in the industrial age must take into account not only incidents of technological change, but also new understandings of women and work produced by such shifts. Alterations in attitudes toward poor women interacted with the decline in the material welfare of the laboring classes; views of women's customary work in agriculture informed the introduction of new methods in farming; a discussion of current perceptions of women workers accompanied innovation in spinning technology and the reorganization of produc ion in

128

factories and domestic settings. While new discourses about female labor could not by themselves transform the position of women in industrial society, they informed and legitimated the processes taking place.

In order to recover another important set of discussions ushering working women into industrial society at the beginning of the nineteenth century, we must turn to theories of political economy. Circulating within learned circles and derived largely from the French and Scottish Enlightenments, this body of knowledge contributed many new ideas to the continuing evaluation of the role of women in industrial production. The term "political economy" itself originated in the 1760s in the writings of François Quesnay and the French Physiocrats, a group of economic theorists in favor of free trade. This new field of inquiry involved the comprehensive study of the economy and the state, informed by related branches of moral and scientific philosophy. Its concerns were thus wide-ranging: concepts of labor, value, the organization of production, the role of mechanization, and the questions raised by wealth and poverty were all subjects addressed by diverse theorists. Popularized through the many learned societies and periodical publications, the ideas of political economists were influential in the recasting of women workers in the industrial economy.[1]

Previous views of laboring women, largely charitable and tolerant, belonged to an older, corporate notion of society. For at least the first half of the eighteenth century, public opinion generally supported such attitudes and saw the vast ranks of the laboring poor, including women, as a potential source of national prosperity. But these views receded in the face of an individualistic perspective advanced by political economists. Advocating the emancipation of economic activity from protective statutes, theories of "classical economics" promoted enterprising individualism as a rationale for economic and social life. Laborers should be free and independent; responsible for their own well-being, they could reap the benefits of the economic system or face the consequences of their failure to do so. Codifying notions that were just coming into being, theories presumed that the "worker" was male and, as a breadwinner, supported a wife and children at home. This separation of public and domestic spheres, which effectively assigned women to nonproductive roles, would form a cornerstone of liberal economic theory of the nineteenth century.

This was precisely the time when public opinion castigated many laboring women, rendered unemployed by recent developments, for their idleness. In his travels through parts of rural England, Arthur Young claimed, "Idleness is the chief employment of women and children," who "drink tea and fly to the parish for relief;" inquiring "what was the employment of the laborer's wives and children" in a district of the South, Young reported that a small farmer replied, "Drinking tea."[2] Displaced from some employments and considered unsuitable for others, they were now responsible for their own predicament. Viewing them as morally lax, ignorant, or idle, popular opinion identified them with problems of poverty rather than habits of industry, and failed to see how recent events had left them little alternative.

Despite their former economic importance, laboring women were not perceived as displaced members of the work force; more likely, they were measured by the yardstick of prosperous housewifery now projected as the province of middle-class women. "Whoever is at all acquainted with the actual state of poor families," wrote one landowner, "must often have had occasion to observe how greatly the internal comfort and well being of such families depend upon the industry, skill, good management, and economical habits of the wife[.]"[3] Whereas older tracts would have praised the productivity of the laboring woman, the new attitude emphasized the domestic failures of the lower-class wife and mother. "[C]onsiderable earnings often prove insufficient for the comfortable support of a family merely because she knows not how to make the most of such articles as she has the management of," this writer argued. (The noted surveyor of the poor, Sir Frederic Eden, had also resorted to this explanation for widespread poverty and went to the length of supplying suitable recipes for laboring women in his three-volume study.) Critics associated such shortcomings in laboring women with more general moral deficiencies—in this case, profligacy and ignorance:

> It too often happens, that the cottager marries a young girl, who, perhaps, he has first seduced, and who, having never been at service, knows little more than how to manage her wheel; and, consequently, is very ill qualified to fulfill the duties of that station which she has undertaken.[4]

Managing the wheel, now a peripheral activity, was supposed to give way to the more important "duties" of creating a respectable household—a mixture of "habits of modesty and industry," "principles of religion," and "all those arts" of servants, wives, and mothers.[5] Unremunerative domestic prescriptions left little room for discussion of their role in the larger economy.

I

Adam Smith and his Scottish contemporaries, recognized later as founders of the British school of political economy, devoted much attention to problems of unemployment and indigence. Smith's famous declaration against the injustice of poverty resounded for generations after the appearance of *The Wealth of Nations.* "No society can surely be flourishing and happy," he averred, "of which the far greater part of the members are poor and miserable. It is but equity, besides," he added, "that they who feed, cloath and lodge the whole body of the people, should have such a share of the produce of their own labor as to be themselves tolerably well fed, cloathed and lodged."[6] Before a coherent movement materialized in the first quarter of the nineteenth century, the study of political economy contributed a unique combination of ideas to the debate on poverty: a belief in liberal individualism coupled with a moral commitment to the poor.[7]

In early writings on political economy, a sense of duty to the larger polity superceded the interests of the individual. According to Scottish philosophers, the study of political economy should lead to the optimal organization of the production of wealth for the entire community. As James Steuart pointed out,

> The principal object of this science is to secure a certain fund of subsistence for all the inhabitants, to obviate every circumstance which may render it precarious; to provide every thing necessary for supplying the wants of the society, and to employ the inhabitants (supposing them to be free-men) in such a manner as naturally to create the reciprocal relations and dependencies between them, so as to make their several interests lead them to supply one another with their reciprocal wants.[8]

Steuart's expectation of a "natural" reciprocity between people resembled Smith's "invisible hand," a mechanism that expected individuals to meet each other's economic needs through ordinary interaction. Steuart left far less to the free market system than Smith later did in *The Wealth of Nations*, permitting some intervention by a paternalist state. But both writers recognized the definitive role of human relationships, in all their diversity, in determining how subsistence was achieved. These "dependencies," as Steuart called them, were key to admitting the world of customary work carried on by laboring women.[9]

So it is not surprising that Adam Smith's writings acknowledged the contribution of women laborers to the eighteenth-century economy. From his native Scotland, Smith gained an appreciation for the household economy of the independent laboring household and its female laborers. Though not always uncritical, Smith nevertheless understood the importance of native cottage industries to the laboring classes. Throughout the *Wealth of Nations*, he makes reference to the presence of women workers in essential domestic industries: for example, the unremunerative but incessant efforts of female spinners and knitters ("they earn but a very scanty subsistence, who endeavour to get their whole livelihood by either of those trades"[10]), the clothing industries, button making, and (though women are not mentioned as laborers) his cherished pin making industry. Alert to their industriousness, Smith was not adverse to laboring women's fecundity—an increasing population, along with wages, was "the liberal reward of labor." In fact, Smith adhered to the older positive view of the benefits of a large population, and though he obviously understood the strain that large numbers might have on subsistence, he came to a conclusion very different from the later one of Malthus. "To complain of [increasing population], is to lament over the necessary effect and cause of the greatest public prosperity," he argued. Under conditions of a "progressive state," subsistence needs would be automatically taken care of.[11]

Optimism like Smith's dissipated over the course of the eighteenth century, facilitated, in part, by theories akin to his own. The unqualified charity inspired by subsistence crises became a thing of the past, as a rise in agricultural productivity in the late seventeenth century eradicated the threat of famine. Thus a time of plenty "rendered moot the question of the poor man's right to bread in times of dearth" and paved the way for the ethos of a profit-oriented market economy.[12] The absence of serious food shortages facilitated efforts to commercialize the grain trade and enclose farmlands; these were the very policies that removed protective regulations from the price of bread and eliminated common land and use rights. Until the hard times of the 1750s, popular resistance and public debate did not modify the course of government legislation. Critics of the poor laws had always advocated a form of free individualism over state assistance, and by the late eighteenth century, arguments for what amounted to laissez-faire policy rested on a long legacy.

Historians have highlighted the paradox that in spite of rising national wealth in the eighteenth century, "a new bitterness superseded the old sense of responsibility towards the Poor." "[T]he system of just prices, fair wages and adequate poor relief," all linked to time-honored notions of community and benevolence, "began to unravel remarkably quickly" during the final decades of the [eighteenth] century."[13] In addition to the withdrawal of statutes regulating bread and apprenticeship, poor law legislation reflected an intransigent mood. A law of 1722, denying relief to the poor who would not enter workhouses, established a punitive strategy for dealing with able-bodied paupers in the following era of unprecedented underemployment. Poor rates continued their upward climb, in large part because of the decline in the practice of living in among agricultural laborers and the effects of enclosures. After the war years of midcentury, increasing animus was visible in the debate over the price of provisions during the late 1760s and early 1770s. Population pressures only added to the problems of feeding and employing the displaced laboring poor. But few contemporaries understood these root causes of distress. Certainly by the troubled times of the 1790s, the tide had turned against the indigent.[14] The "sharp curtailment of the influence of traditional benevolence" as well as the "transformation of the meaning of benevolence" became explicit with the appearance of Malthus's dire commentary in 1798.[15]

Laboring women stood to lose their claim to respect from this erosion of public sympathy for the poor. More often subject to idleness, more likely to seek aid without being able to work for it, women represented much of what critics denounced in the behavior of the poor. With their reputation for unreliability and immorality already part of a public discourse about women of the lower classes, the issues of improvident marriages and numerous offspring could only ring down further charges of irresponsibility. One writer recognized the pessimism of the ordinary Briton with regard to the future prospects of married life for the poor:

When a minister marries a couple, tho' but a poor couple, he rightly prays "that they may be fruitful in procreation of children." But many of the Parishioners pray for the very contrary, and perhaps complain of him for marrying Persons, that, should they have a family of Children, might likely become chargeable.[16]

In matters pertaining to reproduction and "excess population," laboring women shouldered the blame. Though chargeable offspring belonged to both father and mother, the continuing furor over the settlement laws revealed how failed romantic liaisons discredited laboring women; most persons ordered removed from parishes were pregnant laboring women. As their productive powers receded from view, they became linked more closely to their reproductive roles.[17]

Several influential spokesmen of the eighteenth century endorsed arguments for encouraging—or forcing—the poor to stand on their own. "The distresses of the Poor," averred Defoe in his scathing diatribe, *Giving Alms No Charity* (1704), "are either owing to infirmities merely providential, as sickness and old age, or to the improvidence of the laboring classes."[18] Thomas Alcock's early attack on the poor laws in 1752 opened the way for more widespread and unapologetic criticism of the poor.[19] Even more forceful were the arguments of another clergyman, Joseph Townsend, whose *Dissertation on the Poor Laws* (1786) constituted an unprecedented and "unqualified invective" against the system of publicly relieving the poor. Anticipating Malthus's argument that government provisions "promote the evils they mean to remedy," Townsend castigated the poor laws for undermining the incentive of the poor.[20] "Hope and fear are the springs of industry," he stated pithily. "It is the part of a good politician to strengthen these: but our laws weaken the one and destroy the other." As striking was his explicit acknowledgment of class differences in discussing the problem of human motivation:

The poor know little of the motives which stimulate the higher ranks to action—pride, honour, and ambition. In general it is only hunger which can spur and goad them on to labour; .... hunger is not only a peaceable, silent, unremitted pressure, but, as the most natural motive to industry and labour, it calls forth the most powerful exertions.[21]

Incentive differed according to rank. Townsend anticipated Malthus in his depiction of the poor as lacking the mental capacities that made individualism a viable motor of economic and social progress. Inhabiting a world closer to nature, the poor thus responded to a biological stimulus to work—the physical need to eat. This connection between the lower classes and nature had great potential as a subject of scientific discussion and would reappear in the arguments of Malthus a little over a decade later.[22]

During the 1790s, the urgency of published debate over poverty reached a new pitch. Bad harvests, economic dislocation, and the effects of war with France, continuing through the first two decades of the nineteenth century, generated some of the most famous tracts of the age. A legion of writers offered as many different solutions. Most accounts display a remarkable familiarity with the intricacies of poor relief and show how public opinion and practical experience informed one another in early industrial England. Quite often, the contentious authors of tracts were also lawmakers, local magistrates, or religious leaders working to combat the evils of poverty from day to day. For this reason, the public forum provides insight into the mentality of the times, as it both reflected and shaped the context in which laborers found employment or public relief from poverty.[23]

Thomas Ruggles's *History of the Poor* (1793), the Rev. David Davies's *Case of the Labourers in Husbandry Stated and Considered* (1795), and Sir Frederic Morton Eden's *State of the Poor* (1797), to name the most renowned, were published widely and relatively inexpensively. Arthur Young's *Annals of Agriculture*, a monthly serial that enjoyed a wide audience, ran innumerable pieces bearing similar titles. And a flurry of pamphlets on every dimension of poverty and employment for the poor provoked continued controversy. In indirect dialogue with these popular publications, theoretical discussion appeared after 1800 in new elite periodicals such as the *Edinburgh Review* and the *Quarterly Review*.

Adam Smith's thoughts on poverty, rooted in earlier notions of the public sphere, cannot stand as typical of late eighteenth-century viewpoints. More representative were the views of Sir Frederic Morton Eden, who applied new economic theories to plans for the poor more consistently than Adam Smith himself.[24] Inveighing against projects for employing the indigent, Eden eschewed such works as interference with the natural demands of the market. In Eden, we can detect the dominant strain in Smith's legacy: an optimism in the joint operation of self-interest and liberty in economic life. Predictably, Eden favored improvements in agriculture, especially enclosure, and criticized the poor for impeding innovation that promised a greater production of wealth. Given his faith in the invisible prod of self-interest, he reserved his greatest enmity for the harmful effects of the Poor Law on the incentive of the laboring poor. "A legal provision for the Poor," he contended, ". . . seems to check that emulative spirit of exertion, which the want of necessities, or the no less powerful demand for the superfluities, of life gives birth to: for it assures a man that, whether he may have been indolent, improvident, prodigal, or vicious, he shall never suffer want." Even as Eden's work appeared in print, parish officers at Speenhamland enacted a plan to supplement low wages with payments. But criticism of the Poor Law was growing. Eden's argument was a testimony to the impending triumph of the ideal of individualism over a corporate vision of society.[25]

Though not directly addressing the subject, Thomas Robert Malthus's *Essay on Population* (1798) inevitably diminished the public good will offered to laboring women. Its articulation of common perceptions helped to crystalize latent hostility toward the poor and the supportive policies that offered them relief. Its power to shape the terms of discussion went unrivaled; an admirer of the *Essay* claimed that there was "scarcely any other instance in the history of the world of so important a revolution affected in public opinion, within the compass of a single life and by a single mind."[26] Though surprisingly unoriginal in its exposition of current opinions toward the poor, the *Essay* enjoyed considerable influence owing to the baldness of its arguments and the timing of its appearance. As a rejoinder to William Godwin's radical prophecy of endless progress, Malthus sounded a blast on behalf of the enduring force of nature in the new world of the French and industrial revolutions.

Referring throughout to the laws of nature, Malthus identified himself as a successor to enlightened promoters of rational science. The bodily impulses of food consumption and procreation, features of the biological aspects of existence, determined the fate of humanity; this was especially true for the future of the laboring poor.[27] Malthus may have woefully misjudged the potential of industrial developments affecting the economic life of his nation, but his view of the perdurable natural inclination of the lower classes was perfectly in harmony with most of his contemporaries. By joining this powerful source of legitimation to his otherwise typical criticisms of the poor, Malthus was able to mount a relatively unassailable argument.[28]

Women of the laboring class are present in the *Essay on Population* in passing references to their primary function as wives and, more significantly, mothers. All females are objects of choice in the selection of marriage partners—a selection carried out by men. In his discussion of "virtuous attachment," Malthus makes "early attachment to one woman" the means to producing many offspring; theoretically, all women, regardless of class, contribute to "a constant effort towards an increase of population."[29] But in Malthus's account, women of the higher classes had fewer children owing to the practice of postponing marriage until prospective husbands had attained a sufficient livelihood. By marrying early and giving birth to numerous children, members of the lowest classes exercised no such restraint. Malthus called attention to this fact, preparing the ground for a discussion of the laboring woman's reproductive activity and dependence.

Malthus deliberately joined the century-old debate over the benefits of a large population and thus revised the context in which women laborers would be judged. Gone was the celebration of a limitless army of laborers producing wealth; without this standard of prosperity, women of the laboring classes no longer appeared as potentially beneficial to the economic well-being of the nation. "The happiness of a country does not depend, absolutely, upon its poverty or its riches, upon its youth or its age, upon its being thinly or fully inhabited," he asserted, "but upon the rapidity with which it is increasing, upon the degree in which the yearly increase of food approaches to the yearly increase of an unrestricted population."[30] In the new age of Malthus, women came to be seen as more directly linked to their biological rather than their economic functions. Gone, too, were the positive attributes of the industrious female noted by Smith and others, which had entitled laboring women to customary benevolence. An emphasis on the natural world enabled Malthus and later political economists to break away from the moral philosophy—and the humanity—of Scottish political economy.[31]

The behavior of laboring women was now perceived as proof of the domination of nature over their fragile social identity. Since improvident marriages and numerous offspring now seemed to lie at the very heart of the problems of the day, laboring women were accordingly vulnerable to charges of irresponsibility. "[I]t seems difficult to suppose that a labourer's wife who has six children," Malthus comments in a famous passage, "and who is sometimes in absolute want of bread, should be able always to give them the food and attention necessary to support life. The sons and daughters of peasants will not be found such rosy cherubs in real life as they are described to be in romances."[32] That many poor children fell sick and died was not surprising, but in this instance, Malthus implied that their lower-class mothers were responsible. In a later summary view of the *Essay*, Malthus listed "bad nursing" as one of the positive checks to population.[33] Rubbing away the sentimental coloring of customary depictions of the laboring classes, Malthus reconstituted a portrait that precluded sympathy: the lower-class woman, subjected to the inevitable consequences of her reproductive activity in the face of poverty, was inevitably a failure as a mother.

Excluded from a productive role in society, the laboring woman compared unfavorably with the model of woman as mother taking shape from discussions about the middle ranks. Like theorists who had advocated a large population for the good of the nation, Malthus conceived of motherhood in terms of its service to the wider society. But unlike his predecessors, Malthus believed in judicious restraint (a later century would call the tendency "bourgeois") and attentiveness as important aspects of maternal behavior. Malthus undoubtedly knew of the current antipathy toward lower-class wet nurses, generated to improve the child-rearing practices of the aristocracy in the eighteenth century. A sharper sense of the importance of social distinctions challenged the use of wet nurses. Medical expertise concurred with growing popular opinion in criticizing the practice of employing poor women to suckle the children of the wealthy, believing that exposure to poor women posed the threat of disease and infection.[34] But in addition to dangers pertaining to health, offspring might suffer neglect at the hands of a common mother. As Lady Sarah Pennington pointed out, it was "almost impossible to make the lower class of people who are hired to take the care of children, believe the utility of this uncommon method" of a "mother's close inspection."[35] A good mother was both civilized and devoted. Malthus's writings reflected similar views, which were part of a new ideology of domesticity coming into being in the eighteenth century.[36]

In depicting bifurcated roles of mother-as-nurturer and father-as-provider, the *Essay* furnishes one of the clearest and earliest expositions of the nineteenth-century notion of separate spheres. Central to this concept was the male breadwinner, who, according to Malthus, was the only wage earner in the laboring family. A vivid illustration of the male's economic centrality appears in Malthus's account of the deliberations the laborer must make before deciding to marry:

> The labourer who earns eighteen pence a day and lives with some degree of comfort as a single man, will hesitate a little before he divides that pittance among four or five, which seems to be just sufficient for one. Harder fare and harder labour he would submit to for the sake of living with the woman that he loves, but he must feel conscious, if he thinks at all, that should he have a large family, and any ill luck whatever, no degree of frugality, no possible exertion of his manual strength could preserve him from the heart-rending sensation of seeing his children starve, or of forfeiting his independence, and being obliged to the parish for their support.[37]

Malthus's model of male attitudes and gender relations within the laboring classes was patently middle class. The ideal of the male breadwinner had emerged as a reality for well-to-do families during the eighteenth century, as women withdrew from family businesses and other commercial activities.[38] This process, at least for Malthus, was carried out in a spirit of chivalry. Malthus believed that by emulating the middle classes and postponing marriage, laborers could achieve similar results: a higher standard of living and a more civilized existence. The realities of laboring life—the need for female labor and the propensity of the economy to exploit it—were nowhere in evidence in his calculations.[39]

Malthus was not alone in believing that the laboring classes should privilege the male wage earner. A common assumption was that laboring women were (or should be) occupied in caring for young children; if they earned anything, such income was evidently too small to constitute a significant part of the total family income.[40] It was, after all, a fact that male wages were often twice that of women in most occupations, and this alone can account for the hierarchy imposed on male and female earnings in contemporary thinking. Yet earlier poor law provision had reflected a different understanding of laboring life: examining each case individually, the parish allocated assistance according to family need, thus acknowledging the earnings of mothers and children. Late seventeenth- and early eighteenth-century discussions reveal a wide category of wage earner, noting relief given to "parents over burthen'd with children," the wage earner who is "man or woman," and the more general category of family to designate the unit of income. The notion of a dominant male breadwinner seems to have emerged within later debates over "able-bodied" laborers, as opposed to the "poor and impotent."[41]

The development of wage theory, growing out of the early eighteenth-century controversy over the level of the British laborer's wages, gave a more discernible shape to the theoretical male breadwinner. The dispute over a tax on salt in 1732 revealed a typical presentation of the view: "Every workman must be able to maintain himself and his family."[42] Philanthropists relied upon a similar assumption: they believed that the role of *pater familias* inspired the male laborer to work harder from a sense of duty to his dependents. According to Jonas Hanway, the "laboring man, who has a *large family*" tended to work "*two, three,* or *four* hours in the day more than him that has none, and generally in a more *spirited* and *masterly* manner."[43] Another philanthropist added the love of property to the panoply of instincts that inspired the male household head:

> One great source of comfort to the poor man is, HIS WIFE AND CHILDREN, if he can but earn the means of maintaining them. Humble and insignificant abroad, he is of consequence and authority at home. . . . The poor man, poor as he is, loves to cherish the idea of PROPERTY. To talk of *my* house, *my* garden, *my* furniture, is always a theme of delight and pleasure.[44]

These views went a long way toward promoting high wages as part of the new liberal economy.[45]

Male laborers themselves helped to build a general consensus that held they were responsible for the lion's share of the household income. The notion of a male breadwinner can be traced back to the demands of early trade combinations. By presenting themselves as the only providers for their families, organized male workers legitimated their demand for the restriction of entry to their trades, for protection against imports, and for reasonable payment for their work. In explaining the reasons for the formation of Lancashire check weavers' combination in 1758, an apologist reported that a journeyman, if lucky, could earn "Four Shillings and Three Pence, for House-rent, Provisions and all other Necessaries for him, his Wife and perhaps Four or Five small Children." In his lengthy discussion of "Family" expenses, the writer never mentioned the earnings of women and children in spinning and carding.[46] Such instances give further credence to the view that the construct of a male breadwinner, far from being a "natural" arrangement, rested on multiple excisions and silences.[47]

Eighteenth-century economic writers had long since engaged in a lively debate over the question of high wages as a means to further incentive among laborers, and here, too, one finds the persistent assumption that the wage earner was exclusively male. Deriving much from Humean theories of psychology, "high-wage" advocates argued that a positive stimulus to work would be more effective than coercive measures. Their position was far more compatible with emerging beliefs in individual freedom and economic liberalism than that of "low-wage" enthusiasts. The free individual also acted as an acquisitive purchaser of goods, and his activity of getting and spending was crucial to emerging theories of classical political economy. This constituted a relatively radical position, given the liberty that was necessarily ascribed to theoretical participants in the market economy. This fact may have helped to solidify a restrictive, gendered notion of the wage earner since such freedom was seldom, if ever, associated with women.[48]

The new wage theories ascribed different psychological motivation to the worker, but like discussions about wage earning in general, they did not conceive of the individual as female. "High-wage" advocates strove to overturn earlier assumptions that posited that laborers would work only as long as it took to supply themselves with necessities. (Economists now call this apparent pattern the "leisure preference.") They instead argued that too much hardship diminished the laborer's will to toil and resulted in poor productivity and even profligacy. By definition, women became part of the burden of family responsibilities shouldered by the male worker. At worst, they were identified with the very cause of the wage earner's despondency. In his *Elements of Commerce, Politics and Finances* (1772), Thomas Mortimer offered a glimpse of this portrait of gender relations when he discussed the ill effects of hardship on the incentive of the male wage earner:

> [when a labourer is] oppressed by the combined plagues of dearness of provisions, incessant labour and low wages, . . . indifference will take place of emulation, and thus the main springs of industry will be destroyed . . . . he will carry his industry no further, than to procure [his family] temporary and partial relief; and out of the little he earns by constant labour, he will retain a reserve, to purchase the cup of oblivion, to enable him to forget, for a few hours occasionally, *the galling yoke of double bondage*, to a hard-hearted, mercenary master, and a numerous, distressed family.[49]

The identity of laboring women vanished behind the collective image of the dependent family. Though such responsibilities ennobled the philanthopists' image of the male worker, in the age of Malthus, their apparent effect was to jeopardize his standard of living.

Contemporaries had great faith in the potential of male individual incentive and autonomy, which explains the multitude of references to "independence" in the writings of Malthus and other writers on poverty. These sentiments seemed to evolve from conviction to dogma as the years of scarcity carried into the nineteenth century. Most discourses on the virtues of independence originated in the hope that laborers would relinquish their attachment to parochial support, but the issue had wider implications. In praising commerce over agriculture, Adam Smith provided strong arguments in favor of individualism over the dependent relations associated with traditional rural society. "Nothing tends so much to corrupt and enervate and debase the mind as dependency and nothing gives such noble and generous notions of probity as freedom and independency," he asserted. "Commerce is the one great preventative of this custom."[50] One can hear echoes of earlier discourses in these late eighteenth-century arguments for individual freedom. Arthur Young, a loyal adherent to Smithian views, offered his revision of the national wealth theme. "Those are the most fruitful resources of a government," he insisted, "which flow from the exuberant wealth and prosperity of individuals. Remove an obstacle of private industry you create a public resource."[51] Advocates of economic liberalism jettisoned paternalistic notions of economic regulation and social obligation that had supported the poor. This world of attachment and dependency, associated with more traditional social relations, became devalued—and even despised— by the theorists of the new industrial era.[52]

As the problem of female unemployment became more conspicuous, observers highlighted the dependency of women upon male wage earners. "I observe that for the most part, amongst us," an estateholder of Devon commented, "a family of boys chiefly, do pretty well; and where the girls have been early instructed in any manufacture that they can dispose of, and are industrious, comfort pervades the whole cottage." But when women were unemployed, they were "dead weights on the father's labour." The domestic work of women, at least according to this writer, was a decisive factor in determining the conditions of poverty. Female idleness was a source of "misery and wretchedness." New understandings of women's work, based on a notion of the male breadwinner, would be couched in similar terms of dependency and reprobation.[53]

The idea of the laboring woman as a producer apart from her family seemed to vanish from sight. Her fate was intimately associated with the declining strength of a corporate vision of society as it surrendered before a more individualistic, capitalist orientation toward labor. No longer would plans for an industrious nation include explicit discussion of harnessing the productivity of women. For the next three decades, public consideration of these problems would be shaped by the insights of a new generation of political economists. The question of what to do about laboring women, excluded from an increasing number of productive activities and repeatedly thrust into poverty, became subsumed under the larger project of creating a civilized female sex.

8

Recasting Women
in the Workshop of the World:
Middle-Class Authority
and the Female Poor

[I]t appears that those plans have been most successful, in which LADIES
have taken an active part in the arrangement and execution. Their
habits of life, and their exemption from political and professional
engagements, give them very considerable advantages, —not merely in
the detail, but in the peculiar kind of attention and interest, which
subjects of this nature require. —In one very important part, that
which concerns the education and employment of the Female Poor, it is
most obvious that very little can be done effectually or decorously,
without the intervention of their own sex.

Address to the Lady Subscribers, Society for
Bettering the Condition of the Poor (1804)

The theories of Malthus and the early political economists did not exist in
a vacuum; they arose from and informed social contexts peopled by
women and men with particular interests. How did the ideas discussed in
the previous chapter actually relate to the new industrial society as it
evolved at the turn of the century? The work of Malthus converged with
a wider effort, though not always a self-conscious one, to construct the
cultural and political authority of the middle classes. Women were very
much a part of this endeavor, especially as enlightenment ideals inspired
them to make forays into the realms of education and reform. The following chapter discusses the formative role of the nascent science of economics in shaping the values of middle-class women. Notions about

wealth, industry, and the working classes were fused to their understandings of their identities as women. As they worked out their positions in
writings and reform, middle-class women found that their relationships
to working-class women were an intrinsic part of their social universe.

While comprising divergent interests, the middle classes congealed into
an increasingly coherent group in the late eighteenth century.[1] Malthus
recognized this fact. "[A]bove all," he pointed out, the new economic
interests of the age "give a new and happier structure to society, by
increasing the proportion of the middle classes, that body on which the
liberty, public spirit and good government of every country must mainly
depend."[2] The question of the poor facilitated this process by enabling
the middle ranks to differentiate themselves from those beneath them.
Malthus believed that the middle classes followed distinct marriage and
family practices, work habits, and leisure activities. Though many might
have disagreed with Malthus's particular arguments about population,
they nevertheless shared his values and believed them suitable to the
needs of the laboring classes. As benefactors, civic and religious leaders,
and self-appointed tutors of the poor, they promoted many of the same
assumptions about work, family duty, and social behavior deemed useful
to a new industrial society.[3]

From the start, ideas about appropriate gender roles informed this
enterprise. The construction of new models of masculinity and femininity
emerged from discussions about public duties, domestic life, and social
problems. While ushering in freedom in economic life, eighteenth-century writers imposed the strictest controls within prescribed gender roles.
The growing affluence and material culture associated with late eighteenth-century capitalism generated an urgent moral imperative: the middle ranks were to take a custodial role in steering society through the
shoals of industrial capitalism. Personal relations at times assumed the
functions of public charity. As paternalism receded from the economic
arena, hierarchy and deference were reinscribed within relationships
between classes.[4]

The debate over luxury, a favorite preoccupation of eighteenth-century
English people, exposes the middle ranks' understanding of their unique
social mission. No other discussion fused so perfectly the twin concerns
of wealth and work that were born of industrialism. Fired by the publication of Bernard Mandeville's controversial *Fable of the Bees* in 1714, commentary worried over the role of luxury consumption in creating a thriv-
ing nation. How could virtuous asceticism "pay" in a society based on
trade, when the demand for commodities would keep workers busy?
Challenging moralists who regularly warned against the threat of deca-
dence to the survival of the British nation, Mandeville argued that private
vices created public benefits:

> . . . [W]hilst Luxury
> Employ'd a Million of the Poor,
> And odious Pride a Million more.

> Envy it self, and Vanity
> Were Ministers of Industry;
> Their darling Folly, Fickleness
> In Diet, Furniture, and Dress,
> That strange ridic'lous Vice, was made
> The very Wheel, that turn'd the Trade.[5]

In endeavoring to sever economics from morality, Mandeville shocked most of his contemporaries. Many were still eager to impose restrictions on consumption, and as the century progressed, a new generation of moralists, some of them avowed evangelicals, adopted their own ascetic practices. Upon reading Mandeville, John Wesley reacted with predictable disfavor. "'Till now I imagined there had never appeared in the world such a book as the works of Machiavel," he recorded in his journal. "But de Mandeville goes far beyond it."[6]

Consternation about the nation's increasing wealth gave cause for a rallying of moral leadership within the ranks of the middle classes. John Brown's *An Estimate of the Manners and Principles of the Times* (1757), which went into six editions in six months, argued that nothing less than a wholesale degeneration of present-day manners "[has] arisen from our exorbitant Trade and Wealth, left without Check, to their natural Operations and uncontrouled Influence." Immediate evidence of Britain's spiritual and moral decline, likened to the fall of Rome, could be found in the "effeminacy" of wealthy townspeople, who displayed a love of dress, excess comforts, and too rich a diet; the "landed Ranks" of nobility and gentry suffered from the same characteristics. In striving to distinguish themselves from aristocrats, the new middle classes needed to reinvigorate traditional notions of masculinity. Characterizing "luxurious" tastes as womanish and denouncing leisure, Brown called upon "Men of *Capacity, Courage,* and *Virtue*"—namely, men of more modest means—to establish a new kind of leadership.[7]

Women of the middle ranks had a more onerous legacy to live down before they could assume the authority due to their rank. The eighteenth-century critique of luxury depended upon an idea of human imperfection embodied in the feminine. Originating in Genesis, the notion of feminine evil encompassed the traits of unbridled appetite, deception, and fickleness. Just as Machiavelli's *fortuna* was a woman, so, too, were certain forms of luxury so apparent in Mandeville's "private vices." Luxury threatened to "effeminate" and "enervate" the nation by drawing men into "whoring" and "drinking." On a more mundane level, an excess of refinement simply undermined robust masculine activity and even rationality. The "two little adjectives" of "sweet and clean," Mandeville quipped, "are so comprehensive, especially in the Dialect of some Ladies, that no body can guess how far they may be stretcht."[8] Such refinements required the purchase of exotic toiletries, as well as imported fabrics and foods. As sentiment against unregulated consumption waxed strong in the eighteenth century, antipathy found a vehicle of expression in metaphors about female behavior. Bishop Berkeley's depiction of the state as a spendthrift matron is one example:

> Whether it be possible for this country to grow rich so long as what is made by domestic industry is spent in foreign luxury?
>
> Whether she would not be a very vile matron, and justly thought either mad or foolish, that should give away the necessaries of life from her naked and starving children in exchange for pearls to stick in her hair, and sweetmeats to please her own palate?[9]

Foreign or alien influences were often conflated with images of woman, as in the anonymous *Trial of the lady Allured Luxury* (1757), in which a notorious foreign "lady" spy is found guilty of multiple charges of deceit. Whenever the government softened its restrictions on foreign imports, protest against luxuries proliferated in pamphlet literature. Advocates of protection often pinned the blame on female purchasers of such commodities.[10]

Weavers certainly understood the problem in a more concrete sense. Petitions on behalf of the woolen and silk trades, to name but a few, expressed indignation toward female purchasers of foreign luxuries. Invoking national interests to promote their cause, tradespeople beseeched women to wear simpler fabrics made by English laborers.[11] Moralists could only concur: not yet accustomed to a wider social distribution of wealth, they feared that luxuries would corrupt one part of the population while starving the other. In this regard, women were often seen as "the principal channel by which . . . most of our miseries proceed."[12]

The special calling of middle-class women was clear: they were to eschew flagrant display, which suggested moral and sexual laxity, and embrace simplicity and the duties of domestic life. Long before the Victorian age propagated the principles of virtuous womanhood, eighteenth-century moralists reasoned that "the Female Frame of *Person* and *Mind* tends chiefly to fit and qualify the Sex for domestic Life only." So complete is the portrait of female virtue supplied by a cleric in 1765 that one suspects it already constituted familiar rhetoric:

> . . . [T]he great and final Virtue of the Sex is . . . that of a tender and steady Affection for their Husbands and Children: An Affection which leads them to center their Wishes on this great Object, "to make doubly happy the prosperous State of their Family, and to sooth and chear it in the Day of Affliction and Distress." This is the Virtue which compleats and crowns the rest: And which results so clearly from the true Female Constitution here delineated, that to illustrate it farther is almost a needless Labour. For to this great End the ingenuous Spirit of Gentleness, of honourable Subordination, Gratitude for Protection, with all its pleasing Labours, do naturally lead the softer Sex. To this tends no less the guarded Deportment which Modesty and Chastity inspire; which lead the virtuous Wife to purify every Desire of the Heart, to view her Husband as the sole Object of personal Regard. To this great Purpose the tender and compassionate Quality of the Female Mind tends still more strongly to conduct her, while she sees, and feels, and

relieves the Distresses of her beloved Family. And lastly, in this Affection the Principle of Religion confirms her Heart; while it teaches her to regard this domestic Love and Care, as the first Duty of her Life, the very Purpose of her Being.[13]

Women were named guardians not only of the domestic sphere but of morality itself. "[T]oo soon would even the name of virtue be extinct among us, did women not uphold it," one author averred. Young men in need of moral improvement were advised to associate with virtuous women.[14] Middle-class women were flanked on either side by inappropriate models of their sex: aristocratic women flaunted moral proscriptions while plebeian women were completely ignorant of them. The cause of domestic purity and simplicity was theirs alone, and from the late eighteenth century on, they and their menfolk joined in establishing their authority in this domain.[15]

Earnest women of the middle ranks had ample opportunity to put virtue to the test: "polite" society of the eighteenth century was as yet more Rabelaisian than Victorian in its manners. Moralists' debates called attention to the male habit of urinating in streets, women who spoke frankly of bodily functions, and general sexual promiscuity. Novels commonly reproduced the theme of seduction, for which audiences seemed to have an insatiable appetite. Convention freely acknowledged the predatory habits and sexual prowess of men; it was a rare moralist who recognized that only women suffered from the consequences.[16] Women's fashions were as yet relatively revealing. For those inclined or unlucky enough to live in London, the urban world offered "one intire and enormous scene of enchantment, where Fashion, Opulence, and Ostentation, are incessantly practising their witchcraft."[17] The middle-class woman was best advised to devote herself to a circumscribed life and, if possible, a modest, useful education as "a check upon luxury, dissipation, and prodigality." Priscilla Wakefield, a Quaker advocate of education for women, argued that in this way, women of the "respectable" classes could "retard the progress of that general dissoluteness, the offspring of idleness, which is deprecated by all political writers, as the sure forerunner of national decay."[18]

These vague entreaties evolved into a more clearly defined role for women of the middling ranks: that of friend and preceptress of women of the lower classes. Both secular and religious plans for the poor called upon middle-class women for assistance, on theoretical and practical grounds. Jonas Hanway recommended that even wealthy women "should be taught to knit and spin: the *rich*, that they may be the more induced, as they grow up, to superintend the poor, as the piety of the sex should lead them to do."[19] Others understood the custodial role of women of means in a more literal sense. In publicizing his *Plan for a Preservatory and Reformatory, For the Benefit of Deserted Girls, and Penitent Prostitutes* (1758), the London magistrate John Fielding made clear his need for "the kind Attention, the friendly Approbation, and the generous Assistance of the Ladies." Their unsalaried help represented no small contribution in launching his "preservatory" (which was actually a public laundry), but more important, their sympathies were essential in creating the bond between classes that philanthropy strove to forge. The "tender Feelings" of women "will give them a much juster Idea of the Sufferings of these poor Creatures than any Thing the warmest Imagination can suggest," Fielding explained. And as all philanthropists and public servants insisted, such ventures were meant to join human sympathies when economic and social circumstances had severed them.[20]

London philanthropists discovered that one of their pet projects, the rescuing of prostitutes, might serve multiple purposes: while recovering a lost portion of the female laboring population for the good of the nation, the cause could promote female virtue among the middling as well as the lower ranks of society. The latter goal appears to have gotten the upper hand in the world of print. Polemical pamphlets, advice books, sermons, and charity reports counseled women of the higher ranks to demonstrate feminine virtues for their less fortunate sisters. In publishing sermons delivered to its officers, the Magdalen Hospital for penitent prostitutes used the polarities of virtue and vice in order to expatiate on the duties of the well-to-do woman:

> This, we are convinced, will be the amiable conduct and proceeding of those of the SAME SEX, for whom we now plead; and who, we are satisfied, can never be inattentive to the welfare, never unaffected by the calamities, of their fellow-creatures. You who have happily persevered in the pleasing paths of virtue, can best tell the comforts arising from so delightful a conduct, and may easily guess the miseries of a different state. You, who have known the fatal pleadings of passion, can more easily pity them, whom those pleadings have seduced and destroyed. And you, who are possessed of all the sweetnesses and delicacies of the tender mind, and a happier state, can more easily guess the extreme misery which must arise to a female heart, from the foulness and horror of promiscuous prostitution; and will, on these accounts, be the more ready to reach out your pitying hand, and save from distress beyond the reach of description, many of your own sex, for whom, till this happy opportunity, no redress was provided.[21]

Philanthropic writings through the end of the century established this same relationship between virtuous middle class and "lost" lower-class women. The female pattern of perfection could not function without its opposite, for the norm often defined itself through contrary example. "[I]f such horrid wretches, who, from a life of looseness and debouchery, become a scandal to the name of woman . . . what cannot the delicate and more accomplished sex inspire?" queried one author. "[W]ould ladies of rank and condition set them properer examples, it is probable they would as readily follow such, as those they are now so punctual in."[22]

Handbooks for the middle-class woman abounded, perhaps because as a nouveau riche, her ignorance of domestic and social protocol was lamentably conspicuous. She could choose from a wide variety of literary styles, from the cautionary fiction of Eliza Haywood in *The Female Spectator* (vol. I, bk. I, 1744) to the more explicit formulas of John Gregory in *A Father's Legacy to his Daughters* (1774). Priscilla Wakefield offered a list of suggestions, which included works by Sarah Trimmer, Hannah More, Defoe's *Robinson Crusoe* (1719), and Jonas Hanway's *Virtue in humble Life* (1774).[23] Authors were male as well as female, and in almost all cases, their discourse was profoundly patriarchal. As literary critic Elizabeth Kowaleski-Wallace has shown for Hannah More's works, women were complicit in furthering relations that were far from progressive.[24] The larger common goal of uplifting the female sex erased many differences, including denominational, that separated writers from one another.[25]

Hanway's *Virtue in humble Life* stands as an interesting prototype: cast as a dialogue between "Thomas Trueman, a Farmer and his Daughter, Mary," who is about to set out for service, the book offers the benevolent patriarch's idea of the ideal mistress/servant relationship.[26] As such, it appears to be aimed at two audiences. The frontispiece depicts a portly gentleman gesturing with a didactic forefinger at a simple and solemn young woman. Her humble status is reinforced by the beehive at the top of the page, emblazoned with the tag "Instinctive Virtue the Reward of Industry." In spite of this, Hanway justifies his two-volume work of nearly seven hundred pages by making the case for teaching the "lady" how to be a good mistress to the untutored but not irretrievable laboring girl. "No lady can appear in a point of view more charming, than . . . [when] she shews a maternal care of young female servants," recommends the introduction:

> I am sensible how . . . a work of this kind is to be treated as an ebullition of pious zeal: nor should I be surprized to hear it said by a female acquaintance, perhaps in most respects highly valuable, "Lord! what *good* will you do, by taking so much pains to build this *monstrous pile* of piety?" My answer is, "Your *ladyship* will be best able to determine this question, if you should condescend to read what I have written; otherwise I can possibly do you no good: Your women servants may perhaps become the better for it, and *you* may reap some benefit from their virtues.[27]

Hanway's dissatisfaction with "ladies," apparent in the book's lengthy harangues against their habits of sleeping late and idling away time, must have inspired him to take on the role of preceptor himself. He conveniently removed Mary's mother from the picture: on page one, Trueman informs Mary that her mother's last words, before dying, were "*O be careful of my daughter!*" ("More she would have said," he apologizes, "but her heart swelled up too high.") Hanway's book would replace the unfortunate mother.

Women themselves contributed to the vast prescriptive literature of the eighteenth century; indeed, they created a prescriptive genre of their own through their prolific educational and feminist writings.[28] Their messages were often equivocal. Conduct books held much in common with other types of literature, particularly those encouraging women to improve themselves; while recommending passive conformity, some texts introduced tantalizing accounts of female initiative and transgression. Their representation of class relations, however, was relatively unambiguous: middle-class women exerted power over laboring women and, regardless of their common gender, reproduced subordination in all its facets through their interactions. In carving out a middle-class identity for themselves, women delineated identities of inferiority for laboring women. These relations often came alive in educational literature, in which fictional characters enacted relationships between mistresses and servants, or instructed young ladies in their conduct toward social inferiors. Feminist writers, usually women of the middle classes, were not exempt from such attitudes; while espousing reformed relations between the sexes, they stopped far short of spreading enlightenment across class lines. This is hardly surprising, given that many women writers relied upon a middle-class readership for their works. In this sense, Mary Wollstonecraft's *Original Stories from Real Life* (1788) and *Thoughts on the Education of Daughters* (1787) are not dissimilar from the moralistic writings of her conservative contemporary, Hannah More. Both women sought to provide improving literature for a middle-class female audience.[29]

Hannah More's tracts, fabulously successful during the 1790s and the early 1800s, provided a vehicle for the new science of economics. They have generally been considered lessons of morality suitable for the new industrial work force; certainly her teachings included deference to authority, punctuality, and frugality, all values of the work-discipline associated with industrialism. Yet this places the tracts in too narrow a context. Viewed from the perspective of late eighteenth-century economic thought, her writings are a near-perfect reflection of current thinking on the subjects of labor and the source of national wealth. The basic doctrines of political economy—free trade, free competition, free labor, and above all, the principle of self-interest—are all evident in her publications.

Moreover, More's avid interest in the subject, and, one must add, the activity of the characters of her stories, prove that political economy was not just the business of men. Her tracts, particularly her "Stories for Persons of Middle Rank," provide a veritable handbook for the middle-class woman in search of an up-to-date understanding of how economic activity was carried on—its motivations, its pitfalls, and especially its rewards. This was female philanthropy addressing the problem of the poor in the latter half of the eighteenth century. More was projecting a decidedly gendered, middle-class strategy.[30]

One might argue that More's stories offer a window into the fantasies of a middle-class woman concerning the optimal relationship between herself and those obdurate females of the lower classes. More's interest in cultivating middle-class women as a national army of philanthropists was everywhere in evidence in her writings. Repeatedly, she employed the scenario of the assiduous female philanthropist rescuing the misguided working-class girl from ignorance and penury. The middle-class woman of charitable mind was justly rewarded for her exertions; the lady always got her girl and won a considerable degree of power and prestige in the bargain.

Admittedly, Hannah More was only one middle-class woman; but her popularity should be considered in light of the fact that her voluminous sales probably owed most to the interest of women of her own class. One can hardly believe that the tracts were read in great numbers by the actual poor. Most likely, they were purchased and distributed by better off benefactors—mistresses who might hope to read them to their servants, for example, or wives of rural landowners who distributed them among laborers. The tracts read like "how-to" manuals, punctuated repeatedly by instructions and advice to the reader, delivered in a familiar tone that assumed a common set of assumptions. The efficacy with which More's middle-class female characters reconstructed their worlds is astonishing and wholly captivating. Viewed from this advantageous perspective, these accounts offer an intoxicatingly simple solution to private and public quandaries.

"A Cure for Melancholy. Showing the way to do much good with little money," first printed under the less revealing title of "The Cottage Cook, or Mrs. Jones's Cheap Dishes," follows a pattern common to many of More's tracts for the middle ranks. The central character, Mrs. Jones, is the widow of "a great merchant" who, at the outset of the story, is paralyzed by what Hannah More presciently (for a woman of the 1790s) termed melancholy. Mrs. Jones's late husband had "lived in a grand manner" until his business failed owing to recent economic distress; he died from the shock. Mrs. Jones, similarly, had been "too much taken up with the world," and now, making ends meet on "a very narrow income," she hardly ventured outside, "except to church," in the small village of Weston in Somerset. This middle-class woman of leisure and sufficient piety undergoes a change of heart when her local Evangelical clergyman delivers a sermon on the good Samaritan. In tears, she complains to the good vicar that she has nothing to give.

> "Nothing! madam," replied the clergyman, "do you call your time, your talents, your kind offices, nothing? I will venture to say that you might do more good than the richest man in the parish could do by merely giving his money."

And here, the vicar opens the door to state-of-the-art advice:

> "You have lately studied oeconomy for yourself; instruct your poor neighbours in that important art. They want it almost as much as they want money."

And finally, mixing the old with the new:

> "You have influence with the few rich persons in the parish; exert that influence."[31]

Henceforth, the coalition of middle-class woman and clergy goes forward, the plain Christian of "sense and leisure" extending and even assuming the work of the parish minister.

If the story seems predictable, the assiduousness with which Mrs. Jones sets about her "new plan of life" is less so. The meek and retiring widow becomes a ubiquitous virago who soliloquizes at every opportunity. Mrs. Jones's reflections on social relations are too shrewd to be called, as More intended, "good sense."[32] A contrast between the failings of the "thoughtless, lavish, and indolent" local lord, Sir John, and the "over frugal, but active, sober, and not ill-natured" local squire punctuates the entire story. No insight goes to waste: Mrs. Jones resolves never to ask "Sir John for advice, or the Squire for subscriptions," though one gathers that she engaged in the reverse on a regular basis.[33] She uses each confrontation with the two men as an opportunity for further soliloquy, and she never passes up the chance to make a judgmental remark about either one. More's heroines beautifully demonstrate the paradox of power relations in women's work in religion.

It is necessary to get beyond this observation, however, and attempt a more specific characterization of More's philanthropic message. Always amusing in the Cheap Repository Tracts is the savvy displayed by middle-class benefactresses. These characters are not otherworldly creatures with no mind for business or politics, but rather, women who calculate, surmise, and make deals. In "The Sunday School," a sequel to "A Cottage Cook," Mrs. Jones sets out to find a mistress for her school, and her quest begins with a rather lengthy disquisition on the worth of recommendations. Mrs. Jones's wisdom would prove quite useful to any woman looking for hired help; she advises us to investigate ulterior motives that might exist in friends' desires to recommend persons for a position. "When I lived in London," she begins (a very telling introduction), "I learned to be much on my guard as to recommendations. I found people often wanted to impose on me some one who was a burthen to themselves."[34] Sometimes More's calculations are quite literal. In "Betty Brown, the St. Giles's Orange-Girl: with some Account of Mrs. Sponge, the Money-Lender," a lady purchasing produce figures out Betty's losses at the hand of a crafty moneylender in seconds flat. "My poor girl," she offers in response to Betty's brief account of her financial arrangement with Mrs. Sponge, "do you know that you have already paid for that single five shillings the enormous sum of 7l. 10s?"[35] She proceeds to lay out an alternative plan for Betty, complete with another rapid flourish of arithmetical prowess. (The plan, of course, included Betty's giving up gin and saving her pence.) No wonder Hannah More advocated improved education for young women.

Mrs. Jones's agenda in "A Cottage Cook" includes investigating fraud at the local bakery, where loaves are being sold short. (Mrs. Jones presses both the vicar and the squire to work on her behalf to correct the matter.) Another project involves setting up a parish oven, requiring more exercise of influence on Mrs. Jones's part; addressing the problem of the public house; and of course attending to the requisite charity school for servants. One might easily say that the good middle-class woman extended her household, quite literally, to the larger arena of the village, usually by way of relations between ladies and poor women.

Hannah More made charity "the calling of a lady," as her definitive biographer, M. G. Jones, readily points out, or, as More herself put it, "The care of the poor is her profession."[36] Contemporaries soon remarked upon the visible impact of More's writings, not on the poor, but on women of the middle class. "It has always been the practice of the better kind of country ladies to distribute benefactions," wrote Lucy Aikin to William Ellery Channing, "but Hannah More . . . has unfortunately made it a fashion and a rage."[37] Likewise, Hannah More strove to communicate her passion for Sunday schools, though she was by no means the only person doing so, and middle-class women responded. She mapped out an exact strategy in two tracts, one for the person of the middle rank ("The Sunday School") and another ("The History of Hester Wilmot") aimed at "the common people." The grid of relationships is the same: a middle-class benefactress must exert her influence above and below her in order to establish a school that effectively roots out lower-class values and habits. The teacher, carefully handpicked by the benefactress, is, significantly, a woman (the clergyman's housekeeper, a totally trustworthy type) and the young person duly transformed by the experience of Sunday school is also female. In fact, the vast majority of teachers enlisted in the More sisters' Sunday school campaign were women. The venture must have mobilized literally thousands of women, all of them implicated in the cross-class relationship characterized above.

More significant than numbers is the attitude toward teaching the poor that emerges from More's accounts. Her solid middle-class women triumph over the poor girls they seek to teach; compare this to Sarah Trimmer's gingerly thoughts on the same subject: "Perhaps it may be thought improper to take young ladies from whom genteel behaviour and elegance of expression is expected, among a set of vulgar, low bred children. [But] I do not apprehend any disagreeable consequences will arise from this circumstance[.]"[38] Hannah More improved on this rather contemptuous attitude by expecting middle-class women to stand up to threats posed by the eighteenth-century social environment. But such boldness did not extend out of woman's proper sphere. We need only return to "A Cure for Melancholy" to find Hannah More's brand of domestic ideology at work with a vengeance. When asked by the squire why her girls were not spinning and carding or attending to other manufactures, Mrs. Jones astutely answers, "[O]urs is not a manufacturing county."

But there is a[nother] manufacture, which I am carrying on, and I know of none within my own reach which is so valuable. What can that be? said the Squire. *To make good wives for working men*, said she. Is not mine an excellent staple commodity? I am teaching these girls the arts of industry and good management. It is little encouragement to an honest man to work hard all the week, if his wages are wasted by a slattern at home. Most of these girls will probably become wives to the poor, or servants to the rich; to such the common arts of life are of great value[.][39]

It is not so much the ultimate end of Mrs. Jones's activity—good wives and male breadwinners—that jars in this passage. We can expect that More hoped to wean working-class women from their habit of going out to work. It is Mrs. Jones's (and Hannah More's) assumption that working-class women were hers to remake. This proves to be a rather troubling and lasting feature of the world sketched out by "that bishop in petticoats."

An apotheosis of these social and literary developments can be seen in *Conversations on Political Economy* (1816), by Jane Haldiman Marcet (1769–1858). The daughter of a Swiss merchant of London and the wife of a doctor, Marcet established herself as a writer on scientific subjects, which she tailored for women and the young. *Conversations on Political Economy*, her most successful work, went through many editions and received plaudits from luminaries ranging from Lord Macaulay to the French economist Jean-Baptiste Say. The leading Victorian political economist, McCulloch, later called it "on the whole perhaps the best introduction to the science that has yet appeared." Like Hanway's *Virtue in humble Life* and Wollstonecraft's *Original Stories from Real Life*, the book relates the enlightenment of a young woman through a series of talks with a knowing adult; in this case, an erudite Mrs. B. illuminates Caroline, who bears, perhaps not coincidentally, the same name as the pupil in Wollstonecraft's *Original Stories*. But rather than imploring the reader to consider the higher virtues of humane treatment of animals and servants, as Wollstonecraft did, or proper domestic practices, as Hanway attempted, this work provides the theoretical rationale behind economic and class relations of the new industrial society.[40]

At first glance, the young (ostensibly middle-class) woman seems a rather surprising target for the subject of political economy. But Marcet's text illustrates how the act of acquiring "female" identity, an indispensable part of the construction of a middle-class elite, was implicated in the economic circumstances of the time. In her introductory remarks, Mrs. B. employed a trope of political theory that reached back to Aristotle: political economy did not differ very much from "household economy." Mrs. B. encouraged Caroline to think in familiar terms and then she "need only extend . . . [her] idea of the economy of a family to that of a whole people[.]" Neither was political economy antithetical to the religious and moral principles that every good girl learned at school: the distinction lay between "the thirst of gain," which political economy did not endorse, and the wholly necessary quest of "articles of commerce," which it celebrated. "Such commodities . . . are useful or agreeable to mankind," the book explains. Desire took on a domesticated appearance: Mrs. B. argued that the "necessaries of life" must be extended to include such things as windows and stockings. Another conversation explained how property and laws, not simply labor, created wealth. Those in command of an inordinate share of the nation's wealth earned their privileged position by their superior sense of how to apply their (or someone else's, the reader might add) labor. Men of property have learned how "to augment the stock of subsistence, as to transform a country which contained but a few poor huts and a scanty population into a great and wealthy nation." Mrs. B. invoked the concept of "protection" when she explained that the laws of the nation must uphold the notion of property. This, indeed, was a concept familiar to the female reader.[41]

The subjects of wages and population demanded rather lengthier treatment in two entire chapters. Here Mrs. B. and Caroline grappled with the arguments for high and low wages (opting for the latter), and besides using Malthusian arithmetic, they focused on the male breadwinner:

> If besides furnishing subsistence for himself, the wages of the labourer would not enable him to maintain a wife and bring up a family, the class of labourers would gradually diminish, and the scarcity of hands would then raise their wages, which would enable them to live with more comfort and rear a family[.]

Marcet's conclusion was Panglossian: pressure on the means of subsistence, though a necessary part of society, civilized tribes into nations. "If then it produces want and wretchedness to some part of the community, it feeds millions of industrious happy beings, and in a well constituted society, the evil will always tend to diminish, and the good to increase." Though she moderated the pessimism of Malthus, Marcet pointed out, "No amelioration of the condition of the poor can be permanent, unless to industry they add prudence and foresight." With this maxim, she echoed the teachings of her Evangelical contemporary, Hannah More.[42] A kind of Protestant ethic writ secular, these were the values of a new middle class.

As models of domesticity and virtue, rescuers of prostitutes and poor women, mistresses of servants, and generally cultivated ladies, women of the middle classes helped to usher the ideas of political economy into the new industrial age. Though literary evidence does not prove widespread belief or action, a plethora of printed advice nevertheless reveals the extent to which certain options were pressed upon females. Moralists, philanthropists, clergymen, and women writers informed them of their first responsibility: to discipline themselves and other women with values appropriate to the new industrial order. The major concern of the day, the problem of the poor, provided the substance from which they carved their new identities. Equipped with notions that were, in many instances, diluted principles of political economy, women of the middle class found themselves acting as custodians of laboring women. As studies of philanthropy show, women's work in their communities, as well as in their own homes, gave them ample opportunity to put these principles into practice.[43]

9

The Other Victorian Woman: The Domestic Servant in the Industrial Age

Independence, like happiness, is always comparative. There is no class of society but has its power 'to will and to do,' restricted variously, and in different degrees. Each class and each individual composing it is under subordination of some kind or other .... When subordination is so based, society must be both generally and individually benefited. Without it what would be the state either of public or private life? The struggles and contentions of ungoverned passions, the clashings of different interests, the wilfulness of the powerful, would assail and overcome all the quiet and peaceful influences of domestic life, and be in perpetual opposition to the order and justice by which society is held together.

Isabella Beaton, "On the Establishment of Household Servants, and Their Duties," *The Book of Household Management* (1861)

Adam Smith was among the first to call attention to the seemingly superfluous nature of modern domestic service. Cleaning, cooking, and waiting on employers produced no "vendible commodity"; such work simply maintained the upper classes in their ease and turned potentially productive laborers into inconsequential dependents. "A man grows rich by employing a multitude of manufacturers: he grows poor, by maintaining a multitude of menial servants," Smith advised in *The Wealth of Nations*.[1] Smith had in mind the aristocratic model of conspicuous expenditure; he overlooked the extent to which domestic labor was necessary, albeit without "value" in an exchangeable sense. In the 1850s,

Marx reflected with similar disparagement on the subject of servants, but in the context of the bourgeois home. The fact that servants did not create wealth themselves but lived off surplus wealth enjoyed by the bourgeoisie placed them in a separate, parasitic category of labor.[2]

These views provide a useful barometer of changing attitudes toward domestic labor and the women who performed it. Smith and Marx relied on a narrow, "modern" definition of service as menial domestic work, which by the nineteenth century was assigned to women of the lower classes. They also reversed a preindustrial hierarchy of considerations by ranking productive economic activity above the need to maintain households and the social order. From a more contemporary point of view, neither addressed the central problem of the lack of valuation of household work, which can be studied in the "wages for housework" literature that has appeared in recent years.[3]

For our purposes, it is important to examine domestic service for the light it sheds on the place of working-class women in the economy of industrial England. The fact that domestic service was the largest single category of employment of women points up themes in previous chapters: that work for women wage earners was in short supply, and that domestic service would reinforce an association of working-class women with nonproductive activity. Just as important, the dynamics of service promised to recapitulate relations of deference and subordination between women of different classes.

Formerly, the general category of service included participation in the economic functions as well as the essential upkeep of domestic settings. Since households were units of production, the terms of "family" and "servants" were interchangeable. In agricultural settings, male and female servants in husbandry included ploughmen, carters, dairymaids, and household servants who usually doubled as outdoor laborers.[4] Servants in villages and towns might assume tasks related to commercial activities, such as vending produce or assisting in a trade. Little distinction existed between assistance and production, particularly in the case of female service, which often entailed preparing food and caring for others. Such "invisible" work was not classified as productive; it remains similarly unrecognized by economists today.[5]

Above all, service in earlier times had provided a stable structure of authority that rested on the patriarchal notion of the family. Servants passed almost ritualistically from their households of birth to those of their betters, where they received employment, training, and supervision; they have been described as "an offering, so to speak, of the children of the poor to those above them."[6] Eighteenth-century tracts employed the language of patriarchy, speaking of duties and privileges of the servant, and recalled an almost feudal subservience. Mistresses and masters demanded obedience, deference, and respect in return for wages, room, and board. Apologists presented the relationship as a "mutual contract" or "covenant," "founded on a reciprocation of benefit"; but such language was always tinctured by an awareness of the employer's right of domination. Drawing authority from their superior social class, employers were allowed by law to beat or dismiss servants at will for infractions of household rules or disobeying orders.[7] More commonly, they simply dictated the terms of the social and sexual lives of their servants and did their best to enforce them.[8]

Gradually separating itself from this old framework of obligations and responsibilities, modern domestic service made a slow transition from relations of duty to those of contract. In eighteenth-century France, the character of domestic service changed as a result of the rise of individualism in public life and the strengthening of the nuclear family within the home. Both developments contributed to a decline in patriarchal relations between servant and master.[9] Because aristocratic influence was far less important in Britain, some have argued, contractual relations seemed more in evidence earlier on.[10] But it is difficult to say whether the trend was either definitive or welcomed. As late as 1862, the *Edinburgh Review* noted the passing of "the old aristocratic feeling which made the dependent proud of the trust of his master, and identified him with the honour of the house he served." "Service," the author lamented, "is becoming a mere contract for wages."[11]

The history of domestic service is full of such contradictions. The early industrial age of Adam Smith championed productive labor; it also witnessed the general emergence of domestic service as exclusively indoor employment aimed at the upkeep of a household, bereft of an income-producing function. Domestic chores were tainted by their association with perhaps the most unacknowledged form of women's work, that of simply attending to the needs of others. The trend toward hiring servants to maintain a particular style of life became apparent among the middle and lower middle ranks at the end of the eighteenth century. The wealthier wives of tradesmen and farmers began to express distaste for the hard labor of housewifery and afix greater value to the domestic accoutrements of gentility. Londoners frequently commented upon the practice of keeping "maid servants," which especially suited the growing affluence of middle-class households. Provincial habits would soon catch up with those of the metropolis.[12]

By the 1830s, domestic service assumed its modern definition on a grand scale. A substantial middle class, largely urban and professional, cultivated a domestic life that required the constant attendance of menials. The expansion of industry and commerce after midcentury boosted even larger numbers of people to higher levels of security and comfort, at least in relation to the laboring poor. The number of people who earned what would have been considered a middle-class income (usually figured as roughly £150 annually) doubled between 1851 and 1871, while the general population increased by only 11.9 percent between 1851 and 1861, and by 13.2 percent by 1871. Though not every middle-class family employed a servant, many did; added to these numbers were lower-class households needing "another pair of hands in the workshop or at the counter," making domestic service a widely extended form of employment.[13]

The female nature of nineteenth-century domestic service was one of its predominant features. Compared with the early modern period, when service included many male apprentices and young people of both sexes drawn from the general laboring population, the ratio of male to female servants in the industrial age was dramatically reversed: according to the 1851 census, it was 13:100.[14] This was owing not only to the decline of apprenticeship, but also a falloff in the popularity of male servants. Male servants customarily commanded higher wages, though in some cases, marginally so. Nevertheless, "maids of all work" who would perform general housework designated as unskilled at the behest of others were in ever greater demand.[15]

It is impossible to discuss nineteenth-century domestic service without focusing on the question of gender. Maintaining a household that was separated from commercial and industrial activity became almost exclusively "women's work." Though today this statement may seem tautological, the exclusion of men from housework is a product of historical changes of the eighteenth century.[16] Female servants became widely employed partly because of the evolution of "housework" as we now know it, and partly as a result of the "feminization" of housework on a wide scale.[17] The rise of domestic service in the narrow sense "favoured female rather than male servants" because of the nature of the new standards of housekeeping that accompanied the increasing wealth of the middle ranks in the eighteenth century. Household and personal cleanliness, caring for the details of domestic furnishings, and waiting on the needs of others were subordinate tasks often requiring meticulousness; thus they were gendered as female. Generating its own hierarchy, the work required the woman of greater means acting as supervisor over one or more lower-class servants. Her leisure became a measure of her gentility; servants, likewise, a measure of her wealth. The hierarchy absolutely depended on the denigration of household tasks as unbefitting a true lady. These developments make the relationship between mistress and maid one of the most revealing employer–worker relations in the nineteenth century.[18]

The fact that a servant's duties involved her in maintaining a culture of domesticity renders the subject of gender doubly significant. Some have argued that the commonalities of female identity created a special rapport between mistress and maid: functioning as a "bridging occupation," domestic service facilitated the dissemination of middle-class values throughout the working class, while acquainting the middle classes with working-class ways. Female servants thus have been cast in the role of conciliators between classes, particularly as they appeared to demonstrate a conservative, individualistic outlook in their struggle for upward mobility.[19]

But when viewed through concepts of both class and gender, the occupation of service appears fraught with tensions and conflict. Of course we cannot know exactly what kinds of relationships existed between mistresses and servants, but we can surmise attitudes and expectations from the scanty surviving evidence. The right to exercise power appears to have signified a great deal to women on both sides of the divide; for mistresses, it became important not to relinquish "old-fashioned" terms of employment that demanded childlike subordination and loyalty from servants. Current attitudes toward the laboring classes must have influenced employers' expectations, and at the end of the eighteenth century, these inevitably shed a negative light upon women of the laboring classes. For servants, judging from the outcry against their growing demands for "independence," few relished the degree of self-effacement demanded by their position. The domestic context probably accentuated any differences of wealth and power between women. Far from uniting mistresses and servants under the banners of domesticity and womanhood, the ideals of Victorianism drove them apart.

Yet the supply of servants from the late eighteenth to the late nineteenth century was plentiful. Poor women with few other options swelled the ranks of the servant class. In rural areas, young women in need of work had little choice but to look for a "place" in some nearby village or town. No wonder that Londoners reported "waggon loads of poor servants arriving every day from all parts of the kingdom."[20] In the context of the late eighteenth century, when unemployment, poverty, or economic displacement affected much of the laboring classes, service was regarded as a safe occupation that promised the security of a domestic setting and (in theory, at least) the assurance of food, shelter, and some supervision. As Bridget Hill has pointed out, board and lodging during a time of steep inflation "meant a great deal" to the poor. "[W]hether or not she lived well, a girl going to domestic service was *fed*."[21] Though historians have used "advantages" and "rewards" to explain the laboring girl's move into service, these terms may be making virtues out of necessity. Domestic service was often not a choice but a refuge, one which is painfully distorted when described in the language of possessive individualism. So typical was the move into service for working-class girls that few, upon reaching a reasonable age, expected to do anything else.

I

One of the most common occupations in the eighteenth century, domestic service carried the heaviest of social responsibilities. Many people saw service as the sensible solution to the problem of the female poor. Parishes apprenticed girls in "housewifery" in the belief that such skills would train them in habits of industry while insuring their future ability to contribute to their families' self-sufficiency. As many as 40 percent of female parish apprenticeships in the South at the end of the eighteenth century were in housewifery, reflecting the diminishing number of trades open to females as well as the consequent desperation to equip the poor for later hardships.[22] The schemes of charitable institutions also reveal the extent to which service offered a safety net for the laboring female.[23] The Lambeth Asylum for female orphans believed that domestic economy, in and of itself, acted as an antidote to the effects of poverty and degradation. "[H]ow valuable therefore, and how truly laudable is an institution which . . . teaches the children entrusted to its care (and that at an age when they are most capable of learning) every useful branch of houshold [*sic*] oeconomy," eulogized one minister in 1768, "instructs them in every thing that they *ought* to know, and which is perhaps peculiar to this charity, in nothing which they ought *not!*"[24] John Fielding's plan for deserted girls likewise assumed that training for service would set poor girls on the right track. "Servants bred in this Laundry must exceed all others," he claimed, "as they will have a general Knowledge of Housewifery, and will set out in the World free from the Prejudices of evil Habits."[25]

Perhaps part of this hopefulness arose from the belief that women of the higher ranks could naturally improve poor young women. Contemporaries commonly assumed that indigent mothers could not or would not properly train their daughters in the skills of housewifery. Employing the female poor in more prosperous households would provide a salutory normative influence, with more competent women filling the gap. The parish sought expedient placements, usually in the families of tradespeople. Charities adopted the more deliberate strategy of engaging women of the middle classes as mentors. Championing an ideology of separate spheres, the Ladies Society of the Society for Bettering the Condition of the Poor prided itself in its special capacity. "In one very important part," they announced in 1804, "that which concerns the *education* and *employment* of the Female Poor, it is most obvious that very little can be done effectually or *decorously*, without the intervention of their own sex." The ladies' "habits of life, and their exemption from political and professional engagements, give them very considerable advantages, —not merely in the detail, but in the peculiar kind of attention and interest, which subjects of this nature require." In an age when all trades required an apprenticeship, this personal relationship was conceived of as an essential part of education. One also has the sense that the relationship was intended to improve the woman of the middle ranks as much as the female poor by giving her an acceptable and useful occupation.[26]

Such optimism countered the more skeptical opinion that servants, at least the lower sort in London, inevitably ended up as prostitutes. From the mid eighteenth century, urban commentators conceded that because so few trades were left open to women, many poor girls fell into service and just as easily into prostitution. In a reversal of tradition, these servants were not an offering of the poor to those above them, but rather, in the words of a contemporary, "a sacrifice to the metropolis, offered by the thirty-nine counties."[27] Jonas Hanway candidly advised that charitable institutions should avoid placing women in service for just these reasons. "As domestic servitude is the fruitful supply of *prostitutes*, and *female* servants in this metropolis, generally much more numerous than can be accommodated . . . it shall be the *constant maxim* of this charity, that every other method of procuring a comfortable support for those who have approved themselves worthy, under this institution, shall be preferred to that of sending them to *service*." Seduction narratives only confirmed the truth of his apprehension.[28]

Many different types of service existed, with just as great a variety of expectations attached to them. Wealthy households in the country commanded large staffs with a great deal of differentiation among servants, while urban families of modest means might keep one or two maids-of-all-work. Conditions at the top of the profession could be rather comfortable, while the more numerous places at the bottom spelled an anonymous, harsh, and menial life. "In a society that was intensely aware of class distinctions and becoming more so," Bridget Hill has pointed out, "the domestic service hierarchy in the eighteenth century is a sort of microcosm of the society it served."[29] Thus the girl who, through fortunate connections, obtained a place in the local squire's household might dream of gentility. The poor country girl in London, on the other hand, had to navigate hazardous waters before she could be assured of adequate food and shelter.

Strict hierarchies of class and gender governed every moment of a servant's life. Households depended upon a structure of authority and status, and servants were advised to keep well within expected roles. Samuel Pepys's diary describes the labyrinth of negotiations required of female servants who were admitted into the society of their superiors while having to show the correct degree of deference. One upper servant was "not proud, but will do what she is bid; but for want of being abroad, knows not how to give that respect to her mistress as she will do when she is told it." She also made the mistake of making "herself equall with the ordinary servants of the house."[30] Outside her place of work, a young woman was more aware of where she stood with regard to other occupations. In one recorded instance, at least, this was not high: when visiting relatives, a woman in service reported that "if any one came in, I was requested to step into another room, and kept in the background, because I was a servant."[31]

Within the hierarchy of servants, women nearly always fell into the lowest ranks. Among the retinue maintained by noble and upper gentry families, only the lady's maid and housekeeper, and perhaps the female cook, qualified as upper servants. The lady's maid, privileged by polite breeding and special skills in hairdressing and attire, acted as a helpful companion to her mistress. The supervisory capacity of the housekeeper, along with her wide-ranging capablities in every aspect of household maintenance, earned a relatively high status among women servants. But compared to male servants, all of whom contributed to the visible status and prestige of a household, women counted for less. Contemporary accounts measured grand households by the number of men in attendance, counting house stewards, butlers, valets, down to the most insignificant lackey or footboy; females went virtually unnoticed. Descriptions reported "thirty or forty men-servants" at the largest households, without any reference to the number of women employed; one might only guess, as one observer did, that "female ones" (chambermaids, scullery maids, and washerwomen) were "in proportion." Their lower status derived directly from their general sexual subordination: while the subservience of a man-servant conferred indubitable power upon a master or mistress, that of a woman servant signified a more ordinary kind of authority.[32]

Such disparity in status highlights the minimal value placed on the manual and often menial tasks ordinarily performed by women in the household. Their toil, largely unpleasant and unsightly, was a feature of mundane reality rather than an ornament of fortune. The significance of gender among lower servants was the mirror-opposite of that of their employers: men-servants were regarded as decorative, while women servants were seen as utilitarian. In a world far removed from commodity production, prestige was accorded to those who were furthest from dirt and toil. Knowing correct modes of behavior and deference (and having access to positions in which to use them) constituted "skill." Relative wages reflected disparities in status: the most conspicuous and least functional of the male entourage, the footman, could earn as much as £10 per annum in 1750, while a housemaid earned as little as £5. A valet's earnings might reach £30 in the 1770s, compared to the £16 earned by a lady's maid in 1775.[33]

Parliament officially recognized male servants as an item of luxury consumption when it introduced a tax of one guinea per head in 1777. Intended as a way of raising revenue during the American War of Independence, the matter threw up much fascinating evidence of attitudes and practices regarding domestic service. Lord North expected that roughly 100,000 servants would fall into this category, though owing to administrative difficulties, income from the levy never satisfied these expectations. Female servants, in contrast, were clearly more of a necessity and far too common to justify such financial penalties. When the younger Pitt tried to impose an additional tax on female domestics in 1785, he met with much resistance. Jettisoning his original plan, which would have taxed single-servant households more lightly than those with two or more, he conceded that one tax-free female servant should be allowed to every two children, and bachelors should pay double for their maids. The measure was adopted; yet owing to its unpopularity, the tax on female servants was ultimately repealed in 1792.[34]

Female servants by necessity learned the distance between their place and those of their male counterparts. Young servant maids had better maneuver their way round them. One manual advised "a great deal of Circumspection" when in a household with men servants; its author indirectly acknowledged the difference between the sexes among servants. "As these Fellows live high, and have little to do, they are for the most

Part very pert and saucy where they dare, and apt to take Liberties on the least Encouragement; you ought therefore to carry yourself at a Distance towards them."[35] Women servants did in fact often marry other lower servants, and a match with a man of higher status was more risky and less common. Stewards and valets occupied a class apart and their administrative and personal tasks transformed them, in effect, into the very hands of their masters. Their responsibilities were far from being "manual" labor; on the contrary, such servants enjoyed as much intimacy with their masters as their social betters. Thus they generally assumed a superior air and adopted the attitudes and behavior of their masters when dealing with women servants at the bottom of the hierarchy. The chance of seduction and betrayal ran higher in this case, and women were wise to use caution.

Women, too, strove to imitate their employers; or so we are told by countless eighteenth-century observers. Endeavoring to match one's mistress in appearance constituted but one aspect of a larger problem, that of the female servant's not knowing her place. While indignant nineteenth-century critics believed such transgression was unique to their era, the insubordinate servant was a constant feature of the eighteenth century. The besetting sin of male servants, according to one book of advice, was that of speaking out of turn: "There are perhaps no kind of Transgressions which Men are apter to fall into . . . than those of the Tongue."[36] For women, the struggle took place within the realm of clothing. "Apeing the Fashion" was equated with "ambition," and as Eliza Hayward pointed out, its consequences were as anarchic. "The greatest pleasure" accorded to such servants is "in being called *Madam* by such as do not know you," she chided in her book of advice to servants; "and," she added, "you fear nothing so much as being taken for what you are." Clothing could function as a passport into another class, at least in appearances.[37]

While men servants wore uniforms, or livery, women servants did not. Eighteenth-century service offered lower-class women the opportunity to study and adopt certain features of upper-class attire. Free to dress as well as they could manage, they strove to follow fashion "as closely as possible." Servants frequently wore the cast-off's of their mistresses, who through their solicitude often unwittingly fed servants' ambitions. To observers of the 1740s, the "Folly" of wearing fancy attire was "epidemic" among women servants. Foreign visitors to England often remarked on their "handsome and well clothed" appearance.[38] Daniel Defoe was probably not alone in mistaking a maid for her mistress, an error which led to his embarrassment on one occasion. "I remember I was put very much to the Blush," he recalled, "being at a Friend's House, and by him required to salute the Ladies, and I kiss'd the chamber Jade into the bargain, for she was as well dressed as the best." In order to avoid such impious fraudulence, Defoe recommended that female servants wear liveries, "as our Footmen do; or obliged to go in a Dress suitable to their Station. Our Charity Children," he added, "are

distinguished by their Dresses, why then may not our Women Servants?"
As a frank avowal of the stigma attached to service for women of the
lower classes, his proposal acknowledged that female servants used clothing to escape their identities.[39]

The question of appropriate attire led to debates over what constituted
proper behavior for female servants. Ornaments such as "Ribbands,
Ruffles, Necklaces, Fans, Hoop-Petticoats, and all those Superfluities in
Dress" not only cost money that would be better saved, but also required
a considerable outlay of effort. A mistress was bound to be displeased by
her maid when "the Time she pays and feeds her for, and expects should
be employ'd in her Business, shall be trifled away in curling her own
Hair, pinching her Caps, tying up her Knots, and setting her self forth, as
tho' she had no other thing to do, but to prepare for being look'd at."
Only the upper-class woman should expect to be an object of attention,
"[w]hereas nothing looks so handsome in a Servant," the manual
advised, "as a decent Plainness."[40] The discussion of the servant maid's
right to be looked at constituted a debate over her very status as a
woman. Stripped of her fancy attire, the female servant presumably would
lack sexual appeal and thus pose no threat to her mistress's domain. It
was no secret that female employers reneged from hiring attractive young
women for fear of their husband's wayward behavior. The struggle
between servant and mistress threatened to become a battle over sexual
identity and advantage, and the servant's subordination was supposed to
be obvious to all.[41]

Yet a number of forces worked against this subordination in the eighteenth century and created havoc within the seemingly confined world of
domestic life. Aping one's betters was a symptom of a larger phenomenon of the rise of "consumer sovereignty" and the resulting evidence of a
love of luxury for which eighteenth-century England was notorious. The
English state had abandoned sumptuary legislation that restricted the
wearing of certain types of clothing by the beginning of the seventeenth
century. With the expansion of trade and the retailing of food and wares,
something approaching mass consumption soon evolved. Masters
retained the use of payment in kind as a paternalistic way of restricting
free consumption, particularly in the case of servants who lived in. But as
greater numbers of servants existed outside the prescribed constraints of
service in husbandry, many received cash wages that they could dispose of
as they saw fit. Their freedom in spending generated much discussion in
the eighteenth century, if not paranoia. The historian consequently must
avoid exaggerating both the freedom and the extent of the spending:
most purchases were limited to rather ordinary food and clothing, and
not everyone enjoyed the privilege of having money for much beyond
necessities. Yet their spending nevertheless had a considerable impact—
mainly negative—on public opinion.[42]

One rather superficial but noticeable effect was a blurring of visible
class distinctions. "It is the curse of this nation that the labourer and the

mechanic will ape the lord," complained Jonas Hanway; "the different ranks of people are too much confounded: the lower orders press so hard on the heels of the higher, if some remedy is not used the Lord will be in danger of becoming the valet of his Gentleman."[43] Foreigners always commented on the striking homogeneity of English dress, something which would have been inconceivable on the Continent. Von Archenholz's famous account of his travels in England in the 1790s reaffirmed the same impression, noting that "the accumulation of riches, luxury and pleasures are enjoyed by all classes."[44] The new consumer articles of commercial capitalism gave women servants access to relatively inexpensive reproductions of upper-class fashions and, as a result, to postures and occasional attitudes that challenged their employers' superiority. "[C]an you believe any Mistress can be pleased to find," asked Haywood rhetorically, "that she no sooner puts on a new thing, than her Maid immediately jumps into something as like it as she can?" The competition in fashion threatened the hierarchy of ranks in the eighteenth century.[45]

Such challenges extended beyond dress to food and drink. Eighteenth-century servants consumed coffee and tea, as well as "dainties" such as cakes and nuts, either purchased and brought home from shops, or pilfered from their employers' pantry. "It is now usual with many Female Servants to insist on Tea in their Agreement," complained a critic of the poor, "and to refuse serving where this is not allowed." These voices obviously exaggerated the extent to which servants enjoyed "luxuries," but their objections were related to the general concerns rising from new forms of consumption in the eighteenth century. Because service was seen as a nursery for the laboring classes, such extravagance threatened to have a pernicious effect on the nation at large. "And when from Servants they go to be poor Men's Wives, we may naturally suppose they carry the same expensive Appetites and Habits with them, which being propagated by Example to the Offspring, the Evil becomes still more epidemical."[46] The use of these articles required time, so employers might rightly object to them. Possibly as irksome was the air of delicacy and leisure adopted by servants as they partook of beverages and foods. Sitting over tea was a waste of time; and when women servants, like their mistresses, sought to limit their breakfasts to liquid alone, they threatened to diminish their own strength. Mistresses were more apt to encourage their servant maids to eat heartily, even if—or precisely because—it appeared unwomanly.[47]

The mood of getting and spending invaded the close quarters of servant-keeping households like an obnoxious odor. According to Haywood's manual, the tendency to spend rather than save was new among servants. "Enquire of your Mothers and Grandmothers," she intoned, "how the Servants of their Times were drest, and you will be told that it was not by laying out their Wages in these Fopperies they got good Husbands, but by the Reputation of their Honesty, Industry and Frugality, in saving what they got in Service."[48] Once servants appeared to abandon their habit of saving in order to consume, their entire identity was thrown into question. A mistress could not assume that the lowly servant would strive as hard to please in order to retain her position, or accept restrictions or pay without question. The freedom to participate in the consumption of the new world of commodities worked as a powerful solvent of relations of hierarchy and deference.

The habits of commerce inspired a constant search for improvement and might also have contributed to the tendency of women servants to quit one job and look for another. In effect, some eighteenth-century servants "shopped" for places, acquiring and discarding positions as they pleased. "Some of you are apt to [say], *There are more Places than Parish Churches,* and on the least Occasion presently give Warning," chided Haywood in her advice to young women of the 1740s. Judging from advice books, the tendency to "give warning" was exceedingly common in the eighteenth century and appeared to be the result of servants wanting "every Thing exactly to [their] Mind." Employers complained volubly of the grasping self-interest of servants as well as a "roving disposition." "They see others in full ascent, which makes them uneasy and ready to do whatever they can for themselves," pointed out a contemporary in 1785. The average length of stay in any one position, according to one historian, was between three and four years; household account books and servants' memoirs corroborate this estimate.[49]

The practice of servants hiring "chairs" or chars to assist them in their work, another aspect of the relative autonomy of service in the eighteenth century, was common enough to warrant discussion in Haywood's manual. On occasions when mistresses demanded too much within an allotted time, servants subcontracted tasks to women whom they hired from outside the household. Because this introduced an unknown and possibly dishonest character into the household, it was greatly discouraged. A better solution was to "remonstrate it to [the] Mistress" modestly, and if she did not permit any assistance, then a servant could legitimately give warning and expect a good character upon her leaving.[50]

Situations like this show how eighteenth-century service, despite its obvious servile characteristics, was forced to accommodate aspects of a contractual relationship. Widespread evidence led J. Jean Hecht to conclude that "[e]ven when allowance is made for the inevitable exaggeration, the barrage of criticism directed at them by employers leaves the impression that as a group servants were highly insubordinate and very far from identifying their interests with those of their masters."[51] Allowed some degree of self-assertion and autonomy, maids made known their differences with mistresses. The breakdown of what economic historians have termed "hierarchically structured demand," which freed many (though not all) servants from the constraints of payment in kind, enabled some to undermine strict deference through habits of dress and small expenditures. Of course not all servants enjoyed such freedoms, but the sheer possibility gave the profession a certain gloss, at least to observers.

Yet by the end of the eighteenth century, the disappearance of other forms of employment, particularly in the countryside, flooded the servant market. At the nadir of employability, laboring women were seen as destined for little other than service. Studies have shown that female apprenticeship in a relatively wide range of trades was on the decline by the end of the century.[52] "[A]s there are not any little trades which the lower classes of women can be taught," one female philanthropist concluded in 1800, "the best thing that can be done for girls in that rank of life, is to make them fit for servants."[53] Such lack of imagination was not uncommon: typical workhouse rules of the 1790s also implied that service was the likely future employment of most young female inhabitants.[54] To a critical public, such women perpetually sought poor relief and bore illegitimate children. All women of the lower classes became vulnerable to the negative stereotype applied to servants: the intransigent, servile worker who preferred idleness to productivity, or pilfering and sponging to self-sufficiency.

II

In the nineteenth-century contest between mistress and maid, the middle-class woman forced the surrender of her working-class servant. No longer seen as productive, the working-class woman was defined by subordination within the dominant relationships in her life.[55] Servants were cast as petty thieves and lazy lay-abouts, and they were generally believed to be self-serving and scheming unless proven otherwise. Popular literature made the image appealing to servants themselves. The eighteenth-century chapbook, *The Parson and the Fowls: or, the maid too cunning for her master*, showed a servant gleefully outfoxing her rather bumbling employer. According to the standard script, servants "delighted in bamboozling" masters and mistresses, who were repeatedly outwitted by an inexhaustible store of cunning. Rowlandson's prints, dated slightly later, give visual testimony to a similar repertory, but in the form of employers' obsessions and fears: an illustration of 1822 shows servants busily stealing behind the back of an oblivious sated master who has fallen asleep at his table. Of course, such incidents did occur, as in the case of Thomas Wright, a clothier and weaver of Yorkshire, who complained of abuse by his two servants after the death of his wife in 1777. One woman "turned the house upside down, and plundered it through every time I turned my back, and carried out (whenever I was absent) to her father's and relations, meal, flour, butter, eggs, ribbons, small linen, beer and bottles of rum . . . ."[56] As the status of service declined in the nineteenth century, the belief that theft was inevitable only furthered the erosion of master-servant relations.

The battle between the demanding mistress and the impudent servant only magnified the most unattractive attributes of both women. The middle-class woman fared little better than her servant: she became known for her ability to find fault rather than satisfaction, and perhaps because the relationship was one between women, her passionate tendencies were often in evidence. This was precisely what Rowlandson sought to portray in a series of etchings intended to caricature female emotions. In one entitled "Anger," Rowlandson points out in the caption, "this unruly passion shews itself in a forcible degree in a termagant mistress scolding her maid servant." His choice of relationship reveals how open and distasteful the conflict between the two women could be; in this case, the employer, hideous and shrewish, gets the brunt of Rowlandson's brutal pen.[57] Yet her unattractiveness did not diminish the difference in power between the two women.

The critical view of servants contributed greatly to a more general negative image of women of the lower classes in the nineteenth century. Literary and popular images provide a gauge of the changing view of the servant: she was typically a stock figure, an uninteresting, simple girl who posed no threat to the prosperous household. A sketch by Leigh Hunt, published in 1826, described features that readily contrasted with eighteenth-century depictions of servants. The new servant appeared domesticated and lacked any individuality or cunning. Replacing the ambiguous, sometimes ornate attire of previous years was a uniform: unobtrusively simple, dark, and forever remindful of the servant's place:

> The maid servant, in her apparel, is either slovenly or fine by turns, and dirty always; or she is at all times snug and neat, and dressed according to her station. In the latter case, her ordinary dress is black stockings, a stuff gown, a cap, and neck-handkerchief pinned corner-wise behind. . . . On Sundays and holidays, and perhaps of afternoons, she changes her black stockings for white, puts on a gown of better texture and fine pattern, sets her cap and her curls jauntily, and lays aside the neck-handkerchief for a high body, which, by the way, is not half so pretty.

Distanced by her weekday wear, the servant could now appear "pretty" on the weekend without offense. If she resembled her betters in any way, her behavior was construed as silly rather than annoying:

> In her manners, the maid servant sometimes imitates her young mistress; she puts her hair in papers, cultivates a shape and occasionally contrives to be out of spirits.

None of these actions altered her natural self and therefore proved futile:

> But her own character and condition overcome all sophistications of this sort; her shape, fortified by the mop and scrubbing-brush, will make its way; and exercise keeps her healthy and cheerful.

Incapable of low spirits and never physically in need, the maidservant was stalwart and decent. She could never be other than what she was, even in mere figure or hairstyle. The question of improvement was a moot one, for she would find fulfillment through marriage, as the wife of "the butcher, the butler, or her cousin"—unless, of course, she lost her virtue on an outing to the fair.[58]

By the beginning of the nineteenth century, women servants outnumbered men by almost eight to one; by the 1880s, their predominance would grow to twenty-two to one. The expense of keeping male servants, including the continuing increase in taxes applied to their employment, fed this decline, though the fall in their proportion did not represent an absolute numerical decrease. (Coachmen, for example, multiplied three times more rapidly than the rate of growth of new households, and gardeners, categorized as outdoor servants, continued to grow in number.) Their ranks simply failed to keep up with the remarkable rise in female servants: the largest female occupation of the mid-Victorian period, domestic service employed one out of every four working women in 1851.[59] This suggests that running a Victorian household demanded a great deal of labor power and, in addition, that a greater number of women were turning over domestic responsibilities to others.[60]

Many of these employers were quintessential Victorian women striving to fulfill the expectations of bourgeois culture: their image rested upon the absence of any form of paid employment or arduous work and a sumptuous or at least heavily accoutered style of living. "The large family, the large and over-furnished house, the entertainment of guests at lavish dinner-parties, and the economic ability to keep one's wife in genteel idleness" represented the ideal attributes of the Victorian middle-class household.[61] The wives of professionals such as bankers, doctors, and businessmen numbered among these women, and their responsibility in upholding the status of their husbands and households called for the conventionally prescribed trio of servants: the cook, the housemaid, and the parlormaid (or, in the case of a family with children, the nursemaid). This classic Victorian middle-class existence, representing solidity and prosperity, gave birth to the powerful norms that governed the age.[62]

The insatiable demand for servants rose more generally from the increasing ranks of the moderately wealthy and lower middle classes, where one or two servants were the norm. This sector of the Victorian population could range in income anywhere from a base of £60 (the salary of an average business clerk in Manchester in 1860), through the bottom line of income taxation at £150 (a clerk in a very responsible position might earn this much or slightly more) to roughly £300 described in one survey as a "small mercantile income."[63] Where lower middle-class incomes overlapped with those of the upper working classes, historians have used servant keeping as an index of middle-class status. As part of the "paraphernalia of gentility," domestic servants indicated aspirations to a decidedly middle-class way of life. J. A. Banks's influential study, *Prosperity and Parenthood*, employed this method, among others, in order to mark the growth of the middle-class proportion of the population, which expanded at a faster rate than the population at large.[64]

The employment of servants did not necessarily indicate middle-class status, or, for that matter, gentility.[65] Frank Prochaska has added an important qualifying perspective on Banks's assumption by revealing the ready availability of the "cut-price domestic," which working-class families could obtain through charity institutions at rates as low as three pounds a year. Often the former inmates of workhouses or prisons, these girls made unlikely candidates for service in the homes of the upper middle classes, who would be loathe to trust them. Their willingness (though this term must be used with caution) to work for low sums of pay enabled people lower down the social scale to hire them. "Artisans and small tradespeople were the usual customers at the workhouses and the charitable institutions; when they went away empty-handed it was more likely to be because of a shortage of supply, not because of the price." Keeping a servant might indicate a very modest expenditure.[66]

The Victorian domestic servant thus eludes historians, as well as census enumerators and the authors of servant manuals; yet the data must not be disregarded entirely. Table 9.1 gives some sense of the numerical dimensions of the female servant class.[67] The most common of all categories of female domestics was the "general servant" or "maid-of-all-work." By the 1860s, general servants were nine times as numerous as cooks.[68] Higgs's research on Rochdale revealed that 68 percent of all servants came under this classification in 1851, and in twenty districts studied by Ebery and Preston, 54 percent were declared as such in 1871. For the entire servant population of Great Britain for that year, nearly two-thirds of the 1.2 million women were "general servants."[69] Though the term sometimes functioned as a catchall, other studies confirm that the great majority of servants worked alone (and therefore became designated as "general") or with only one other servant.

The prevalence of general servants reveals how the affluence of most Victorian households must have fallen far short of the ideal. For most of these women worked not in the households of professional or landowning gentlemen, but rather, in the more modest establishments of small businessmen, clerks, and the like; at the lower end of the spectrum, the

Table 9.1 Female Indoor Domestic Servants in England and Wales, 1851–1871

	1851	1861	1871
General servants	575,162	644,271	780,040
Housekeepers	46,648	66,406	140,836
Cooks	44,009	77,822	93,067
Housemaids	49,885	102,462	110,505
Nurserymaids	35,937	67,785	74,491
Laundrymaids	—	4,040	4,538
TOTAL	751,641	962,786	1,204,477

class also included "grocers, bakers, beer house keepers, and . . . huckster[s]," as well as artisans and tradesmen whose status was more fluid and precarious.

Servants' autobiographies, chock-full of descriptions of physical hardship and petty economies, support this impression. "My mother was glad for me to go out for food alone," Mrs. Wrigley (b. 1858), a Welsh servant, recalled; but when her first employers rationed her food and locked everything up, she soon left. In her next position, she "had no wages," "only a few clothes."[70] Lilian Westall's discerning assessment of her many places pointed to the insufficient income of some who nevertheless hired servants:

> My employers didn't seem to have much money themselves; he was a clerk of some sort, but they liked the idea of having a 'nurse-maid' and made me buy a cap, collar, cuffs and apron. The mistress took me to have a photograph taken with the children grouped around me.

Her next position entailed general housework for a dentist's family in Chiswick. As the only servant, she was up at six in the morning and busy till eleven o'clock at night. "The mistress explained that she was very particular; the house had to be spotless always. After all, they were professional people and used to very high standards."[71]

Working alone, general servants led an arduous, dreary life of toil. Hours of work stretched from 6:00 or 6:30 in the morning till 11:00 or 12:00 at night, with irregular breaks for tea or a brief meal. Because her responsibilities covered almost every department of general housekeeping, from scrubbing the flags in front of the house to preparing and delivering the supper upstairs, the general maid's work was never done. Hannah Cullwick provided a detailed account of the endless labor of the maid-of-all-work while she was employed at the home of a beer merchant in London. Her recital of one day's responsibilites, even when abbreviated, seems endless:

> Saturday, 7 March (1863) Got up early, for they all went to Temple Bar to see the princess come through. They all got off in carriages before 9 o'clock—Mary the housemaid & Sarah as well & I was left, & it was a first-rate chance for me to get some cleaning done. I black'd the grates & that & clean'd 3 pairs of boots. Took the breakfast up & Mr Garle came done & ask'd me to brush his trousers & I did 'em for him, kneeling on the floor & wi' him putting his foot on a chair for the bottoms. . . . I had some breakfast. Clean'd away upstairs & wash'd the things up. Put coals on the fire. Went up & made all the beds & emptied the slops. Came down & swept the dining room all over & dusted it. Swept the hall & steps & shook the mats & then I had a mutton chop & some beer for my dinner. Clean'd the windows in the hall & passage & clean'd the hall & steps . . . I took the matting out & shook it. Swept the passage & took the things out of the hole under the stairs . . . & swept the walls down . . . .
>
> The first part of the family came back at six & was ready for tea. . . . I carri'd the tea things up & all that & waited on them all they wanted, & then a lot

more came in & I wash'd up & took up fresh tea. Clean'd away again &
then laid the cloth for supper & cook'd the potatoes. Carried the supper up
& waited on them. Clean'd more knives and wash'd plates. Clean'd away &
laid the kitchen cloth for Mary & the waiter & us all. Had supper. Put way
& then I went to bed very tired . . . .[72]

As even Mrs. Beeton admitted, "A general servant's duties are so multifarious, that unless she be quick and active, she will not be able to accom-
plish this. To discharge these various duties properly is a difficult task,
and sometimes a thankless office."[73]

III

As the nineteenth century progressed, the business of service more exclusively involved relationships between women. The role of guardian of the
middle-class home, the repository of Victorian virtue and prosperity, fell
naturally to the female sex. One need only glance at the copious literature
on the subject of household management to comprehend the weight of
this burden, whether real or imagined. The art of housekeeping
demanded more than mere manual exertion. In the words of Mrs. Ellis,
author of the bestselling *Women of England* (1838), "household management" should aspire to the level of "philosophy."[74] In instructing and
supervising servants, the mistress became, in the words of Thorsten
Veblen, "the chief menial of the house." Such women could channel
boundless energy, often otherwise untapped, into their office. For those
who could not afford so much assistance, the exactions of economy could
demand as much time and trouble as a full complement of domestic
responsibilities and servants. Excessive vigilance resulted directly, some
believed, in the shortage of good servants complained of at the end of the
nineteenth century. The zeal of the aspiring Victorian woman was perhaps the servant's greatest enemy.[75]

Imbued with this philosophy, middle-class women made domestic service a vehicle for the expression of class consciousness and, more to the
point, class antagonism. To the servant, the more prosperous middle-
class woman owed her independence, or at least her freedom from manual labor. Yet required as she was to live with this visitor from another
class, she could hardly tolerate her. As Frank Prochaska has cleverly
quipped, while the Victorians cherished the precept "Servants talk about
People: Gentlefolk discuss Things," "one of the 'things' much discussed
. . . was the servant question." Victorian women devoted endless energy
to addressing the purported shortage of "good servants." Bristling with
criticisms and complaints, middle-class women made their experiences
with servants the centerpiece of their daily lives. Servants became the
scapegoats of all their animus, "the greatest plague connected with
housekeeping," or, in the words of a popular humorous novel of the
1840s, which based its entire plot around the servant–mistress relationship, "the greatest plague of life."[76]

"Nearly 'worried to Death' by the Greatest Plagues of one's Life." Frontispiece from Henry and Augustus Mayhew, *The Greatest Plague of Life: Or, the Adventures of a Lady in Search of a Good Servant* (1847). (Courtesy of Widener Library, Harvard University)

Mistresses viewed servant girls across a chasm of class difference. Attitudes of indifference and contempt enabled employers to distance themselves psychologically from the strangers with whom they shared close quarters; if servants could be seen as less than human, employers need not feel self-conscious or embarrassed to carry on their intimate lives in front of them.[77] Reports of interaction between servants and their mistresses, admittedly scarce and not always reliable, nevertheless deserve close analysis. The language and tone of such evidence suggests deeper meaning rooted in an ideology of class and race. For in the eyes of many masters and mistresses, class did operate in ways parallel to racial categories; lower-class people were closer to nature and less pure and clean than the more civilized middle-classes. Female servants suffered from the double stigma of gender and class, and the effect was a foreignness approaching racial difference. The framework of Victorian sexuality subjected lower-class women to inferior status from every point of view. As Leonore Davidoff has argued, "the dual vision of women, as woman and lady, becomes mixed with other polarities such as those between white and black, familiar and foreign, home and empire." Using the unusual and somewhat bizarre relationship between maidservant Hannah Cullwick (b. 1833) and Arthur Munby, barrister and man of letters, Davidoff intricately illustrates how men employed these assumptions to maintain power over women. Less explored is the way in which middle-class women, enmeshed in many of the same beliefs, exercised much the same power over servants through their role as mistresses.[78]

More prosperous Victorian women reserved their greatest contempt for the lowest class of servants, those from the workhouse. Debates raged over the worth of programs to educate female workhouse and prison inmates for domestic service. Critics doubted the efficacy of such training and wondered if the better class of employers would ever admit such girls into their homes. "If workhouse schools were, as it is hoped they will be, separated from pauper life and conditions," observed the *Edinburgh Review*, we should have [the servants] we require."

> It is only in extremity that employers will receive into their houses girls from either [workhouse or ragged schools]. Girls brought up in the workhouse are reasonably objected to; and so are the odds and ends of pupils from ragged schools: and thus, at present, while one class is growing too high for service, the next class remains too low for it.[79]

Popular opinion reiterated the belief that workhouse girls would only end in the Magdalen ward of the workhouse, the sick ward of a hospital (inevitably with venereal disease), or in the street. Philanthropists and government officials, accustomed to the way in which physical differences heightened the barrier of class, casually referred to the stigma borne by these girls. "The [workhouse] girls in service repeatedly tell me," reported Mrs. Nassau Senior, "that they would have no chance of getting into a 'good family' because they are so little."[80] Even the more enlightened middle-class feminist spared few words on girls who fell into the hands of the parish and then moved into domestic service; this was "a system," claimed the *English Woman's Journal* in 1859, "which turns those children first into destructive creatures preying on their fellow-beings, next into expensive claimants for food and medicine."[81]

Just as typical were the complaints of the lack of training among "raw" girls fresh from the country. Though admittedly the most desirable pool of applicants, as town girls showed too little deference and respect, the well-to-do employer nevertheless expressed exasperation at their ignorance and clumsiness. Their rural accents, always rather mockingly reproduced in middle-class accounts, underscored the status of servants as foreign creatures. "What the task [of training] is can be understood only by those who have witnessed the bewilderment of any raw girl amidst the furniture and the methods of a middle-class house," reported one reviewer.

> She has to learn the use of a hundred things she never saw before, and to take care of articles which seem made only to be broken. She does not even understand the language of educated people; she sees no meaning in their daily arrangements, and cannot remember a tithe of what she is told and must not forget. The drawing-room which she would once "have given sixpence to see," if she had not got in gratis, because "it was as good as a play," she has herself to take more or less charge of; and so on through the whole system of the house.[82]

If such a servant in the end turned out to be competent, she owed her value to the mistress who trained her. Middle-class women credited themselves with the creation of good girls since they firmly believed that the "apprentice-servant" arrived from her own home with no knowledge of cleanliness whatsoever. A tract published by the Society for the Promotion of Christian Knowledge, *Little Servant Maids* (1851), by Charlotte Adams, revealed typical middle-class assumptions about working-class girls. Raised in degradation, these girls did not know how to dust, sweep, whiten steps, or wash up tea things; the only chores their mothers taught them were how to nurse babies, fetch water, scour floors, mend clothes, and light fires. Very few lower-class skills could be transferred to the middle-class household.

Corresponding to the distinctions of class within the ranks of servants was a hierarchy of mistresses; the social distance between mistresses could be almost as great as that between mistress and servant. The type of servant that a woman hired often indicated her social status. Mild condescension was reserved for "the humblest class of mistresses—the wives of farmers and tradesmen, the widows and single ladies of small means who cannot afford to take qualified servants."[83] Yet these women maintained a rightful, if fragile claim to gentility. Occasionally a board of guardians turned down an application for a child servant on the grounds of a lack of morality evidenced by the prospective family. Even the tastefully discreet

Mrs. Beeton added a word of criticism of the lower middle-class mistress: the general servant, she carefully noted, was likely to start off in the household of "some small tradesman's wife . . . just a step above her in the social order; and although the class contains among them many excellent kind-hearted women, it also contains some very rough specimens of the feminine gender, and to some of these it occasionally falls to give our maid-of-all-work her first lessons in her multifarious occupations."[84] The prescriptions of Victorian femininity and domesticity subjected women to constant judgment, often at the hands of other women. Few lower middle-class or working-class women could meet such standards.

For most servants, actuality probably seldom conformed to the ideal. The wages and conditions of work for general servants contradicted all the most sacred tenets of certain Victorian myths. The proficiency of the general servant stood little chance of improvement over time, despite the constant talk of Victorian ladies of how much energy was devoted to teaching household chores. The demands of the job made meticulousness impossible and expertise in any one area of work unfeasible. In the case of the lodging-house maid, who worked without supervision, she was more likely to follow orders than instructions, with little time for the completion of basic chores. Owing to the heaviness of her responsibilities, the servant-of-all-work often grew less rather than more competent. She possessed a poor reputation, for employers of larger households believed her to be careless and untidy as a result of her poor "management of their household duties." The maid-of-all-work, according to more generous observers, was "conscious of having fallen into the habit of doing everything badly, and of having ceased to be able to do things well."[85]

Moreover, the general servant's pay was hardly enough to live on, let alone save. "Of the 400,000 maids-of-all-work," reported the *Edinburgh Review* for 1862, "few have more than 10l. a-year, and many have no more than 8l." When "the plainest and most economical style of dress" cost at least "6l. in the country, and 7l. in town," the maidservant had hardly enough left to spend on postage for correspondence with her family.[86] Mrs. Beeton reported a range of £7 10s to £11, with an allowance for tea, sugar, and beer, for the same decade. The Carlyles employed a long string of general servants in the 1830s at £8 a year for long hours of work under constant supervision. One survey recorded a range of £16 to £30 for general maids, but Mrs. Beeton's averages remained between £10 to £16, plus allowances.[87]

These estimates appear generous compared to the irregular wages anecdotally reported by servants themselves. At the age of nine, one girl obtained no wages, "only a few clothes," as a maid-of-all-work at Stockport in the 1860s. For general cleaning and nursing, another girl received three shillings a week around 1870. "My wages were very small," she reported, "and I often bought myself some food as I always felt I could eat more than was given to me. I tried to dress nicely . . . . My sister who worked at a factory always seemed to be better dressed than I was, and I suppose I envied her a little."[88] The most important factor in determining wage rates appeared to be the affluence and size of the household; lesser establishments were likely to deviate from the norm in the demands placed on a servant and the pay she received for meeting them. Here, too, housing and diet were likely to be much poorer than in wealthier homes.[89]

Hannah Cullwick's diaries provide an unmatched source of firsthand experiences of a servant's life. Scant education in a charity school equipped her with writing skills adequate to supply her suitor and later husband with daily reports of her routine work and personal life. Because convention, as well as Munby's peculiarities, dictated that the couple carry on their courtship in secret, "correspondence" through Hannah's diary entries often took the place of ordinary meetings. Hannah obliged Munby in his demands that she supply reports of her life in copious detail, but she repeatedly expressed doubts of the value of her untutored observations and accounts of her daily drudgery. She never enjoyed writing and seemed to long for her obligations to stop; they continued, however, from 1854 to 1873. While some of what she wrote was tailored according to Munby's specifications (he particularly wished to hear the details of her dirtiest chores), her natural candor and shrewd powers of observation gave rise to a wealth of fascinating material on relations between mistress and servant.

Hannah's daily records show how the servant's routine demanded constant dealings with middle-class women. The process of securing positions, fulfilling responsibilities, and terminating jobs placed her under the power of female authority. In the course of her career, Hannah passed through literally a score of places of employment, ranging from country estates to lodging houses. The treatment she received was as varied, and sometimes Hannah benefited from the kindnesses and charity of a good mistress. Yet even in the best of situations, her account concurred with middle-class representations of servants' lives. She lived under constant scrutiny, and apart from Munby and a few of his associates, the gaze was most often a female one. Mistresses regularly measured and exerted power over her physical person. "I needn't ask about your temper, your face looks good & Miss Margaret spoke so highly of you I'm sure you'll be an excellent creature," one of Hannah Cullwick's employers said to her in their first interview. "What *arms* you've got!" a woman innkeeper exclaimed upon first addressing her. "I like the looks of you—you look honest & strong. I like your face too."[90] Other servants commented on the same blatant inspection of their bodies in interviews. The servant girl was, in effect, a beast of burden, and employers unblinkingly examined them as such.[91]

Hannah Cullwick's experience at a servants' registry, a highly regarded form of female philanthropy, yielded similar impressions. "I felt very nervous till one lady spoke to me & she ask'd me to follow her, & that was to another room where the ladies sat & hir'd you or ask'd you questions after they'd walk'd round and pick'd you out," Hannah reported.[92] Nothing promoted the livelihood of a servant as much as good looks (or, more accurately, features that could be construed as middle-class), and in her youth, Hannah had the good fortune of a pleasing countenance. "Miss J. told me that she herself thought the first time she see me at Mrs Eastlands how that she thought me the best-looking servant she ever saw, & that her sister said I was very different to servants in general, not at all *common*," Hannah assured herself when wondering if a particular mistress liked her. Like the ideal Victorian woman, a servant needed to be mindful of her appearance; but in this case, the judgement of women, not men, was at issue.[93]

Perhaps the most striking of Hannah's revelations was the humiliation, unclouded by resentment, that she experienced as a servant. Middle-class observers seldom explicitly recognized this aspect of service, preferring to see the degradation of domestics within the framework of required discipline rather than a function of middle-class preferences. Even the most polite employer assumed that the servant's position was, at bottom, menial and inferior and therefore unworthy of the same considerations given to other people. Few would have imagined that the servant girl actually minded the treatment that this implied. But Hannah noticed and felt all the abuse meted out to her. Throughout her career, she developed a sharp eye for differences between "ladies" and "real ladies"—those who behaved badly toward her, and those who used politeness to get what they wanted. Her job at a lodging house generated some of the worst encounters. In laying carpets "as the lady wanted 'em," "one proud one stood over me as I knelt & was crawling on the floor once," she recorded. "Instead of her showing me how with her hand she kick'd me with her foot & pointed. I dare say she thought I *sh'd* feel hurt & vex'd with her but I didn't." But then she added, "I was glad she thought me humble enough without kicking again." Such was the attitude of the mistress "determined to be dissatisfied"—and she encountered several such employers—who "made . . . reason to be angry, instead of thanking me as I thought she would."[94]

For Hannah, experiences such as these made her ponder the possibility of someday leaving service for other work. "I am thirty years old this month," she recorded in May of 1863, "must be quite a woman now, though I don't feel any different than I ever did except in feeling lower in heart I think, for I've been a servant now 20 years or more." For reasons of his own, Munby encouraged Hannah to remain a domestic. "He has taught me, though it's been difficult to learn thoroughly, the beauty in being nothing but a common drudge & to bear being despised by others what don't have to work the same way." Popular opinion held that the typical servant was always nurturing some ambition of rising in the world, and Hannah confirmed the belief, though more for emotional than material reasons. "I have hardly ever met wi' a *servant* yet who wasn't

ashamed o' dirty work & who would be glad to get out of it for something they think is *better*," she averred.[95] Other servants' autobiographies,
though far less detailed, reveal the same abhorrence of "dirty work" and
what came with it—the humiliating posture required to clean steps, the
disdainful treatment handed out by employers' children, the sexual
advances of masters and their sons, the constant truck with slops, grime,
and sweat—all added up to an unsavory and often unendurable lot that
every woman dreamed of escaping.

Victorians, including servants themselves, regarded domestics within
a finely graded social hierarchy. All common servants were "low" on
the larger ladder of social class, but some were lower than others. In
some rural districts, servants retained a weak claim to respectability and
still managed to make advantageous marriages. But in urban areas, and
particularly in factory districts where other employment options for
women existed, servants were viewed as virtual slaves lacking autonomy
and self-respect. Many employers carefully prohibited visitors through
the notorious "no followers" dictum, limited servants' time off, and
prescribed what that time would be used for. (Sunday churchgoing
sometimes constituted the only leisure time a servant might obtain.)
The typical factory girl and, later in the century, the shop girl enjoyed
far more freedom in determining their personal lives, lending added
ignominy to the already heavy burden of contempt reserved for most
Victorian servants.

The hierarchy exerted a palpable influence on the day-to-day inter-
course of servants. Female servants were forced to navigate between the
condescension of employers and the disdain of other servants. Like their
mistresses, female servants sometimes absorbed the value system of the
dominant class and judged their peers almost as harshly as middle-class
employers might, if only to obtain a modicum of self-respect. Hannah
noted how servants of holiday lodgers at Margate "despised us for being
lodging house servants rather than having pity for us." And for women,
the gradations of class applied in special ways. In another post, a fellow
servant looked down on her for dressing shabbily and "talking so
plain."[96]

Different standards of womanhood applied to each class; struggling
with an awareness of this, Hannah frequently ruminated on her relations
with other women. Her accounts of her mistresses reveal a wisdom that
came from her marginalization. One of her employers, exhibiting characteristics that were typically female, inspired mixed feelings. "Miss Henderson would send for me to her room sometimes, to ask me questions
about the books or some trivial thing or other," Hannah recalled. "I was
humble and respectful to her & we generally parted on good terms. But I
couldn't help thinking her very fussy for all I like'd her principle, & felt
she was a real lady, but not over wise in not trusting me more & leaving
me to go & do as I lik'd on Sundays so long as I was in good time for
prayers." Miss Henderson's daughter inspired less affection:

She was fussy and *whining* like, & yet so small & feeble. It seem'd hard to be provoked so by her, & for me to be patient & meek to one as I could crush with one hand almost & I so much taller nor her. But she knew she was the lady & I knew I was her servant & I pitied her too, for being not well through a love affair, that I never forgot my place & was as quiet as ever I could be with her, & I think she did not dislike me.

Hannah readily accepted kindnesses from her mistresses, so her diaries tended to reflect their best features. Yet interspersed throughout her accounts were numerous records of less pleasant encounters. "I used to see some young ladies (Miss Perkins's) as I stood looking out in the area," she wrote while visiting Brighton. "They was so proud & would look so disdainfully down at me." Without the cushion that came from a working relationship, contact with ladies could prove wounding.[97]

Class conflict, always straining at the boundaries of domestic service, broke into full view during the second half of the nineteenth century. "Good servants" had always been difficult to find and harder to keep; but now the dilemma took the shape of an open breach between employers and servants. "We hear that domestic servants have become so 'insolent,' and even domineering, that it is difficult to deal with them, and impossible to be on comfortable terms with them," was the report in 1862. Still more galling to the middle class was "the servants' notion . . . that we require them more than they require us."[98] Contemporaries registered servants' preferences for more contractual relations and greater independence. Clearly this was not all that was needed to rescue domestic service from criticism and condemnation from every quarter of society.

Conclusion

No matter how hard the challenge of successive generations, the conventions of the Victorian age endure. The work ethic, the ethos of self-help and individualism, the sublimation and suppression of sexuality, and pervasive sexual divisions flourished in the halcyon days of mid nineteenth-century prosperity and are with us today. They owe their durability, at least in part, to the economic miracle of industrialization. Nowadays, any ambitious nation must take into account the systems of behavior that played a part in English industrialization: the resulting material rewards have sealed their success.

How difficult, then, must be the task of untangling those conventions that impinged on the material life and status of working-class women. The resulting account risks sounding unremittingly grim and predictable. Industrialization brought about the subordination of women in many realms of production, but can this account change the larger picture of industrial history without seeming to elevate an illusory "golden age" of the preindustrial past? In what ways can a reevaluation of industrialization be helpful, particularly in an era that has jettisoned wholesale critiques of capitalism? Many alternative views of British industrialization celebrate the evolution of labor relations, for example, or the recognition of government responsibility for the health and safety of its workers. What has this study told us with regard to general questions about economic development and the inclusion of women?

This book has aimed to dislodge the "whig history" of industrialization—an unbroken narrative of progress—from its dictatorial role. The study of women and work, to paraphrase feminist Patricia Hill Collins, can "create possibilities for new versions of truth." We have charted a different history of industrial innovation, full of unexpected twists and turns, rather than a course of progress toward the present. The route has involved conflicts not always apparent in the "winners' history" of industrialization. At times, the elisions and silences involving the interests of women and the laboring poor have left us with an inadequate sense of the concerns that were obvious to contemporaries. Focusing on issues of gender and class has forced us to cast our net widely in determining the context of industrial transformation. Easy assumptions about material success bear reexamination in light of the most general questions about economic justice and social well-being.

The history of women workers highlights the link between poverty and progress. Attitudes toward the laboring poor during the critical period of early industrialization informed important determinations about who would work, how well they performed, and how they were to be remunerated. Earlier views stressed an inclusive attitude toward the laboring population; women as well as men were seen as potentially productive and necessary to the nation's economic welfare. Large-scale unemployment and growing poverty eroded this perspective and opened the way for a reevaluation of the poor. Idleness came to be seen as the result of laziness and lack of moral fiber among the poor at precisely the time when changes in agriculture and domestic spinning rendered women unemployed and dependent. Perhaps as definitive was the deterioration of good will toward the poor after 1780. This was to impinge on women in especially deleterious ways, as certain special categories of sympathy and charity that had helped to compensate for their customary disabilities as women (their responsibility for children, the infirm, and the old) were swept aside.

The eighteenth century saw laborers as mainly an undifferentiated mass, and women claimed a rightful place, however unstable, within the realm of the industrious nation. As long as they inhabited a household and worked within the aegis of a productive "little commonwealth," they could enjoy a fair share of security and praise. The paternalistic nature of eighteenth-century society circumscribed the experience of women, but it also allowed for some negotiation between propertied classes and rural laborers. In agrarian society, laboring women could work within the interstices: a loose system of property ownership enabled them to gather subsistence needs, and a local, *ad hoc* system of poor relief provided material aid without confining them in an institution. Discourses about a moral economy and a village community provided a basis for discussion of their productive lives and maintenance.

Into this context the modernization of agriculture introduced a welter of new values. Changes in property ownership and land use made women's customary work in agriculture illegal if not impossible. At the same time, new patterns in employment announced a hierarchy of labor: male laborers claimed whatever job security and skill acquisition that were available (which in agriculture amounted to very little), while female laborers were consigned to seasonal, unskilled, and low-paid work. The transformation of dairying demonstrated the ways in which the commercial advancement of agriculture promoted a set of skills and knowledge identified with male management, while attributing backwardness and unreliability to female labor.

The revolution in the production of textiles, the centerpiece of most studies of industrialization, enables us to witness a similar reconceptualization of women's work. Once a widespread employment thoroughly identified with women, spinning became mechanized; housed in factories; and managed, supervised, and carried out largely by men in the early industrial period. Though women workers found jobs operating large mules in factories during the 1820s and 1830s, for the most part, they obtained work on the lowest rungs of the employment ladder—in picking, tenting, and carding—where they earned "wages approximating one-third to one-half of men's at best."[1]

But the story reveals more than simply the displacement of female labor in one industry. The transformation of spinning gave another occasion for the reevaluation of female labor as inferior. As this highly influential form of production established, women workers proved ill-suited to the rational, ends-oriented production of large-scale textile manufacturing. Women's handwork was construed as irregular and unreliable, their demands as workers were considered disruptive, and the autonomous nature of female domestic industry was deemed incompatible with the requirements of economic expansion. Already existing prejudices toward women were mobilized in an effort to eliminate the bottleneck in the production of spun thread for weavers. Mechanization appeared as a triumph against entrenched systems of production populated by women and children, thereby setting at odds new forms of production against the people who were responsible for the old.

One result of this defamation of women workers was the reinscription of what we now call "wage differentials" in the new industrial context. The seemingly timeless assumption that woman's labor demanded little remuneration gained new currency in a series of industrial decisions and improvements. Though the spinning jenny was named, according to legend, for a woman, and though its earliest versions were suitable for home use, it soon became the archetype for revolutionary textile machinery: large jennies, too costly for widespread use, offered advantages to the wealthy investor interested in organizing a factory. In their institutional setting, they were made to be mastered by male labor deemed as skilled. For most women, the mechanization of spinning spelled widespread unemployment.

A careful reading of the history of women and work thus must move away from the simple formulation, so easily cited by students, of "woman moved out of the home and into the factory." For the relatively limited number of women who took jobs in the early spinning factories, terms of employment were less than advantageous. Women were excluded from male unions and so were caught between employers and better-paid male workers. By the 1830s, power-loom weaving admitted a fair number of women workers into the factories at equal pay, but their reputations as well as their claims to skill came under siege. It was impossible for women workers to escape the limitations imposed on them as women, whether through exclusion from higher-paid positions, or denigration of their reputation on account of their purported sexual and social freedom. With government intervention in the 1840s, explicit definition of women workers within protective legislation confirmed in law that they constituted a secondary work force.

Perhaps the most important corrective to the formulaic view of women in factories is the paradoxical extension of handwork and cottage industry that occurred during the industrial era. This book covers only a fraction of the many kinds of employment outside the factory in which women constituted a major part of the work force. While the expansion of women's work in domestic industries between 1780 and 1815 had particular relevance to industrial development, this form of female employment recurred through the nineteenth century and remains prevalent around the world today. Women provided a plentiful, cheap supply of labor. Given the exigencies of their familial roles, they needed work that could be done at home, at irregular intervals during the day, and seasonally if need be. Such employments became categorized as unskilled (whether or not they were in fact) and low-paid, offering little predictability and no security. Often women who engaged in such activity became stigmatized by their association with "low" forms of employment. Cottage industry also influenced the status of women workers in factories by promoting the definition of women as unskilled and low-paid secondary wage earners. Their invisibility, then and today, only compounds the problem of identifying their labor as productive activity worthy of life-sustaining remuneration.

An examination of the emerging science of political economy has helped to ground this study of women workers in changing notions of wealth and poverty at the beginning of the nineteenth century. The erosion of sympathy for the poor became evident at the end of the eighteenth century. Rising poor rates, high unemployment, urbanization and its attendant anxieties, and widespread chronic poverty contributed to this general decline. Conflict between radicals and conservatives during the period of the French Revolution only sharpened hostilities. The population theories of Malthus fueled contentious debate over the merits of supporting the poor in their unemployment and need. These discussions occurred in the context of economic dislocation and war with France, yet they are noteworthy for their abandonment of an older perspective that held society accountable for its large population of laborers, who served as the defenders of the nation. Emerging as a dominant theme was the ethos of individualism, which resonated so well with industrial expansion and the call for an independent, free work force.

With regard to gender, such thinking contributed to a more general promotion of an ideal of a male breadwinner. What had been a partial and constantly contradicted assumption in relation to the laboring classes nevertheless became part of formal economic theory. The social construction of the male breadwinner, of course, took place mainly within the English middle classes at the end of the eighteenth century. Malthus's writings helped to identify some of the ideas about women associated with this allegedly universal construct, which was so clearly the product of a historical context. The ideals of marriage and the family carried very specific prescriptions: for women, these included a nonproductive domestic identity and vigilant attention to household and family, especially in the area of child rearing. Working-class women, living within very different circumstances, would find this model irrelevant, if not an obstruction to their efforts to provide for themselves and their families. Hard times at the turn of the century proved the miseries attendant upon the economic dependency of women. But from the point of view of middle-class surveyors of the poor, this only magnified the sense of "discovery" of the working-class female as an object in need of reform.

The project of civilizing the working-class female became a central concern of industrial society. As the customary productive image of the laboring woman waned, nineteenth-century opinion rushed to fill the void. A flurry of philanthropic activity, accompanied by a barrage of literary productions, urged the reform of working-class women. Middle-class women made up the vanguard: exploiting the ambiguity of their defined roles as protectors of female virtue, they extended their sphere of influence to women of the lower classes. As benefactresses, reformers, writers, or simply as employers, they promoted habits of thrift, diligence, and deference to authority. This, they felt, would ensure the security and social success of the working-class female.

A summary look at the massive employment of working-class women in domestic service brings together two strands prevalent throughout our examination: the difficulty that working-class women experienced in finding productive work and worth outside the home and the significance of the subordination embedded in relations between mistress and maid. The extent of domestic service as the largest employment of working-class women reflects the narrowing of definitions of women's work and opportunities open to them since the middle of the eighteenth century. These developments coincided with the vast accumulation of wealth among the middle classes, making possible an unprecedented elaboration of the domestic sphere. Households required more meticulous and regular attendance, much of which was passed on to a variety of female servants. At the same time, the ranks of people able and willing to afford domestic servants grew, swelling the numbers of women employed in menial domestic work. Bereft of skills marketable in the industrial work place, many working-class women had no choice but to enter domestic service.

Given the decline in their status, public opinion regarded service as a desirable solution to the problem of working-class women. Domestic service facilitated the communication of skills of household maintenance, while exacting proper female behavior and social deference from women who needed discipline and training. Domestic relations between mistresses and servants reveal the importance of class differences between women in industrial England. Though the hopeful student of feminism might argue that women of all classes suffered a lack of opportunities and status, the dynamics of domestic service prove this context to be no foundation for an identification of interests. Middle-class employers of servants claimed priority to power and authority, familial attachments, and individual fulfillment. The spell cast by domestic service over the fate of working-class women would not be broken until society addressed the larger question of their rightful place within the economic life of the first industrial nation.

Notes

Introduction

1. One of the earliest analytical discussions of this problem in historiography can be found in Eric Richards, "Women in the British Economy Since About 1700: An Interpretation," *History* 59 (1974): 337–57; for a more recent synthesis, see Janet Thomas, "Women and Capitalism: Oppression or Emancipation?" *Comparative Studies in Society and History* 30 (1988): 534–49; Leonore Davidoff, "The Role of Gender in the 'First Industrial Nation': Agriculture in England, 1780–1850," in *Gender and Stratification,* ed. Rosemary Crompton and Michael Mann (Cambridge: Polity Press, 1986), pp. 190–213; and for the problem in an American setting, see Carol J. Haddad, "Technology, Industrialization, and the Economic Status of Women," in *Women, Work, and Technology: Transformations,* ed. Barbara Drygulski Wright et al. (Ann Arbor: University of Michigan Press, 1987), pp. 33–57.

2. Ester Boserup, *Women's Role in Economic Development* (New York: St. Martin's Press, 1970), p. 5.

3. Richards, "Women in the British Economy," p. 342; for a critique of Richards's use of census data, see Thomas, "Women and Capitalism," pp. 542–43.

4. An example of such a view is Neil McKendrick, "Home Demand and Economic Growth: A New View of the Role of Women and Children in the Industrial Revolution," in *Historical Perspectives: Studies in English Thought and Society in Honour of J. H. Plumb,* ed. Neil McKendrick (London: Europa, 1974), pp. 152–210. Tables I.1, I.2, and I.3 give the number of women in the work force and where they worked. Figures for Table I.1 are adapted from B. R. Mitchell and P. Deane, *Abstract of Historical Statistics* (Cambridge: Cambridge University Press, 1971), pp. 6, 60. Those for Table I.2 are also from Mitchell and Deane, p. 60, and N. L. Tranter, "The Labour Supply, 1780–1860," in *The Eco-*

nomic History of Britain since 1700, 2 vols., ed. Roderick Floud and Donald McCloskey (Cambridge: Cambridge University Press, 1981), I: p. 208.

5. Sonya O. Rose, *Limited Livelihoods: Gender and Class in Nineteenth Century England* (Berkeley: University of California Press, 1992); Judy Lown, *Women and Industrialization: Gender at Work in Nineteenth-Century England* (Minneapolis: University of Minnesota Press, 1990).

6. Maurice Godelier, "Work and Its Representations: A Research Proposal," *History Workshop Journal* 10 (1980): 164–68. See also Patrick Joyce, ed., *The Historical Meanings of Work* (Cambridge: Cambridge University Press, 1987), p. 6.

7. Harold Perkin, *Origins of Modern English Society* (1969; reprint, London: Routledge, 1991), p. 112.

8. Ibid., pp. 156–57.

9. David Landes, *The Unbound Prometheus: Technological Change and Industrial Development in Western Europe from 1750 to the Present* (Cambridge: Cambridge University Press, 1972), p. 41.

10. Ibid., pp. 15, 21, 24. On women, nature, and technology, see Carolyn Merchant, *The Death of Nature: Women, Ecology and the Scientific Revolution* (New York: Harper and Row, 1980); Joan Rothschild, ed., *Machina Ex Dea: Feminist Perspectives on Technology* (New York: Pergamon Press, 1983).

11. For a full discussion of the historiography of the industrial revolution, see David Cannadine, "The Present and the Past in the English Industrial Revolution, 1880–1980," *Past and Present* 103 (1984): 130–72.

12. Raphael Samuel, "Workshop of the World: Steam Power and Hand Technology in Mid-Victorian Britain," *History Workshop Journal* 3 (1977): 17–18.

13. On the new labor history, see Ava Baron, ed., *Work Engendered: Toward a New History of American Labor* (Ithaca, NY: Cornell University Press, 1991), esp. her introduction, pp. 1–46; Ava Baron, "Contested Terrain Revisited: Technology and Gender Definitions of Work in the Printing Industry, 1850–1920," in *Women, Work, and Technology,* ed. Wright et al., pp. 58–83. For feminist analysis of technology, see Diane Elson and Ruth Pearson, "'Nimble Fingers Make Cheap Workers': An Analysis of Women's Employment in Third World Export Manufacturing," *Feminist Review* 7 (1981): 87–107; Anne Phillips and Barbara Taylor, "Sex and Skill: Notes Towards a Feminist Economics," *Feminist Review* 6 (1980): 79–88; Cynthia Cockburn, *Machinery of Dominance: Women, Men and Technical Know-How* (London: Pluto Press, 1985); Wendy Faulkner and Erik Arnold, eds., *Smothered by Invention: Technology in Women's Lives* (London: Pluto Press, 1985).

14. See William Cadogan, *Essay on Nursing* (London, 1750), p. 3; Randolph Trumbach, *The Rise of the Egalitarian Family: Aristocratic Kinship and Domestic Relations in Eighteenth-Century England* (New York: Academic Press, 1978), pp. 188–91.

15. For a lucid and inspiring call for an application of theory to the study of women in history, see Joan Wallach Scott, *Gender and the Politics of History* (New York: Columbia University Press, 1988), esp. chaps. 1 and 2.

Chapter 1

1. For a general discussion of women's work in the preindustrial economy, see Alice Clark, *Working Life of Women in the Seventeenth Century* (1919; reprint, London: Routledge & Kegan Paul, 1982); Lindsey Charles and Lorna Duffin, eds., *Women and Work in Pre-Industrial England* (Beckenham, Kent: Croom

Helm, 1985); Ivy Pinchbeck, *Women Workers and the Industrial Revolution 1750–1850* (1930; reprint, London: Frank Cass, 1969); Bridget Hill, *Women, Work, and Sexual Politics in Eighteenth-Century England* (Oxford: Blackwell, 1989); Susan Cahn, *Industry of Devotion* (New York: Columbia University Press, 1987); Margaret George, *Women in the First Capitalist Society* (Urbana: University of Illinois Press, 1988); Mary Prior, "Women and the Urban Economy: Oxford 1500–1800," in *Women in English Society 1500–1800*, ed. Mary Prior (London: Methuen, 1985), pp. 93–117; Eric Richards, "Women in the British Economy Since About 1700: An Interpretation," *History* 59 (1974): 337–57; K. D. M. Snell, *Annals of the Labouring Poor: Social Change and Agrarian England, 1600–1900* (Cambridge: Cambridge University Press, 1985), pp. 287–90; Peter Earle, "The Female Labour Market in London in the Late Seventeenth and Early Eighteenth Centuries," *Economic History Review*, 2d ser., 42, no. 3 (1989): 328–53; Carole Shammas, "The World Women Knew: Women Workers in the North of England During the Late Seventeenth Century," in *The World of William Penn*, ed. Richard S. Dunn and Mary Maples Dunn (Philadelphia: University of Pennsylvania Press, 1986), pp. 99–115.

2. A. W. Coats, "The Relief of Poverty, Attitudes to Labour, and Economic Change in England, 1660–1782," *International Review of Social History* 21 (1976): 104. That labour was the source of the nation's wealth was a "sentiment . . . reiterated again and again." On this point, see Edgar S. Furniss, *The Position of the Laborer in a System of Nationalism: A Study in the Labor Theories of the Later English Mercantilists* (1920; reprint, New York: Augustus M. Kelley, 1965), pp. 18; 37–38.

3. Expounded at length in Thomas Filmer's famous tract *Patriarcha* (1680), these ideas enjoyed their fullest political expression in the earlier part of the seventeenth century. In a more general social sense, patriarchal assumptions continued to inform attitudes toward the family, women, and children through the eighteenth and nineteenth centuries.

4. *Populousness with Oeconomy, the Wealth and Strength of a Kingdom* (London, 1759), pp. 11, 21–22.

5. Gordon J. Schochet, *Patriarchalism in Political Thought: The Authoritarian Family and Political Speculation and Attitudes Especially in Seventeenth-Century England* (New York: Basic Books, 1975), p. 65, on the ideological basis of patriarchalism in general, see chaps. 1, 4, and 5. For a discussion of the social realities interacting with these prescriptions, see Susan Amussen, *An Ordered Society: Gender and Class in Early Modern England* (Oxford: Blackwell, 1988), esp. pp. 134–79. On patriarchal ideas and political theory, see Susan M. Okin, *Women in Western Political Thought* (Princeton, NJ: Princeton University Press, 1979); Mary Lyndon Shanley, *Feminism, Marriage, and the Law in Victorian England, 1850–1895* (Princeton, NJ: Princeton University Press, 1989); Lawrence Stone, *The Family, Sex and Marriage in England, 1500–1800* (New York: Harper & Row, 1977).

6. For a discussion of the family economy of the working classes, see Louise A. Tilly and Joan W. Scott, *Women, Work, and Family* (New York: Holt, Rinehart and Winston, 1978), pp. 4–5, 14–15.

7. Even the status of "unemployed" was imprecise, for as one historian has pointed out, "perhaps two-fifths of the whole population . . . could be described as both laboring and idle because the same person could expect at any time to be either." Joyce Oldham Appleby, *Economic Thought and Ideology in Seventeenth-Century England* (Princeton, NJ: Princeton University Press, 1978), p. 152.

8. King's estimates have been challenged by recent reassessments, particularly with reference to his undercounting of persons in commerce, building, and industry. See Peter Lindert, "English Occupations, 1670–1811," *Journal of Economic History* 40, no. 4 (Dec. 1980): 685–712. Lindert admits, however, that his own calculations may seriously underestimate the number of cottagers and the poor. P. 709.

9. On the reassessment of poor women in contemporary surveys, see Shammas, "The World Women Knew," p. 112. Like Shammas, I have calculated the figures from Lindert, "Occupations," p. 703. On women as a predominant proportion of the poor, see Dorothy Marshall, *The English Poor in the Eighteenth Century* (London: George Routledge & Sons, 1926), p. 166; Pamela Sharpe, "Literally Spinsters: A New Interpretation of Local Economy and Demography in Colyton in the Seventeenth and Eighteenth Centuries," *Economic History Review* 44 (1991): 46–65, esp. pp. 57–62.

10. Sidney and Beatrice Webb, *English Poor Law History*, pt. 1, *The Old Poor Law* (London: Longmans, Green, & Co., 1927), pp. 170, 340–49; Edgar Furniss made the same point: "They treated of the laboring class as a group, to be handled in the mass by the state. The individual laborer was lost sight of . . . . In all this it is apparent that the rapidly spreading individualistic concept of society did not extend to the laboring class." Furniss, *The Position of the Laborer*, p. 114, see also p. 87.

11. The contemporary literature on this phenomenon is vast, but there is little for the eighteenth century. The best place to start is Marshall, *The English Poor;* and Ursula R. Q. Henriques, "Bastardy and the New Poor Law," *Past and Present* 37 (1967): 103–29.

12. Joan Thirsk, *Economic Policy and Projects: The Development of a Consumer Society in Early Modern England* (Oxford: Clarendon Press, 1978).

13. Henry Fielding, *A Proposal for Making an Effectual Provision for the Poor, for Amending their Morals, and for Rendering them useful Members of the Society* (London, 1753), p. 6.

14. Josiah Tucker, *Manifold Causes of the Increase of the Poor Distinctly set forth* (London, [1760]), p. 32.

15. Carew Reynel, *The True English Interest,* 'Preface' and p. 19, quoted in vol. 5, pt. 2, of *The Agrarian History of England and Wales,* ed. Joan Thirsk p. 383; Appleby, *Economic Thought,* p. 113.

16. Francis Moore, *Considerations on the Exorbitant Price of Provisions,* (London, 1773), pp. 54–55, 57. Moore borrowed the table from the famous economic theorist Postlethwaite.

17. Ibid., p. 58.

18. Firmin, *Some Proposals For the Imployment [sic] of the Poor* (London, 1681), p. 14.

19. Pamela Sharpe has argued the same for seventeenth- and eighteenth-century Colyton, where the tradition of domestic industry helped to construct a veritable sub-society of single women. Sharpe, "Literally Spinsters," pp. 60–62.

20. Firmin, *Proposals,* p. 12. Firmin's discussion is notable for the absence of a punitive attitude toward the unemployed, as well as its focus on exogenous causes of poverty. Writers of the late seventeenth century, more than the generations to follow, believed that poverty generally stemmed from misfortune rather than individual failure. Later tracts would place far more responsibility on laborers themselves. See Donna Andrew, *Philanthropy and Police: London Charity in the*

Eighteenth Century (Princeton, NJ: Princeton University Press, 1989), pp. 135–62.

21. Chris Middleton, "Women's Labour and the Transition to Pre-Industrial Capitalism," in *Women and Work in Pre-Industrial England,* ed. Lindsey Charles and Lorna Duffin (London: Croom Helm, 1985), pp. 181–206; Margaret George, "From 'Goodwife' to 'Mistress': The Transformation of the Female in Bourgeois Culture," *Science and Society* 37 (1973): 152–77. Women were thought to be particularly vulnerable to idleness, "the devil's playground," and seventeenth-century prescriptive literature advised that women pursue labor in order to avoid sin. See Cahn, *Industry of Devotion,* pp. 72–74.

22. Firmin, *Proposals,* pp. 11, 36. Sharpe gives as example women receiving poor relief for tending relatives. "Literally spinsters," p. 61.

23. Marshall, *The English Poor,* p. 114.

24. *English Society in the Eighteenth Century* (Harmondsworth, Middlesex: Penguin, 1982), p. 144.

25. For an excellent discussion of housewifery, see Hill, *Women, Work, and Sexual Politics,* pp. 89, 98–99, and chap. 7; also G. E. and K. R. Fussell, *The English Countrywoman: A Farmhouse Social History 1500–1900* (London: Andrew Melrose, 1953), esp. chap. 5.

26. Millinery and mantua making, as Ivy Pinchbeck pointed out, "were the favoured occupations for those in the class 'a little above the vulgar,'" *Women Workers,* p. 289; Snell, *Annals of the Labouring Poor,* chap. 6, esp. pp. 276–95.

27. Marshall, *The English Poor,* pp. 161–63.

28. Ibid., p. 212.

29. Figures from ibid., pp. 164–65.

30. For the Act of 1744 [17 Geo. II c.5], see Sir Frederic Morton Eden, *The State of the Poor,* 3 vols. (London, 1797), pp. 55–56.

31. Rex v. Inhabitants of Hensingham, *Caldecott's Reports* (1782), p. 206.

32. Ibid., pp. 206–7.

33. Rex v. Inhabitants of Ryton, *Caldecott's Reports* (1778), pp. 39–41. See also James Stephen Taylor, *Poverty, Migration, and Settlement in the Industrial Revolution: Soujourners' Narratives* (Palo Alto, CA: Society for the Promotion of Science and Scholarship, 1989), esp. pp. 52, 66–67.

34. Andrew, *Philanthropy and Police,* pp. 57–71, 98–134. The Society for Bettering the Condition and Increasing the Comforts of the Poor, founded in 1798, published numerous proposals for schools of industry. See their *Reports* for 1797 to 1805; *An Address to the Public, on the Propriety of Establishing Schools for Spinning* [1795] for Lincoln. On setting families to work, see Richard Burn, *Observations on the Bill Intended to be offered to Parliament for the Better Relief and Employment of the Poor* (London, 1776), esp. pp. 37–40.

35. John Fielding, *A Plan for a Preservatory and Reformatory, for the Benefit of Deserted Girls, and Penitent Prostitutes* (London, 1758), pp. 19–20. Fielding was one of the early members of the Marine Society for boys and he helped to organize the Lambeth Asylum for orphan girls, founded in 1759. Andrew, *Philanthropy and Police,* p. 115.

36. John Fielding, *Plan,* p. 3. For the problem of female unemployment at the end of the century, see *Reports of the Society for Bettering the Condition and Increasing the Comforts of the Poor,* vols. 2 and 3; David Davies, *The Case of the Labourers in Husbandry* (London, 1795); Sir Frederic Morton Eden, *State of the Poor,* 3 vols. (London, 1797). See also Hill, *Women, Work, and Sexual Politics,*

pp. 67–68; Andrew, *Philanthropy and Police*, p. 188; A. F. J. Brown, *Essex at Work 1700–1815* (Chelmsford: Tindal Press, 1969), pp. 133, 153.

37. Priscilla Wakefield, *Reflections on the Present Condition of the Female Sex* (London, 1798), pp. 150–51. Jonas Hanway believed that if women were "to be educated in an industrious manner," their options could be more numerous. "There are many trades, now in the hands of men, in which women might do as well, and some which their natural ingenuity would enable them to carry on much better," he claimed. *A Plan for Establishing a Charity-House, or Charity-Houses, for the Reception of Repenting Prostitutes* (London, 1758), p. 30.

38. [Anon.], *Populousness with Oeconomy*, pp. 26–27; Thomas Alcock voiced a typical view when he argued that the law "has a Tendency to hurt Industry, Care and Frugality" and "tends to destroy the Principle it proceeds from, the Principle of Charity." Alcock, *Observations on the Defects of the Poor Laws* (London, 1752), pp. 10–11.

39. On definitions of charity and philanthropy, see Andrew, *Philanthropy and Police*, pp. 5–7; 12–22.

40. Ibid., p. 131.

41. [Rev.] Gregory Sharpe, *A Sermon Preached before the Guardians of the Asylum, at their Chapel, on the Queen's Birth-Day, May 19, 1770* (London, 1770), p. 21.

42. *An Account of the Rise, Progress, and Present State of the Magdalen Hospital, for the Reception of Penitent Prostitutes*, 4th ed. (London, 1770), pp. 12–13.

43. Ibid., pp. 14, 24.

44. John Fielding, *Plan*, p. 8.

45. J. Massie, *A Plan for the Establishment of Charity-Houses for Exposed or Deserted women and girls, and for penitent prostitutes* (London, 1758), p. 3.

46. Massie, *Plan*, pp. 3, 4–5.

47. Hanway, *Plan*, p. 1.

48. Fielding, *Plan*, p. 5. The Rev. Sharpe (see above) was echoing Fielding in his sermon of 1770.

49. R. D. Lee and R. S. Schofield, "British Population in the Eighteenth Century," in vol. 1 of *The Economic History of Britain since 1700*, 2 vols., ed. Roderick Floud and Donald McCloskey (Cambridge: Cambridge University Press, 1981), pp. 17–35.

50. E. P. Thompson, *Customs in Common* (New York: New Press, 1991), pp. 185–351; John Bohstedt, *Riots and Community Politics in England and Wales* (Cambridge, MA: Harvard University Press, 1983); Carole Shammas, *The Pre-Industrial Consumer in England and America* (Oxford: Clarendon Press, 1990), pp. 145–48; Walter J. Shelton, *English Hunger and Industrial Disorders* (Toronto: University of Toronto Press, 1973); John Walter and Keith Wrightson, "Dearth and the Social Order in Early Modern England," *Past and Present* 71 (1976): 22–42. See also John Brewer and John Styles, eds., *An Ungovernable People? The English and Their Law in the Seventeenth and Eighteenth Centuries* (London: Hutchinson, 1980), pp. 12–20.

51. E. A. Wrigley, "A Simple Model of London's Importance in Changing English Society and Economy, 1650–1750," in *Towns in Societies*, ed. Philip Abrams and E. A. Wrigley (Cambridge: Cambridge University Press, 1978), pp. 215–43; P. J. Corfield, *The Impact of English Towns 1700–1800* (Oxford: Oxford University Press, 1982), esp. chap. 5.

52. Peter Linebaugh, *The London Hanged: Crime and Civil Society in the*

Eighteenth Century (Cambridge: Cambridge University Press, 1992), pp. 402–41 and passim.

53. "The Criminality of Women in Eighteenth-Century England," *Journal of Social History* 8 (1975): 106–7.

54. John Trusler, ed., *The Works of William Hogarth*, 2 vols. (London, [1840?]), 2: pp. 223–24.

55. Beattie, "Criminality of Women," pp. 92–93. Women were also among those arrested for more serious crimes, such as larceny, which Peter Linebaugh has shown were often related to impoverished circumstances. *The London Hanged*, pp. 336–42.

56. John Styles, "Embezzlement, Industry and the Law in England, 1500–1800," in *Manufacture in Town and Country Before the Factory*, ed. Maxine Berg, Pat Hudson, and Michael Sonenscher (Cambridge: Cambridge University Press, 1983), pp. 173–210; H. Heaton, *The Yorkshire Woollen and Worsted Industries* (Oxford: Clarendon Press, 1920), pp. 429–30; Linebaugh, *The London Hanged*, pp. 378–80.

57. Massie, *Plan*, p. 17.

58. Andrew, *Philanthropy and Police*, pp. 156–60.

Chapter 2

1. On the power of the country in producing images and ideals, see Raymond Williams, *The Country and the City* (London: Chatto and Windus, 1973); for the same phenomenon at a later date, Martin J. Wiener, *English Culture and the Decline of the Industrial Spirit, 1850–1980* (Cambridge: Cambridge University Press, 1981); on population and the countryside, see N. Tranter, *Population Since the Industrial Revolution: The Case of England and Wales* (London: Croom Helm, 1973); Roy Porter, *English Society in the Eighteenth Century* (Harmondsworth, Middlesex: Penguin, 1982), pp. 69–78.

2. J. Massie, *A Plan for the Establishment of Charity-Houses for Exposed or Deserted women and girls, and for penitent prostitutes* (London, 1758), p. 69.

3. On such "independent spirit" and its later disappearance, see Thomas Davis, *General View of the Agriculture of Wiltshire* (London, 1811), p. 215. These discussions closely mirror the contemporaneous debate in England and America over republicanism. Among the many works on this subject are Caroline Robbins, *The Eighteenth-Century Commonwealthman* (Cambridge, MA: Harvard University Press, 1959); J. G. A. Pocock, *The Machiavellian Moment: Florentine Political Thought and the Atlantic Republican Tradition* (Princeton, NJ: Princeton University Press, 1975).

4. E. J. Hobsbawm, *Industry and Empire* (Harmondsworth, Middlesex: Penguin, 1969), p. 98; see also G. E. Mingay, *English Landed Society in the Eighteenth Century* (London: Routledge & Kegan Paul, 1963), pp. 5–10, 26.

5. Eric Kerridge, *The Agricultural Revolution* (London: George Allen & Unwin, 1967), pp. 41–180; Keith Wrightson and David Levine, *Poverty and Piety in an English Village: Terling, 1525–1700* (New York: Academic Press, 1979); J. R. Wordie, "The Chronology of English Enclosure, 1500–1914," *Economic History Review*, 2d ser., 34 (1983): 483–505; Robert W. Malcolmson, *Life and Labour in England 1700–1780* (London: Hutchinson, 1981), pp. 136–43.

6. Robert Malcolmson has pointed out for the eighteenth century, "It is

important to appreciate that the notion of absolute private ownership of land and its resources was not yet fully triumphant." *Life and Labour,* pp. 24, 32.

7. Ivy Pinchbeck, *Women Workers and the Industrial Revolution 1750–1850* (1930; reprint, London: Frank Cass, 1969), p. 25.

8. Sir William Pulteney, "Account of a Cottager," *Annals of Agriculture* 44 (1806): 97–101.

9. Dorothy Marshall, *The English Poor in the Eighteenth Century* (London: George Routledge & Sons, 1926), pp. 21, 108.

10. Olwen Hufton, "Women Without Men: Widows and Spinsters in Britain and France in the Eighteenth Century," *Journal of Family History* 9 (1984): 363; George R. Boyer, *An Economic History of the English Poor Law* (Cambridge: Cambridge University Press, 1990), pp. 248–49.

11. Mr. Robert Gourlay, "An Inquiry into the State of the Cottagers in the Counties of Lincoln and Rutland," *Annals of Agriculture* 37 (1801): 523.

12. Olwen Hufton, "Women and the Family Economy in Eighteenth-Century France," *French Historical Studies* 9 (1975): 1–22; Bridget Hill, *Women, Work, and Sexual Politics in Eighteenth-Century England* (Oxford: Blackwell, 1989), pp. 37, 253–55.

13. The gentry, courts, and Parliament redefined the terms of landownership at the end of the seventeenth century. With the introduction of strict settlements and entail, heads of families were prohibited from selling any part of their estates, excepting on account of bankruptcy. At the same time, new mortgage laws enabled them to raise money by mortgaging their estates. All of these changes increased the interest of landowners in making more money from their holdings. Peter Mathias, *The First Industrial Nation,* 2d ed. (London: Methuen, 1983), pp. 50–52; Mingay, *English Landed Society in the Eighteenth Century,* pp. 50–79.

14. Mathias, *The First Industrial Nation,* p. 441. See also Roderick Floud and Donald McCloskey, ed., *The Economic History of Britain Since 1700,* 2 vols. (Cambridge: Cambridge University Press, 1981), I: pp. 52ff.

15. William Marshall, *Rural Economy of Gloucestershire,* 2 vols. (Gloucester, 1789), II: p. 96. See also Stuart Macdonald, "The Diffusion of Knowledge Among Northumberland Farmers, 1780–1815," *Agricultural History Review* 27 (1979): 30–39; Nicholas Goddard, "The Development and Influence of Agricultural Periodicals and Newspapers, 1780–1880," *Agricultural History Review* 31 (1983): 116–31.

16. Phyllis Deane, *The First Industrial Revolution* (Cambridge: Cambridge University Press, 1965), p. 46; on the interest of the Hanoverian kings in farming, see Joan Thirsk, "Agricultural Innovations and Their Diffusion," in vol. 5, pt. 2, of *The Agrarian History of England and Wales,* ed. Joan Thirsk (Cambridge: Cambridge University Press, 1985), p. 575.

17. Thirsk, "Agricultural Innovations and Their Diffusion," pp. 571–89; J. D. Chambers and G. E. Mingay, *The Agricultural Revolution 1750–1880* (New York: Schocken, 1966); G. E. Mingay, ed., *Arthur Young and His Times* (London: Macmillan, 1975); on the relationship between agricultural innovation, science, and industrialism, see Maureen McNeil, *Under the Banner of Science* (Manchester: University of Manchester Press, 1987), pp. 168–88.

18. J. A. Yelling, *Common Field and Enclosure in England, 1450–1850* (Hamden, CT: Archon, 1977), p. 5.

19. Wordie, "English Enclosure," pp. 494–95.

20. The county of Leicestershire, which had no commons or waste by 1844, is often used as an example. Wordie, "English Enclosure," p. 497, but cf. p. 501.

21. The literature on the debate over enclosure is voluminous. Apologists include J. D. Chambers, "Enclosure and the Labour Supply in the Industrial Revolution," *Economic History Review* 5 (1953): 319–43; Chambers and Mingay, *The Agricultural Revolution*; G. E. Mingay, *Enclosure and the Small Farmer in the Age of the Industrial Revolution* (London: Macmillan, 1968); E. C. K. Gonner, *Common Land and Enclosures* (London: Macmillan, 1912); Donald N. McCloskey, "The Enclosure of Open Fields: Preface to a Study of Its Impact on the Efficiency of English Agriculture in the Eighteenth Century," *Journal of Economic History* 32 (1972): 15–35. The classic critique of enclosure is J. L. Hammond and Barbara Hammond, *The Village Labourer* (1911; reprint, London: Longman, 1978), pp. 1–65; see also K. D. M. Snell, *Annals of the Labouring Poor: Social Change and Agrarian England 1660–1900* (Cambridge: Cambridge University Press, 1985), pp. 138–227; J. M. Martin, "Village Traders and the Emergence of a Proletariat in South Warwickshire, 1750–1851," *Agricultural History Review* 32 (1984): 179–88; Jane Humphries, "Enclosures, Common Rights, and Women: The Proletarianization of Families in the Late Eighteenth and Early Nineteenth Centuries," *Journal of Economic History* 50 (1990): 17–42; Boyer, *An Economic History of the English Poor Law*, pp. 32–35 and passim.

22. J. Houghton, *A Collection for the Improvement of Husbandry and Trade*, rev. ed., 3 vols. (London, 1727), I: p. 296, quoted in P. R. Edwards, "The Development of Dairy Farming on the North Shropshire Plain in the Seventeenth Century," *Midland History* 4 (1978): 182.

23. Bob Bushaway, *By Rite: Custom, Ceremony and Community in England 1700–1800* (London: Junction Books, 1982), p. 213.

24. Douglas Hay, "Property, Authority and the Criminal Law," in *Albion's Fatal Tree: Crime and Society in Eighteenth-Century England,* Douglas Hay et al. (New York: Pantheon, 1975), pp. 17–63; Peter King, "Decision-Makers and Decision-Making in the English Criminal Law, 1750–1800," *Historical Journal* 27 (1984): 25–58; Bushaway, *By Rite.*

25. Bennett, "Misogyny, Popular Culture, and Women's Work," *History Workshop Journal* 31 (1991): 166–88. For a lucid argument calling attention to the place of women in primary production before enclosure, see Humphries, "Enclosures, Common Rights, and Women," esp. pp. 35–41.

26. "It has been said, that by common law and custom of England, the poor are allowed to enter and glean upon another's ground after the harvest, without being guilty of trespass," Blackstone noted. William Blackstone, *Commentaries on the Laws of England,* 4 vols. (London, 1857), 3: p. 220n.

27. Bushaway, *By Rite,* p. 138; Susan D. Amussen, *An Ordered Society: Gender and Class in Early Modern England* (Oxford: Blackwell, 1988), pp. 156–57.

28. Bushaway, *By Rite,* p. 138.

29. Arthur Young, *A General View of the Agriculture of Norfolk* (London, 1813), p. 494; Bushaway, *By Rite,* p. 43. Another estimate, documented in 1730, reported that gleaning "secured 15 shillings to a family." Quoted in J. M. Martin, "Village Traders and the Emergence of a Proletariat in South Warwickshire, 1750–1851," p. 183. See also Peter King, "Customary Rights and Women's Earnings: The Importance of Gleaning to the Rural Labouring Poor, 1750–1850," *Economic History Review* 44 (1991): 461–76.

30. Pinchbeck, *Women Workers,* p. 22.

31. Bushaway, *By Rite,* p. 142.

32. The Hammonds were the first to discuss at length the significance of this case. See J. L. and Barbara Hammond, *The Village Labourer,* pp. 67–68. For a

more recent and fuller analysis of the controversy over gleaning, see Peter King, "Gleaners, Farmers and the Failure of Legal Sanctions, 1750–1850," *Past and Present* 125 (1989): 116–50; E. P. Thompson, *Customs in Common* (New York: New Press, 1991), pp. 138–44.

33. Steel v. Houghton et Uxor (1788), 1 *H. Bl. Rep.* 52, 62.

34. Steel v. Houghton et Uxor (1788), 1 *H. Bl. Rep.* 61.

35. According to the Hammonds, Lofft was "struck off the Commission for the Peace a few year later, apparently at the instance of the Duke of Portland, for persuading the Deputy-Sheriff to postpone the execution of a girl sentenced to death for stealing." *The Village Labourer,* p. 67.

36. *Annals of Agriculture* 10 (1788): 220, 227.

37. *Annals of Agriculture* 9 (1788): 13, 640.

38. King, "Gleaners, Farmers and the Failure of Legal Sanctions."

39. 136 *English Reports* 32, quoted in David H. Morgan, "The Place of Harvesters in Nineteenth-Century Village Life," in *Village Life and Labour,* ed. Raphael Samuel (London: Routledge & Kegan Paul, 1975), p. 57.

40. Bushaway, *By Rite,* p. 215. In the case of Scotland, where peasants reacted against capitalist sheep farming, "to a remarkable degree Highland riots were women's riots." E. Richards, "Patterns of Highland Discontent, 1790–1860," in *Popular Protest and Public Order,* ed. R. Quinault and J. Stevenson (London: Allen & Unwin, 1974), p. 106. For an extensive exploration of the role of women in agrarian and industrial protests, see Malcolm I. Thomis and Jennifer Grimmett, *Women in Protest 1800–1850* (London: Croom Helm, 1982); on the viability of associating women with subsistence riots, see John Bohstedt, "Gender, Household and Community Politics: Women in English Riots 1790–1810," *Past and Present* 120 (1988): 88–122.

41. C. Vancouver, *Report to the Board of Agriculture on Hampshire* (1808), p. 389, quoted in Bushaway, *By Rite,* p. 209.

42. Bushaway, *By Rite,* pp. 213–14. See also M. J. Ingram, "Communities and Courts: Law and Disorder in Early Seventeenth-Century Wiltshire," in *Crime in England, 1550–1800,* ed. J. S. Cockburn (Princeton, NJ: Princeton University Press, 1977), pp. 110–34.

43. Bushaway, *By Rite,* p. 217.

44. Norma Landau, *The Justices of the Peace, 1679–1760* (Berkeley: University of California Press, 1984), p. 195.

45. Bushaway, *By Rite,* p. 230.

46. *Annals of Agriculture* 4 (1785): 181.

47. Sir Frederic Morton Eden, *State of the Poor,* 3 vols. (London, 1797), 3: p. 797.

48. Jeanette 'M. Neeson, "Opposition to Enclosure in Northamptonshire c. 1760–1800," in *An Atlas of Rural Protest in Britain 1548–1900,* ed. Andrew Charlesworth (Philadelphia: University of Pennsylvania Press, 1983), p. 60; see also Neeson, "The Opponents of Enclosure in Eighteenth-Century Northamptonshire," *Past and Present* 105 (1984): 114–39.

49. John Bohstedt, *Riots and Community Politics in England and Wales, 1790–1810* (Cambridge, MA: Harvard University Press, 1983), p. 198.

50. Neeson, "The Opponents of Enclosure," pp. 130, 129.

51. A. Young, *General Report on Enclosures* (1808), quoted in Snell, *Labouring Poor,* p. 175.

52. Carole Shammas, *The Pre-Industrial Consumer in England and America*

(Oxford: Clarendon Press, 1990), p. 42. See also David Levine, *Reproducing Families: The Political Economy of English Population History* (Cambridge: Cambridge University Press, 1987), pp. 38–93.

53. John Burnett, *Plenty and Want*, rev. ed. (London: Scolar Press, 1979), pp. 30–47; J. C. Drummond and Anne Wilbraham, *The Englishman's Food*, rev. ed. (London: Jonathan Cape, 1958), pp. 180–81; Redcliffe Salaman, *The History and Social Influence of the Potato* (1945; new ed., Cambridge: Cambridge University Press, 1985), pp. 487–517.

54. Quoted in Snell, *Labouring Poor*, p. 178; see also John Burnett, "The Country Diet," in *The Victorian Countryside*, 2 vols., ed. G. E. Mingay (London: Routledge & Kegan Paul, 1981), 2: p. 555; Pamela Horn, *The Rural World 1780–1850: Social Change in the English Countryside* (New York: St. Martin's Press, 1980), pp. 37–38.

55. George Sturt, *Change in the Village* (1912), quoted in Snell, *Labouring Poor*, p. 167.

56. D. Davies, *The Case of the Labourers in Husbandry* (London, 1795), pp. 56–57.

57. On wages and the male laborer, see A. W. Coats, "Changing Attitudes to Labour in the Mid-Eighteenth Century," *Economic History Review*, 2d ser. 11 (1958): 35–51; see also Michele Barrett and Mary McIntosh, "The 'Family Wage,'" in *The Changing Experiences of Women*, ed. Elizabeth Whitelegg et al. (Oxford: Martin Robinson, 1982), pp. 71–87; Pat Thane, "Women and the Poor Law in Victorian and Edwardian England," *History Workshop Journal* 6 (1978): 29–51; Hilary Land, *The Family Wage* (Liverpool: University of Liverpool, 1979).

58. *Report from Commissioners on the Employment of Women and Children in Agriculture, Parliamentary Papers* (hereafter abbreviated as *PP*) (1843), 12: pp. 112, 109.

59. Jennie Kitteringham, "Country Work Girls in Nineteenth-Century England," in *Village Life and Labour*, ed. Raphael Samuel (London: Routledge & Kegan Paul, 1975), pp. 73–138; Pinchbeck, *Women Workers*, pp. 44–45.

60. Ann Kussmaul, *Servants in Husbandry in Early Modern England* (Cambridge: Cambridge University Press, 1981), p. 3; Hill, *Women, Work, and Sexual Politics*, p. 71. Hill cites Arthur Young's estimates of servants in 1770, which were 222,996 for menservants and 167,247 for female servants. See *A Six Months' tour through the North of England*, 4 vols. (1770), 4: p. 517, in Hill, *Women, Work, and Sexual Politics*, p. 71.

61. Louise A. Tilly and Joan W. Scott, *Women, Work, and Family* (New York: Holt, Rinehart and Winston, 1978), pp. 25, 29; Bridget Hill, *Eighteenth-Century Women: An Anthology* (London: Allen & Unwin, 1984), p. 125; Hill, *Women, Work, and Sexual Politics*, pp. 73, 240–43. In 1696 Gregory King estimated that one-sixth of all adult females were widows.

62. Pinchbeck, *Women Workers*, pp. 17, 24; Snell, *Labouring Poor*, p. 22; Hill, *Women, Work, and Sexual Politics*, pp. 53–45. See also Martine Segalen, *Love and Power in the Peasant Family*, trans. Sarah Matthews (Chicago: University of Chicago Press, 1983), chap. 3.

63. Stephen Duck, *The Thresher's Labour* (1730), ed. and intro. by E. P. Thompson (London: Merlin, 1989), p. 8.

64. Mary Collier, *The Woman's Labour: An Epistle to Mr. Stephen Duck; In Answer to his late Poem, called The Thresher's Labour* (1739), ed. and intro. by E.

P. Thompson (London: Merlin Press, 1989), pp. 16–17. See also Roger Lonsdale, ed., *Eighteenth Century Women Poets: An Oxford Anthology* (Oxford: Oxford University Press, 1990), pp. 171–72.

65. Jethro Tull, *The Horse-Hoing [sic] Husbandry* (London, 1733), 226n.

66. Stuart Macdonald, "Agricultural Improvement and the Neglected Labourer," *Agricultural History Review* 31 (1983): 83–85. Macdonald notes that for Tull, "who loathed agricultural labourers with all the strength his ailing health allowed, the perfidy of his employees was a major inspiration for his horse-hoeing husbandry." P. 84.

67. Macdonald, "Agricultural Improvement and the Neglected Labourer," p. 84.

68. Sturt, *Change in the Village* (1912), p. 109, cited in Snell, *Labouring Poor*, p. 8; see also pp. 5–9, for several "definitions" of "Hodge."

69. See, e.g., William Ellis, *The Country Housewife's Family Companion* (London, 1750), pp. 12, 176, 311, 344–45, 332; Richard Bradley, *The Country Gentleman and Farmer's Monthly Director*, 2d ed. (London, 1727), pp. vii–ix; Richard Bradley, *A Complete Body of Husbandry* (London, 1727), pp. 172–73. See also Macdonald, "Agricultural Improvement and the Neglected Labourer," p. 84; Deborah Valenze, "The Art of Women and the Business of Men: Women's Work and the Dairy Industry c. 1740–1840," *Past and Present* 130 (1991): 142–69.

70. Snell, *Labouring Poor*, pp. 74–94; Raphael Samuel, "Village Labour," in *Village Life and Labour*, ed. Samuel, pp. 10–11; Alun Howkins, "In the Sweat of Thy Face: The Labourer and Work," in vol. 2 of *The Victorian Countryside*, ed. Mingay, p. 509.

71. Snell, *Labouring Poor*, pp. 155, 158; Howkins, "In the Sweat of Thy Face," p. 514.

72. Pinchbeck, *Women Workers*, pp. 19, 54–62.

73. Eden, *State of the Poor*, 2: p. 47.

74. As Raphael Samuel has pointed out, "The agricultural revolution of the eighteenth and early nineteenth centuries had nothing to do with machinery, but demanded instead a prodigious number of hands." "Workshop of the World: Steam Power and Hand Technology in mid-Victorian Britain," *History Workshop Journal* 3 (1977): 17–18.

75. Mabel Ashby, e.g., recorded the use of sickles by women at Tysoe late in the nineteenth century, noting that "a dozen or maybe twenty reapers, largely women would work in one field, with men following to tie up the sheaves." Mabel K. Ashby, *Joseph Ashby of Tysoe 1859–1919* (1961), p. 25, quoted in David H. Morgan, "The Place of Harvesters in Nineteenth-Century Village Life," in *Village Life and Labour*, ed. Samuel, p. 33.

76. Michael Roberts, "Sickles and Scythes: Women's Work and Men's Work at Harvest Time," *History Workshop Journal* 7 (1979): 3–28; E. J. T. Collins, "Harvest Technology and Labour Supply in Britain, 1790–1870," *Economic History Review*, 2d ser., 22 (1969): 453–67; W. A. Armstrong, "The Workfolk," in *The Victorian Countryside*, ed. Mingay, 2: p. 496.

77. *Reports of the Society for Bettering the Condition and Increasing the Comforts of the Poor* (London, 1802), III: 91.

78. Ibid., p. 91.

79. Sidney O. Addy, *Household Tales with other Traditional Remains* (London, 1895), p. 127.

Chapter 3

1. Max Weber, *The Protestant Ethic and the Spirit of Capitalism*, trans. Talcott Parsons (New York: Charles Scribner's Sons, 1958), p. 62.

2. See Sherry B. Ortner, "Is Female to Male as Nature is to Culture?" in *Women, Culture, and Society*, ed. Michelle Zimbalist Rosaldo and Louise Lamphere (Stanford, CA: Stanford University Press, 1974), pp. 67–87; see also Carolyn Merchant, *The Death of Nature: Women, Ecology and the Scientific Revolution* (New York: Harper and Row, 1980); L.J. Jordanova, "Natural Facts: A Historical Perspective on Science and Sexuality," in *Nature, Culture and Gender*, ed. Carol P. MacCormack and Marilyn Strathern (Cambridge: Cambridge University Press, 1980), pp. 42–69.

3. Little work on women in the dairy industry exists; see Joan M. Jensen, *Loosening the Bonds: Mid-Atlantic Farmwomen* (New Haven, CT: Yale University Press, 1986), and "Butter Making and Economic Development in Mid-Atlantic America from 1750 to 1850," *Signs: Journal of Women in Culture and Society* 13 (1988): 813–29; Lena Sommestad, "Able Dairymaids and Proficient Dairymen: Education and De-feminization in the Swedish Dairy Industry," *Gender and History* 4 (1992): 34–48.

4. Sir Anthony Fitzherbert, *Boke of Husbandrye* (1534), quoted in Alice Clark, *Working Life of Women in the Seventeenth Century* (1919; reprint, London: Routledge & Kegan Paul, 1982), p. 48; G.E. Fussell, *The English Dairy Farmer, 1500–1900* (London: Frank Cass, 1966), esp. chap. 5; Martine Segalen, *Love and Power in the Peasant Family*, trans. Sarah Matthews (Chicago: University of Chicago Press, 1983), pp. 112–27; though Segalen points out that "the cow is not an incontestably feminine animal in the way that the chicken is," for in Central France, men took the cows into the high pastures and managed "dairies" there. She notes, however, that this is "an extreme example" of male management, for in many other cases, dairying was the responsibility of women. Pp. 97–98. I know of no similar instances in England.

5. Ivy Pinchbeck, *Women Workers and the Industrial Revolution, 1750–1850* (1930; reprint, London: Frank Cass, 1969), pp. 22–23.

6. George Eliot, *Adam Bede* (1859; reprint, New York: Signet, 1961), p. 186. The novel is set in the early nineteenth century.

7. Peter J. Bowden, "Agricultural Prices, Wages, Farm Profits, and Rents," in vol. 5, pt. 2, of *The Agrarian History of England and Wales*, ed. Joan Thirsk (Cambridge: Cambridge University Press, 1985); Eric Kerridge, *The Agricultural Revolution* (London: George Allen & Unwin, 1967), pp. 123–28; Adrian Henstock, "Cheese Manufacture and Marketing in Derbyshire and North Staffordshire, 1670–1870," *Derbyshire Archeological Journal* 84 (1969): 35.

8. For a discussion of the differentiation between small- and large-scale dairying operations, see P. R. Edwards, "The Development of Dairy Farming on the North Shropshire Plain in the Seventeenth Century," *Midland History* 4 (1978): 175–90. See also John Billingsley, *General View of the Agriculture of Somerset*, 2d ed. (Bath, 1798), pp. 53–54, 142–43, 157–58.

9. William Ellis, *Modern Husbandman* 2 (June 1744): 167–68; Billingsley, *General View of Somerset*, pp. 142–43, 157; William Marshall, *The Rural Economy of Gloucestershire*, 2 vols. (Gloucester, 1789), 1: p. 263, 2: pp. 137, 153. Marshall indicates that some female managers were hired and paid wages. Dairymen may also have participated in the production of cheese. He compares a "Mrs. Badon of

Deyhouse near Swindon [Wilts.]," "a most experienced and intelligent manager," to "Mr. Rich, of Foxham . . . a skilful and attentive dairyman," who also appears to be responsible for the making of cheese on his farm. *Rural Economy of Gloucestershire,* 2: p. 156. See also John Lawrence, *The New Farmer's Calendar,* 4th ed. (London, 1802), pp. 135–36.

10. Thomas Tusser, *Five Hundred Points of Good Husbandry,* ed. W. Mavor (1812), as quoted in Fussell, *English Dairy Farmer,* p. 161. Tusser devoted a good deal of attention and wit to the dairy, giving advice on everything from servants to mousetraps.

> Good dairie doth pleasure
> Ill dairie spendes treasure.
>
> Good huswife in dairie, that needes not be tolde,
> deserueth hir fee to be paid hir in golde.
>
> Ill seruant neglecting what huswiferie saies,
> deserueth hir fee to be paid hir with baies [reproof].

T. Tusser, *Fiue Hundred Pointes of Good Husbandrie* (1580 ed.), reprint, English Dialect Society (London, 1878), p. 172.

11. William Ellis, *Modern Husbandman* 3 (July 1744): 62.

12. Marshall, *Rural Economy of Gloucestershire,* 2: pp. 104–5, 1: p. 263.

13. William Ellis, *Agriculture Improv'd* 1 (June 1745): 133–34; 2 (August 1745): 92–93; Fussell, *English Dairy Farmer,* p. 251.

14. Marshall, *Rural Economy of Gloucestershire,* 2: p. 96; Ellis, *Modern Husbandman* 2 (May 1744): 134; Lawrence, *The New Farmer's Calendar,* pp. 135–36. Milk production and marketing, though obviously related to this discussion, cannot be treated at length here, but see William Harley, *The Harleian Dairy System* (1829); see also [Anon.], *A Treatise on Milk, As an Article of the First Necessity to the Health and Comfort of the Community* (London, 1825); P. J. Atkins, "The Retail Milk Trade in London, c. 1790–1914," *Economic History Review,* 2d ser., 33 (1980): 522–37. J. A. Chartres points out that "cheese reaching London may have at least doubled between the mid seventeenth and the mid eighteenth" centuries. "The Marketing of Agricultural Produce," in vol. 5, pt. 2, of *Agrarian History of England and Wales,* ed. Thirsk, p. 447.

15. Kerridge, *Agricultural Revolution,* pp. 332–35; J. C. Drummond and Anne Wilbraham, *The Englishman's Food* (1939; rev. ed., London: Jonathan Cape, 1958), p. 55; Fussell, *English Dairy Farmer,* pp. 270–71; John Burnett, *Plenty and Want,* rev. ed. (London: Scolar Press, 1979), chaps. 2 and 3. Whey was also consumed in great quantities by the coffee houses of London. See John Houghton, ed., *A Collection for the Improvement of Husbandry and Trade,* rev. ed., 3 vols. (London, 1727), 1: p. 409.

16. Drummond and Wilbraham, *Englishman's Food,* pp. 193–95, 303–4; Fussell, *English Dairy Farmer,* p. 206; Burnett, *Plenty and Want,* chap. 4. Adulteration unfortunately was very much a part of the ordinary marketing of butter in the eighteenth century. Only the advent of railway transport and, later on, refrigeration ushered in a widespread taste for liquid milk outside the immediate vicinity of dairying regions. Drummond and Wilbraham, *Englishman's Food,* pp. 193–94; 299–300; Fussell, *English Dairy Farmer,* pp. 300 ff.

17. Chartres, "Marketing of Agricultural Produce," pp. 406–7, 486–87. Henstock, "Cheese Manufacture and Marketing," p. 44. Riots protesting the transport of butter were frequent; see, e.g., John Bohstedt, "Gender, Household

and Community Politics: Women in English Riots 1790–1810," *Past and Present* 120 (1988): 103.

18. Drummond and Wilbraham, *Englishman's Food,* p. 195; on male managers, especially in Dorset, Devon, Somerset, Wiltshire, and Hampshire, see Pinchbeck, *Women Workers,* pp. 41–42 and H. Levy, *Large and Small Holdings* (Cambridge: Cambridge University Press, 1911), pp. 177–78.

19. One author complained that the books on agriculture were "too numerous to be purchased." See David Henry, *The Complete English Farmer, or, A Practical System of Husbandry* (London, 1771), p. iii; Lawrence, *The New Farmer's Calendar,* p. v. For the diffusion of scientific knowledge in the eighteenth century, see Margaret Jacob, *The Cultural Meaning of the Scientific Revolution* (New York: Knopf, 1988), pp. 152–53; Roy Porter, "The Enlightenment in England," in *The Enlightenment in National Context,* ed. Roy Porter and Mikulas Teich (Cambridge: Cambridge University Press, 1981), pp. 1–18; Keith Thomas, *Man and the Natural World* (New York: Pantheon, 1983), pp. 87–91.

20. Marshall, *Rural Economy of Gloucestershire,* 2: p. 186.

21. William Marshall, *Rural Economy of Norfolk,* 2 vols. (London, 1787), 1: p. vii; Fussell, *English Dairy Farmer,* pp. 203–4, 206, 223.

22. Josiah Twamley, *Dairying Exemplified* (Warwick, 1784), pp. 28–29. Thermometers were costly and scarce until the mid nineteeneth century. See Fussell, *English Dairy Farmer,* pp. 230–37; Joseph Harding, "Recent Improvements in Dairy Practice," *Journal of the Royal Agricultural Society* 21 (1860): 85.

23. Twamley, *Dairying Exemplified,* p. 10; *Annals of Agriculture* 17 (1792): 48–49; Young quoted in Fussell, p. 211. Young's tirade against "minutiae" was never repeated with reference to the detail of knowledge required of men in dairying. John Lawrence praised this aspect of the breeder's qualities and disposition: "He must enter fully into the spirit of a thousand little niceties, both of judgment and practice, which it would take a good volume to describe." *The New Farmer's Calendar,* pp. 137–38.

24. Fussell, *English Dairy Farmer,* p. 209.

25. Marshall, *Rural Economy of Gloucestershire,* 2: pp. 111, 126–27, 164.

26. Ibid., p. 111.

27. Ibid., p. 128; Ellis, *Agriculture Improv'd* 2 (August 1745): 95–98; Pinchbeck, *Women Workers,* p. 15.

28. *The New Farmer's Calendar,* pp. 510, 507. Lawrence published an earlier treatise addressing the humane treatment of animals and promoted the cause throughout his life. See his *Philosophical and Practical Treatise on Horses; and on the Moral Duties of Man towards the Brute Creation* (London, 1796).

29. Lawrence, *The New Farmer's Calendar,* p. 510.

30. James Anderson, *Recreations in Agriculture, Natural-History, Arts, and Miscellaneous Literature,* 6 vols. (1799–1802), 4 (Oct. 1801): 89.

31. Marshall, *Rural Economy of Gloucestershire* 2: p. 185.

32. Kerridge, *Agricultural Revolution,* p. 122; Celia Fiennes, *Journey of Celia Fiennes* (London, 1947), p. 177, quoted in David Hey, "The North-West Midlands: Derbyshire, Staffordshire, Cheshire, and Shropshire," in vol. 5, pt. 1, of *The Agrarian History of England and Wales,* ed. Thirsk (Cambridge, 1984) p. 153.

33. Ellis, *Agriculture Improv'd* 2 (August 1745): 97–98.

34. Ellis, *Agriculture Improv'd* 1 (June 1745): 132.

35. Henry Holland, *General View of the Agriculture of Cheshire* (London, 1808), p. 282; Marshall, *Rural Economy of Gloucestershire*, 2: 156; Twamley, *Dairying Exemplified*, pp. 12–13, 20; Fussell, *English Dairy Farmer*, pp. 228–29. Such work was still being performed by women in the mid nineteenth century. See *Report from Commisioners on the Employment of Women and Children in Agriculture*, *PP* (1843), 12: pp. 61–62.

36. Marshall, *Rural Economy of Gloucestershire*, 1: p. 263; James Jackson, *A Treatise of Agriculture and Dairy Husbandry* (Edinburgh, 1840), quoted in Fussell, *English Dairy Farmer*, p. 170; Levy, *Large and Small Holdings*, p. 173.

37. Marshall, *Rural Economy of Gloucestershire*, 1: p. 264.

38. Twamley, *Dairying Exemplified*, pp. 52–53, 92–95; Pinchbeck, *Women Workers*, p. 12.

39. See, e.g., Houghton, *A Collection for the Improvement of Husbandry and Trade*, 1: pp. 394–95, 406.

40. *Rural Economy of Gloucestershire*, 2: pp. 106–7. Bigland was declared bankrupt in 1800. See *Victoria History of the County of Gloucestershire*, ed. C. R. Elrington and N. M. Herbert (Oxford: Oxford University Press, 1972) 10: p. 174.

41. Twamley, *Dairying Exemplified*, pp. 7–9.

42. Ibid., pp. 7, 11, 75.

43. Ibid., pp. 78–81.

44. Ibid., pp. 74–75.

45. Ibid., pp. 70, 72.

46. Ibid., pp. 71–72.

47. *Report from Commisioners on the Employment of Women and Children in Agriculture*, *PP* (1843), 12: pp. 61–62, 65. Fussell reckoned that "the growth of population and the comparatively small proportion of imports indicate that the home dairy industry, so far from decreasing, must have expanded to a quite notable degree." *English Dairy Farmer*, p. 284. Certain localities, such as Derbyshire, obviously increased cheese production to meet the needs of a growing working-class population. The rate of expansion, according to one midcentury account, went from 2,000 tons annually in the first decade of the nineteenth century, to 8,000 tons in 1846, and 10,000 tons in 1857. Henstock, "Cheese Manufacture and Marketing," pp. 39–43.

48. James Obelkevich, *Religion and Rural Society* (Oxford: Clarendon Press, 1974), p. 66; J. Chalmers Morton, "On Cheese-making in Home Dairies and in Factories," *Journal of the Royal Agricultural Society*, 2d ser., 11 (1875): 270; Jennie Kitteringham, "Country Work Girls in Nineteenth-Century England," *Village Life and Labour*, ed. Raphael Samuel (London: Routledge & Kegan Paul, 1975), pp. 95–96. Kitteringham points out that larger farmers would hire a "milking gang for the duration of the milking season and then lay off most of the workers when the cows were due to calve." A select number of maids would be retained and would live in at the farmer's residence. P. 95.

49. Charles Phythian-Adams, "Milk and Soot: The Changing Vocabulary of a Popular Ritual in Stuart and Hanoverian London," in *The Pursuit of Urban History*, ed. Derek Fraser and Anthony Sutcliffe (London: Edward Arnold, 1983), p. 99. I am indebted to Edward Thompson for this reference.

50. Stephen Glover, *History of the County of Derby*, 2 vols. (Derby, 1829), 1: pp. 210–11; Henstock, "Cheese Manufacture and Marketing," pp. 43–44.

51. Harding, "Recent Improvements in Dairy Practice," pp. 85, 90.

52. Morton, "On Cheese-making in Home Dairies and in Factories," p. 74.

53. Ibid., p. 269. See also Gilbert Murray, "The Origin and Progress of the Factory System of Cheese-making in Derbyshire," *Journal of the Royal Agricultural Society,* 2d ser., 7 (1871): 43.

54. Morton, "On Cheese-making in Home Dairies and in Factories," pp. 269–70. See also Obelkevich, *Religion and Rural Society,* p. 53.

55. Pinchbeck, *Women Workers,* pp. 41–42. Pinchbeck follows the assessment made by Billingsley in 1798:

> This practice of letting dairies must have originated either from *pride* or *indolence* on the part of the farmer's hous[e]hold, and ought, in my opinion, to be checked by the landlord.
>
> When the female part of a farmer's family is unemployed, (and, without a dairy, that must be the case throughout [a] great part of the year) dissipation, folly, and extravagance, take the lead, and domestick care and industry are entirely forgotten.

Billingsley's enthusiasm for female labor in the dairy was based on his belief that "arduous domestick labour and incessant employment" provided a check on population growth. See *General View of Somerset,* pp. 205–6, 252.

56. M. Godelier, "Work and its Representations: A Research Proposal," *History Workshop Journal* 10 (1980): 166, 170.

Chapter 4

1. Joseph Bland, *An Essay in Praise of Women* (London, 1733), p. 20; *The Spinster in Defence of the Woollen Manufactures* (London, 1719), pp. 2–3. Exceptions to the rule of female spinsters did exist. Contemporaries noted that men span in eighteenth-century Silesia (Andrew Gray, *A Treatise on Spinning Machinery* [Edinburgh, 1819], p. 90), and historians have since located occasional instances, which they have associated with the proto-industrial economy. See Peter Kriedte, Hans Medick, and Jürgen Schlumbohm, *Industrialization Before Industrialization,* trans. Beate Schempp (Cambridge: Cambridge University Press, 1981), p. 62. This point is also discussed in Gay L. Gullickson, *Spinners and Weavers of Auffay: Rural Industry and the Sexual Division of Labor in a French Village, 1750–1850* (Cambridge: Cambridge University Press, 1986), p. 69. Gullickson provides an excellent close account of the spinning and weaving industries.

2. Sir A. Fitzherbert, *Boke of Husbandrye* (1555), quoted in Alice Clark, *Working Life of Women in the Seventeenth Century* (1919; reprint, London: Routledge & Kegan Paul, 1982), p. 48.

3. Ivy Pinchbeck, *Women Workers and the Industrial Revolution 1750–1850* (1930; reprint, London: Frank Cass, 1969), p. 124.

4. A. P. Wadsworth and J. de Lacy Mann, *The Cotton Trade and Industrial Lancashire 1600–1780* (1931; reprint, New York: Augustus M. Kelley, 1968), p. 274.

5. Daniel Defoe, *A Tour Through the Whole Island of Great Britain,* 2 vols. (1724–26; reprint, London: Dent, 1962); 1: pp. 62, 266; in *Every-Body's Business is No-Body's Business* (London, 1725), Defoe complained that servants showed too much audacity in expecting the same wages as spinsters.

6. John Dyer, *The Fleece* (1757).

7. Maxine Berg, *The Age of Manufactures: Industry, Innovation and Work in Britain 1700–1820* (London: Fontana, 1985), p. 142.

8. Pinchbeck, *Women Workers,* p. 129; Berg, *Age of Manufactures,* pp. 137, 139–43.

9. Gray, *A Treatise on Spinning Machinery,* pp. 86–87. On the tendency to naturalize this aspect of women's work, see Chris Middleton, "Women's Labour and the Transition to Pre-Industrial Capitalism," in *Women and Work in Pre-Industrial England,* ed. Lindsey Charles and Lorna Duffin (Beckenham, Kent: Croom Helm, 1985), pp. 181–206. Middleton quotes Thomas Tusser, who understood the problem as early as the sixteenth century:

> Some respit to husbands the weather may send
> But huswiues affaires haue neuer an end.
>
> P. 198.

10. J. James, *Continuation and Additions to the History of Bradford* (1866), p. 221, quoted in Paul Mantoux, *The Industrial Revolution in the Eighteenth Century,* trans. Marjorie Vernon (1928; rev. ed., Chicago: University of Chicago Press, 1983), p. 70.

11. Pamela Sharpe, "Literally Spinsters: A New Interpretation of Local Economy and Demography in Colyton in the Seventeenth and Eighteenth Centuries," *Economic History Review* 44 (1991): 60.

12. *Remarks upon Mr. Webber's Scheme and the Drapers' Pamphlet,* 1741, quoted in Pinchbeck, *Women Workers,* p. 136.

13. See Hans Medick, "Village Spinning Bees: Sexual Culture and Free Time Among Rural Youth in Early Modern Germany," in *Interest and Emotion: Essays on the Study of Family and Kinship,* ed. Hans Medick and David Warren Sabean (Cambridge: Cambridge University Press, 1984), pp. 317–39; Berg, *Age of Manufactures,* pp. 164–65.

14. Wadsworth and Mann, *The Cotton Trade and Industrial Lancashire,* p. 274. See also Richard Guest, *A Compendious History of the Cotton Manufacture* (Manchester, 1823).

15. Pinchbeck, *Women Workers,* p. 137; Wadsworth and Mann, *The Cotton Trade and Industrial Lancashire,* pp. 273–77, on woolens, see pp. 277–83.

16. Gullickson, *Spinners and Weavers,* p. 84.

17. *Annals of Agriculture* 9 (1788): 267, quoted in Pinchbeck, p. 139.

18. E. Lipson, *The History of the Woollen and Worsted Industries* (London: A. & C. Black, 1921), pp. 65–66.

19. John Kirby, *Letter to a Member of Parliament Stating the Necessity of an Amendment in the Laws relating to the Woollen Manufactory, so far as respect to the wages of spinners* (Ipswich, 1787), p. 21.

20. Herbert Heaton, *Yorkshire Woollen and Worsted Industries* (Oxford: Clarendon Press, 1920), pp. 418–19; on the history of laws against "bugging" and other forms of appropriation of raw materials, see Peter Linebaugh, *The London Hanged: Crime and Civil Society in the Eighteenth Century* (Cambridge: Cambridge University Press, 1992), pp. 239–41, 264–67; a different point of view can be found in John Styles, "Embezzlement, Industry and the Law in England, 1500–1800," in *Manufacture in Town and Country Before the Factory,* ed. Maxine Berg and Pat Hudson (Cambridge: Cambridge University Press, 1983), pp. 173–210; John Rule, *The Experience of Labour in Eighteenth-Century Industry* (London: Croom Helm, 1981), pp. 124–46.

21. Wadsworth and Mann, *The Cotton Trade and Industrial Lancashire,* p. 419.

22. *Manchester Magazine,* 11 September 1750, quoted in Wadsworth and Mann, *The Cotton Trade and Industrial Lancashire,* p. 398.

23. Wadsworth and Mann, *The Cotton Trade and Industrial Lancashire,* p. 421. The act operated with mixed success, owing to the ambivalence of inspectors and magistrates. One case against a number of women was stymied simply because the magistrate balked at punishing them, claiming that "the Act of Parliament was arbitrary and not fit to be put into execution." Heaton, *Yorkshire Woollen and Worsted Industries,* pp. 429–30.

24. Heaton, *Yorkshire Woollen and Worsted Industries,* pp. 429–31.

25. Heaton, *Yorkshire Woollen and Worsted Industries,* pp. 315ff; J. L. Hammond and Barbara Hammond, *The Skilled Labourer 1760–1832* (1919; reprint, New York: Augustus M. Kelley, 1967).

26. Wadsworth and Mann, *The Cotton Trade and Industrial Lancashire,* p. 277.

27. Wadsworth and Mann, *The Cotton Trade and Industrial Lancashire,* p. 277; Julia de Lacy Mann, *The Cloth Industry in the West of England from 1640 to 1880* (Oxford: Oxford University Press, 1971), pp. 131–32.

28. Wadsworth and Mann, *The Cotton Trade and Industrial Lancashire,* pp. 415–31. Paul's claim to authorship was contested by descendents of his associate, John Wyatt.

29. By the 1760s, when obtaining a patent for more sophisticated machinery, Richard Arkwright offered no apologies or proposals for the much greater displacement of labor that was to result from the introduction of the power loom. Wadsworth and Mann, *The Cotton Trade and Industrial Lancashire,* pp. 417–18.

30. Wadsworth and Mann, *The Cotton Trade and Industrial Lancashire,* pp. 476–78; Phyllis Deane, *The First Industrial Revolution* (Cambridge: Cambridge University Press, 1965), pp. 86–87.

31. William Bailey, *The Advancement of Arts, Manufactures, and Commerce* (London, 1772); Jonas Hanway, *A Plan for Establishing a Charity-House, or Charity-Houses, for the Reception of Repenting Prostitutes* (London, 1758), mentions "inventions to facilitate labor, not yet commonly known," and adds "the judicious use of them will be a means to increase the profits of these *Magdalens,* as well as render the expence of supporting the house so much the lighter." He had in mind the double-handed wheel for spinning flax. P. 32. The majority of early writers on technology were optimistic that machinery could be introduced without harmful effects. See A. W. Coats, "Changing Attitudes to Labour in the Mid-Eighteenth Century," *Economic History Review,* 2d ser., 11 (1958): 47–48.

32. Dyer, *The Fleece,* bk. III, pp. 356–57.

33. Thomas Bentley, *Letters on the Utility and Policy of Employing Machines to Shorten Labour* (London, 1780), pp. 14, 2–3. Later political economists discussed and criticized the use of female labor in factories, which to Tories and Radicals of the early nineteenth century, appeared to disrupt customary divisions of labor and displace male workers. Maxine Berg, *The Machinery Question and the Making of Political Economy 1815–1848* (Cambridge: Cambridge University Press, 1980), pp. 264–65, 282.

34. Pinchbeck, *Women Workers,* p. 114; Guest, *History of the Cotton Manufacture,* p. 12.

35. Edward Baines, *History of the Cotton Manufacture in Great Britain,* 2 vols. (London, 1835), 1: p. 115.

36. Quoted in ibid., 1: pp. 115–16n.

37. Wadsworth and Mann, *The Cotton Trade and Industrial Lancashire*, p. 276.

38. David Landes, *The Unbound Prometheus: Technological Change and Industrial Development in Western Europe from 1750 to the Present* (Cambridge: Cambridge University Press, 1972), p. 85.

39. Deane, *The First Industrial Revolution*, p. 86.

40. Berg, *Age of Manufactures*, p. 237.

41. [Thomas Barnes], *Thoughts on the Use of Machines* (Manchester, 1780), p. 14. T. S. Ashton noted that by 1788, an estimated 20,000 jennies were in use in England. He also pointed out that the jenny's small size and cheapness meant that its "effect was to strengthen, rather than weaken, the family economy." *The Industrial Revolution 1760–1830* (1948; rev. ed., Oxford: Oxford University Press, 1969), pp. 50–51. On the subject of job segregation by sex in the cotton textile industry, see Mary Freifeld, "Technological Change and the 'Self-acting' Mule: A Study of Skill and the Sexual Division of Labour," *Social History* 11 (1986): 319–43.

42. Baines, *History*, 1: pp. 158–60.

43. W. C. and Ralph Mather, *An Impartial Representation of the Case of the Poor Cotton Spinners in Lancashire* (London, 1780), p. 4.

44. Pinchbeck, *Women Workers*, pp. 150–51; quote from Hammond and Hammond, *The Skilled Labourer*, p. 56.

45. Baines, *History*, 1: p. 159.

46. Mann, *Cloth Industry*, p. 130.

47. Baines, *History*, 1: p. 160.

48. Robert Sadler, *The Discarded Spinster; or, a Plea for the Poor, on the impolicy of Spinning Jennies* (London, 1791), pp. 2, 8, 9.

49. W. C. and R. Mather, *Impartial Representation*, p. 12.

50. Malcolm I. Thomis and Jennifer Grimmett, *Women in Protest 1800–1850* (London: Croom Helm, 1982), p. 51.

51. Hammond and Hammond, *The Skilled Labourer*, pp. 55–56.

52. Mann, *Cloth Industry*, p. 128.

53. Quoted in Hammond and Hammond, *The Skilled Labourer*, pp. 147–48.

54. Sir Frederick Morton Eden, *The State of the Poor*, 3 vols. (London, 1797), 3: p. 796; W. C. and R. Mather, *Impartial Representation*, p. 3; Hammond and Hammond, *The Skilled Labourer*, p. 149.

55. Stark empirical evidence of this appears in A. F. J. Brown, *Essex at Work 1700–1815* (Chelmsford: Tindall Press, 1969), pp. 133–34.

56. Rev. David Davies, *The Case of the Labourers in Husbandry* (London, 1795), p. 86.

57. *Annals of Agriculture* 5 (1786): 418–20. *An Address to the Public, on the Propriety of Establishing Schools for Spinning* [1795] told of a Society of Industry that taught the poor habits of industry, but also reported the intractable problem of false reeling, which "entirely defeated" efforts to introduce jersey spinning into certain neighborhoods. *Address*, pp. v, 58–59.

58. *Observations . . . on the loss of woollen spinning* (c. 1794). I am grateful to E. P. Thompson for sharing this pamphlet with me.

59. Sadler, *Discarded Spinster*, p. 27.

60. Mantoux, *The Industrial Revolution*, p. 70.

61. Heaton, *Yorkshire Woollen and Worsted Industries*, p. 23.

62. An alternative approach can be found in Gullickson, *Spinners and Weavers*, chap. 5.

Chapter 5

1. Historians, sociologists, and anthropologists joined in these debates from an early date. For general discussions, see Ivy Pinchbeck, *Women Workers and the Industrial Revolution 1750–1850* (1930; reprint, London: Frank Cass, 1969); Eric Richards, "Women in the British Economy Since About 1700: An Interpretation," *History* 59 (1974): 337–57; Louise A. Tilly and Joan W. Scott, *Women, Work, and Family* (New York: Holt, Rinehart and Winston, 1978); Edward Shorter, *The Making of the Modern Family* (Huntington, NY: Fontana, 1975); Janet Thomas, "Women and Capitalism: Oppression or Emancipation?" *Comparative Studies in Society and History* 30 (1988): 534–49. American historians have provided a lively, informative basis for comparison. See Thomas Dublin, *Women at Work: The Transformation of Work and Community in Lowell, Massachusetts, 1826–1860* (New York: Columbia University Press, 1979); Alice Kessler-Harris, *Out to Work: A History of Wage-Earning Women in the United States* (New York: Oxford University Press, 1982); Christine Stansell, *City of Women: Sex and Class in New York, 1789–1860* (New York: Knopf, 1986).

The contemporary debate over the relationship between capitalism and women's oppression can be found in Michele Barrett, *Women's Oppression Today* (London: Verso, 1980); Johanna Brenner and Maria Ramas, "Rethinking Women's Oppression," *New Left Review* 144 (March–April, 1984): 33–71; Michele Barrett, "Rethinking Women's Oppression: A Reply to Brenner and Ramas," *New Left Review* (July–Aug. 1984): 123–28; Jane Lewis, "The Debate on Sex and Class," *New Left Review* 149 (Jan.–Feb. 1985): 108–20.

2. Wanda F. Neff, *Victorian Working Women: An Historical and Literary Study of Women in British Industries and Professions, 1832–1850* (1929; reprint, New York: AMS Press, 1966), p. 11. Sonya Rose refers to this phenomenon as "the working mother problem," though the critique extended beyond mothers to young single women as well; see Sonya O. Rose, *Limited Livelihoods: Gender and Class in Nineteenth Century England* (Berkeley: University of California Press, 1992), pp. 61–62.

3. For contemporary commentary, see Peter Gaskell, *The Manufacturing Population of England* (London, 1833); *Reports of the Factory Commission* (1833), 20, give a sense of the broad range of opinion among employers, medical men, and some working men; Frederick Engels, *Condition of the Working Class in England* (1845; St. Albans: Panther, 1969); more recent analysis of the Victorian woman of the working classes include Frank Mort, *Dangerous Sexualities: Medico-Moral Politics in England Since 1830* (London: Routledge & Kegan Paul, 1987); Lynda Nead, *Myths of Sexuality: Representations of Women in Victorian Britain* (Oxford: Blackwell, 1988); see also Martha Vicinus, ed., *Suffer and Be Still: Women in the Victorian Age* (Bloomington: Indiana University Press, 1972).

4. For an example of this point of view, see David Landes, *The Unbound Prometheus: Technological Change and Industrial Development in Western Europe from 1750 to the Present* (Cambridge: Cambridge University Press, 1969).

5. Alfred P. Wadsworth and Julia de Lacy Mann, *The Cotton Trade and Industrial Lancashire 1600–1780* (1931; reprint, New York: Augustus M. Kelley, 1968), p. 492n.

6. On alternative perspectives on technological development, see Maxine Berg, *The Machinery Question and the Making of Political Economy 1815–1848* (Cambridge: Cambridge University Press, 1980), pp. 179–97, 236–37. See also

Catherine Hall, "The Home Turned Upside Down? The Working Class Family in Cotton Textiles, 1780–1850," in *The Changing Experience of Women,* ed. Elizabeth Whitelegg et al. (Oxford: Martin Robertson, 1982).

7. Wadsworth and Mann, *The Cotton Trade and Industrial Lancashire,* pp. 493–94.

8. Ibid., pp. 492–93.

9. Stanley D. Chapman, *The Early Factory Masters: The Transition to the Factory System in the Midlands Textile Industry* (Newton Abbot: David and Charles, 1967), pp. 50–56.

10. Maxine Berg, *The Age of Manufactures: Industry, Innovation and Work in Britain 1700–1820* (London: Fontana, 1985), pp. 231–32.

11. Wadsworth and Mann, *The Cotton Trade and Industrial Lancashire,* pp. 492–93; Edward Baines, *History of the Cotton Manufacture in Great Britain,* 2 vols. (London, 1835), 1: 184–85.

12. The opposition to protective patents in Lancashire was "intense," yet Arkwright persevered even to the point of battling other manufacturers in court, a practice that remained relatively unusual until the nineteenth century. Wadsworth and Mann, *The Cotton Trade and Industrial Lancashire,* p. 490. On the career of Richard Arkwright, see R. S. Fitton, *The Arkwrights: Spinners of Fortune* (Manchester: Manchester University Press, 1989); R. S. Fitton and A. P. Wadsworth, *The Strutts and the Arkwrights 1758–1830: A Study of the Early Factory System* (Manchester: Manchester University Press, 1958).

13. R. L. Hills, "Hargreaves, Arkwright and Crompton. Why Three Inventors?" *Textile History* 10 (1979): 123.

14. Judy Lown, *Women and Industrialization: Gender at Work in Nineteenth-Century England* (Minneapolis: University of Minnesota Press, 1990), p. 18; Rose, *Limited Livelihoods,* pp. 23–24; Hilary Land, "The Family Wage," *Feminist Review* 6 (1980): 55–77; Michele Barrett and Mary McIntosh, "The 'Family Wage,'" in *The Changing Experience of Women,* ed. Elizabeth Whitelegg et al., pp. 71–87.

15. As quoted in Chapman, *Early Factory Masters,* p. 159.

16. Lown, *Women and Industrialization,* p. 29.

17. Chapman, *Early Factory Masters,* pp. 156–57, 184; Frances Collier, *The Family Economy of the Working Classes in the Cotton Industry 1784–1833* (Manchester: printed for the Chetham Society, 1965), p. 43; J. T. Ward, *The Factory Movement, 1830–1855* (London: Macmillan, 1962), pp. 15–19.

18. Collier, *Family Economy,* p. 16.

19. Ibid., pp. 17–20, 32.

20. Chapman, *Early Factory Masters,* pp. 30–31; for later years, see Lown, *Women and Industrialization,* p. 50.

21. Neff, *Victorian Working Women,* p. 29; see also Michael Anderson, *Family Structure in Nineteenth Century Lancashire* (Cambridge: Cambridge University Press, 1971), p. 23.

22. At the Courtauld silk mills in the 1860s, women's wages for operating powerlooms were roughly one-half those of male attendants, and less than one-fourth those of male supervisors. Judy Lown, "Not So Much a Factory, More a Form of Patriarchy: Gender and Class During Industrialisation," in *Gender, Class and Work,* ed. Eve Gamarnikow et al. (London: Heinemann, 1983), p. 38; Lown, *Women and Industrialization,* pp. 53–58.

23. Quoted in Neff, *Victorian Working Women,* pp. 30–31.

24. Table taken from Fitton and Wadsworth, *The Strutts and the Ark-wrights*, pp. 231–32.

25. Fitton and Wadsworth, *The Strutts and the Arkwrights*, pp. 230–34.

26. Lown, *Women and Industrialization*, p. 33; see also D. C. Coleman, *The Courtaulds: An Economic and Social History*, 2 vols. (Oxford: Clarendon Press, 1969), 1: p. 64.

27. B. L. Hutchins and A. Harrison, *A History of Factory Legislation* (London, 1911), p. 19. They point out that after the wars, "[t]he whole subject . . . assumes a somewhat different aspect. The factories for the most part were much larger affairs, and much more before the eye of the public." P. 19.

28. Thomas Bentley, *Letters on the Utility and Policy of Employing Machines to Shorten Labour* (London, 1780), p. 9.

29. Andrew Ure, *Philosophy of Manufactures* (London, 1835), p. 23.

30. Quoted in Barbara L. Hutchins, *Women in Modern Industry* (1915; reprint, EP Publishing, 1978), p. 54.

31. *PP* (1833), 20: p. 46.

32. Hutchins, *Women in Modern Industry*, pp. 54–55; William Lazonick, "Industrial Relations and Technical Change: The Case of the Self-acting Mule," *Cambridge Journal of Economics* 3 (1979): 231–62.

33. "Gender and Labor History: Learning from the Past, Looking to the Future," in *Work Engendered: Toward a New History of American Labor*, ed. Ava Baron (Ithaca, NY: Cornell University Press, 1991), p. 13.

34. On women and trade unions in Britain, see Barbara Drake, *Women in Trade Unions* (London, 1921); Sheila Lewenhak, *Women and Trade Unions* (London: Ernest Benn, 1977); Norbert C. Soldon, *Women in British Trade Unions, 1874–1976* (Dublin: Gill and Macmillan, 1978); Jane Lewis, *Women in England, 1870–1950* (Brighton: Wheatsheaf Books, 1984), pp. 175–78; Hutchins, *Women in Modern Industry*, pp. 92–177; Rose, *Limited Livelihoods*, pp. 69, 143–44, 175–76.

35. Sidney and Beatrice Webb, *English Poor Law History*, Pt. I, *The Old Poor Law* (London: Longmans, Green & Co., 1927), pp. 104–5, quoted in Drake, *Women in Trade Unions*, p. 93. As Jane Lewis has pointed out, "skilled work . . . become[s], by definition, work that is not performed by women." *Women in England*, pp. 171, 177. For a cogent analysis of the question of gender and skill, see Anne Phillips and Barbara Taylor, "Sex and Skill: Notes towards a Feminist Economics," *Feminist Review* 6 (1980): 79–88.

36. William Lazonick, "Industrial Relations and Technical Change," pp. 231–62; see also Mary Freifeld, "Technological Change and the 'Self-acting' Mule: A Study of Skill and the Sexual Division of Labour," *Social History* 11 (1986): 319–43; Mariana Valverde, "'Giving the Female a Domestic Turn': The Social, Legal and Moral Regulation of Women's Work in British Cotton Mills, 1820–1850," *Journal of Social History* 21 (1988): 619–34; Rose, *Limited Livelihoods*, pp. 143–46; Lown, *Women and Industrialization*, pp. 184–85. On the exclusion of women from British trade unions, see Harold Benenson, "Victorian Sexual Ideology and Marx's Theory of the Working Class," *International Labor and Working Class History* 25 (1984): 5–8.

37. For a discussion of the concerns of women workers in the history of labor relations, see Carole E. Morgan, "Women, Work and Consciousness in the Mid-Nineteenth-Century English Cotton Industry," *Social History* 17 (1992): 23–41.

38. Lewenhak, *Women and Trade Unions,* p. 29.

39. On the ways in which men were able to gain advantage of women workers in Lancashire textile factories, see Rose, *Limited Livelihoods,* pp. 159–60; on trade union politics, see ibid., pp. 166–83. For an analysis of the exceptional nature of this type of labor organization, see Benenson, "Victorian Sexual Ideology," pp. 6–7.

40. Barbara Taylor, *Eve and the New Jerusalem* (London: Virago, 1983); Benenson, "Victorian Sexual Ideology," pp. 1–5; Drake, *Women in Trade Unions,* p. 5.

41. Dorothy Thompson, *The Chartists: Popular Politics in the Industrial Revolution* (New York: Pantheon, 1984), pp. 134–35.

42. Quoted in Thompson, *The Chartists,* p. 136.

43. Morgan, "Women, Work and Consciousness," p. 36.

44. Quoted in Lewenhak, *Women in Trade Unions,* pp. 34–35.

45. Ibid., p. 33.

46. Tilly and Scott, *Women, Work and Family,* p. 64.

47. Richards, "Women in the British Economy," p. 346.

48. Geoffrey Best, *Mid-Victorian Britain* (New York: Schocken, 1971), p. 107.

49. Wally Seccombe, "Patriarchy Stabilized: The Construction of the Male Breadwinner Wage Norm in Nineteenth-Century Britain," *Social History* 11 (1986): 53–76. For the important and lasting influence of discussion of women workers in factories during the debates over protective legislation in the 1840s, see Rose, *Limited Livelihoods,* chap. 3.

50. Ure, *Philosophy of Manufactures,* p. 354. On Ure and the relationship of machinery to political economy, see Berg, *The Machinery Question,* pp. 181, 197–202.

51. Travers Twiss, *Two Lectures on Machinery* (Oxford, 1844), pp. 33, 50–51; *Hickson's Report, Handloom Weavers' Report, PP* (1840), 24: p. 44. Twiss also cited Hickson's Report in his lectures.

52. Sir Egerton Brydges, *The Population and Riches of Nations* (London, 1819), p. 58.

53. Gaskell, *Manufacturing Population of England,* pp. 61–68, 93–94, 162–68; Charles Bray, *The Industrial Employment of Women* (London, 1857), pp. 5–8; Twiss, *Two Lectures on Machinery,* p. 29; Neff, *Victorian Working Women,* pp. 55–56; Engels, *Condition of the Working Class,* p. 144; on middle class ideology, see Leonore Davidoff and Catherine Hall, *Family Fortunes: Men and Women of the English Middle Class, 1780–1850* (London: Hutchinson, 1987), chap. 3.

54. Gaskell, *Manufacturing Population of England,* pp. 163–65; see also Bray, *Industrial Employment of Women,* pp. 13–15.

55. *PP* (1833), 20: p. 48.

56. *Philosophy of Manufactures,* p. 475.

57. See Chapter 8.

58. On the passage of the Factory Acts, see Ward, *The Factory Movement;* Cecil Driver, *Tory Radical: The Life of Richard Oastler* (New York: Oxford University Press, 1946). The achievement of the Act of 1833 "[wrote] the problem of mill women in capital letters" by bringing about an increase in the employment of women. Neff, *Victorian Working Women,* p. 70.

59. See Benenson, "Victorian Sexual Ideology"; Rose, *Limited Livelihoods,*

pp. 55–59; Valverde, "Giving the Female A Domestic Turn," pp. 623–31; Morgan, "Women, Work and Consciousness," pp. 27–29; Brenner and Ramas, "Rethinking Women's Oppression," pp. 40–47.

60. Frances Place, Letter to James Turner, Cotton Spinner, Brompton, London, September 29, 1835, quoted in Neff, *Victorian Working Women*, p. 31.

61. Jane Humphries, "'Class Struggle and the Persistence of the Working–Class Family," *Cambridge Journal of Economics* 1 (1977): 241–58; Valverde, "Giving the Female a Domestic Turn," p. 620.

62. Quoted in Valverde, "Giving the Female a Domestic Turn," p. 628, from 1842 Short-Time Committee of the West Riding of Yorkshire.

63. As Harold Benenson has argued, "Among skilled working men, this male breadwinner concept had its roots in the value of artisan respectability of many early nineteenth century trades." "Victorian Sexual Ideology," p. 7. Charles Bray's discussion of the proper role of factory women points out the same conviction: that women have work to do, "but not in competition with men." Bray was explicit in expressing disapproval of the independence of factory women who "refused to take upon themselves the responsibility of husbands." *Industrial Employment of Women*, pp. 8, 12.

64. Jane Humphries, "The Working Class Family, Women's Liberation, and Class Struggle: The Case of Nineteenth Century British History," *Review of Radical Political Economics* 9 (1977): 34–36; Taylor, *Eve and the New Jerusalem*, pp. 110–11; for examples in the watch and ribbon trades, see Bray, *Industrial Employment of Women*, pp. 4, 11.

65. Horner's Report of October 1843, quoted in Hutchins and Harrison, *History of Factory Legislation*, p. 84. Leonard Horner, a Lancashire factory inspector, was "a key figure in the shaping of factory legislation." Valverde, "'Giving the Female a Domestic Turn,'" pp. 626–27.

66. See Rose, *Limited Livelihoods*, pp. 50–75; Valverde, "Giving the Woman a Domestic Turn," p. 627.

67. Horner's Report, quoted in Hutchins and Harrison, *History of Factory Legislation*, p. 84.

68. The phrase "withdrawn from their domestic duties" is from Horner's testimony. Mariana Valverde argues that it became "a common cliche" by the 1840s, when Lord Ashley and others took up the cause of restricting women's work in the mills owing to its offense to "the order of nature, and the rights of labouring men." Valverde, "'Giving the Female a Domestic Turn,'" pp. 626–27; see also Rose, *Limited Livelihoods*, pp. 56–59; Ward, *The Factory Movement*; Hutchins and Harrison, *A History of Factory Legislation*.

69. On the implications of the Factories (Health of Women, etc.) Act of 1874 and the Factory and Workshops Consolidation Act of 1878, see Rose, *Limited Livelihoods*, pp. 71–75. She argues that "such legislation made individual women responsible for the welfare of babies and children," blamed them for infant mortality, and "vilified working-class men whose wives were working in factories." Pp. 71–72.

70. Tilly and Scott, *Women, Work and Family*, p. 114.

71. Neil McKendrick, "Home Demand and Economic Growth: A New View of the Role of Women and Children in the Industrial Revolution," in *Historical Perspectives: Studies in English Thought and Society in honour of J. H. Plumb*, ed. Neil McKendrick (London: Europa, 1974), pp. 167–68.

72. The literature on American women is extremely helpful in understand-

ing the subjectivity and autonomy of factory workers. See Dublin, *Women at Work*; Kessler-Harris, *Out to Work,* esp. p. 34.

73. Elizabeth Gaskell, *Mary Barton* (1848; Harmondsworth, Middlesex: Penguin, 1970), p. 43.

74. Quoted in Anderson, *Family Structure,* p. 124.

75. Ibid., pp. 124–25.

76. Ibid., p. 54.

77. Many such households took in lodgers who were "secondary kin." See Lown, *Women and Industrialization,* pp. 86–88.

78. Neff, *Victorian Working Women,* p. 14.

79. McKendrick, "Home Demand and Economic Growth," p. 164.

80. *PP* (1833), 20: p. 35.

81. On the moral meanings attached to the working-class woman's mode of dress, see Mariana Valverde, "The Love of Finery: Fashion and the Fallen Woman in Nineteenth-Century Social Discourse," *Victorian Studies* 32 (1989): pp. 169–88.

82. Joan W. Scott and Louise A. Tilly, "Women's Work and the Family in Nineteenth Century Europe," *Comparative Studies in Society and History* 17 (1975): 54.

83. Anderson, *Family Structure,* p. 153

84. Neil Smelser, *Social Change in the Industrial Revolution* (Chicago: University of Chicago Press, 1959), pp. 188–89.

85. Anderson, *Family Structure,* pp. 56ff; 101ff.

86. Neff, *Victorian Working Women,* p. 27.

87. *PP* (1833), 20: p. 39.

88. Jane Humphries, "The Working Class Family," pp. 25–41; Humphries, "Class Struggle," pp. 241–58.

89. *PP* (1833), 20: pp. 34–35.

90. *PP* (1833), 20: p. 35.

91. Anderson, *Family Structure,* pp. 30–32.

92. John Foster, *Class Struggle and the Industrial Revolution: Early Industrial Capitalism in Three English Towns* (London: Methuen, 1974), p. 30.

93. Collier, *Family Economy,* p. 17.

94. Margaret Hewitt, *Wives and Mothers in Victorian Industry* (1958; reprint, Westport, CT: Greenwood Press, 1975), p. 11.

95. Leonore Davidoff, "The Separation of Home and Work? Landladies and Lodgers in Nineteenth- and Twentieth-Century England," in *Fit Work for Women,* ed. Sandra Burman (London: Croom Helm, 1979), pp. 64–97; Elizabeth A. M. Roberts, "Women's Strategies, 1890–1940," in *Labour and Love: Women's Experiences of Home and Family, 1850–1940,* ed. Jane Lewis (Oxford: Blackwell, 1986), pp. 232–33; on the multiplicity of ways in which working-class women were forced to make ends meet, see Ellen Ross, "Survival Networks: Women's Neighbourhood Sharing in London Before World War I," *History Workshop Journal* 15 (1983): 4–27.

96. Engels, *Condition of the Working Class,* pp. 162, 164–65; Bray, *Industrial Employment of Women,* p. 11.

97. *PP* (1830), 20: pp. 36–37.

98. Anderson, *Family Structure,* p. 131.

99. Engels concluded that "the binding tie of this family was not family affection, but private interest lurking under the cloak of a pretended community of possessions." Engels, *Condition of the Working Class,* pp. 174–75; see also

Frederick Engels, *The Origin of the Family, Private Property and the State,* Alec West, trans. (New York: International Publishers, 1972), esp. chap. 2.

100. Hutchins, *Women in Modern Industry,* pp. 53, 73.

101. Jane Humphries, "Protective Legislation, the Capitalist State, and Working Class Men: The Case of the 1842 Mines Regulation Act," *Feminist Review* 7 (1981): 1–33; Angela V. John, *By the Sweat of Their Brow: Women Workers at Victorian Coal Mines* (London: Routledge & Kegan Paul, 1984).

102. Millicent Garrett Fawcett, champion of women's suffrage, believed that female factory workers should be allowed to determine the question of their work lives themselves. See Rosemary Feurer, "The Meaning of 'Sisterhood': The British Women's Movement and Protective Labor Legislation, 1870–1900," *Victorian Studies* 31 (1988): 233–60; Rose, *Limited Livelihoods,* pp. 65–66; Lewis, *Women in England,* pp. 201–2.

103. Lown, "Not So Much a Factory"; Sonya Rose, "'Gender at Work': Sex, Class and Industrial Capitalism," *History Workshop Journal* 21 (1986): pp. 113–31; Seccombe, "Patriarchy Stabilized," pp. 56–59; Nancy Grey Osterud, "Gender Divisions and the Organization of Work in the Leicester Hosiery Industry," in *Unequal Opportunities: Women's Employment in England 1800–1918,* ed. Angela V. John (Oxford: Blackwell, 1986), pp. 45–68.

104. *PP* (1833), 20: p. 9.

105. See Chapman, *Early Factory Masters,* pp. 196–98; Fitton and Wadsworth, *The Strutts and the Arkwrights,* pp. 99–100; J. F. C. Harrison, *Quest for the New Moral World: Robert Owen and the Owenites in Britain and America* (New York: Charles Scribner's Sons, 1969), pp. 151–63.

106. From this time, the textile factories of the North swept into their orbit many village and town handworkers. See Patrick Joyce, *Work, Society and Politics: The Culture of the Factory in Later Victorian England* (Brighton, Sussex: Harvester Press, 1980), pp. xv–xvi, pp. 55–59.

107. Parkes, "Preface," in Mary Merryweather, *Experience of Factory Life, Being a Record of Fourteen Years' Work, Mr. Courtauld's Silk Mill at Halstead, in Essex,* 3d ed. (London: Emily Faithfull, 1862), p. xxi.

108. Quoted in Chapman, *Early Factory Masters,* p. 197.

109. Letter from George Courtauld to Joseph Wilson, 24 September 1814, cited in Lown, *Women and Industrialization,* p. 29.

110. A factory master's wife offered revealing evidence of his origins. Peter Gaskell called attention to her "vulgar" speech and "tawdry" dress; her daughters were often expensively educated but still *nouveau. Manufacturing Population of England,* p. 60. As Lown points out, "Those born in the 1780s or 1790s, like Samuel Courtauld's generation, were very active proselytizing ideals of gentility and domesticity for their own womenfolk early in the nineteenth century even if they were not yet in a position to live fully according to such principles themselves." Ibid., pp. 32–33. Arkwright's daughters were undergoing the same transformation in the 1770s, but apparently with less involvement with the factory hands. Chapman, *Early Factory Masters,* p. 77.

111. *Women and Industrialization,* pp. 141–51. Lown's discussion of Merryweather is one of the few and by far the best analyses of the role of middle-class women in creating the culture of paternalism in factory towns. This subject warrants further investigation. See Jane Rendall, "'A Moral Engine'? Feminism, Liberalism and the *English Woman's Journal,*" in *Equal or Different? Women's Politics, 1800–1914,* ed. Jane Rendall (Oxford: Blackwell, 1987), pp. 114–15.

Davidoff and Hall have emphasized the tendency of factory owners' families to avoid direct involvement with the work force, seeking instead a spatial as well as a social distance from the work place. See Davidoff and Hall, *Family Fortunes,* p. 251. On the rise of the female philanthropist, see Frank Prochaska, *Women and Philanthropy in Nineteenth-Century England* (Oxford: Clarendon Press, 1980).

112. Merryweather, *Experience of Factory Life,* pp. 7–8.

113. Ibid., pp. 16, 17, 20, 23–24.

114. Bessie Rayner Parkes, "Preface," in ibid., pp. iii–iv.

115. Ibid., pp. iii–iv.

116. On Parkes, see Rendall, "'A Moral Engine'?" pp. 112–38; Rendall, *The Origins of Modern Feminism: Women in Britain, France and the United States, 1780–1860* (New York: Schocken, 1984), pp. 266–67, 314; Diane M. C. Worzala, "The Langham Place Circle: The Beginnings of the Organized Women's Movement in England, 1854–1870" (Ph.D. diss., University of Wisconsin, 1982). Parkes was a friend of Mary Merryweather, who wrote numerous articles for the *Journal*. Emily Faithfull, publisher of *Experience of Factory Life,* founded the Victorian Press, which was devoted to the feminist ideals of the Langham Place Circle.

117. Bray, *Industrial Employment of Women,* p. 16.

118. Gaskell, *Manufacturing Population of England,* p. 165.

Chapter 6

1. Quoted in John G. Dony, *A History of the Straw Hat Industry* (Luton: Gibbs, Bamforth, 1942), p. 21.

2. For the background of English cottage industries, see Joan Thirsk, "Industries in the Countryside," in *Essays in the Economic and Social History of Tudor and Stuart England,* ed. F. J. Fisher (Cambridge: Cambridge University Press, 1961), pp. 70–88; Maxine Berg, *The Age of Manufactures: Industry, Innovation and Work in Britain, 1700–1820* (London: Fontana, 1985), pp. 92–107; Maxine Berg, Pat Hudson, and Michael Sonenscher, *Manufacture in Town and Country* (Cambridge: Cambridge University Press, 1983), pp. 1–32.

3. The dates are implicit in most discussions of proto-industrialization, but David Levine has demarcated this period as "the efflorescence of *proto-industrialization.*" *Reproducing Families: The Political Economy of English Population History* (Cambridge: Cambridge University Press, 1987), p. 131. For figures, see Berg, *Age of Manufactures,* pp. 23–47. Employment and wages in several industries, such as lace making and straw plait, declined after 1815 owing to changes in import policies and foreign competition. On the decline of cottage industries after 1815, see George R. Boyer, *An Economic History of the English Poor Law* (Cambridge: Cambridge University Press, 1990), pp. 38–40; Joan Thirsk, *Economic Policy and Projects: The Development of a Consumer Society in Early Modern England* (Oxford: Clarendon Press, 1978); Carole Shammas, *The Pre-Industrial Consumer in England and America* (Oxford: Clarendon Press, 1990); cf. Roderick Floud and Donald McCloskey, *The Economic History of Britain Since 1700,* 2 vols. (Cambridge: Cambridge University Press, 1981), 1: pp. 36–65.

4. Adam Smith, *Wealth of Nations,* ed. by Edwin Cannan (1776; reprint, Chicago: University of Chicago Press, 1976), bk. 4, chap. 8, p. 161; Berg, *Age of Manufactures,* pp. 62–3. Smith was not simply voicing sympathy when he pointed out the disparity of power between cottage workers and merchant manufacturers; he wished to demonstrate the larger social ramifications of economic

dependency. Ideally, rural producers should exist in independence, a state that was far more likely to engender political and moral virtue.

5. Peter Kriedte, Hans Medick, and Jürgen Schlumbohm, *Industrialization Before Industrialization,* trans. Beate Schempp (Cambridge: Cambridge University Press, 1981), p. 55; Levine, *Reproducing Families,* pp. 112–13.

6. A. W. Coats, "Changing Attitudes to Labour in the Mid-Eighteenth Century," *Economic History Review,* 2d series, 11 (1958): 35–51.

7. For the early debate on proto-industrialization, see E. L. Jones, "The Agricultural Origins of Industry," *Past and Present* (1968): 58–71; Franklin F. Mendels, "Proto-industrialization: The First Phase of the Industrialization Process," *Journal of Economic History* 32 (1972): 241–61; Hans Medick, "The Proto-Industrial Family Economy: The Structural Function of Household and Family During the Transition from Peasant Society to Industrial Capitalism," *Social History* 3 (1976): 291–318; Berg, *Age of Manufactures,* p. 77.

8. Kriedte et al., *Industrialization Before Industrialization,* p. 62.

9. Whether the wife became active as a spinner engaging in production of commodities for the market or whether she increased the marginal returns from petty agrarian production by intensive cultivation or by tending the livestock on the commons, often it was only her activity that assured the vital margin of the family economy's subsistence.

Medick, "The Proto-industrial Family Economy," p. 311.

10. Robert Malcolmson, *Life and Labour in England 1700–1780* (London: Hutchinson, 1981), pp. 38, 39; see also Joan Thirsk, "Seventeenth-Century Agriculture and Social Change," *Agricultural History Review* 18 (1970): pp. 171–72.

11. Kriedte et al., *Industrialization Before Industrialization,* pp. 61–62.

12. Kriedte, p. 62.

13. Medick, "The Proto-industrial Family Economy," pp. 311n.

14. Dorothy Thompson, "Women and Nineteenth-Century Radical Politics: A Lost Dimension," in *The Rights and Wrongs of Women,* ed. Juliet Mitchell and Ann Oakley (Harmondsworth, Middlesex: Penguin, 1976), pp. 112–38.

15. Jeanette M. Neeson, "The Opponents of Enclosure in Eighteenth-Century Northamptonshire," *Past and Present* 105 (1984): 114–39; John Bohstedt, *Riots and Community Politics in England and Wales, 1790–1810* (Cambridge, MA: Harvard University Press, 1983); Malcolm I. Thomis and Jennifer Grimmett, *Women in Protest 1800–1850* (London: Croom Helm, 1982); John Knott, *Popular Opposition to the 1834 Poor Law* (London: Croom Helm, 1986).

16. Deborah M. Valenze, *Prophetic Sons and Daughters: Female Preaching and Popular Religion in Industrial England* (Princeton, NJ: Princeton University Press, 1985).

17. For an insightful discussion of women's work in framework knitting, see Nancy Grey Osterud, "Gender Divisions and the Organization of Work in the Leicester Hosiery Industry," in *Unequal Opportunities: Women's Employment in England 1800–1918,* ed. Angela V. John (Oxford: Blackwell, 1986), pp. 45–68; for the metal trades and the Birmingham toy trades, see Berg, *Age of Manufactures,* pp. 264–314.

18. Ivy Pinchbeck, *Women Workers and the Industrial Revolution 1750–1850* (1930; reprint, London: Frank Cass, 1969), p. 207; Fanny Bury Palliser, *A History of Lace,* 2d ed. (London, 1869), pp. 229–30. Women in Bedfordshire could earn as much by lace making as reaping at the end of the seventeenth century,

which placed the cottage industry among the most remunerative forms of female labor as well as making it sufficiently high to attract men. G. F. R. Spenceley, "The Origins of the English Pillow Lace Industry," *Agricultural History Review* 21 (1973): 92.

19. Daniel Defoe, *A Brief State of the Inland or Home Trade* (London, 1730; reprint, 1967), pp. 288–89.

20. Quoted by Dony, *History of the Straw Hat Industry,* pp. 24–25.

21. David Levine, *Family Formation in the Age of Nascent Capitalism* (London: Academic Press, 1977); Thirsk, "Industries in the Countryside."

22. *PP* (1843), pp. 295, 327.

23. W. G. Hoskins, *The Midland Peasant: The Economic and Social History of a Leicestershire Village* (London: Macmillan, 1957), pp. 227–28; Jones, "Agricultural Origins of Industry," p. 63; Malcolmson, *Life and Labour,* p. 44; Osterud, "Gender Divisions," pp. 45–68.

24. Spenceley, "Origins of the English Pillow Lace Industry," p. 90.

25. K. D. M. Snell, *Annals of the Labouring Poor: Social Change and Agrarian England 1660–1900* (Cambridge: Cambridge University Press, 1985), pp. 65, 164–65.

26. *PP* (1843), 13: d.39.

27. Pinchbeck, *Women Workers,* pp. 222–23.

28. Dony, *History of the Straw Hat Industry,* pp. 19, 30–34.

29. Numbers, when available, were significantly high: by 1780, around 140,000 carried on lace making in Bedford, Buckinghamshire, and Northampton and in the neighboring districts of Huntingdon, Hertfordshire, and Oxford. Berg, *Age of Manufactures,* p. 123.

30. Pinchbeck, *Women Workers,* pp. 222–23.

31. R. Campbell, *The London Tradesman* (London, 1747), p. 152.

32. T. S. Ashton, "The Records of a Pin Manufactory, 1814–21," *Economica* 5 (1925): 290–92.

33. Pinchbeck, *Women Workers,* p. 225.

34. William Hull, *History of the Glove Trade* (London, 1834), p. 135.

35. Thomas G. Austin, *The Straw Plaitting and Straw Hat and Bonnet Trade* (Luton, 1871), p. 16; Pinchbeck, *Women Workers,* pp. 215–22; *The Pioneer,* 26 April 1834, quoted in Dony, *History of the Straw Hat Industry,* p. 50; see also pp. 25, 41–42; Duncan Bythell, *The Sweated Trades: Outwork in Nineteenth-Century Britain* (London: Batsford, 1978) pp. 119–20. Pinchbeck dates the decline in straw plaiting from 1820. *Women Workers,* p. 221.

36. Dony, *History of the Straw Hat Industry,* p. 68.

37. Charles Tomlinson, *Illustrations of Useful Arts, Manufactures, and Trades* (London, 1860), p. 107, Pinchbeck, *Women Workers,* p. 231; *PP* 1843, vol. 12, p. 87.

38. Palliser, *History of Lace,* p. 361; Pamela Horn, "Child Workers in the Pillow Lace and Straw Plait Trades of Victorian Buckinghamshire and Bedfordshire," *Historical Journal* 17 (1974): 786, on abuses.

39. Dony dates the appearance of dealers at around 1785, noting that they became "the pulse of the industry." *History of the Straw Hat Industry,* pp. 25, 63.

40. Berg, *Age of Manufactures,* p. 123; Bythell, *The Sweated Trades,* p. 98.

41. Bythell, *The Sweated Trades,* pp. 99–100.

42. Inventions, if inexpensive, could work in favor of the laborer. The introduction of brass straw-splitters, sold at sixpence each, "within easy reach of the

plaitters," enabled English plaiters to compete more successfully with foreign imports. Austin, *Straw Plaitting Trade,* p. 16.

43. *PP* (1843), 14: f.42.

44. Mistresses were notoriously exploitative in the pin industry. See Ashton, "Records of a Pin Manufactory" pp. 283, 286.

45. *PP* (1843), 14: f.43.

46. Even though a bill forbidding truck abuses in the lace industry had been passed in 1779, for example, the practice continued. Long into the nineteenth century, lace "schools" continued to disguise the exploitation of child labor and payments in kind. See Horn, "Child Workers," pp. 779–96.

47. *PP* (1843), 14: d. 29, 30.

48. E. P. Thompson, "Patrician Society, Plebeian Culture," *Journal of Social History* 7 (1974): 385–86. See also Levine, *Reproducing Families,* p. 53; Kreidte et al., *Industrialization Before Industrialization,* pp. 64–71.

49. Levine, *Reproducing Families,* pp. 117, 120. Pamela Sharpe has argued just the opposite, pointing out that cottage industry enabled the female part of the population to choose *not* to marry since it gave them a means of self-support. Pamela Sharpe, "Literally Spinsters: A New Interpretation of local economy and demography in Colyton in the Seventeenth and Eighteenth Centuries," *Economic History Review* 44 (1991): 46–47.

50. Rudolf Braun, "Protoindustrialisation and demographic changes in the canton of Zurich," in *Historical Studies of Changing Fertility,* ed. Charles Tilly (Princeton, NJ: Princeton University Press, 1978), pp. 289–334; Levine, *Reproducing Families,* pp. 130–31. Levine qualifies this argument, however, by adding that "some proto-industrial areas were superseded and reverted to a later age at marriage and a more prudential replacement rate." P. 130.

51. Quoted in John R. Gillis, *For Better, For Worse: British Marriages, 1600 to the Present* (New York: Oxford University Press, 1985), p. 119.

52. Ibid., p. 153; Bridget Hill, *Women, Work, and Sexual Politics in Eighteenth-Century England* (Oxford: Blackwell, 1989), p. 189.

53. Spenceley, "Origins of the English Pillow Lace Industry," pp. 88–89. Spenceley points out that some confusion exists over whether the Katherine at issue was Queen Katherine of Aragon, who has been credited by some to be the originator of the lace making industry in Ampthill, Bedfordshire, where she was incarcerated in 1532–33. According to legend, "when the trade was dull," the "good Queen" was said to have "burnt all her lace and ordered new to be made." The story was popularly held to be true, but the festival day, November 25, commemorates Katherine of Alexandria.

54. Sharpe, "Literally Spinsters," pp. 46–65; A. Young, *Agriculture of Hertfordshire,* pp. 222, 223, quoted by R. C. Richardson, "Metropolitan Counties: Bedfordshire, Hertfordshire, and Middlesex," in vol. 5, pt. 1, of *The Agrarian History of England and Wales,* ed. Joan Thirsk (Cambridge: Cambridge University Press, 1984), p. 267; see also Pamela L. R. Horn, "The Buckinghamshire Straw Plait Trade in Victorian England," *Records of Buckinghamshire* 19 (1971): 43.

55. *PP* (1843), 13: p. 131, quoted in Horn, "Buckinghamshire Straw Plait Trade," p. 50.

56. "Lace Making," *Annals of Agriculture* 37 (1801): 449.

57. Quoted in J. L. Hammond and Barbara Hammond, *The Skilled Labourer 1760–1832* (1919; reprint, New York: Augustus M. Kelley, 1967), p. 262.

58. Temma Kaplan, "Female Consciousness and Collective Action: The Case of Barcelona, 1910–1918," *Signs: Journal of Women in Culture and Society* 7 (1982): 585; Ruth L. Smith and Deborah M. Valenze, "Mutuality and Marginality: Liberal Moral Theory and Working-Class Women in Nineteenth-Century England," *Signs: Journal of Women in Culture and Society* 13 (1988): 277–98.

59. Knott, *Popular Opposition to the 1834 Poor Law*, pp. 67–68; Dony, *History of the Straw Hat Industry*, pp. 56–57.

60. Quoted in Valenze, *Prophetic Sons and Daughters*, p. 67.

61. Census figures on religious affiliation in straw plaiting districts shows a strong correlation with Methodism, both Wesleyan and Primitive. See Austin, *The Straw Plaitting Trade*, pp. 22ff.

62. *PP* (1843), 14: d. 29, 30.

63. *PP* (1843), 14: f. 45; f. 42.

64. Quoted in Horn, "Child Workers," p. 779.

65. *PP* (1867–68), 17: p. 515.

66. *PP* (1867–68), 17: p. 499.

67. *PP* (1867–68), 17: p. 515.

68. *PP* (1864), 22: p. 203.

69. PP (1867), 17: pp. 498–99. Similar criticisms were aimed at lace makers, who were seen as "unwilling to take part in home duties, which they look upon as drudgery, and thus they never acquire habits which will fit them for the married state, and are unable to cook a dinner, clean a house, or generally make home comfortable." *PP* (1864), 22: p. xvii.

70. Osterud, "Gender Divisions," p. 65. The history of cottage industries reminds us that "cheap labour rather than invention was the fulcrum of economic growth." Raphael Samuel, "Workshop of the World: Steam Power and Hand Technology in Mid-Victorian Britain," *History Workshop Journal*, no. 3 (1977): 17.

Chapter 7

1. Gary Langer, *The Coming of Age of Political Economy, 1815–1825* (Westport, CT: Greenwood Press, 1987); Harold Benenson, "The Origins of the Concept of Class and Gender Ideology," Paper presented at the Conference on Feminism: Theory and Politics, Pembroke Center for Research and Teaching on Women, Brown University, 1986. For an excellent collection of studies on eighteenth-century political economy, see Istvan Hont and Michael Ignatieff, eds., *Wealth and Virtue: The Shaping of Political Economy in the Scottish Enlightenment* (Cambridge: Cambridge University Press, 1983).

2. *Northern Tour* (1770), III: p. 317; and *Southern Tour*, 2d ed. (1769), p. 257, quoted in Edgar S. Furniss, *The Position of the Laborer in a System of Nationalism: A Study in the Labor Theories of the Later English Mercantilists* (1920; reprint, New York: Augustus M. Kelley, 1965), p. 155.

3. *Annals of Agriculture* 34 (1800): 613.

4. Ibid.

5. Ibid., p. 614.

6. *An Inquiry into the Nature and Causes of the Wealth of Nations*, 2 vols., ed. Edwin Cannan (1776; reprint, Chicago: University of Chicago Press, 1976), I: bk. 1, chap. 8, p. 88.

7. For an analytical treatment of Smith as a moral philosopher, see Istvan

Hont and Michael Ignatieff, "Needs and Justice in the 'Wealth of Nations,'" in *Wealth and Virtue,* Hont and Ignatieff, pp. 1–44; for later developments in political economy, see Langer, *Coming of Age;* Raymond G. Cowherd, *Political Economists and the English Poor Laws* (Athens, OH: Ohio University Press, 1977); Barry Gordon, *Political Economy in Parliament 1819–1823* (London: Macmillan, 1976); Frank Whitson Fetter, *The Economist in Parliament: 1780–1868* (Durham, NC: Duke University Press, 1980).

8. J. Steuart, *An Inquiry into the Principles of Political Oeconomy,* 2 vols., ed. A. S. Skinner, (Edinburgh: Oliver and Boyd, 1966), I: p. 17.

9. Historians of economic thought concur that unalloyed economic individualism begins not with Smith, but rather, with Malthus and Ricardo. Keith Tribe, *Land, Labour and Economic Discourse* (London: Routledge & Kegan Paul, 1978), pp. 146–58; Hont and Ignatieff, "Needs and Justice," p. 19.

Adam Smith consciously refuted the paternalism of Steuart's notion of the state. "I flatter myself," he wrote to William Pulteney in 1772, "that every false principle in [Steuart's *Inquiry into the Principles of Political Oeconomy* (1767)], will meet with a clear and distinct confutation in [*Wealth of Nations*]." Ernest Campbell Mossner and Ian Simpson Ross, eds., *The Correspondence of Adam Smith* (Oxford: Clarendon Press, 1977), p. 164. I am grateful to Herbert Sloan for this reference.

10. Vol. I, bk. I, chap. 10, p. 131.

11. Vol. I, bk. I, chap. 8, pp. 88–90. Smith offers a rather amusing class analysis of the procreative power of women, pointing out that "[a] half-starved Highland woman frequently bears more than twenty children, while a pampered fine lady is often incapable of bearing any, and is generally exhausted by two or three." He then added that poverty "is extremely unfavourable to the rearing of children" and that such a Highland mother may only be left with two surviving children. P. 88. For a discussion of Smith's ambivalence toward "domestic industry," see Joan Thirsk, *Economic Policy and Projects: The Development of a Consumer Society in Early Modern England* (Oxford: Clarendon, 1978), pp. 148ff.

12. "Without rejecting the moral economy of production and sustenance," Joyce Oldham Appleby has shown, economic writers "prepared the ground for its irrelevance" by the turn of the century. *Economic Thought and Ideology in Seventeenth-Century England* (Princeton, NJ: Princeton University Press, 1978), pp. 52, 57.

13. Dorothy Marshall, *The English Poor in the Eighteenth Century* (London: George Routledge & Sons, 1926), pp. 22–23, 78–79; Gregory Claeys, *Machinery, Money and the Millennium* (Princeton, NJ: Princeton University Press, 1987), p. 18.

14. John Sekora, *Luxury: The Concept in Western Thought, Eden to Smollett* (Baltimore, MD: Johns Hopkins University Press, 1977), pp. 89–90, 124–31. J. R. Poynter argues that the advocacy of independence over dependent poverty came and went throughout the period, though he points out that "genuine revulsion against pauperism as a way of life grew rapidly, especially after 1815." His discussion of "the lessons of scarcity" (which includes the obvious result of Malthus's writings) focuses on the experience of the years after 1795. *Society and Pauperism: English Ideas on Poor Relief, 1795–1834* (London: Routledge & Kegan Paul, 1969), pp. xviii, 45–105. For a succinct summary of the declining situation of the poor, see Roy Porter, *English Society in the Eighteenth Century* (Harmondsworth, Middlesex: Penguin, 1982), pp. 108–12.

15. Daniel A. Baugh, "Poverty, Protestantism, and Political Economy: English Attitudes Toward the Poor, 1660–1800," in *England's Rise to Greatness, 1660–1763,* ed. Stephen B. Baxter (Berkeley: University of California Press, 1983), p. 91; Deborah Valenze, "Charity, Custom and Humanity: Changing Attitudes Towards the Poor in Eighteenth-Century England," in *Revival and Religion Since 1700: Essays for John Walsh,* ed. Jane Garnett and Colin Matthew (London: Hambledon Press, 1993), pp. 59–70.

16. Thomas Alcock, *Observations on the Defects of the Poor Laws* (London, 1752), pp. 19–20.

17. Sir Frederick Morton Eden, *The State of the Poor,* 3 vols. (London, 1797). See also J. L. Hammond and Barbara Hammond, *The Village Labourer* (1911; reprint, London: Longman, 1978), p. 79n; Ursula R. Q. Henriques, "Bastardy and the New Poor Law," *Past and Present* 37 (1967): 103–29.

18. Daniel Defoe, *Giving Alms No Charity,* quoted in Eden, *State of the Poor,* 1: 44. Criticisms of the poor, as well as attacks on the poor laws, appeared at the beginning of the eighteenth century, when high wages and labor shortages led many contemporaries to see the laboring classes as lacking in discipline and the desire to work.

19. Alcock, *Observations on the Defects of the Poor Laws*; Poynter, *Society and Pauperism,* p. 40.

20. Joseph Townsend, *A Dissertation on the Poor Laws* (1786; reprint, Berkeley: University of California Press, 1971), p. 17; "unqualified invective" are the words of T. Ruggles, *History of the Poor,* ii: pp. 33–34, quoted in Poynter, *Society and Pauperism,* p. 43.

21. Townsend, *Dissertation,* pp. 23–24.

22. On Alcock and Townsend, especially the latter's anticipation of Malthus, see Poynter, *Society and Pauperism,* pp. 39–44.

23. Langer, *Coming of Age,* pp. 5–6; Cowherd, *Political Economists,* passim; Poynter, *Society and Pauperism,* chaps. 3–4.

24. Poynter, *Society and Pauperism,* pp. 111–17. The following is indebted to his discussion of Eden and the poor laws.

25. Sir Frederic Morton Eden, *The State of the Poor,* abridged and ed. A. G. L. Rogers (New York: Dutton, 1929), pp. 92–93.

26. Quoted in Langer, *Coming of Age,* p. 37.

27. On the significance of a discourse of the body in Malthus, see Catherine Gallagher, "The Body Versus the Social Body in the Works of Thomas Malthus and Henry Mayhew," *Representations* 14 (1986): 83–106.

28. Donald Winch, *Malthus* (New York: Oxford University Press, 1987), pp. 27–30; Cowherd, *Political Economists,* pp. 2, 27–46.

29. Malthus, *Essay,* pp. 73, 77.

30. Ibid., p. 118.

31. Malthus's position on nature and morality eludes simple explanation. See Cowherd, *Political Economists,* p. 33; Winch, *Malthus,* pp. 27–28, 102; Nicholas Phillipson, "Adam Smith as Civic Moralist," in *Wealth and Virtue,* ed. Hont and Ignatieff, pp. 179–202. On Malthus's unorthodox arguments about the body, see Gallagher, "The Body Versus the Social Body," pp. 83–106.

32. *Essay,* pp. 93–94.

33. Published in 1830. *Essay,* p. 250.

34. On medical testimony in favor of breast-feeding, see Jones, *Women in the Eighteenth Century,* p. 59; *The Ladies Dispensatory; or Every Woman her own Physician* (1740), exerpted in ibid., pp. 83–85. On changing attitudes toward

breast-feeding, see Ruth Perry, "Colonizing the Breast: Sexuality and Maternity in Eighteenth-Century England," in *Forbidden History: The State, Society, and the Regulation of Sexuality in Modern Europe*, ed. John C. Fout (Chicago: University of Chicago Press, 1992), pp. 107–37.

35. Lady Sarah Pennington, *Letters on Different Subjects*, 4 vols. (London, 1767), 3: 124–26, quoted in Randolph Trumbach, *The Rise of the Egalitarian Family: Aristocratic Kinship and Domestic Relations in Eighteenth-Century England* (New York: Academic Press, 1978), pp. 197–98.

36. On the new role of mothers of the middle ranks, see Jonas Hanway, *A Candid Historical Account of the Hospital for the Reception of Exposed and Deserted Young Children* (London, 1759), pp. 60–61; also relevant are the innumerable tracts on midwifery: e.g., see Martha Mears, Practitioner in Midwifery, *The Pupil of Nature, or Candid Advice to the Fair Sex on the Subject of Pregnancy* (London, 1791); Sequin Henry Jackson, M.D., *Cautions to Women, respecting the State of Pregnancy* (London, 1791).
On the promotion of middle-class motherhood, see Elizabeth Kowaleski-Wallace, *Their Fathers' Daughters: Hannah More, Maria Edgeworth, and Patriarchal Complicity* (New York: Oxford University Press, 1991), pp. 101–3; on the new ideology of domesticity, see Trumbach, *Rise of the Egalitarian Family*, pp. 65–66; Margaret George, "From 'Goodwife' to 'Mistress': The Transformation of the Female in Bourgeois Culture," *Science and Society* 37 (1973): 152–77.

37. *Essay*, p. 91.

38. Leonore Davidoff and Catherine Hall, *Family Fortunes: Men and Women of the English Middle Class, 1780–1850* (London: Hutchinson, 1987), esp. chap. 3. On the fusion of romanticism and capitalism, see John C. Holley, unpublished MS.

39. Keith Tribe points out that "economic discourse makes possible the constitution of specifically economic agents, agents that are not related to 'real persons,' rational calculators or whatever: they are constituted discursively by relations of capital and labour, categories which themselves are formulated discursively." Tribe, *Land, Labour and Economic Discourse*, p. 145.

40. Evidence appears in various tracts in the last quarter of the century. "The mother is supposed to be chiefly employed in tending the younger children. But as she may have some vacant time, and the elder children may be able to assist her and also to do some other kind of service[.]" Richard Burn, *Observations on the Bill Intended to be offered to Parliament for the Better Relief and Employment of the Poor* (London, 1776), p. 39.

41. See Marshall, *English Poor in the Eighteenth Century*, pp. 104–7; Ursula R. Q. Henriques, *Before the Welfare State: Social Administration in Early Industrial Britain* (London: Longmans, 1979), esp. chap. 2. See also Sidney and Beatrice Webb, *English Poor Law History*, Part I, *The Old Poor Law* (London: Longmans, Green & Co., 1927). On the connection between Malthus and the ideas behind the revisions of the 1834 Poor Law, see Anne Digby, "Malthus and Reform of the Poor Law," in *Malthus Past and Present*, ed. J. Dupaquier and A. Fauve-Chamoux (London: Academic Press, 1983), pp. 97–109.

42. William Pultney, *Case of . . . the Salt Duty* (1732), p. 56, quoted in Furniss, *The Position of the Laborer*, p. 193.

43. Hanway, *Candid Historical Account of the Hospital for Children*, p. 47. For these reasons, Hanway opposed the establishment of a foundling hospital, which he believed would enable male laborers to avoid acknowledging their familial duty. Malthus, of course, reversed this assumption, arguing that large families were a drain on incentive.

44. "Of the Comforts of the Poor," *Reports of the Society for Bettering the Condition and Increasing the Comforts of the Poor,* vol. 2 (London, 1800), pp. 81–82.

45. On the reversal of later wage theorists, see A. W. Coats, "Changing Attitudes to Labour in the Mid-Eighteenth Century," *Economic History Review,* 2d ser., 11 (1958): 35–51.

46. From a check weavers' *Apology* of 1758, quoted in Alfred P. Wadsworth and Julia de Lacy Mann, *The Cotton Trade and Industrial Lancashire 1600–1780* (1931; reprint, New York: Augustus M. Kelley, 1968), p. 350. Wadsworth adds, "Curiously the estimate quite ignores the possible earnings of the rest of the family in spinning and carding."

Custom defined the level of their wages: ordinary laborers' wages were related to the cost of subsistence; skilled workers, differing in proficiency and prestige, could claim the right to about twice as much as the minimum necessary for survival.

47. Michele Barrett and Mary McIntosh, "The 'Family Wage,'" in *The Changing Experience of Women,* ed. Elizabeth Whitelegg et al. (Oxford: Martin Robinson, 1982), pp. 71–87; Wally Seccombe, "Patriarchy Stabilized: The Construction of the Male Breadwinner Wage Norm in Nineteenth-Century Britain," *Social History* 11 (1986): 53–76; Michele Barrett, *Women's Oppression Today: Problems in Marxist Feminist Analysis* (London: Verso, 1980); cf. Jane Humphries, "The Working Class Family, Women's Liberation, and Class Struggle: The Case of Nineteenth Century British History," *Review of Radical Political Economics* 9 (1977): 25–41.

48. The debate over high wages emerged from the discussion of the high prices of staples and the unequal distribution of luxury commodities. See, e.g., Nathaniel Forster, *An Enquiry into the Causes of the Present High Price of Provisions* (1767). For a discussion of the contemporary debate, see Sekora, *Luxury,* pp. 125–27; A. W. Coats, "Changing Attitudes to Labour in the Mid-Eighteenth Century," pp. 49–51.

49. Pp. 90–91. Emphasis mine.

50. *Lectures on Jurisprudence* (A) vi. 6–7, quoted in Nicholas Phillipson, "Adam Smith as Civic Moralist," in *Wealth and Virtue,* ed. Hont and Ignatieff, p. 188.

51. *Annals of Agriculture* 1 (1784): 74. He added, "Upon the same principle, those laws that burthen the nation with poor rates, ought to be revised."

52. The discussions of the virtue of independence within contemporary literature on poverty and the poor laws are legion. For a theoretical discussion of the decline of paternalism, see Appleby, *Economic Thought,* pp. 61–62; on the attack on dependency within philanthropic circles, see Donna Andrew, *Philanthropy and Police: London Charity in the Eighteenth Century* (Princeton, NJ: Princeton University Press, 1989), pp. 141–43, 153ff; Poynter, *Society and Pauperism,* pp. xvii–xix and passim.

53. Lord De Dunstanville, "State of the Poor," *Annals of Agriculture* 34 (1800): 273.

Chapter 8

1. Catherine Hall, "The Early Formation of Victorian Domestic Ideology," in *Fit Work for Women,* ed. Sandra Burman (New York: St. Martin's Press, 1979), pp. 15–32; Leonore Davidoff and Catherine Hall, *Family Fortunes: Men and*

Women of the English Middle Class, 1780–1850 (London: Hutchinson, 1987), esp. chap. 10.

2. *Pamphlets of Thomas Robert Malthus,* quoted in Donald Winch, *Malthus* (New York: Oxford University Press, 1987), p. 61.

3. Judy Lown, "Not So Much a Factory, More a Form of Patriarchy: Gender and Class during Industrialisation," in *Gender, Class and Work,* ed. Eve Gamarnikow et al. (London: Heinemann, 1983), pp. 28–45.

4. Randolph Trumbach, *The Rise of the Egalitarian Family: Aristocratic Kinship and Domestic Relations in Eighteenth-Century England* (New York: Academic Press, 1978), pp. 65–66.

5. Bernard Mandeville, *The Fable of the Bees* (1714; reprint, Harmondsworth, Middlesex: Penguin, 1970), p. 68.

6. *The Journal of the Rev. John Wesley,* ed. Nehemiah Curnock (London, 1909–16), IV: p. 157 (14 April 1756), quoted in Phillip Harth, "Introduction," in Mandeville, *Fable of the Bees,* p. 8. On Mandeville, see John Sekora, *Luxury: The Concept in Western Thought, Eden to Smollett* (Baltimore, MD: Johns Hopkins University Press, 1977), pp. 66–67, 113–15.

7. *An Estimate of the Manners and Principles of the Times.* 2 vols. 6th ed. (1757), i: pp. 209–10. The same concern became evident in books and pamphlets denouncing the "immorality" of the times. The term extended to matters of furniture, food, sports, and language, often using gender-specific behavior as its point of reference.

8. Mandeville, *Fable of the Bees,* pp. 137–48.

9. George Berkeley, *The Querist* (1750 ed.), pp. 55, 19, quoted in Edgar S. Furniss, *The Position of the Laborer in a System of Nationalism: A Study in the Labor Theories of the Later English Mercantilists* (1920; New York: Augustus M. Kelley, 1965), p. 62. On the question of gender in Machiavelli's political thought, see Hanna Fenichel Pitkin, *Fortune Is a Woman: Gender and Politics in the Thought of Niccolo Machiavelli* (Berkeley: University of California Press, 1984).

10. Sekora, *Luxury,* pp. 66–67, 93.

11. Petitions in the Goldsmith-Kress Collection attest to the intense interest that many groups of manufacturers showed in the frequent alterations in trade policy. For a general discussion of changes in trade during the period, see D. C. Coleman, *The Economy of England, 1450–1750* (Oxford: Oxford University Press, 1977), chap. 10.

12. [Anon.], *Reflections Arising From the Immorality of the Present Age* (London, 1756), p. 4. See also [Francis Foster], *Thoughts on the Times, but chiefly on the Profligacy of Our Women, and It's [sic] Causes* (London, 1779). Not all attacks were aimed at women of the middle and upper ranks; public opinion also excoriated the lower-class woman, often a servant, who paid too much attention to dress and other articles of adornment. Donna Andrew, *Philanthropy and Police: London Charity in the Eighteenth Century* (Princeton, NJ: Princeton University Press, 1989), pp. 116–17.

13. John Brown, D. D., *On the Female Character and Education* (London, 1765), pp. 13–14.

14. [Anon.], *Reflections Arising From the Immorality of the Present Age,* p. 10; Priscilla Wakefield, *Reflections on the Present Condition of the Female Sex* (London, 1798), pp. 69–70. James Fordyce, *The Character and Conduct of the Female Sex* (London, 1776). Fordyce's description of women gives further insight into the new ideals of womanhood in the eighteenth century:

That Providence designed women for a state of dependance [*sic*] and consequently of submission, I cannot doubt, when I consider their timidity of
temper, their tenderness of make, the many comforts and even necessaries of
life which they are unable to procure without our aid, their evident want of
our protection upon a thousand occasions, their incessant study, at every
age, in every state, by every means, to engage our attention, and ensure our
regard. (p. 40)

15. Scottish political economist John Millar recommended a similar way of
life for "ladies" of the higher ranks. See *The Origin of the Distinction of Ranks,* 3d
ed. (1779), reprinted in William C. Lehmann, *John Millar of Glasgow 1735–1801*
(Cambridge: Cambridge University Press, 1960), pp. 220–23.
16. References to "the snares laid for [the Fair Sex] by designing Men" (R.
Campbell, *The London Tradesman* [London, 1747], p. 228) appear in literature
aimed at both middling and lower ranks of society. On the "superior *advantages*" of
the male sex, "whose reputation suffers no stain even from an avowed indulgence in
. . . vice," see the first and third sermons of Dr. Dodd in *An Account of the Rise,
Progress, and Present State of the Magdalen Hospital* (London, 1770), pp. 71, 151.
17. [Anon.], *Reflections Arising From the Immorality of the Present Age,* pp.
33–35; Mandeville, "Enquiry into the Origin of Moral Virtue," *Fable of the Bees,*
pp. 103–6; Fordyce, *Character and Conduct of the Female Sex,* pp. 55–56. The
covert use attributed to the hoop petticoat indicates how deceptive eighteenth-
century fashion could be. As the author of a trade journal put it, "We see they are
Friends to Men, for they have let us into all the Secrets of the Ladies Legs, which
we might have been ignorant of to Eternity without their Help; they discovert to
us indeed a Sample of what we wish to purchase, yet serve as a Fence to keep us at
an awful Distance." Campbell, *The London Tradesman,* p. 212.
18. Wakefield, *Reflections,* pp. 69–70.
19. Hanway, *The Defects of Police, the Cause of Immorality, and the Contin-
ual Robberies Committed, Particularly in and about the Metropolis* (London,
1775), p. 189.
20. John Fielding, *A Plan for a Preservatory and Reformatory, For the Benefit
of Deserted Girls, and Penitent Prostitutes* (London, 1758), pp. 8–9. Sir Thomas
Bernard, Treasurer of the Foundling Hospital and founder of the Society for Bettering the Condition of the Poor, also set out to engage the energies of women of
the middle ranks by founding a Ladies Committee for the Employment and Education of the Female Poor. See Thomas Bernard, *Pleasure and Pain (1780–1818),*
ed. J. Bernard Baker, (London: John Murray, 1930), pp. 67–68. See also
Andrew, *Philanthropy and Police,* p. 195.
21. William Dodd, "A Sermon, preached before the President, Vice-Presi-
dents, Treasurer and Governors of the Magdalen-House," in *An Account of the
Rise, Progress, and Present State of the Magdalen Hospital,* 4th ed. (London,
1770), p. 80.
22. [Anon.] *Reflections Arising From the Immorality of the Present Age,* pp.
10, 21.
23. Wakefield, *Reflections,* p. 143.
24. Elizabeth Kowaleski-Wallace, *Their Fathers' Daughters: Hannah More,
Maria Edgeworth, and Patriarchal Complicity* (New York: Oxford University
Press, 1991), p. 84.
25. As a Quaker, Wakefield's interests were distinct from those of Jonas
Hanway, described below, or Evangelical Hannah More.

26. Jonas Hanway (1712–1786) began his career in trade with Russia, but retired in 1750 to devote his time to philanthropy. He helped to establish the Marine Society in 1756, the Magdalen House for Penitent Prostitutes in 1758, and acted as the vice-president of the Foundling Hospital for fifteen years. He was also responsible for the passage of the Act (later called the Hanway Act) for the Better Regulation of the Parish Poor Children, passed in 1767. See Ruth K. McClure, *Coram's Children: The London Foundling Hospital in the Eighteenth Century* (New Haven, CT: Yale University Press, 1981), pp. 106–11, 144, 170.

27. Jonas Hanway, *Virtue in humble Life*, 2 vols. (London, 1774), pp. xix, xxxii.

28. Nancy Armstrong and Leonard Tennenhouse, eds., *The Ideology of Conduct: Essays on Literature and the History of Sexuality* (London: Methuen, 1987); Mary Poovey, *The Proper Lady and the Woman Writer: Ideology as Style in the Works of Mary Wollstonecraft, Mary Shelley, and Jane Austen* (Chicago: University of Chicago Press, 1984); Kathryn Shevelow, *Women in Print Culture: The Construction of Femininity in the Early Periodical* (London: Routledge, 1989).

29. On Hannah More's writings for the middle-class woman, see Kowaleski-Wallace, *Their Fathers' Daughters*; Mitzi Meyers, "Hannah More's Tracts for the Times: Social Fiction and Female Ideology," in *Fetter'd or Free?: British Women Novelists 1670–1815*, ed. Mary Anne Schofield and Cecilia Macheski (Athens, OH: Ohio University Press, 1986).

30. Hannah More wrote her Cheap Repository Tracts between 1795 and 1798. They were collected and reprinted repeatedly in England and America through the first half of the nineteenth century, and it was in these compilations that the stories came under headings addressed to persons of various ranks. See M. G. Jones, *Hannah More* (Cambridge: Cambridge University Press, 1952), chap. 6; and Susan Pedersen, "Hannah More Meets Simple Simon: Tracts, Chapbooks, and Popular Culture in Late Eighteenth-Century England," *Journal of British Studies* 25 (1986): 84–113.

31. Hannah More, "A Cure for Melancholy" and "The Cottage Cook" in *Cheap Repository Tracts; Entertaining, Moral, and Religious* [hereafter *CRT*] (London, 1798), pp. 304–06.

32. Ibid., pp. 306–7.

33. Ibid., p. 307.

34. "The Sunday School," in *CRT*, p. 325.

35. "Betty Brown," in *Cheap Repository Shorter Tracts* (London, 1798), p. 121.

36. Jones, *Hannah More*, p. 195.

37. Quoted in ibid., p. 265n.

38. Sarah Trimmer, *Oeconomy of Charity*, p. 41. I owe this citation to Kelly Dermody.

39. "The Cottage Cook," pp. 317–18.

40. The following quotations from *Conversations on Political Economy* are taken from the third edition (London, 1819). On Marcet's life, see S. J. Hale, *A Cyclopaedia of Female Biography* (1857); Dorothy Lampen Thompson, *Adam Smith's Daughters* (New York: Exposition Press, 1973), chap. 1; *Dictionary of National Biography* (Oxford: Oxford University Press, 1967–68), 12: 1007–8; J. R. Poynter, *Society and Pauperism: English Ideas on Poor Relief, 1795–1834* (London: Routledge & Kegan Paul, 1969), pp. 237–39.

41. Marcet, *Conversations on Political Economy* (1816), pp. 17–18; 23–29; 34–51; 129–30.

42. Ibid., pp. 121–22.

43. Jones, *Hannah More,* p. 195. No full-length study of eighteenth-century women and philanthropy exists. See Frank K. Prochaska, *Women and Philanthropy in Nineteenth-Century England* (Oxford: Clarendon Press, 1980), pp. 21–46; Prochaska, "Women in English Philanthropy, 1790–1830," *International Review of Social History* 19 (1974): 426–45.

Chapter 9

1. *Wealth of Nations,* ed. Edwin Cannan (1776; reprint, Chicago: University of Chicago Press, 1976), I: bk. 1, chap. 3, p. 351. Smith was paraphrasing French authors when he wrote this.

2. Karl Marx, *Grundrisse: Foundations of the Critique of Political Economy,* trans. Martin Nicolaus (New York: Vintage, 1973), p. 401. Seel also John R. Gillis, "Servants, Sexual Relations and the Risks of Illegitimacy in London, 1801–1900," in *Sex and Class in Women's History,* ed. Judith L. Newton, Mary P. Ryan, and Judith R. Walkowitz (London: Routledge & Kegan Paul, 1983), p. 123.

3. See Wally Seccombe, "The Housewife and Her Labour Under Capitalism," *New Left Review* 83 (1973), and replies in following issues. For a general treatment, see Ann Oakley, *Woman's Work: The Housewife, Past and Present* (New York: Vintage, 1974); on America, Susan Strasser, *Never Done: A History of American Housework* (New York: Pantheon, 1982).

4. Ann Kussmaul, *Servants in Husbandry in Early Modern England* (Cambridge: Cambridge University Press, 1981), p. 4.

5. The great majority of the population passed through some form of service before entering adulthood, and at any one time, as much as 18.2 percent of a village community might be considered engaged as such. Affecting the broad spectrum of the laboring classes, service was an accepted part of the life of work that many young women and men faced before reaching maturity. Peter Laslett, *The World We Have Lost: England Before the Industrial Age,* 3d ed. (New York: Charles Scribner's Sons, 1984). On parish apprentices in housewifery, see Bridget Hill, *Women, Work, and Sexual Politics in Eighteenth-Century England* (Oxford: Blackwell, 1989), p. 100.

6. Laslett, *The World We Have Lost,* p. 65.

7. J. Jean Hecht, *The Domestic Servant Class in Eighteenth-Century England* (London: Routledge & Kegan Paul, 1956), p. 71. Whipping appears in several eighteenth-century accounts of female servants' misbehavior. See Hill, *Women, Work, and Sexual Politics,* p. 142; Peter Earle, *The Making of the English Middle Class: Business, Society and Family Life in London, 1660–1730* (Berkeley: University of California Press, 1989), p. 226.

8. Hill, *Women, Work, and Sexual Politics,* pp. 136–38; Earle, *Making of the English Middle Class,* pp. 225–26; Gillis, "Servants, Sexual Relations and the Risks of Illegitimacy," pp. 122–23, 129–30.

9. Cissie Fairchilds, *Domestic Enemies: Servants and Their Masters in Old Regime France* (Baltimore, MD: Johns Hopkins University Press, 1984); Sarah C. Maza, *Servants and Masters in Eighteenth-Century France* (Princeton, NJ: Princeton University Press, 1983).

10. Theresa M. McBride, *The Domestic Revolution: The Modernisation of Household Service in England and France 1820–1920* (New York: Holmes & Meier, 1976), pp. 32, 119.

11. "Modern Domestic Service," *Edinburgh Review* 115 (April 1862): p. 415.

12. Hill, *Women, Work, and Sexual Politics,* pp. 124, 126; Leonore Davidoff and Catherine Hall, *Family Fortunes: Men and Women of the English Middle Class, 1780–1850* (London: Hutchinson, 1987), pp. 388–96; for evidence of similar practices in the late seventeenth and early eighteenth century, see Earle, *The Making of the English Middle Class,* pp. 218–19, 222. Hill cites a letter in *The Lady's Magazine* for May 1771, regarding "the eldest daughter of a tradesman who had acquired a considerable fortune": she was "entirely ignorant of everything belonging to that vulgar character a good housewife." P. 124. See also Ivy Pinchbeck, *Women Workers and the Industrial Revolution 1750–1850* (1930; reprint, London: Frank Cass, 1969), pp. 34–37. On the proliferation of consumer goods that made a genteel style of life possible, see Carole Shammas, *The Pre-Industrial Consumer in England and America* (Oxford: Clarendon Press, 1990), pp. 169–88; Lorna Weatherill, "A Possession of One's Own: Women and Consumer Behavior in England, 1660–1740," *Journal of British Studies* 25 (1986): 131–56; Neil McKendrick, John Brewer, and J. H. Plumb, *The Birth of a Consumer Society: The Commercialization of Eighteenth-Century England* (London: Europa, 1982).

13. McBride, *The Domestic Revolution,* pp. 18–33; Geoffrey Best, *Mid-Victorian Britain 1851–1875* (New York: Schocken, 1971), pp. 82–83; J. F. C. Harrison, *The Early Victorians 1832–51* (New York: Praeger, 1971); J. A. Banks, *Prosperity and Parenthood* (London: Routledge & Kegan Paul, 1954). On servant keeping among tradesmen and shopkeepers, see D. A. Kent, "Ubiquitous But Invisible: Female Domestic Servants in Mid-Eighteenth Century London," *History Workshop Journal* 28 (1989): 119. Based on his examination of the censuses of 1871–91 in Rochdale, Edward Higgs has shown that not all middle-class homes registered a servant; conversely, some working-class households did. Higgs, "Domestic Servants and Households in Victorian England," *Social History* 8 (1983): 201–10.

14. Studies of the period from the sixteenth to the eighteenth century have shown a nearly even ratio of male to female servants, estimated at 107:100. Including those serving as apprentices within trades, males predominated even more: among craftsmen's households, the ratio was as high as 171:100. Kussmaul, *Servants in Husbandry,* p. 4.

15. Kent, "Ubiquitous But Invisible," pp. 123–24. Earle points out the huge demand for such servants in early eighteenth-century London; this led to a rise in wages and advantageous conditions for female servants. Earle, *Making of the English Middle Class,* p. 219.

16. See Bridget Hill's excellent chapter on housework: *Women, Work, and Sexual Politics,* pp. 103–24, esp. pp. 122–24; see also Leonore Davidoff, "The Rationalization of Housework," in *Sexual Divisions Revisited,* ed. Diana Leonard and Sheila Allen (New York: St. Martin's Press 1991), pp. 59–94.

17. McBride, *The Domestic Revolution,* pp. 38–39.

18. Hill, *Women, Work, and Sexual Politics,* p. 127; Davidoff and Hill, *Family Fortunes,* pp. 380–96.

19. McBride argues that as a "means of the modernisation of rural labour and particularly of women," domestic service functioned as a bridging occupa-

tion. *The Domestic Revolution,* pp. 48, 82–83; 117. On bridging occupations, see L. Broom and J. H. Smith, "Bridging Occupations," *British Journal of Sociology* 14 (1963): 321–34. Nineteenth-century female philanthropists felt somewhat the same way; see Brian Harrison, "For Church, Queen and Family: The Girls' Friendly Society 1874–1920," *Past and Present* 61 (1973): 107–38.

20. From *London Chronicle,* 1762, quoted in Hecht, *Domestic Servant Class,* p. 12, and Kent, "Ubiquitous But Invisible," p. 124.

21. Hill, *Women, Work, and Sexual Politics,* p. 142.

22. Hill, pp. 99–100; K. D. M. Snell, *Annals of the Labouring Poor: Social Change and Agrarian England 1660–1900* (Cambridge: Cambridge University Press, 1985), pp. 281.

23. See Chapter 1, p. 24.

24. Rev. Thomas Francklin, *A Sermon Preached in the Chapel of the Asylum for Female Orphans* (London, 1768), p. 11.

25. John Fielding, *A Plan for a Preservatory and Reformatory, For the Benefit of Deserted Girls, and Penitent Prostitutes* (London, 1758), p. 14.

26. J. Fielding, *Plan,* pp. 8–9; also, at a later date, *Report of the . . . Guardian Society* (London, 1815), pp. 14–15; *Society for Bettering the Condition of the Poor. Extract from an Account of the Ladies Society, for the Education and Employment of the Female Poor* (London, 1804), p. 12.

27. William Hutton, *A Journey to London* (London, 1785), quoted in Bridget Hill, *Eighteenth-Century Women: An Anthology* (London: Allen & Unwin, 1984), pp. 41–42. Joseph Massie was of the same opinion regarding the connections between lack of employment, domestic service, and prostitution. See *A Plan for the Establishment of Charity-Houses for Exposed or Deserted women and girls, and for penitent prostitutes* (London, 1758), pp. 3–5.

28. [Jonas Hanway], *A Plan for Establishing a Charity-House, or Charity-Houses, for the Reception of Repenting Prostitutes* (London, 1758), p. 39. For an example of a seduction narrative set in a religious context, see Rev. William Dodd, *The Magdalen, or History of the First penitent received into that charitable asylum; in a series of letters to a lady* (London, [1763]).

29. Hill, *Women, Work, and Sexual Politics,* p. 132.

30. Quoted in Earle, *Making of the English Middle Class,* pp. 226–27.

31. Mary Ann Ashford, *Life of a Licensed Victualler's Daughter, Written by Herself* (1844), quoted in Hill, *Women, Work, and Sexual Politics,* p. 143.

32. Hecht, *Domestic Servant Class,* pp. 5–6.

33. Hecht, *Domestic Servant Class,* pp. 142–49.

34. Pamela Horn, *The Rise and Fall of the Victorian Servant* (Dublin: Gill and Macmillan, 1975), pp. 8–9.

35. Eliza Haywood, *A Present for a Servant-Maid* (1743; reprint, New York: Garland, 1985), p. 36.

36. Thomas Seaton, *The Conduct of Servants in Great Families* (1720; reprint, New York: Garland, 1985), p. 184.

37. Haywood, *Present for a Servant-Maid,* pp. 24–25. See also Daniel Defoe, *The Behaviour of Servants* (London, 1724).

38. Hecht, *Domestic Servant Class,* p. 119; Neil McKendrick, "Home Demand and Economic Growth: A New View of the Role of Women and Children in the Industrial Revolution," in *Historical Perspectives: Studies in English Thought and Society in Honour of J. H. Plumb,* ed. Neil McKendrick (London: Europa, 1974), p. 193.

39. Andrew Moreton [Daniel Defoe], *Every-body's Business is No-Body's Business; or, Private Abuses, Publick Grievances: Exemplified in the Pride, Insolence, and Exorbitant Wages of our Women Servants, Footmen, &c.*, 4th ed. (London, 1725), pp. 6, 16–18; Horn, *Rise and Fall of the Victorian Servant*, p. 12.

40. Haywood, *Present for a Servant-Maid*, pp. 24–25.

41. Hill points out the example in Sarah Scott's *Millenium Hall* (1762), in which a young and beautiful girl in need of a place is told that she will not find work in a family as long as she appeared so attractive. Hill, *Women, Work, and Sexual Politics*, p. 142.

42. Neil McKendrick, "The Commercialization of Fashion," in McKendrick, Brewer and Plumb, *Birth of a Consumer Society*, pp. 58–60. For a discussion of hierarchically structured demand in early modern England, see Shammas, *The Pre-Industrial Consumer*, pp. 210–19.

43. J. Hanway, "Essay on Tea," in *A Journal of Eight Days' Journey* (1756), p. 224, quoted in McKendrick, "Home Demand and Economic Growth," p. 192.

44. J. W. von Archenholz, *A Picture of England* (1791), pp. 75–83, quoted in McKendrick, "Home Demand and Economic Growth," p. 193; see also Earle, *Making of the English Middle Class*, p. 284; McKendrick, "The Consumer Revolution," in McKendrick, Brewer, and Plumb, *Birth of a Consumer Society*, pp. 20–22.

45. Haywood, *Present for a Servant-Maid*, p. 25.

46. Thomas Alcock, *Observations on the Defects of the Poor Laws* (London, 1752), p. 48. Alcock also objected to "the wearing of *Ribbands, Ruffles, Silks*, and other slight foreign Things," which "contributed greatly to make Labour and Servants Wages run so high." P. 48.

47. Haywood, *Present for a Servant-Maid*, pp. 9–10.

48. Haywood, *Present for a Servant-Maid*, p. 25.

49. Hecht, *Domestic Servant Class*, pp. 77, 82; Hill, *Women, Work, and Sexual Politics*, p. 136; Earle, *Making of the English Middle Class*, p. 221.

50. Haywood, *Present for a Servant-Maid*, pp. 7, 29–30.

51. Hecht, *Domestic Servant Class*, p. 78.

52. Snell, *Annals of the Labouring Poor*, pp. 309, 313.

53. Catharine Cappe, *An Account of Two Charity Schools* (London, 1800), pp. 103–4, app. no. 6, quoted in Hill, *Eighteenth-Century Women*, p. 68.

54. F. M. Eden, *The State of the Poor*, 3 vols. (London, 1797), vol. 2: p. 347, quoted in Hill, *Eighteenth–Century Women*, p. 67.

55. Leonore Davidoff, "Mastered for Life: Servant and Wife in Victorian and Edwardian England," *Journal of Social History* 7 (1974): 406–28.

56. Quoted in Caroline Davidson, *A Woman's Work is Never Done: A History of Housework in the British Isles 1650–1950* (London: Chatto and Windus, 1982), p. 172.

57. Ibid., pp. 166, 172.

58. Leigh Hunt, "The Maid-Servant," in *The Every-Day Book*, ed. William Hone (London, 1835), pp. 481–85. Discussion of servants' insubordination through clothing continued even after the general assignment of uniforms. See "Why Do Servants of the Nineteenth Century Dress as They do?" 2d ed. (London, 1859), pp. viii, cited in McBride, *The Domestic Revolution*, p. 25.

59. Horn, *Rise and Fall of the Victorian Servant*, p. 10; John Burnett, *Useful Toil: Autobiographies of Working People from the 1820s to the 1920s* (Harmondsworth, Middlesex: Penguin, 1984), p. 137.

60. An even larger proportion of *young* women came under the heading of domestic servant: in 1861, one in every three women between the ages of fifteen and twenty-four years of age was a domestic servant. McBride, *The Domestic Revolution*, p. 14; Edward Higgs, "Domestic Service and Household Production," in *Unequal Opportunities: Women's Employment in England 1800–1918*, ed. Angela V. John (Oxford: Blackwell, 1986), p. 137.

Historians have recognized the problems with using census data on domestic servants; for example, a significant proportion of the women recorded as housekeepers and servants were in fact relatives of the members of the household. See Higgs, "Domestic Servants," pp. 201–10. But as Mark Ebery and Brian Preston have pointed out, many women could not be classified in any other way. *Domestic Service in Late Victorian and Edwardian England 1871–1914*, Reading Geographical Papers (Reading: University of Reading, 1973).

61. Burnett, *Useful Toil*, p. 136.

62. But such arrangements were less common than Mrs. Beeton's well-known *Book of Household Management* implied. Relatively few families enjoyed the requisite income—over £300 per year—to employ as many as three or more servants at average wages. Of the entire range of families regarded as middle class, such wealthy persons constituted 9.7 percent in 1867. These households, Patricia Branca has pointed out, "although not negligible in terms of numbers, are not typical of the middle class." "Image and Reality: The Myth of the Idle Victorian Woman," in *Clio's Consciousness Raised*, ed. Mary Hartman and Lois W. Banner (New York: Harper and Row, 1974), p. 183.

63. Best, *Mid-Victorian Britain*, pp. 89–90.

64. Banks, *Prosperity and Parenthood*, pp. 70–102.

65. More recent historians have cautioned against unqualified acceptance of statistics regarding service. Higgs, "Domestic Service and Household Production," pp. 125–50; "Domestic Servants;" see also Frank Prochaska, "Female Philanthropy and Domestic Service in Victorian England," *Bulletin of the Institute of Historical Research* 54 (1981): 79–85.

66. Prochaska, "Female Philanthropy and Domestic Service," p. 83.

67. Adapted from Best, *Mid-Victorian Britain*, p. 88.

68. "Modern Domestic Service," *Edinburgh Review* (1862), p. 417.

69. Higgs, "Domestic Service and Household Production," p. 136; Ebery and Preston, *Domestic Service*, p. 70; Horn, *Rise and Fall of the Victorian Servant*, p. 18.

70. Mrs. Wrigley, "A Plate-Layer's Wife," in Margaret Llewelyn Davies, *Life as We Have Known It* (1931; reprint, London: Norton, 1975), p. 58.

71. Burnett, *Useful Toil*, p. 216. See also Horn, *Rise and Fall of the Victorian Servant*, p. 23.

72. Liz Stanley, ed., *The Diaries of Hannah Cullwick, Victorian Maidservant* (New Brunswick, NJ: Rutgers University Press, 1984), pp. 118–19.

73. Quoted in Horn, *Rise and Fall of the Victorian Servant*, pp. 18, 52.

74. Sarah Stickney Ellis, *The Women of England*, 2 vols. (Philadelphia, 1839), 1: 31–32.

75. Thorsten Veblen, *The Theory of the Leisure Class* (London: Allen & Unwin, 1970), p. 128.

76. [Henry and Augustus Mayhew], *The Greatest Plague of Life: or The Adventures of a Lady in Search of a Good Servant* (London, [1847]); Prochaska, "Female Philanthropy and Domestic Service," p. 79; McBride, *The Domestic Revolution*, p. 19.

77. Fairchilds, *Domestic Enemies,* pp. 144–45.

78. Leonore Davidoff, "Class and Gender in Victorian England," in *Sex and Class in Women's History,* ed. Judith L. Newton et al. (London: Routledge & Kegan Paul, 1983), p. 21.

79. "Modern Domestic Service," *Edinburgh Review,* p. 416.

80. Quoted in Prochaska, "Female Philanthropy and Domestic Service," p. 83.

81. "Mrs. Robinson's Housemaid," *The English Woman's Journal* 3 (1859): 125.

82. "Modern Domestic Service," *Edinburgh Review,* p. 418.

83. Ibid., p. 435.

84. Quoted in Horn, *Rise and Fall of the Victorian Servant,* pp. 18–19.

85. Thomas Webster and Mrs.Parkes, *An Encyclopedia of Domestic Economy* (London, 1847), p. 341; "Modern Domestic Service," *Edinburgh Review,* p. 426.

86. "Modern Domestic Service," *Edinburgh Review,* pp. 426–27.

87. Burnett, *Useful Toil,* pp. 157–62.

88. Mrs. Layton, "Memories of Seventy Years," in Davies, *Life as We Have Known It,* pp. 25–27; Mrs. Wrigley, "A Plate-Layer's Wife," ibid., p. 58.

89. Burnett, *Useful Toil,* pp. 158.

90. Stanley, *Diaries,* pp. 51, 63.

91. "Open your mouth," one mistress demanded of Lilian Westall (b.1893). "Let's see your teeth." Burnett, *Useful Toil,* p. 217.

92. Stanley, *Diaries,* pp. 54–55.

93. Ibid., p. 67.

94. Ibid., pp. 46, 91.

95. Ibid., pp. 125–26.

96. Ibid., pp. 77, 146.

97. Ibid., pp. 89, 126.

98. Quoted in "Modern Domestic Service," *Edinburgh Review,* pp. 409, 419.

Conclusion

1. Carol E. Morgan, "Women, Work and Consciousness in the Mid-Nineteenth-Century English Cotton Industry," *Social History* 17 (1992): 25.

Bibliography

Alexander, Sally. "Women, Class and Sexual Differences in the 1830s and 1840s: Some Reflections on the Writing of a Feminist History." *History Workshop Journal* 17 (1984): pp. 125–49.

———. *Women's Work in Nineteenth-Century London: A Study of the Years 1820–50.* London: Journeyman Press, 1983.

Amussen, Susan. *An Ordered Society: Gender and Class in Early Modern England.* Oxford: Blackwell, 1988.

Anderson, Michael. *Family Structure in Nineteenth-Century Lancashire.* Cambridge: Cambridge University Press, 1971.

Andrew, Donna. *Philanthropy and Police: London Charity in the Eighteenth Century.* Princeton, NJ: Princeton University Press, 1989.

Appleby, Joyce Oldham. *Economic Thought and Ideology in Seventeenth-Century England.* Princeton, NJ: Princeton University Press, 1978.

Ashton, T. S. *The Industrial Revolution 1760–1830.* 1948. Rev. ed. Oxford: Oxford University Press, 1969.

Baines, Edward. *History of the Cotton Manufacture in Great Britain.* 2 vols. London, 1835.

Banks, J. A. *Prosperity and Parenthood.* London: Routledge & Kegan Paul, 1954.

Baron, Ava, ed. *Work Engendered: Toward a New History of American Labor.* Ithaca, NY: Cornell University Press, 1991.

Barrett, Michele. "Rethinking Women's Oppression: A Reply to Brenner and Ramas." *New Left Review* (July–Aug., 1984): 123–28.

———. *Women's Oppression Today: Problems in Marxist Feminist Analysis.* London: Verso, 1980.

Barrett, Michele, and Mary McIntosh. "The 'Family Wage.'" In *The Changing Experience of Women*, edited by Elizabeth Whitelegg et al., pp. 71–87. Oxford: Martin Robinson, 1982.

Baugh, Daniel A. "Poverty, Protestantism, and Political Economy: English Attitudes Toward the Poor, 1660–1800." In *England's Rise to Greatness, 1660–1763*, edited by Stephen B. Baxter, pp. 63–107. Berkeley: University of California Press, 1983.

Beattie, J. M. *Crime and the Courts in England 1660–1800.* Princeton, NJ: Princeton University Press, 1986.

Benenson, Harold. "The 'Family Wage' and Working Women's Consciousness in Britain, 1880–1914." *Politics and Society* 19 (1991): 71–108.

———, "Victorian Sexual Ideology and Marx's Theory of the Working Class." *International Labor and Working Class History* 25 (1984): 1–23, and 26 (1984): 45–51.

Bennett, Judith. "Misogyny, Popular Culture, and Women's Work." *History Workshop Journal* 31 (1991): 166–88.

Berg, Maxine. *The Age of Manufactures: Industry, Innovation and Work in Britain 1700–1820.* London: Fontana, 1985.

———. *The Machinery Question and the Making of Political Economy 1815–1848.* Cambridge: Cambridge University Press, 1980.

———. "Women's Work, Mechanisation and the Early Phases of Industrialization in England." In *The Historical Meanings of Work,* edited by Patrick Joyce, pp. 64–98. Cambridge: Cambridge University Press, 1987.

Best, Geoffrey. *Mid-Victorian Britain 1851–1875.* New York: Schocken, 1971.

Blackstone, William. *Commentaries on the Laws of England.* 4 vols. London, 1857.

Bohstedt, John. *Riots and Community Politics in England and Wales, 1790–1810.* Cambridge, MA: Harvard University Press, 1983.

Boserup, Ester. *Women's Role in Economic Development.* New York: St. Martin's Press, 1970.

Boyer, George R. *An Economic History of the English Poor Law.* Cambridge: Cambridge University Press, 1990.

Branca, Patricia. "Image and Reality: The Myth of the Idle Victorian Woman." In *Clio's Consciousness Raised,* edited by Mary Hartman and Lois W. Banner, pp. 179–91. New York: Harper & Row, 1974.

Braun, Rudolf. "The Impact of a Cottage Industry on an Agricultural Population." In *The Rise of Capitalism,* edited by David S. Landes, pp. 53–64. New York, 1966.

Bray, Charles. *The Industrial Employment of Women.* London, 1857.

Brenner, Johanna, and Maria Ramas. "Rethinking Women's Oppression." *New Left Review* 144 (March–April, 1984): 33–71.

Brewer, John, and John Styles, eds. *An Ungovernable People? The English and Their Law in the Seventeenth and Eighteenth Centuries.* London: Hutchinson, 1980.

Brown, A. F. J. *Essex at Work 1700–1815.* Chelmsford: Tindall Press, 1969.

Burman, Sandra, ed. *Fit Work for Women.* London: Croom Helm, 1979.

Bushaway, Bob. *By Rite: Custom, Ceremony and Community in England 1700–1880.* London: Junction Books, 1982.

Bythell, Duncan. *The Handloom Weavers.* Cambridge: Cambridge University Press, 1969.

———. *The Sweated Trades: Outwork in Nineteenth-Century Britain.* London: Batsford, 1978.

Cahn, Susan. *Industry of Devotion.* New York: Columbia University Press, 1987.

Cannadine, David. "The Present and the Past in the English Industrial Revolution, 1880–1980." *Past and Present* 103 (1984): 131–72.

Chambers, J. D., and G. E. Mingay. *The Agricultural Revolution 1750–1880.* New York: Schocken, 1966.

Chapman, Stanley D. *The Early Factory Masters: The Transition to the Factory System in the Midlands Textile Industry.* Newton Abbot: David and Charles, 1967.

Charles, Lindsey, and Lorna Duffin, eds. *Women and Work in Pre-Industrial England.* Beckenham, Kent: Croom Helm, 1985.

Clark, Alice. *Working Life of Women in the Seventeenth Century.* 1919. Reprint, London: Routledge & Kegan Paul, 1982.

Coats, A. W. "Changing Attitudes to Labour in the Mid-Eighteenth Century." *Economic History Review,* 2d ser., 11 (1958): 35–51.

———. "The Relief of Poverty, Attitudes to Labour, and Economic Change in England, 1660–1782." *International Review of Social History* 21 (1976): 98–115.

Cockburn, Cynthia. *Machinery of Dominance: Women, Men and Technical Know-How.* London: Pluto Press, 1985.

Cockburn, J. S., ed. *Crime in England, 1550–1800.* Princeton, NJ: Princeton University Press, 1977.

Collier, Frances. *The Family Economy of the Working Classes in the Cotton Industry 1784–1833.* Manchester: printed for the Chetham Society, 1965.

Collier, Mary. *The Woman's Labour: An Epistle to Mr. Stephen Duck; In Answer to his late poem, called The Thresher's Labour.* London, 1739. Edited and introduction by E. P. Thompson. London: Merlin, 1989.

Cowherd, Raymond G. *Political Economists and the English Poor Laws.* Athens, OH: Ohio University Press, 1977.

Davidoff, Leonore. "Class and Gender in Victorian England." In *Sex and Class in Women's History,* edited by Judith L. Newton et al., pp. 17–71. London: Routledge & Kegan Paul, 1983.

———. "Domestic Service and the Working-class Life Cycle." *Bulletin of the Society for the Study of Labour History,* no. 26 (Spring 1973).

———. "Mastered for Life: Servant and Wife in Victorian and Edwardian England." *Journal of Social History* 7 (1974): 406–28.

Davidoff, Leonore, and Catherine Hall. *Family Fortunes: Men and Women of the English Middle Class, 1780–1850.* London: Hutchinson, 1987.

Davidoff, Leonore, and Ruth Hawthorn. *A Day in the Life of a Victorian Domestic Servant.* London: Allen & Unwin, 1976.

Davidson, Caroline. *A Woman's Work is Never Done: A History of Housework in the British Isles 1650–1950.* London: Chatto and Windus, 1982.

Davies, Margaret Llewelyn. *Life as We Have Known It.* 1931. Reprint. London: Norton, 1975.

Davis, Thomas. *A General View of the Agriculture of Wiltshire.* London, 1811.

Deane, Phyllis. *The First Industrial Revolution.* Cambridge: Cambridge University Press, 1965.

Devine, T.M."Women Workers, 1850–1914." In *Farm Servants and Labour in Lowland Scotland 1770–1914,* edited by T. M. Devine, pp. 98–123. Edinburgh: John Donald, 1984.

Drake, Barbara. *Women in Trade Unions.* London, 1921.

Duck, Stephen. *The Thresher's Labour.* London, 1730. Edited and with an introduction by E. P. Thompson. London: Merlin, 1989.

Dyer, John. *The Fleece.* London, 1757.

Earle, Peter. *The Making of the English Middle Class: Business, Society and Family Life in London, 1660–1730.* Berkeley: University of California Press, 1989.

Ebery, Mark, and Brian Preston. *Domestic Service in Late Victorian and Edwardian England 1871–1914.* Reading Geographical Papers. Reading: University of Reading Press, 1973.

Eden, Sir Frederic Morton. *The State of the Poor.* 3 vols. London, 1797.

Elson, Diane, and Ruth Pearson. "'Nimble Fingers Make Cheap Workers': An Analysis of Women's Employment in Third World Export Manufacturing." *Feminist Review* 7 (1981): 87–107.

Engels, Frederick. *The Condition of the Working Class in England.* 1845. Reprint. St. Albans: Panther, 1969.

———. *The Origins of the Family, Private Property and the State.* Translated by Alec West. 1884. Reprint. New York: International Publishers, 1972.

Fairchilds, Cissie. *Domestic Enemies: Servants and Their Masters in Old Regime France.* Baltimore, MD: Johns Hopkins University Press, 1984.

Faulkner, Wendy, and Erik Arnold, eds. *Smothered by Invention: Technology in Women's Lives.* London: Pluto Press, 1985.

Fitton, R. S. *The Arkwrights: Spinners of Fortune.* Manchester: Manchester University Press, 1989.

Fitton, R. S., and A. P. Wadsworth. *The Strutts and the Arkwrights 1758–1830: A Study of the Early Factory System.* Manchester: Manchester University Press, 1958.

Floud, Roderick, and McCloskey, Donald, eds. *The Economic History of Britain Since 1700.* 2 vols. Cambridge: Cambridge University Press, 1981.

Fordyce, James. *The Character and Conduct of the Female Sex.* London, 1776.

Foster, John. *Class Struggle and the Industrial Revolution: Early Industrial Capitalism in Three English Towns.* London: Methuen, 1974.

Foucault, Michel. *Discipline and Punish: The Birth of the Prison.* Translated by Alan Sheridan. New York: Vintage, 1979.

———. *The History of Sexuality:* Vol. 1, *An Introduction.* Translated by Robert Hurley. New York: Vintage, 1978.

Freifeld, Mary. "Technological Change and the 'Self-acting' Mule: A Study of Skill and the Sexual Division of Labour." *Social History* 11 (1986): 319–43.

Furniss, Edgar S. *The Position of the Laborer in a System of Nationalism: A Study in the Labor Theories of the Later English Mercantilists.* 1920. Reprint. New York: Augustus M. Kelley, 1965.

Fussell, G. E. *The English Dairy Farmer, 1500–1900.* London: Frank Cass, 1966.

Fussell, G. E., and Fussell, K. R. *The English Countrywoman: A Farmhouse Social History 1500–1900.* London: Andrew Melrose, 1953.

Gallagher, Catherine. *The Industrial Reformation of English Fiction.* Chicago: University of Chicago Press, 1985.

George, Margaret. "From 'Goodwife' to 'Mistress': The Transformation of the Female in Bourgeois Culture." *Science and Society* 37 (1973): 152–77.

Gillis, John R. *For Better, For Worse: British Marriages, 1600 to the Present.* New York: Oxford University Press, 1985.

———. "Servants, Sexual Relations and the Risks of Illegitimacy in London, 1801–1900." In *Sex and Class in Women's History,* edited by Judith L. Newton, Mary P. Ryan, and Judith R. Walkowitz. London: Routledge & Kegan Paul, 1983.

Goddard, Nicholas. "The Development and Influence of Agricultural Periodicals and Newspapers, 1780–1880." *Agricultural History Review* 31 (1983): 116–31.

Godelier, Maurice. "Work and Its Representations: A Research Proposal." *History Workshop Journal* 10 (1980): 164–74.

Guest, Richard. *A Compendious History of the Cotton Manufacture.* Manchester, 1823.

Gullickson, Gay R. *Spinners and Weavers of Auffay: Rural Industry and the Sexual Division of Labor in a French Village, 1750–1850.* Cambridge: Cambridge University Press, 1986.

Hall, Catherine. "The Early Formation of Victorian Domestic Ideology." In *Fit Work for Women,* edited by Sandra Burman, pp. 15–32. New York: St. Martin's Press, 1979.

———. "The home turned upside down? The working class family in cotton textiles, 1780–1850." In *The Changing Experience of Women,* edited by Elizabeth Whitelegg et al. Oxford: Martin Robertson, 1982.

———. *White, Male and Middle Class: Explorations in Feminism and History.* New York: Routledge, 1992.

Hammond, J. L., and Barbara Hammond. *The Skilled Labourer 1760–1832.* 1919. Reprint. New York: Augustus M. Kelley, 1967.

———. *The Village Labourer.* 1911. Reprint. London: Longman, 1978.

Harrison, Brian. "For Church, Queen and Family: The Girls' Friendly Society 1874–1920." *Past and Present* 61 (1973): 107–38.

Harrison, J. F. C. *The Early Victorians 1832–51.* New York: Praeger, 1971.

———. *Quest for the New Moral World: Robert Owen and the Owenites in Britain and America.* New York: Charles Scribner's Sons, 1969.

Heidi Hartmann. "Capitalism, Patriarchy, and Job Segregation by Sex." In *Capitalist Patriarchy and the Case for Socialist Feminism,* edited by Zillah R. Eisenstein, pp. 206–47. New York: Monthly Review Press, 1979.

Hartsock, Nancy C. M. "The Feminist Standpoint: Developing the Ground for a Specifically Feminist Historical Materialism." In *Discovering Reality,* edited by Sandra Harding and Merrill B. Hintikka, pp. 283–310. Dodrecht, Holland: D. Reidel, 1983.

Hay, Douglas. "Property, Authority and the Criminal Law." In Douglas Hay et al., *Albion's Fatal Tree: Crime and Society in Eighteenth-Century England,* pp. 17–63. New York: Pantheon, 1975.

Haywood, Eliza. *A Present for a Servant-Maid.* 1743. Reprint. New York: Garland, 1985.

Heal, Felicity. *Hospitality in Early Modern England.* Oxford: Clarendon Press, 1990.

Heaton, Herbert. *Yorkshire Woollen and Worsted Industries.* Oxford: Clarendon Press, 1920.

Hecht, J. Jean. *The Domestic Servant Class in Eighteenth-Century England.* London: Routledge & Kegan Paul, 1956.

Henriques, Ursula R. Q. "Bastardy and the New Poor Law." *Past and Present* 37 (1967): 103–29.

———. *Before the Welfare State: Social Administration in Early Industrial Britain.* London: Longmans, 1979.

Hewitt, Margaret. *Wives and Mothers in Victorian Industry.* 1958. Reprint. West-port, CT: Greenwood Press, 1975.

Higgs, Edward. "Domestic Servants and Households in Victorian England." *Social History* 8 (1983): 201–10.

———. "Domestic Service and Household Production." In *Unequal Opportunities: Women's Employment in England 1800–1918*, edited by Angela V. John, pp. 125–50. Oxford: Blackwell, 1986.

Hill, Bridget. *Women, Work, and Sexual Politics in Eighteenth-Century England.* Oxford: Blackwell, 1989.

Himmelfarb, Gertrude. *The Idea of Poverty: England in the Early Industrial Age.* New York: Knopf, 1984.

Hirschman, Albert O. *The Passions and the Interests: Political Arguments for Capitalism Before Its Triumph.* Princeton, NJ: Princeton University Press, 1977.

Hobsbawm, E. J. *Industry and Empire.* Harmondsworth, Middlesex: Penguin, 1969.

———. *Labouring Men: Studies in the History of Labour.* London: Weidenfeld and Nicolson, 1964.

———. "Scottish Reformers of the Eighteenth Century and Capitalist Agriculture." In *Peasants in History: Essays in Honour of Daniel Thorner*, edited by E. J. Hobsbawm et al., pp. 3–29. Calcutta: Oxford University Press, 1980.

Holcombe, Lee. *Victorian Ladies at Work: Middle-Class Working Women in England and Wales, 1850–1914.* Hamden, CT: Archon Books, 1973.

Hont, Istvan, and Michael Ignatieff, eds. *Wealth and Virtue: The Shaping of Political Economy in the Scottish Enlightenment.* Cambridge: Cambridge University Press, 1983.

Horn, Pamela L. R. "The Buckinghamshire Straw Plait Trade in Victorian England." *Records of Buckinghamshire* 19 (1971): 42–54.

———. "Child Workers in the Pillow Lace and Straw Plait Trades of Victorian Buckinghamshire and Bedfordshire." *Historical Journal* 17 (1974): 779–96.

———. "An Eighteenth-Century Land Agent: The Career of Nathaniel Kent (1737–1810)." *Agricultural History Review* 30 (1982): 1–16.

———. *Labouring Life in the Victorian Countryside.* Dublin: Gill and Macmillan, 1976.

———. *The Rural World 1780–1850: Social Change in the English Countryside.* New York: St. Martin's Press, 1980.

Hoskins, W. G. *The Midland Peasant: The Economic and Social History of a Leicestershire Village.* London: Macmillan, 1957.

Hufton, Olwen. "Women and the Family Economy in Eighteenth-Century France." *French Historical Studies* 9 (1975): 1–22.

———. "Women Without Men: Widows and Spinsters in Britain and France in the Eighteenth Century." *Journal of Family History* 9 (1984): 355–76.

Humphries, Jane. "Class Struggle and the Persistence of the Working-Class Family." *Cambridge Journal of Economics* 1 (1977): 241–58.

———. "Enclosures, Common Rights, and Women: The Proletarianization of Families in the Late Eighteenth and Early Nineteenth Centuries." *Journal of Economic History* 50 (1990): 17–42.

———. "Protective Legislation, the Capitalist State, and Working Class Men: The Case of the 1842 Mines Regulation Act." *Feminist Review* 7 (1981): 1–33.

———. "The Working Class Family, Women's Liberation, and Class Struggle:

The Case of Nineteenth Century British History." *Review of Radical Political Economics* 9 (1977): 25–41.

Hutchins, Barbara L. *Women in Modern Industry.* 1915. Reprint. Wakefield: EP Publishing, 1978.

Hutchins, B. L., and A. Harrison. *A History of Factory Legislation.* London, 1911.

John, Angela V. *By the Sweat of Their Brow: Women Workers at Victorian Coal Mines.* London: Routledge & Kegan Paul, 1984.

———, ed. *Unequal Opportunities: Women's Employment in England 1800–1918.* Oxford: Blackwell, 1986.

Jones, E. L. "The Agricultural Origins of Industry." *Past and Present* (1968): 58–71.

Joyce, Patrick, ed. *The Historical Meanings of Work.* Cambridge: Cambridge University Press, 1987.

Joyce, Patrick. *Work, Society and Politics: The Culture of the Factory in Later Victorian England.* Brighton: Harvester Press, 1980.

Kaplan, Temma. "Female Consciousness and Collective Action: The Case of Barcelona, 1910–1918." *Signs: Journal of Women in Culture and Society* 7 (1982): 545–66.

Kent, D. A. "Ubiquitous But Invisible: Female Domestic Servants in Mid-Eighteenth Century London." *History Workshop Journal* 28 (1989): 111–28.

Kerridge, Eric. *The Agricultural Revolution.* London: George Allen & Unwin, 1967.

King, Peter. "Customary Rights and Women's Earnings: The Importance of Gleaning to the Rural Labouring Poor, 1750–1850." *Economic History Review* 44 (1991): 461–76.

———. "Decision-Makers and Decision-Making in the English Criminal Law, 1750–1800." *Historical Journal* 27 (1984): 25–58.

———. "Gleaners, Farmers and the Failure of Legal Sanctions, 1750–1850." *Past and Present* 125 (1989): 116–50.

Kitteringham, Jennie. "Country Work Girls in Nineteenth-Century England." In *Village Life and Labour*, edited by Raphael Samuel, pp. 75–138. London: Routledge & Kegan Paul, 1975.

Klingender, Francis D. *Art and the Industrial Revolution.* St. Albans: Paladin, 1972.

Knott, John. *Popular Opposition to the 1834 Poor Law.* London: Croom Helm, 1986.

Kowaleski-Wallace, Elizabeth. *Their Fathers' Daughters: Hannah More, Maria Edgeworth, and Patriarchal Complicity.* New York: Oxford University Press, 1991.

Kriedte, Peter, Hans Medick, and Jürgen Schlumbohm. *Industrialization Before Industrialization.* Translated by Beate Schempp. Cambridge: Cambridge University Press, 1981.

Kussmaul, Ann. *Servants in Husbandry in Early Modern England.* Cambridge: Cambridge University Press, 1981.

Land, Hilary. "The Family Wage." *Feminist Review* 6 (1980): 55–77.

Landau, Norma. *The Justices of the Peace, 1679–1760.* Berkeley: University of California Press, 1984.

Landes, David. *The Unbound Prometheus: Technological Change and Industrial Development in Western Europe from 1750 to the Present.* Cambridge: Cambridge University Press, 1969.

Langer, Gary. *The Coming of Age of Political Economy, 1815–1825.* Westport, CT: Greenwood Press, 1987.

Laqueur, Thomas. *Making Sex: Body and Gender from the Greeks to Freud.* Cambridge, MA: Harvard University Press, 1990.

Laslett, Peter. *The World We Have Lost: England Before the Industrial Age.* 3d ed. New York: Charles Scribner's Sons, 1984.

Lazonick, William. "Industrial Relations and Technical Change: The Case of the Self-acting Mule." *Cambridge Journal of Economics* 3 (1979): 231–62.

Letwin, William. *Origins of Scientific Economics.* Westport, CT: Greenwood Press, 1963.

Levine, David. *Reproducing Families: The Political Economy of English Population History.* Cambridge: Cambridge University Press, 1987.

Lewenhak, Sheila. *Women and Trade Unions.* London: Ernest Benn, 1977.

Lewis, Jane. "The Debate on Sex and Class." *New Left Review* 149 (Jan.–Feb. 1985): 108–20.

———. *Women in England, 1870–1950.* Brighton: Wheatsheaf, 1984.

———, ed. *Labour and Love: Women's Experience of Home and Family, 1850–1940.* Oxford: Blackwell, 1986.

Lindert, Peter H. "English Occupations, 1670–1811." *Journal of Economic History* 40, no. 4 (Dec. 1980): 685–712.

Linebaugh, Peter. *The London Hanged: Crime and Civil Society in the Eighteenth Century.* Cambridge: Cambridge University Press, 1992.

Lonsdale, Roger, ed. *Eighteenth-Century Women Poets: An Oxford Anthology.* New York: Oxford University Press, 1990.

Lown, Judy. "Not So Much a Factory, More a Form of Patriarchy: Gender and Class During Industrialisation." In *Gender, Class and Work*, edited by Eve Gamarnikow et al., pp. 28–45. London: Heinemann, 1983.

———. *Women and Industrialization: Gender at Work in Nineteenth-Century England.* Minneapolis: University of Minnesota Press, 1990.

McBride, Theresa M. *The Domestic Revolution: The Modernisation of Household Service in England and France 1820–1920.* New York: Holmes & Meier, 1976.

McCloskey, D. N. "The Persistence of English Common Fields." In *European Peasants and Their Markets: Essays in Agrarian Economic History*, edited by E. L. Jones and W. N. Parker. Princeton, NJ: Princeton University Press, 1975.

McClure, Ruth K. *Coram's Children: The London Foundling Hospital in the Eighteenth Century.* New Haven, CT: Yale University Press, 1981.

Macdonald, Stuart. "Agricultural Improvement and the Neglected Labourer." *Agricultural History Review* 31 (1983): 83–85.

———. "The Diffusion of Knowledge Among Northumberland Farmers, 1780–1815." *Agricultural History Review* 27 (1979): 30–39.

McKendrick, Neil. "Home Demand and Economic Growth: A New View of the Role of Women and Children in the Industrial Revolution." In *Historical Perspectives: Studies in English Thought and Society in Honour of J. H. Plumb*, edited by Neil McKendrick, pp. 152–210. London: Europa, 1974.

McKendrick, Neil, John Brewer, and J. H. Plumb. *The Birth of a Consumer Society: The Commercialization of Eighteenth-Century England.* London: Europa, 1982.

McNeil, Maureen. *Under the Banner of Science.* Manchester: University of Manchester Press, 1987.

Malcolmson, Robert. *Life and Labour in England 1700–1780.* London: Hutchinson, 1981.

Mantoux, Paul. *The Industrial Revolution in the Eighteenth Century.* Translated by Marjorie Vernon. 1928. Rev. ed., Chicago: University of Chicago Press, 1983.

Marshall, Dorothy. *The English Poor in the Eighteenth Century.* London: George Routledge & Sons, 1926.

Martin, J. M. "Village Traders and the Emergence of a Proletariat in South Warwickshire, 1750–1851." *Agricultural History Review* 32 (1984): 179–88.

Martineau, Harriet. "Female Industry." *Edinburgh Review* 172 (1859): 295.

Mather, Ralph, and W. C. *An Impartial Representation of the Case of the Poor Cotton Spinners in Lancashire.* London, 1780.

Mathias, Peter. *The First Industrial Nation.* 2d ed. London: Methuen, 1983.

Maza, Sarah C. *Servants and Masters in Eighteenth-Century France.* Princeton, NJ: Princeton University Press, 1983.

Medick, Hans. "The Proto-industrial Family Economy: The Structural Function of Household and Family During the Transition from Peasant Society to Industrial Capitalism." *Social History* 3 (1976): 291–318.

Mendels, Franklin F. "Proto-industrialization: The First Phase of the Industrialization Process." *Journal of Economic History* 32 (1972): 241–61.

Merchant, Carolyn. *The Death of Nature: Women, Ecology and the Scientific Revolution.* New York: Harper and Row, 1980.

Merryweather, Mary. *Experience of Factory Life, Being a Record of Fourteen Years' Work, Mr. Courtauld's Silk Mill at Halstead, in Essex,* 3d ed. London: Emily Faithfull, 1862.

Mingay, G. E. *English Landed Society in the Eighteenth Century.* London: Routledge & Kegan Paul, 1963.

———, ed. *Arthur Young and His Times.* London: Macmillan, 1975.

———, ed. *The Victorian Countryside.* 2 vols. London: Routledge & Kegan Paul, 1981–82.

"Modern Domestic Service." *Edinburgh Review* 115 (April 1862): 409–39.

Morgan, Carol E. "Women, Work and Consciousness in the Mid-Nineteenth-Century English Cotton Industry." *Social History* 17 (1992): 23–41.

Nead, Lynda. *Myths of Sexuality: Representations of Women in Victorian Britain.* Oxford: Blackwell, 1988.

Neeson, Jeanette M. "The Opponents of Enclosure in Eighteenth-Century Northamptonshire." *Past and Present* 105 (1984): 114–39.

Neff, Wanda F. *Victorian Working Women: An Historical and Literary Study of Women in British Industries and Professions, 1832–1850.* 1929. Reprint. New York: AMS Press, 1966.

Osterud, Nancy Grey. "Gender Divisions and the Organization of Work in the Leicester Hosiery Industry." In *Unequal Opportunities: Women's Employment in England 1800–1918,* edited by Angela V. John, pp. 45–68. Oxford: Blackwell, 1986.

Palliser, Fanny Bury. *A History of Lace.* 2d ed. London, 1869.

Perkin, Harold. *Origins of Modern English Society.* 1969. Reprint. London: Routledge, 1991.

Phillips, Anne, and Barbara Taylor. "Sex and Skill: Notes Towards a Feminist Economics." *Feminist Review* 6 (1980): 79–88.

Pinchbeck, Ivy. *Women Workers and the Industrial Revolution 1750–1850.* 1930. Reprint. London: Frank Cass, 1969.

Porter, Roy. *English Society in the Eighteenth Century.* Harmondsworth, Middlesex: Penguin Books, 1982.

Poynter, J. R. *Society and Pauperism: English Ideas on Poor Relief, 1795–1834.* London: Routledge & Kegan Paul, 1969.

Prochaska, F. K. *Women and Philanthropy in Nineteenth-Century England.* Oxford: Clarendon Press, 1980.

———. "Women in English Philanthropy, 1790–1830." *International Review of Social History* 19 (1974): 426–45.

Quinault, R., and J. Stevenson, eds. *Popular Protest and Public Order.* London: Allen & Unwin, 1974.

Rendall, Jane. *The Origins of Modern Feminism: Women in Britain, France and the United States, 1780–1860.* New York: Schocken, 1984.

———, ed. *Equal or Different? Women's Politics, 1800–1914.* Oxford: Blackwell, 1987.

Richards, Eric. "Women in the British Economy Since About 1700: An Interpretation." *History* 59 (1974): 337–57.

Roberts, Elizabeth. *Women's Work, 1840–1940.* London: Macmillan, 1988.

Roberts, Michael. "Sickles and Scythes: Women's Work and Men's Work at Harvest Time." *History Workshop Journal* 7 (1979): 3–28.

Rose, Sonya O. "'Gender at Work': Sex, Class and Industrial Capitalism." *History Workshop Journal* 21 (1986): 113–31.

———. *Limited Livelihoods: Gender and Class in Nineteenth Century England.* Berkeley: University of California Press, 1992.

Rule, John. *The Experience of Labour in Eighteenth-Century Industry.* London: Croom Helm, 1981.

Samuel, Raphael. "Workshop of the World: Steam Power and Hand Technology in Mid-Victorian Britain." *History Workshop Journal* 3 (1977): 6–72.

———, ed. *Village Life and Labour.* London: Routledge & Kegan Paul, 1975.

Schmiechen, James A. *Sweated Industries and Sweated Labor: The London Clothing Trades, 1860–1914.* Urbana: University of Illinois Press, 1984.

Schochet, Gordon J. *Patriarchalism in Political Thought: The Authoritarian Family and Political Speculation and Attitudes Especially in Seventeenth-Century England.* New York: Basic Books, 1975.

Scott, Joan Wallach. *Gender and the Politics of History.* New York: Columbia University Press, 1988.

Scott, Joan W., and Louise A. Tilly. "Women's Work and the Family in Nineteenth Century Europe." *Comparative Studies in Society and History* 17 (1975): 36–64.

Seaton, Thomas. *The Conduct of Servants in Great Families.* 1720. Reprint. New York: Garland, 1985.

Seccombe, Wally. "Patriarchy Stabilized: The Construction of the Male Breadwinner Wage Norm in Nineteenth-Century Britain." *Social History* 11 (1986): 53–76.

Segalen, Martine. *Love and Power in the Peasant Family.* Translated by Sarah Matthews. Chicago: University of Chicago Press, 1983.

Sekora, John. *Luxury: The Concept in Western Thought, Eden to Smollett.* Baltimore, MD: Johns Hopkins University Press, 1977.

Shammas, Carole. *The Pre-Industrial Consumer in England and America.* Oxford: Clarendon Press, 1990.

———. "The World Women Knew: Women Workers in the North of England During the Late Seventeenth Century." In *The World of William Penn,* edited by Richard S. Dunn and Mary Maples Dunn, pp. 99–115. Philadelphia: University of Pennsylvania Press, 1986.

Shanley, Mary Lyndon. *Feminism, Marriage, and the Law in Victorian England, 1850–1895.* Princeton, NJ: Princeton Univeristy Press, 1989.

Sharpe, Pamela. "Literally Spinsters: A New Interpretation of Local Economy and Demography in Colyton in the Seventeenth and Eighteenth Centuries." *Economic History Review* 44 (1991): 46–65.

Shorter, Edward. *The Making of the Modern Family.* Huntington, NY: Fontana, 1975.

Smith, Ruth L. "Feminism and the Moral Subject." In *Women's Consciousness, Women's Conscience,* edited by Barbara Andolsen, Christine Gudorf, and Mary Pellauer, pp. 235–50. Minneapolis: Winston Press, 1985.

Smith, Ruth L., and Deborah Valenze. "Mutuality and Marginality: Liberal Moral Theory and Working-Class Women in Nineteenth-Century England." *Signs: Journal of Women in Culture and Society* 13 (1988): 277–98.

Snell, K. D. M. *Annals of the Labouring Poor: Social Change and Agrarian England, 1660–1900.* Cambridge: Cambridge University Press, 1985.

Spenceley, G. F. R. "The Origins of the English Pillow Lace Industry." *Agricultural History Review* 21 (1973): 81–93.

The Spinster in Defence of the Woollen Manufactures. London, 1719.

Sturt, George. *Change in the Village.* 1912. Reprint. New York: Augustus M. Kelley, 1959.

Taylor, Barbara. *Eve and the New Jerusalem.* London: Virago, 1983.

Thane, Pat. "Women and the Poor Law in Victorian and Edwardian England." *History Workshop Journal* 6 (1978): 29–51.

Thirsk, Joan. *Economic Policy and Projects: The Development of a Consumer Society in Early Modern England.* Oxford: Clarendon Press, 1978.

———. "Industries in the Countryside." In *Essays in the Economic and Social History of Tudor and Stuart England,* edited by F. J. Fisher, pp. 78–88. Cambridge: Cambridge University Press, 1961.

Thomas, Janet. "Women and Capitalism: Oppression or Emancipation?" *Comparative Studies in Society and History* 30 (1988): 534–49.

Thomis, Malcolm I., and Jennifer Grimmett. *Women in Protest 1800–1850.* London: Croom Helm, 1982.

Thompson, Dorothy. *British Women in the Nineteenth Century.* Historical Association, London, 1989.

———. *The Chartists: Popular Politics in the Industrial Revolution.* New York: Pantheon, 1984.

———. "Women and Nineteenth-Century Radical Politics: A Lost Dimension." In *The Rights and Wrongs of Women,* edited by Juliet Mitchell and Ann Oakley, pp. 112–38. Harmondsworth, Middlesex: Penguin, 1976.

Thompson, E. P. *Customs in Common.* New York: New Press, 1991.

———. *The Making of the English Working Class.* New York: Vintage, 1963.

———. "The Moral Economy of the English Crowd in the Eighteenth Century." *Past and Present* 50 (1971): 76–136.

———. "Patrician Society, Plebeian Culture." *Journal of Social History* 7 (1974): 382–405.

———. "Time, Work-Discipline and Industrial Capitalism." *Past and Present* 38 (1967): 56–97.

Tilly, Louise A., and Joan W. Scott. *Women, Work, and Family.* New York: Holt, Rinehart and Winston, 1978.

Townsend, Joseph. *A Dissertation on the Poor Laws.* 1786. Reprint. Berkeley: University of California Press, 1971.

Tribe, Keith. *Land, Labour and Economic Discourse.* London: Routledge & Kegan Paul, 1978.

Trumbach, Randolph. *The Rise of the Egalitarian Family: Aristocratic Kinship and Domestic Relations in Eighteenth-Century England.* New York: Academic Press, 1978.

Ure, Andrew. *The Philosophy of Manufactures.* London, 1835.

Valenze, Deborah. "Charity, Custom and Humanity: Changing Attitudes Towards the Poor in Eighteenth-Century England." In *Revival and Religion Since 1700: Essays for John Walsh,* edited by Jane Garnett and Colin Matthew. London: Hambledon Press, 1993.

———. *Prophetic Sons and Daughters: Female Preaching and Popular Religion in Industrial England.* Princeton, NJ: Princeton University Press, 1985.

Valverde, Mariana. "'Giving the Female a Domestic Turn': The Social, Legal and Moral Regulation of Women's Work in British Cotton Mills, 1820–1850." *Journal of Social History* 21 (1988): 619–34.

Wadsworth, Alfred P., and Julia de Lacy Mann. *The Cotton Trade and Industrial Lancashire 1600–1780.* 1931. Reprint. New York: Augustus M. Kelley, 1968.

Wakefield, Priscilla. *Reflections on the Present Condition of the Female Sex.* London, 1798.

Ward, J. T. *The Factory Movement, 1830–1855.* London: Macmillan, 1962.

Weatherill, Lorna. "A Possession of One's Own: Women and Consumer Behavior in England, 1660–1740." *Journal of British Studies* 25 (1986): 131–56.

Webb, Sidney, and Beatrice Webb. *English Poor Law History.* Part I, *The Old Poor Law.* London: Longmans, Green & Co., 1927.

Williams, Raymond. *The Country and the City.* London: Chatto and Windus, 1973.

———. *Culture and Society, 1780–1850.* New York: Harper and Row, 1958.

Winch, Donald. *Malthus.* New York: Oxford University Press, 1987.

Wright, Barbara Drygulski, et al., eds. *Women, Work, and Technology: Transformations.* Ann Arbor: University of Michigan Press, 1987.

Wrightson, Keith, and David Levine. *Poverty and Piety in an English Village: Terling, 1525–1700.* New York: Academic Press, 1979.

Yelling, J. A. *Common Field and Enclosure in England, 1450–1850.* Hamden, CT: Archon, 1977.

Index

Adams, Charlotte, 175
Agricultural change. *See also* Dairying;
    Small-scale farming
  dislocation of laboring classes and, 34
  eighteenth-century literature on, 53–64
  role of female labor and, 10, 30, 31–32,
    41, 46, 182–83
  scientific methods and, 33–35, 52–53,
    55
Agricultural writings, 53–55, 57–58, 61–64
Aikin, John, 79
Aikin, Lucy, 151, 226n.43
Alcock, Thomas, 133
American Revolution, 26
"Ancient Virgins," 96
Anderson, James, 54, 57–58
Anderson, Michael, 105, 106
Andrew, Donna, 24
Apprenticeship, 19–20, 159–60, 167
Arkwright, Richard, 87, 88–90, 109,
    205n.29, 208n.12
Ashby, Mabel K., 198n.75
Ashton, T. S., 206n.41
Atkin, Elizabeth, 19
Attitudes toward laboring women
  dairying and, 65–66
  female factory workers and, 98–103
  spinning technology and, 77–78, 79, 81,
    83–84
  theories of political economy and,
    129–30, 132–33

Attitudes toward the poor. *See also*
    Laboring poor; Poverty
  industrialization and, 9, 27, 132, 182
  property rights and, 35–39
  theories of political economy and,
    130–37

Baines, Edward, 79
Banks, J. A., 169
Baron, Ava, 95
Beattie, John, 27
Beeton, Mrs., 172, 176, 230n.62
Benenson, Harold, 211n.63
Benn, Mrs. Anthony, 21–22
Bentley, Thomas, 78
Berg, Maxine, 79
Berkeley, Bishop, 144
"Bidding wedding," 123
Bigland, Mr., 61–62
Billingsley, John, 203n.55
Blackstone, William, 35
Boserup, Ester, 4
Bradford Female Radical Association,
    96
Bradley, Richard, 54
Branca, Patricia, 230n.62
Bray, Charles, 211n.63
Breastfeeding, 8, 220n.34
Brown, John, 143
Button making, 118, 120. *See also* Cottage
    industry

Cadogan, William, 8
Carding engine, 87, 88
Charity, and female poor, 23–24, 29, 159–61. *See also* Customary rights; Parish relief; Philanthropy
Chartres, J. A., 200n.14
Cheese making, 55–56, 59–61, 62–64
Chernock, Thomas, 32
Child care, 8, 136–37, 221n.40
Children, employment of
  cottage industry and, 116, 121
  factory system and, 89, 91, 93–94, 100
  laboring poor and, 16–17
Collier, Frances, 89
Collier, Mary, 43
Collins, Patricia Hill, 182
Combination Acts (1799 and 1800), 95
Community
  cottage industry and, 123
  dairying practices and, 58–59, 62–64
  political economy and, 131
  spinning and, 71–72
Contractual relations, and domestic service, 157, 166, 180
Cottage industry
  economic development and, 4, 7–8, 16, 18, 215n.18
  factory work and, 91
  irregularity of, 118–20
  middlemen and, 120–21
  plebeian culture and, 122–26
  pre-nineteenth century respect for, 116
  protest and, 121–22
  regional variation in, 116–18
  status of women workers and, 11, 113–27, 184
  wage rates and, 114, 120–21, 123, 124, 215n.18
Cotton industry, 79, 90. *See also* Factory system; Spinning
Courtauld, George, 109, 110
Courtauld, Mrs., 110
Courtauld, Samuel, 89, 213n.110
Crime, 27–28, 35–39, 73–74. *See also* Morality
Cullwick, Hannah, 171–72, 174, 177–80
Customary rights, 30, 35–39. *See also* Tradition

Dairying
  agricultural writings and, 54–58
  attitudes toward labor in, 65–66
  authority of women in, 49–52, 57–58, 64–67
  community and, 58–59, 62–64
  displacement of female labor in, 8, 10, 57–58, 61–64, 66–67, 183
  gender roles and, 49, 59–60
Davidoff, Leonore, 174, 213n.111
Davies, David, 41, 134
Deane, Phyllis, 79

Defoe, Daniel, 69, 116, 133, 147, 163–64
Distaff, 70
"Dolphin cheese," 59
Domesticity, ideology of. *See also* Feminine ideal; Victorian conventions
  concept of work and, 6–8
  Malthus and, 135–37
  reform of working women and, 109–12, 145–52, 185, 186
  theories of political economy and, 129–30, 152–54
  working-class life and, 4, 7, 106–7, 185
Domestic outwork. *See* Cottage industry
Domestic service
  age and, 230n.60
  circumstances of laboring women and, 21–22, 24–25
  class relations and, 158–59, 161, 162–65, 167–68, 172–80, 185–86
  clothing and, 163–65, 168, 229n.58
  contractual relations in, 157, 166, 180
  employment opportunities for women and, 76, 156, 159, 167
  female poor and, 159–60, 167, 174–75
  gender and, 158, 161–63, 169, 227n.14
  middle-class culture and, 12
  negative view of, 27–28, 155–56, 167–68
  productive roles of women and, 185
  servants' diaries and, 177–80
  servants' duties and, 171–72, 177
  "service in husbandry" and, 42
  status of women workers and, 161–63, 167–72, 174–75, 185–86
  types of, 161, 170–71
Duck, Stephen, 43
Dyer, John, 70
  The Fleece (poem), 77–78, 81

Ebery, Mark, 170
Eden, Frederic Morton, 39, 45, 82, 130
Education of women. *See also* Apprenticeship
  domestic service and, 160, 174
  laboring poor and, 23, 24
  middle class virtue and, 145
Eliot, George, *Adam Bede*, 50, 126
Ellis, Sarah Stickney, 172
Ellis, William, 51–52, 56–57, 59
Enclosure system, 34–35, 38, 40–41, 45, 115, 134
Engels, Frederick, 99, 107–8, 212n.99
English Woman's Journal, 111
Entrepreneurship, 6–7, 74–75, 88–90
Evans, Elizabeth Strutt, 110

Factor (middleman), 53, 61, 62–64, 65–66. *See also* Middleman
Factory girl
  as archetype, 3, 85
  Victorian ideals and, 4, 86, 98–100

Factory system
  debate over female labor and, 97–103
  female independence and, 86, 103–5,
    107
  labor organization and, 86, 91, 94–97
  proportion of workforce in, 97–98
  small scale production and, 87–88
  wage rates and, 89–91, 95–97
  workers' choices and, 91–93
Family economy, 15
Family employment, 105, 114–16
Family values
  concept of work and, 6–8
  female factory workers and, 104–8
  patriarchalism and, 14–15
Family wage, 100–101. *See also* Male bread-
    winner concept
Farey, John, 88
Fawcett, Millicent Garrett, 213n.102
Female consciousness, 124–25
Female-headed households, 31–33, 107
Female independence
  cottage industry and, 122–26
  factory system and, 86, 103–5, 107
Female labor. *See also* Attitudes toward
    laboring women; Working-class
    women
  agricultural wage work and, 41, 42–44,
    45–47, 65
  contemporaneous debate over, 9, 48–49,
    97–103
  customary rights and, 31–33, 34, 35–39
  dairying as domain of, 49–53, 54–58,
    59–64, 66–67
  degraded view of, 11, 25–26, 27–28,
    118, 120–21
  displacement of, 8, 130, 183–84. *See also*
    under specific industries
  literary representation of, 43–44
  number of women in workforce and, 5
  occupations of, in 1851, 5
  organizational weakness of, 74
  productive potential of, 14–25, 140
  subordination of, 11, 49, 167–72
  textile industry and, 69
Female virtue, 144–45, 146
Feminine evil, notion of, 143–44
Feminine ideal, 223n.14. *See also* Domestic-
    ity, ideology of; Victorian conventions
  dairymaids and, 65
  female factory workers and, 98–101
  servants and, 168, 178
  spinning and, 68–69, 71
Feminist writings, eighteenth-century,
    147–52
Fielding, Henry, 16
Fielding, John, 23, 24, 25, 145–46, 160
Fiennes, Celia, 58–59
Firmin, Thomas, 17–19
Fitton, R. S., 91
Fitzherbert, Anthony, 50, 69

Flying shuttle, 76, 78
Food prices, 33, 41, 52–53, 66
Fordyce, James, 223n.14
Foster, John, 106
Franklin, Benjamin, 71
Fraudulent practices, 73–74
Free Trade Act of 1824, 93
French Physiocrats, 129
French Revolution, 26, 184
Fuel gathering, 31, 38–39
Furniss, Edgar, 190n.10
Fussell, G. E., 202n.47

Gaskell, Elizabeth, 103
Gaskell, Peter, 99, 112, 213n.110
Gender. *See also* Sexual division of labor;
    Wage differentials
  construction of, 6–8, 9, 49
  construction of skill and, 8, 44, 57–58,
    162
  dairying and, 49, 59–60
  domestic service and, 158, 161–63, 169,
    227n.14
  labor organization and, 94–97, 101
George II (king of England), 33
Gibson, Bridget, 21–22
Gibson, William, 22
Gleaning, 35–39
Gloving, 117, 118, 119. *See also* Cottage
    industry
Godelier, Maurice, 67
Godwin, William, 135
Grand General Union of the United
    Kingdom, 95
Grand Lodge of Operative Bonnet Makers,
    96
Grand Lodge of Women of Great Britain
    and Ireland, 96
Grand National Consolidated Trades
    Union of Great Britain and Ireland, 96
Gray, Andrew, 71
Gregory, John, 147

Hacking, Ellen, 87
Hacking, John, 87
Hall, Catherine, 213n.111
Hammond, Barbara, 37
Hammond, J. L., 37
Handbooks for women, 146–47, 148
Hanway, Jonas, 138, 145, 160–61, 165,
    205n.31, 225n.26
  Virtue in humble Life, 147, 152
Harding, Joseph, 66
Hardy, Thomas, 65
Hargreaves, Richard, 76, 79–80
Harrison, A., 209n.27
Haywood, Eliza, 147
  Present for a Serving-Maid (manual),
    163, 165–66
Heaton, Herbert, 73, 74
Hecht, J. Jean, 166

Higgs, Edward, 170, 227n.13
Hill, Bridget, 9, 159, 161, 229n.41
Hogarth, William, "A Woman Swearing a Child to a Rich Merchant" (engraving), 27
Holland, Henry, 59–60
Horner, Leonard, 102
Hume, David, 138
Humphries, Jane, 102
Hunt, Leigh, 168
Hutchins, B. L., 108, 209n.27

Idleness of women, 113–14, 129–30, 191n.21
Individualism, 138–40, 157, 219n.9. *See also* Female independence
  attitudes toward poverty and, 129, 132, 134, 185
Industrialization
  kinship ties and, 105–6
  number of women in workforce and, 4, 5
  occupations of women in workforce and, 5
  standard treatments of, 6–9, 79, 181–82
  status of male workers and, 101–2
Invisible trades, 4. *See also* Cottage industry

James, J., 71
Jones, M. G., 151
Joyce, Patrick, 109

Kaplan, Temma, 124–25
Katherine of Alexandria (patron saint of spinsters), 124, 217n.53
Kidson, Benjamin, 22
Kidson, Sarah, 22
King, Gregory, 15
Kitteringham, Jennie, 202n.48
Kowaleski-Wallace, Elizabeth, 147

Laboring classes
  early eighteenth-century economic identity of, 14–15
  enclosure system and, 34, 40–41
  landholding system and, 30–35
  late eighteenth-century conditions and, 26–28
  male *vs.* female workers and, 100–102
  Malthus and, 134–37
Laboring poor. *See also* Attitudes toward the poor; Poverty
  category of, 15
  factory employment and, 106
  projects for employment of, 16–19, 69, 133, 134
  women among, 15–16, 32–33, 69, 132
Labor organization, 53, 74, 125–26. *See also* Protest
  factory system and, 86, 91, 94–97
  gender and, 94–97, 101

Lace making, 116, 117, 124, 215n.18. *See also* Cottage industry
Ladies Society of the Society for Bettering the Condition of the Poor, 160
Lambeth Asylum, 24
Landes, David, 7, 79
Landholding, system of, 30–35
Lawrence, John, 52, 54, 57, 58, 201n.23
Leased dairy, 53
Legislation
  customary rights and, 34, 35, 39
  factory system and, 100, 102–3
  spinning fraud and, 74
Lewis, Jane, 209n.35
Lindert, Peter, 190n.8
Lofft, Capel, 37
Lown, Judy, 104, 213n.110
Luddite activity, 124
Luxury consumption
  debate over, 142–44
  domestic service and, 162, 164–66
Lying-in Hospital (London), 23

Machiavelli, Niccolò, 143
Magdalen Hospital (London), 23, 24
Malcolmson, Robert, 115
Male breadwinner concept, 11–12, 42, 47, 185, 211n.63
  cottage industry and, 114, 126
  factory system and, 89, 100, 101, 106–7
  theories of political economy and, 129, 137–39, 152, 153
Malthus, Thomas Robert, 11, 14, 100, 102, 131, 132, 134–37
  contemporary debates and, 184
  ideas about women and, 185
  women of the middle classes and, 141–42, 153
Mandeville, Bernard, *Fable of the Bees*, 142–43
Mantoux, Paul, 84
Marcet, Jane Haldiman, 152–53
Marine Society, 24
Marketing
  dairying practices and, 56–57, 64, 200n.16
  spinning and, 71–72
Marshall, Dorothy, 20
Marshall, William, 51, 53, 54, 55, 56, 58, 59–62, 199n.9
Marx, Karl, 67, 156
Massie, Joseph, 22, 24–25, 29–30
Mayhew, Augustus, 173
Mayhew, Henry, 173
Mechanization. *See also* Factory system
  cottage industry and, 121, 127
  human cost of, 89–91, 93–94
  organization of production and, 84, 87
  participation of women in, 87
  of spinning, 72, 75–82, 84
  textile industry and, 88

Mercantilism, 14
Merryweather, Mary, 110–11
Methodist sects, 125
Middle classes
  construction of authority and, 141–42
  domestic service and, 157–58, 169–71
  gender and, 142
  morality and, 142–45
  self-differentiation from the poor and, 142
Middle-class women
  class consciousness and, 172–80, 185–86
  domestic ideal and, 130, 136–37,
    144–45, 185
  feminist writings by, 147–52
  late eighteenth-century literature and,
    146–54
  mistress-servant relations and, 167–68,
    172–80
  paternalism and, 213n.111
  reform of working-class women and,
    11–12, 109–12, 145–54, 185, 186
  theories of political economy and, 141–42
Middleman. *See also* Factor
  cottage industry and, 120–21
  textile industry and, 72, 75
Middleton, Chris, 204n.9
Moore, Francis, 190n.16
Morality. *See also* Prostitution; Theft
  of lower-class women, 130, 146
  middle classes and, 142–45
More, Hannah, 147, 148–52, 153, 154
Mortimer, Thomas, 139
Morton, J. Chalmers, 66
"Mosaical law." *See* Customary rights
Motherhood. *See* Child care; Domesticity,
    ideology of
Munby, Arthur, 174, 177, 178

Neeson, Jeanette, 40
Neff, Wanda, 86
New Poor Law, 115, 125
Nightingale, Florence, 110
North, Frederick, 162

Opportunities for women workers
  cottage industry and, 113
  decline in, 4, 23
  domestic service and, 76, 156, 159, 167
  enclosure and, 45
  factory system and, 86, 94
  machine spinning and, 82–83
  organization of production and, 87–88
Osterud, Nancy Grey, 127
Owen, Robert, 109
Owenism, 96

Parish relief
  apprenticeships and, 19–20, 159–60
  cottage industry and, 118, 123
  eighteenth-century laboring women and,
    19–22

Settlement Laws and, 20–22
  socio-economic class and, 45
  tradition and, 30
Parkes, Bessie Rayner, 110, 111
Parson and the Fowls, The (chapbook), 167
Paternalism, 14–15
  class relations and, 142, 164
  domestic service and, 156–57
  factory system and, 91, 107–8, 213n.111
  pre-industrial views of women workers
    and, 10
Paul, Lewis, 72, 75–76, 77
Payment in kind, 120
Pennington, Sarah, 136
Pepys, Samuel, 161
Perkin, Harold, 6–7
Philanthropy, 23–24. *See also* Charity, and
    female poor; Parish relief
  class relations and, 145–46, 148–52,
    154, 177–78
Phythian-Adams, Charles, 65
Pinchbeck, Ivy, *Women Workers and the
    Industrial Revolution 1750–1850*, 8–9,
    36, 67, 80, 82
Pin trade, 119. *See also* Cottage industry
Place, Francis, 101
Plebeian culture, 122–26
Political economy, theories of
  attitudes toward poverty and, 129–37,
    184–85
  concerns of, 129
  construct of male breadwinner and, 47,
    129, 185
  decline in sympathy for poor and,
    132–34
  early writings and, 130–32
  employment of laboring poor and, 16
  Malthus and, 134–37
  middle-class women and, 148–54
  private property and, 36–37
  technology and, 78, 98
Poor laws, 19–22, 23, 26, 125, 132, 134
Population growth, 26, 131, 135–36, 153
Porter, Roy, 19
Poverty. *See also* Attitudes toward the poor;
    Laboring poor; Parish relief
  agrarian society and, 32–33, 40–41, 46
  assistance and, 19–24, 50
  association of women with, 10, 11,
    16–23, 72–73, 106
  cottage industry and, 117–18
  link between progress and, 182
  mechanization and, 80–82, 83, 98
  theories of political economy and, 98,
    129–34, 184–85
  of working classes, 106–7
Poynter, J. R., 219n.14
Preston, Brian, 170
Private property, 35–39. *See also* Enclosure
    system
Prochaska, Frank, 170, 172

Production, organization of
    change in, *vs.* process of mechanization,
        84
    factory system and, 86, 87–88
    spinning and, 72–75, 84
Progress, and poverty, 182
Prostitution, 23, 24, 25, 160–61
Protest. *See also* Labor organization;
    Resistance
    cottage industry and, 121–22, 124–25
    enclosure system and, 38, 40, 115
    laboring classes and, 115–16
    mill workers and, 96–97
"Proto-industrialization," 114–15, 123. *See
    also* Cottage industry
Public opinion. *See* Attitudes toward labor
    ing women
Public-private distinction, 129
Putting-out system, 72–75, 114

Quesnay, Francois, 129

Radcliffe, William, 88
Radical associations, 96–97
Rational, the, 7–8, 49. *See also* Tradition *vs.*
    reason
Religion, 125–26
Rendall, Jane, 9
Resistance. *See also* Protest
    dairying industry and, 66–67
    textile industry and, 73–74, 78,
        79–82
Reynel, Carew, 16
Ricardo, David, 11
Richardson, Samuel, 28
Rose, Sonya O., 207n.2, 211n.69
Rowlandson, Thomas, 167, 168
Ruggles, Thomas, 37, 134

Sadler, Richard, 81, 83
Scott, Joan, 97, 104
Senior, Mrs. Nassau, 174
Servant autobiographies, 171, 177–80
Service in husbandry, 42, 44–45
Settlement Laws, 20–22
Sexual division of labor
    agricultural change and, 42–43, 47
    apprenticeships and, 19–20
    cottage industry and, 114–16
    dairying and, 49, 59–60, 67
    spinning and, 71
Sharpe, Pamela, 190n.19, 217n.49
Short-Time Movement, 100
Silk industry, 93, 144
Skill, gendered construction of, 8, 44,
    57–58, 162, 209n.35
Small factories, 87–88
Small-scale farming, 16, 46, 50, 64–65
Smith, Adam, 114, 134, 139, 219n.9
    The Wealth of Nations, 6, 130–31, 155

Snell, Keith, 45
Society for Bettering the Condition and
    Increasing the Comforts of the Poor,
    46, 118
Socio-economic class. *See also* Laboring
    classes; Middle classes; Middle-class
    women; Working-class women
    construction of, 6, 11, 27
    domestic service and, 185–86
    parish relief system and, 45
    Victorian ideals and, 185
Spinning. *See also* Textile industry
    displacement of female labor and, 10,
        69, 75–76, 81, 82–83, 183
    mechanization of, 72, 75–82, 84
    traditional methods and, 70–75
    as women's work, 18, 68, 70–72
Spinning jenny, 76–77, 79, 88, 183,
    206n.41
Status of women workers
    in agrarian society, 31–32, 43–44, 47
    change in, 3, 10, 13–14, 25–26,
        129–30
    cottage industry and, 113–27, 184
    dairying and, 49–53, 54–58, 59–60,
        61–64, 65
    debate over female labor and, 48–49,
        98–103
    domestic service and, 161–63, 167–72,
        174–75, 185–86
    enclosure system and, 34–35
    factory system and, 102–3
    wage differentials and, 183–84
Steuart, James, 131
Straw plaiting, 116, 117–18, 119–21, 123,
    124, 216n.42. *See also* Cottage
    industry
Strutt (manufacturer), 91, 92–93, 109

Taylor, Barbara, 96
Taylor, Thomas, 121
Textile industry. *See also* Factory system;
    Spinning
    displacement of female labor and, 10,
        69, 183–84
Theft. *See also* Morality
    customary rights and, 35–39
    domestic servants and, 27–28
    "reeling short" and, 73–74
Thompson, Dorothy, 96–97
Thompson, E. P., 122
Tilly, Louise, 97, 104
Tomlinson, Elizabeth, 125–26
Townsend, Joseph, 133
Tradition
    association of women with, 48–49
    customary rights and, 30
Tradition *vs.* reason
    agricultural writings and, 53–55,
        61–64

concept of work and, 7–8
dairying and, 54–55, 61–64
spinning and, 77, 78
Trial of the lady Allured Luxury (anonymous), 144
Tribe, Keith, 221n.39
Trimmer, Sarah, 147, 151
Tucker, Josiah, 16
Tull, Jethro, 44
Tusser, Thomas, 51, 204n.9
Twamley, Josiah, 62–64

Unemployment
cottage industry and, 118–20, 126
enclosure system and, 45
female breadwinners and, 107
as idleness, 129–30
mid eighteenth-century labor and,
18–19, 23, 26, 129–30
spinning technology and, 80
status of, 189n.7
Unions. *See* Labor organization
Urbanization, 27
Ure, Andrew, 93, 98, 100
Use rights, 31. *See also* Customary rights

Valverde, Marianna, 211n.68
Veblen, Thorsten, 172
Victorian conventions. *See also* Domesticity,
ideology of; Feminine ideal; Middle-
class women
domestic servants and, 169–71
durability of, 181
female factory workers and, 109–12
middle-class culture and, 12, 169–71
status of women workers and, 3,
98–100, 181
Von Archenholz, J. W., 165

Wade, Mrs., 61–62
Wadsworth, A. P., 91
Wage differentials
factory system and, 90–91, 97, 99–101,
107–9, 208n.22
status of women workers and, 127,
183–84

Wage rates
cottage industry and, 114, 120–21, 123,
124, 215n.18
defamation of women workers and, 183
domestic service and, 176–77
factory system and, 89–91
spinning and, 72–74
textile industry and, 69, 183, 222n.46
theories of political economy and,
137–39, 153
Wage theory, development of, 137–40
Wakefield, Priscilla, 23, 145, 147
Warfare, periods of, 26
Wasteland, 32
Watt, James, 87
Webb, Beatrice, 16
Webb, Sidney, 16
Weber, Max, 48
Wesley, John, 143
Westall, Lilian, 171
Wet nurses, 136
Wollstonecraft, Mary, 148, 152
Woolen industry, 16–17, 73, 75, 118, 144.
See also Spinning; Textile industry
Work, concept of
class and, 6, 7
gender and, 6, 7
tradition *vs.* the rational and, 7–8
"work in general" and, 67
Working-class women. *See also* Female
labor; Status of women workers; *specific occupations and industries*
construction of image of, 86, 99
domestic ideal and, 4, 7, 130, 185
formulaic view of, 183–84
ideal of womanhood and, 98–100
middle-class reform of, 11–12, 109–12,
185, 186
morality and, 130, 146
Worsted Act of 1777, 74
Wright, Thomas, 167
Wrigley, Mrs., 171
Wyatt, John, 76

Young, Arthur, 33, 37, 39, 53–54, 56, 57,
83, 129, 134, 139–40

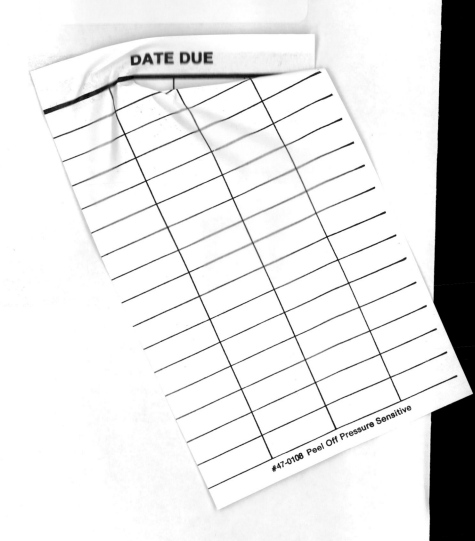

DATE DUE

#47-0108 Peel Off Pressure Sensitive